# Religion and the Secular

# Religion and the Secular

## Historical and Colonial Formations

*Edited by Timothy Fitzgerald*

LONDON   OAKVILLE

Published by:
UK: Equinox Publishing Ltd., Unit 6, The Village, 101 Amies St., London SW11 2JW
USA: DBBC, 28 Main Street, Oakville, CT 06779

www.equinoxpub.com

First published 2007

British Library Cataloguing-in-Publication Data

A catalogue record for this book is available from the British Library.

ISBN:  978 1 84553 266 6   (hardback)
ISBN:  978 1 84553 267 3   (paperback)

Library of Congress Cataloging-in-Publication Data

Religion and the secular : historical and colonial formations / edited by Timothy Fitzgerald.
    p. cm.
    Includes bibliographical references and index.
    ISBN 978-1-84553-267-3 (pb) -- ISBN 978-1-84553-266-6 (hb)
    1. Religion--Philosophy--History--Congresses. 2. Secularism--History--Congresses. 3. Colonies-
-Religious aspects--History--Congresses. I. Fitzgerald, Timothy, 1947-
    BL51.R3478 2007
    200.9--dc22                                                          2006101917

Typeset by Kate Williams, Swansea.
Printed and bound by Antony Rowe Ltd., Chippenham.

In loving memory of my mother,
Angela Dorothea Radford-Rowe Kirk (1914–1970),
stage actress, who died in tragic circumstances.
Alive in our hearts, may she rest in peace.

# Contents

CONTENTS

# Acknowledgements

I would like to thank present and former colleagues in Religious Studies at the University of Stirling (now successfully incorporated into the School of Languages, Cultures and Religions) for their help and cooperation in organising the 2003 conference at Stirling from which the chapters in this book developed. The University of Stirling gave financial support. Many participants at that conference contributed valuable ideas that will have fed into the book as a whole even though their own contributions may not have materialised as papers here. They travelled to Stirling in Scotland from different parts of the world – Japan, South Africa, North America – as well as different universities in the UK. I am grateful to Mahinda Deegalle for his initial help in getting things started and his ideas about the name of the conference, and to Anna Blume for tracking down the image used for the book cover. Thanks especially to the book contributors themselves for their patient devotion to the editorial task over a rather protracted period between conference and publication, and their religious attention to detail in the reworking of ideas, sentences, references and bibliographies. And thanks to Janet Joyce and Valerie Hall of Equinox and Kate Williams for their kind and helpful part in the production of the book. Without their outstanding professionalism, under pressure of externally imposed deadlines, I would not have got this book out in time. Finally, thanks to Noriko, James and Mari for their patience and support during a difficult period.

# Contributors

**Gregory D. Alles** (galles@mcdaniel.edu) is Professor in the Department of Philosophy and Religious Studies, McDaniel College, Westminster, Maryland, USA. He has recently edited *Religious Studies: A Global View* (London: Routledge, 2007).

**Anna Blume** (annablume@mindspring.com) is Professor of Pre-Columbian and American Indian Art in the History of Art Department, FIT, State University of New York. She is the author of *Animal Transformations: The Mixing of Maya and European Fantasy and Belief*, in Jeffrey Quilter and Mary Miller (eds), *A Pre-Columbian World* (Cambridge, MA: Harvard University Press, 2006).

**William T. Cavanaugh** (WTCAVANAUGH@stthomas.edu) is Associate Professor of Theology at the University of St Thomas, St Paul, Minnesota, USA. His forthcoming book is *The Myth of Religious Violence*.

**David Chidester** (davidc@iafrica.com) is Professor of Religious Studies and Director of the Institute for Comparative Religion in Southern Africa at the University of Cape Town. He is the author of *Savage Systems: Colonialism and Comparative Religion in Southern Africa* (Charlottesville, VA: University Press of Virginia, 1996). His most recent book is *Authentic Fakes: Religion and American Popular Culture* (Berkeley, CA: University of California Press, 2005).

**James L. Cox** (J.Cox@ed.ac.uk) is Professor and Head of Religious Studies in the School of Divinity at the University of Edinburgh. He recently published *A Guide to the Phenomenology of Religion* (London: Continuum, 2006) and will shortly publish *From Primitive to Indigenous: The Academic Study of Indigenous Religions* (Aldershot: Ashgate, 2007).

**Timothy Fitzgerald** is Reader in Religion at the University of Stirling. His book *Discourse on Civility and Barbarity: A Critical History of Religion and related Categories* is to be published by Oxford University Press, New York, in 2007.

**Jun'ichi Isomae** (icb74921@hotmail.com) is Associate Professor at the International Research Institute for Japanese Studies, Kyoto. His most recent book is *Japanese Mythology: Hermeneutics on Scripture* (London: Equinox, 2007).

**Thomas Pearson** (pearsont@wabash.edu) is Associate Director of the Wabash Center for Teaching and Learning in Theology and Religion. He recently published "Montagnard-Dega Communities", *Encyclopedia of American Folklife* (Armonk, NY: M. E. Sharpe, 2006).

**Trevor Stack** (t.stack@abdn.ac.uk) is Lecturer in Hispanic Studies at the University of Aberdeen. He is completing a book on the politics of historical knowledge in Mexico, and is beginning a project, also in Mexico, that asks whether citizenship can be conceived as something more than a relationship with the state.

**Will Sweetman** (will.sweetman@gmail.com) is Senior Lecturer in Asian Religions in the Department of Theology and Religious Studies, University of Otago, New Zealand. He is the author of *Mapping Hinduism: 'Hinduism' and the Study of Indian Religions, 1600–1776* (Halle: Verlag der Franckeschen Stiftungen zu Halle, 2003).

**Abdulkader Tayob** (Abdulkader.Tayob@uct.ac.za) is Professor of Islamic Studies at the University of Cape Town. His monograph on religion in modern Islamic discourse will be published by Hurst in 2008.

**Michael S. Wood** (mswood@darkwing.uoregon.edu), who translated Jun'ichi Isomae's chapter, is currently completing a postdoctoral tenure in the Department of Law and Politics at the National University of Hokkaido, Japan and teaching early-modern and modern Japanese history courses at Fuji Women's University. His recent research has focused on Japanese castaway narratives and their links to late-eighteenth- and nineteenth-century colonization in the Pacific.

**Dr John Zavos** (John.Zavos@manchester.ac.uk) is Lecturer in South Asian Studies at the University of Manchester. He is co-author with Jacqueline Suthren Hirst of "Riding a Tiger? South Asia and the Problem of Religion", *Contemporary South Asia*, special issue "Teaching Across South Asian Religious Traditions" (guest-edited by Zavos and Suthren Hirst) 14(1) (2005), 3–20. He is author of *The Emergence of Hindu Nationalism in India* (New Delhi: Oxford University Press, 2002).

# Introduction

## *Timothy Fitzgerald*

> It may be a happy accident that this effort of defining religion converges with the liberal demand in our time that it be kept quite separate from politics, law, and science – spaces in which varieties of power and reason articulate our distinctively modern life. The definition is at once part of a strategy (for secular liberals) of the confinement, and (for liberal Christians) of the defence of religion.      (Talal Asad 1993: 28)

> I would go even further than this: the very concept of religion as such – as an entity with any distinction whatever from other human phenomena – is a function of these same processes and historical moments that generate an individualistic concept of it (in fairness, Asad 1993: 29 hints at this).      (William Arnal 1999: 31)

## INTRODUCTION: THE PROBLEM SITUATION

"A Matter of Power, Not Religion" is the title of a two-page interview with Fred Halliday (2005). Halliday, who is Montague Burton Professor of International Relations at the London School of Economics (LSE) and a fellow of the British Academy, and author of books on Islam, was interviewed about the "war against terrorism" by Adam Holm of the Danish weekly political magazine *Opinion*. Halliday is an interesting writer, but here I draw attention to the implications of the title: that religion and power are distinct and separate alternatives – a matter of power, not religion. In the late seventeenth century, the Quaker William Penn (1680) pursued what in his day was the dangerous heterodox position that religion *ought to be* understood as distinct from the magistrate, with different ends and purposes, against the prevailing view of the meaning of religion at the time. Now this contentious ideological reformulation has become a matter of unquestioned assumption: what ought to be in the minds of a few seventeenth-century radicals has become the uncritically accepted assumption of what is the case. Religion, rather than meaning Christian Truth, or one or another conflicting interpretations of Christian Truth, has become pluralized into generic things in the world, things that have some problematic relationship with a distinct and separate domain of power called 'politics'.

The logic of "A matter of power, not religion" allows in principle for the reverse: a matter of religion, not power. Whatever anyone thinks religion may be, the idea that it is not a matter of power seems counter-intuitive. Yet it follows the same logic as the ideological separation of religion and politics into two essentialized domains, one concerned with power and public order, the other the private inner world of prayer.

In his second question to Halliday, Holm asks "What is required to stop, or minimise, the religiously motivated terrorism that we are now witnessing in parts of the west and in many places in the Arab world?" In this question, the idea of a distinct form of terrorism – *religious* terrorism – is introduced effortlessly into the discussion. This usage, which is widely dispersed throughout the media and academic publications, implies that some terrorism is religious but some is non-religious or secular. In part of his reply, Halliday further underwrites this when he says, "I would not say 'religiously motivated' because the main issues are nationalist and anti-imperialist ones if you read the statements of Al Qaida ... the main issues are eminently understandable, even conventional, political ones". For Halliday "religion provides a means of expressing" these conventional political motives. And in his answer to Holm's third question about Islamic terrorists, Halliday at one point says, "it is not the religion that determines the political means ... it is the political groups of today who select and use religion".

The essential distinction between religion and politics is embedded in this interview by both scholars. Politics is secular, not religious: "terrorism ... is a product of modern, secular, politics", Halliday asserts. "It has long had no relation to religion at all." And he gives as examples of secular (non-religious) political terrorism Palestinian Marxist-Leninists of the 1970s, Kurdish far-left-wing fighters, Tamil Tigers and Peruvians in Sendero Luminoso.

An interview is not the same as an academic paper, yet these published usages are unsurprising since they are part of our common discourse and trip off the tongue effortlessly. They seem entirely natural to us. The assumption, never questioned in this discussion between two distinguished writers, that religion is not about power or politics, and when it becomes so then something is wrong, reflects a wider media and academic discourse about religion in which 'it' is defined as essentially distinct from the secular, and thus as having a problematic relationship to it. The implication is that religion is essentially non-political, and politics is essentially non-religious.

Wilfred Cantwell Smith ([1962] 1978; 1983), is rightly famous for his attempt to critique the reification of religions, but as I have argued elsewhere (2000; 2003: 27), he was never able consistently to purge his own writing of essentializing usages (see Fitzgerald 2000: 43–8). For example, in the introduction to his *The Meaning and End of Religion* he writes, "Yet religion itself continues, and in many parts of the world appears to be ... resurgent" ([1962] 1978: 3). Writers on the subject 'religion' manage to blow life into a category as though it were an autonomous reality in the world, and often take its distinction from 'politics' as both a fact and a value. It simultaneously *is* the case and *ought to be* the case. In his comments on the book *The Desecularization of the World* (1999), edited by Peter Berger, Robert Wuthnow of Princeton University says:

> The myth that religion has become irrelevant dies hard – especially among university faculty who consider themselves too enlightened to be bothered with religion. The essays in this provocative volume prove that religion has not only survived; it is flourishing. From Peru to Guatemala, from China to the Sudan, and from barrios in Los Angeles to temples in New York City, we see the evidence of this resurgence. And in all of these places religion is having an impact on political life. Whether we like it or not, religion must be reckoned with by any serious student of human affairs.

In these comments by Wuthnow (found on the back of the book and designed by the publisher to increase sales), and also in Berger's introduction, 'religion' is spoken of as though it is a thing in the world: religion "dies hard"; religion "has not only survived, it is flourishing". Also, the separation of religion and politics as distinct domains is implicitly assumed: "religion is having an impact on political life". In most publications across the humanities, whether by historians, sociologists, anthropologists or religionists, the categories 'religion' and 'politics' are taken as unproblematic, as though it is self-evident what is meant by these complex, contested and ambiguous terms. They are treated as generic and ahistorical, as though their meaning and the distinction between them is a natural aspect of the world. We all know what 'religion' is and we all know what 'politics' is; the problem is to see how they interact and 'impact' in various places around the world today.

And yet it seems obvious that there are many beliefs and practices in our own Western cultures that might normally be categorized as 'secular' but that could equally be called 'religious'. Nationalism, for example, is a kind of worship of a transcendental imaginary entity that undercuts the supposed distinctions between religion and the secular state. Consider an image that appeared on British television recently in a news report of the inaugural address of the new president of a recently autonomous central Asian state (*More4 News*, 12 January 2006). We saw him finishing his solemnly delivered address; he removed his right hand from the sacred book (it could have been the Koran, it could have been the Bible, it could have been the Constitution), dropped to one knee, and with bowed head reverently gathered up the folds of the national flag and kissed it. Is this not a form of spiritual communion: a public commitment to a transcendental form of life?

Mark Juergensmeyer (1993; 2000) might be tempted to agree. At one point in his provocatively titled *The New Cold War? Religious Nationalism Confronts the Secular State* (1993) he argues that secular nationalism and religion are equivalent in terms of both structure and function within their respective contexts. For example, one characteristic that they share is that:

They both serve the ethical function of providing an overarching framework of moral order, a framework that commands ultimate loyalty from those who subscribe to it ... For this reason I believe the line between secular nationalism and religion has always been quite thin. Both are expressions of faith, both involve an identity with and a loyalty to a large community, and both insist on the ultimate moral legitimacy of the authority vested in the community. (1993: 16)

Unfortunately he then proceeds to discuss a whole range of different kinds of movement in the world by placing them uncritically into two large conflicting boxes, the religions and the seculars, the religions and the non-religions, claiming to be able to make a significant analytical distinction between religious and secular nationalisms, for example, or religious and secular terrorisms, or religious and secular ideologies. The result is analytical confusion (see Fitzgerald, 2000: 106–18 for a detailed analysis). When a highly perceptive scholar of Juergensmeyer's standing grasps such a critical point and then backs away from it, reverting to the discourse on the essentialized religion–secular dichotomy, one is surely justified in trying to identify unacknowledged and indirect motives and interests that may be driving this entrenched discourse that pervades public rhetoric.

Nationalism is one example. But there are others. In his book *Holy Terrors* (2003), Bruce Lincoln points out that the chief actors in the English, American and French revolutions "saw such doctrines as the rights of man, popular sovereignty, and the social contract as no less sacred – in fact, much more so – than the divine right of kings", and he goes on to quote Christopher Dawson that the revolutionaries in France "dreamt of a spiritual republic based on moral foundations" (quoted in Lincoln 2003: 87). And in a footnote he points out that the secular ideologies of Marxism, anarchism and psycho-analysis possess powerful mythic, ritual and soteriological dimensions, whatever their position towards "religion per se" (*ibid.*: 129n10). Unfortunately the expression 'religion per se' is one of the indications that Lincoln cannot follow this important insight about the so-called secular foundations of the modern state through to any satisfactory conclusion, because the overall intention of much of this and other books he has written is to embed the religion–secular dichotomy – into an ahistorical transcendentalism of its own.

For one thing Lincoln never questions the status in this regard of the ideology of liberal capitalism, which finances our scholarly English-language productions and makes ideologically hegemonic the belief in Euro-American standards of scholarly objectivity. That Lincoln's intention is more in the direction of essentializing and naturalizing the religion–secular dichotomy can be seen from something he says near the beginning of the book, where he indicates that he is still searching for "the nature of religion", as though religion has a nature, as when he writes in the preface: "This book represents my attempt to think through the nature of religion, to identify its core components (discourse, practice, community, institution), and to specify its historically changing relation to other aspects of culture (particularly the ethical, aesthetic, and political)" (2003: ix). Why should we assume that religion has a nature distinct from the aesthetic, the ethical or the political? Do all these categories refer to things with natures? If discourse, practice, community and institution are what constitute the core components of the nature of religion (its essence), how does religion differ from secular history, or from secular politics, or from secular anything you like? Do they not all have discourse, practice, community and institution? We come back to this point, because Lincoln claims quite explicitly in his "Theses on Method" (1996: 225–7) to be able to specify the essential differences between religion and the secular, but it is an illusion generated by the mystifying effects of his own brand of transcendentalism.

One finds the assumption of an essential difference between 'religion' and 'the secular' embedded in the writing of perhaps the majority of scholars in religious studies and more widely.[1]

But in the English-language scholarly rhetorics cited above, there are implications that may not translate well into Arabic (see Chapter 9), or Japanese (see Chapter 4), or Tamil (see Chapter 6), or indeed into many non-European languages. In typical English-language press reportage, some imams might be described as 'genuine religious leaders' whereas others are *really* 'political' and therefore by implication not genuine, but only pretending to be 'religious'; in Halliday's terms religion is used by people whose real motives are political: "it is the political groups of today who select and use religion". This kind of reporting shows that (a) it is already assumed that religion and politics are distinct, mutually exclusive categories not only in the English language but also in the minds of people who speak in Arabic (or Urdu, Persian, Japanese, Chinese, Tamil and so on); or, if it is not in their minds, then it should be; and (b) it is assumed that imams are 'religious', and are therefore not genuine if they are involved in 'politics'. But if the imam does not make the same assumption, what kind of communication or miscommunication may be occurring? The essays in this book represent attempts to unravel the illusions generated by these categories to show how they operate and how they originate in colonial or colonial-related situations.

## BACKGROUND TO THE PRODUCTION OF THIS BOOK

This book grew out of a conference, "The Religion–Secular Dichotomy: Historical Formations in Colonial Contexts", held by the Department of Religious Studies at the University of Stirling in July 2003. The general theoretical concern was with the ideological function of the privatization of religion and its separation from politics and other forms of secular discourse, with especial reference to the dominance of Western capitalism and the colonial relationship. One of the central aims was to theorize the religion–secular dichotomy from both the imperial centre and as many of its peripheries as possible, given the expertise available.[2] As with 'religion' and 'politics', so with imperial centre and colonial periphery, it is the *relationship* between categories that is fundamental. Only in this way can we question the assumption of dominance in this formulation.

The theoretical assumptions out of which the idea for the conference grew can be summarized in the following generalizations. It should be stressed that these are not theses to be promulgated so much as generalizations that we hope the papers in this book go some way towards substantiating:

1.  An initial analytical distinction must be made between: (a) religion as a category in general uncritical use for talking about what is assumed unproblematically to be found in the world, namely, religions, religious traditions and religious experiences; and (b) 'religion' as an English-language category in our own and other peoples' actual usages that we find to be problematic and that therefore needs critical analysis in the different texts and contexts of its use. For us the dominant context, and the one least attended to with the exception of a few writers mentioned earlier (such as Talal Asad [1993] and David Chidester [1996]) is the colonial one.

2.  The concept of 'a religion' and its pluralization 'religions' is a modern category, has a specific set of historical conditions for its emergence, most clearly and unambiguously in the second half of the seventeenth century (although see Chapter 11 and Stack's argument in Chapter 2 that secular narration emerged in the sixteenth-century colonial encounter), and is a fundamental part of modern Western ideology. Various important consequences flow from this. One would be that to talk about medieval Christianity as 'a religion' would therefore make no sense, or at least be a distortion suggesting a lack of historical awareness. Even when Samuel Purchas was talking about the religions of the world in the early seventeenth century, he would not have thought of Christianity as one example of a generic type (Purchas [1613] 1626).[3]

3.  Religion did not emerge alone, but in conjunction with other categories, one of them being 'the secular' (non-religion). The conceptualization of 'religion' and 'religions' in the modern sense of private faith, or the related sense of a personal adherence to a soteriological doctrine of God, was needed for the representation of the world as a secular, neutral, factual, comprehensively quantifiable realm whose natural laws can be discovered by scientific rationality, and whose central human activity is a distinct 'non-religious' sphere or domain called 'politics' or 'political economy'. By 'non-religious' I do not necessarily mean 'hostile to religion', but, more often, neutral towards religion, tolerant of religion. This does not exclude hostility but does not entail it either. The crucial logic is separation into two essentially different domains. It is this that makes the plural objectification of 'religions' possible. Probably the most powerful single formulation of the religion–secular ideology is found in the American Constitution (see the argument in Chapter 11), which protects the right to freedom of religion. However, that, and all modern constitutions influenced by it, also protects the state *from* religion. Logically, whether hostile, neutral or indifferent, this amounts to a non-religious domain having jurisdiction over a religious one.

    Although the modern meaning of 'secular' as 'non-religious' did not emerge clearly in actual usage until well into the nineteenth century, it is embryonically present in the seventeenth-century developments in the idea of scientific knowledge as authorized by natural human processes in contradistinction to revelation, and in a new idea of the polity, the magistracy, indicated by a modern discourse on 'politics' conceived as a distinct domain of rational *non-religious* activity.[4] The further idea of political economy, and from this of economics as a distinct sphere, developed in the second half of the eighteenth and the early nineteenth centuries. To read a distinction between 'religious' and 'secular' – in the sense of 'non-religious' – spheres into earlier European formations, or into formations articulated in non-European languages, is to muddy the waters before immersing in them, that is to say is to commit a category mistake.

4. An implication of this is that the assumption that 'religion' or 'religions' can be researched, analysed and compared scientifically as though they are species of a genus is an illusion created by the elision of the function of 'religion' in the construction of 'the secular', and in the construction of so-called non-religious domains such as politics and economics. In this book we propose the necessity of this dichotomy in conceptualizing capitalist markets as universally rational but obscured by the irrational practices of natives and savages in the non Euro-American world. But we do not claim that the construction of capitalist markets was the only motive for colonization. It may be that no one, probably not even Adam Smith, knew they were constructing capitalist markets until Marx and other nineteenth-century theorists told them so. As part of the enlightenment project the classification of 'religions' and 'religious phenomena' was also driven by the desire to dominate the world through the imposition of Euro-American knowledge. To claim that capitalism was the fundamental driving force risks assuming that economic motivation could precede the very idea of 'economics', which was itself a result of this process. The more subtle suggestion must be that the processes of colonialism were profoundly important both in explaining the changes in the categorical structures of European consciousness and in creating a dominant space for 'politics' and 'economics' conceivable as distinct arenas of human action.

5. There is no assumption here that the idea of a world divided between religion and non-religion, understood as neutrality towards 'religion' and therefore as essentially distinct from 'religion', was a simple act of Euro-American imposition on subordinated peoples. Although the general implication of the research and argumentation in this book is consistent with Edward Said's thesis in *Orientalism* (1978), it would also want to accommodate the point made by postcolonial critics of Said, who have suggested that his argument focuses too exclusively on what the imperial powers did and gave to colonized societies, but stress, for example, that subaltern peoples appropriated hegemonic colonial discourse for their own ends in the struggle for freedom (see Chatterjee 1986; 1995; Guha & Spivak 1988; Breckenridge & Veer 1993; King 1999). Charles Hallisey (1995) has used the term "intercultural mimesis" to refer to this kind of process.

It follows from these general principles that the religion–secular distinction is a historically unstable product, put together by complex and contested forces, and is not a static binary with two simple and unchanging meanings. It seems obvious – especially after reading the essays in this book – that what constitutes 'religion' and what constitutes 'the secular' is highly contested and requires historiographical and ethnographic deconstruction. Indeed a central point of this book is that when contemporary sociologists and historians talk about religion and secularization, or the process of secularization, or the separation of religion and politics, or the separation of church and state, they tend to talk as though the meanings of these terms is self-evident, and they refer relatively unproblematically to things or processes that actually exist in the world, and by implication have always existed, at certain times in history being covered up and disguised by the dominance of one domain or the other, but essentially pre-existing in various degrees of relationship with each other.

It is worth considering here that, as late as 1815, the entry on secularization in the *Encyclopaedia Britannica* described it as:

> the act of converting a regular person, place or benefice, into a secular one. Almost all the Cathedral churches were anciently regular, that is, the canons were to be religious; but they have been since secularized. For the secularization of a regular church, there is required the authority of the pope, that of the prince, the bishop of the place, the patron, and even the consent of the people. Religious that want to be released from their vow, obtain briefs of secularization from the pope.
>
> (*Encyclopaedia Britannica*, 5th edn, vol. XIX)

The use of the word 'regular' here is the same as the use of the word 'religious'. The regulars or the religious were, and still are, those who belong to special orders – the monks, nuns and friars – who had taken special vows of obedience. These orders were disbanded in England in the sixteenth century as part of the creation of the Protestant Nation State. The seculars were the priesthood who had not taken special vows. Obviously the secular and the process of secularization described here has an entirely different nuance from the modern concept of the 'non-religious' as being an essentially distinct domain from religion. Yet this article was written 40 years after the publication of Adam Smith's *Inquiry into the Nature and Causes of the Wealth of Nations* in 1776 and the posthumous publication of David Hume's *The Natural History of Religion* in 1777[5] (both in Edinburgh, the city in which the *Encyclopaedia Britannica* was published).

The point I am making here is that while these two authors were major contributors to what came to be called secularization, or at least to the naturalization of the emerging ideological configuration of the 'non-religious' secular, the one in constructing political economy, the other in constructing generic religion, the older usages of 'religious' and 'secular' were still powerfully present and arguably dominant nearly half a century later. I believe that this small piece of evidence, which indicates that profoundly different meanings are being attributed to the same word at the same historical time by individuals thinking within competing paradigms, in combination with much else, makes apparent for us today the importance of critically historicizing and deconstructing reified terminology.

Influential authors of the kind I cite and quote embed in an uncritical, taken-for-granted manner highly contentious aspects of modern ideology as though they represent the natural order of things. This rhetorical habit is not merely misleading but surely dangerous. Such a procedure, and the assumptions on which it is based, seems to constitute a category mistake of sufficiently serious implications to require explanation. For under the guise of neutral and objective description and analysis of highly volatile movements and ideologies, which spring from widespread misery and inequality in the world, such authors reproduce and reconfirm a network of assumptions as though they constitute objective descriptions about what is, rather than ideological discourses that are intentional and persuasive, in the sense that they urge us to believe in what ought to be. They are, if you like, objects of faith that, through chant and ritual repetition, have become clothed in an aura of factuality.

English-language categories such as religion, nation, sacred, secular, politics, economics, law and civil society may have close relations in a number of other European languages, but are often very distant approximations in many non-European ones. The history of these modern concepts can be traced. Most have a degree of continuity with earlier words and ideas. This superficial appearance of continuous meaning has misled historians and others into thinking that it is acceptable to talk about, say, the religion and politics of virtually any society at any time in history as though it is self-evident what is meant. This pitfall is especially easy to fall into when no actual translation into non-European languages is required. Yet even in the English language, the difference in meaning between modern and late-medieval or even early modern usages of terms such as 'religion', 'secular', 'church' or 'state' is profound. It is easier to notice the incommensurability of categories when translation is at stake, especially into a non-European language. The evidence is that few non-European languages contain semantic equivalents, and that the demand of colonial powers for the constitutional separation of church and state, or of religion and politics, and of the 'right to freedom of religion', has turned out to be a demand for the virtual reconstruction of the self-representations of indigenous societies in line with Western ones.

It follows that this book is concerned with the hegemony of English-language, and tacitly other European-language, categories that organize knowledge of the world in a particular way. The colonial aspect is crucial because the idea of a 'secular' realm of natural reason, scientific knowledge, civil society and the nation state is inseparable from the development of constitutions, world trade and capitalist markets. These in turn have a symbiotic relationship with the development of a generic concept of 'religion' and 'religions' based on Protestant Christian origins but projected universally. The imperial powers, missionaries, trade organizations and other agencies have often facilitated the institutionalization of these categories into cultures and languages where they did not previously exist. It is assumed that this was not a one-way process, that is, a process from metropolis to periphery, but that the developments in Europe were partly the result of what was happening in the colonies, a point illuminated by David Chidester (Chapter 8) in the case of southern Africa.

## THEORETICIANS, HISTORIANS AND HISTORIOGRAPHY

In this book we seek to question critically the ideological functions of the religion–secular distinction that so many scholars apparently seek to re-affirm, either consciously or unconsciously. Yet it is important to acknowledge the painstaking and exact analysis of the historically changing usages of 'religion' that we are given by historians and contemporary theorists interested in the emergence of the modern category, such as W. C. Smith (1962), John Bossy (1982; 1985), Jonathan Z. Smith (1982; 1998); Peter Biller (1985), Louis Dumont (1986), Michael Taussig (1987), Fritz Staal (1989), Peter Harrison (1990), Michel Despland and Gérard Vallée (1992), Talal Asad (1993; 2003), S. N. Balagangadhara (1994),[6] David Chidester (1996), Russ McCutcheon (1997), Daniel Dubuisson (1998), Gavin Flood (1999), Richard King (1999), Danièle Hervieu-Léger (2000), Derek Peterson and Darren Walhof (2002),[7] Kim Knott (2005) and Tomoko Masuzawa (2005).[8]

One problem is that in some of the more historical studies, such as the important Despland and Vallée collection (1992), or the detailed studies by Harrison (1990) or Masuzawa (2005), there is a tendency to confine the historiographical enquiry to the way 'religion' appears as an essentially isolated category, or one that is only incidentally and secondarily connected with others. Because of the enormity of the historiographical project we do not always get the illumination that might come from placing those texts in the wider-angled vision, such as the relationship of religion to other shifting categories.

The expansion of Europe into Asia, Africa and America has been a fundamental aspect of more general changes in European self-representations and cosmology, and we are interested here particularly in 'religion' as an interconnected part of those wider changes. The essays in this book are a contribution towards the exploration of that wider colonial context, and that categorical relational network. These two methodological problems are not identical, but they do coexist. By treating 'religion' as though it is a category in its own right, its function in the legitimization and construction of other categories, in particular the idea of the 'non-religious', is missed. Critical studies that focus exclusively on the history of 'religion' as though the issue of 'what religion is not' is *secondary*, miss the importance of the ideological configuration without which we cannot see what 'religion' is 'doing'.

Jonathan Z. Smith was one of the first writers to expose, in a series of seminal essays (1982), the fallacies behind the essentialization of 'religion'. And in a more recent justly famous article (1998), he draws the reader's attention to the colonial and imperial context with which we are concerned in this book. Yet he claims that "'Religion' is not a native term; it is a term created by scholars for their intellectual purposes and therefore is theirs to define" (1998: 281). I find this a strange argument considering Smith initially locates his own in many ways brilliant historiography of the category in the colonial context. 'Religion' – a native English term with close approximations in other European languages – has surely for centuries meant Christian Truth; the essays in this book suggest that it was not only 'scholars' who created its different modern nuances, but people engaged in serious struggles of power who, since the late seventeenth century, wished to redefine current usages in order to gain some specific interest, such as toleration of certain limited (although significant) forms of dissent, or to make possible changes in property rights, or to free trade or finance from existing ideological and/or legal controls, all of which accumulated into a combined challenge to the status quo (see Chapter 11). The idea that scholars can choose to mean what they like by 'religion', as though we can simply say that "this is what we intend to mean by 'religion' for analytical purposes", seems highly questionable, and yet it is a widespread rhetorical ploy. One only has to consider the usages of the term in the media, in politics and in popular discourse to realize that no one has control over its meanings. What scholars can do is to reflect critically on these usages and meanings, subvert them, and refrain from using their authority to legitimize this ideologically weighted language game. This includes critically questioning how religious studies and associated disciplines such as anthropology, philosophy and sociology of religion are framed and taught in the academy and the schools.

W. C. Smith and some of the other contributors to the important Despland and Vallée collection (1992) say little about the wider contexts of the formation of 'religion', but they inadvertently construct the field in the very act of historicizing it.[9] In this work historians of profound knowledge get to grips with actual textual usages from different centuries and in several languages. In this sense they are problematizing the category in historical detail. Yet let us take Vallée's introduction. Vallée says that the book (and the conference from which the book emerged) was concerned with "determining the turning point in the emergence of the modern concept of religion" (Despland & Vallée 1992: 5). He points out that Smith (an inspiration for the conference and also a contributor to the book) "was haunted by the question: How are we to understand that many cultural worlds are religious without having a distinct idea of religion, still less our modern idea?" But the way this question has been formulated here by Vallée encapsulates the problem of circularity that I want to draw attention to. If a cultural world has no distinct idea of religion, then what does it mean to propose that it is religious? Vallée is presumably trying to avoid essentializing 'religion' as though it is a thing, and this would be consistent with a central part of Smith's argument in *The Meaning and End of Religion* ([1962] 1978). The problem is that by attributing personal lives (or cultural worlds) with a 'religious' dimension, and assuming as Smith does that such personal religious consciousness is ubiquitous and universal in place and time, we are still left with the problem of deciding which purportedly universal aspect of human experience is 'religious' and which is not religious (see Tayob, this volume, p. 178).

Smith's seminal work *The Meaning and End of Religion* ([1962] 1978) has been much discussed and analysed, for example by Asad (1993; 2003) in his own outstanding contributions to the field and its critical deconstruction. But a few words here will connect Smith's problematic to the orientation of this book (see my discussion in Fitzgerald 2000; 2003). I have argued elsewhere that *The Meaning and End of Religion*, while giving us a brilliant *historiographical* account of the categories 'religio' and 'religion' as they appear in historically significant texts, is essentially an ecumenical *theology* and as such a foundation text for the twentieth-century myth of 'religion', a myth that has been in the making for about 400 years but now has special academic departments, such as the World Religions programme at Harvard, to ensure its irrefutable respectability. Smith wished to problematize 'religion' and abandon its use in the academy, but he also thought that the adjectival form 'religious' can still be used loosely to talk about any period of history, even at the very point that he is demonstrating the historical and cultural relativity of the concept. In his chapter 2, "'Religion' in the West", Smith shows with impressive learning that at different historical times the word '*religio*' has had different meanings and nuances, and that the emergence of the modern meaning(s) can with scholarly sensitivity be traced through its historical vicissitudes.

Of Latin *religio*, which is frequently cited by many authors as the origin of the English-language term 'religion', he writes:

> To say that such and such a thing was *religio* ... meant that it was mightily incumbent upon me to do it (alternatively, not to do it ...) ... Oaths, family proprieties, cultic observances and the like were each *religio* to a man ... Also the ritual ceremonies themselves were designated *religiones*. Throughout Latin usage right to the end of its development, the sense of rite, the outward observance of a particular practice, is to be found. This is, perhaps, related to a Roman tendency to perceive what we would call the divine or the holy not so much, or not only, in the form of a figure of 'god' as in that of a series of standardised acts. (Smith [1962] 1978: 20–21)

Here Smith gives us a potentially revolutionary idea in the field of religious studies. Instead of legitimizing the English-language term 'religion' as 'belief in God or gods' by claiming descent from Latin *religio*, he suggests that *religio* and its derivatives have always had an important, perhaps fundamental, nuance of ritual practice, which would presumably include state ritual, household rituals, clan rituals and other standardized acts of collective identity. I am not an expert in the field of Roman history but Smith has raised the issue in a potentially fruitful analytical shift. This would involve moving away from the assumption that Roman *religio* was fundamentally about 'belief' in 'gods', a retrospective abstraction perhaps overlaid with Protestant Christian intellectualism and much less clear in meaning than it may seem, and see *religio* more in terms of collective, standardized practices of *civilitas* that confer Roman (or Roman Christian) identity as distinct from those categories of 'other' such as *barbaroi*, *paganus* and *superstitio*.

King (1999), drawing partly on Balagangadhara (1994), has argued that *religiones* in the pre-Christian, Roman Latin context "were simply the ancestral practices of particular communities" (King 1999: 37).[10] Like others King derives an etymology for the word from Cicero relating it to *relegere*, meaning to retrace or reread. He writes:

> ... *religio* involves the retracing of 'the lore of the ritual of one's ancestors'. This understanding of the term seems to have gained provenance in the 'pagan' Roman empire and made *religio* virtually synonymous with *traditio*. As such it represented the teachings of one's ancestors and was essentially not open to question. Primarily *religio* involved performing ancient ritual practices and paying homage to the gods. (King 1999: 36)

One aspect of this understanding of *religio* is that it is not about truth or falsity of beliefs in any propositional sense. It is fundamentally about the customary disciplines of civility of different groups of people who represent themselves as having a collective identity. There was no clash of belief claims. One could honour someone else's gods as a mark of respect to that community on the appropriate ritual occasion without offending one's own.[11]

This line of thinking, initiated by W. C. Smith and added to in the work of writers such as Balagangadhara and King, prompts me to suggest a further thought, although always deferring to those with more expertise in Roman Latin than me. In such a methodological revision, we might look at the practice of those virtues that confer civility (*civilitas*), for *religio* would come to look like a minor term in a larger and more significant discourse on Roman identity, a sense of superior cultivation (*civilitas, romanitas*) as against the barbarians (*barbarus*), especially those Germanic and Celtic tribes and their barbaric, uncultivated *superstitio*. It would, I suppose, be legitimate to ask whether anything was more ultimate and sacred to the Romans than Rome itself; and whether it was not *religio* to practise the civic virtues that made one Roman and civilized.[12]

This is, of course, a question for the experts in Roman Latin culture. But there is a potentially large methodological pay-off in thinking of *religio* as about something more interesting than the cliché 'belief in gods'. 'Belief' is itself a multivalent word that has become overdetermined by Protestant enlightenment intellectualism, which posits belief as a kind of imperfect propositional knowledge. Religion defined as belief in gods and thus as an essentially explanatory construct has been persistently challenged in ethnography, and also by some historians.

John Gould (1985: 7–8) has argued about 'Greek religion' that it was as different from a Christian idea of religion as the 'religion' of the Dinka in South Sudan. Gould argues that "the central *Greek* term, *theous nomizein*, means not 'believe in the gods', but 'acknowledge' them, that is, pray to them, sacrifice to them, build them temples, make them object of cult and ritual ..." (*ibid.*: 14).

By rendering 'belief in gods' differently, as 'acknowledging the gods' or 'honouring the gods', we can move the semantic weight from a propositional concept of belief as a kind of imperfect knowledge to a notion of practice. Acknowledging the gods means performing what W. C. Smith meant when he referred "to a Roman tendency to perceive what we would call the divine or the holy not so much, or not only, in the form of a figure of 'god' as in that of a series of standardised acts" (Smith [1962] 1978: 21); also see Zavos, Chapter 7 on 'performance' in the context of Indian 'politics' and 'religion').

If *religio* is taken as referring to those collectively recognized, self-identifying performances and cultivations whereby one's own *civilitas* is symbolically constructed as against the barbarity of various others, there would be a methodological pay-off. The pay-off would derive from the well-established interconnectedness of Greek, Roman and medieval Catholic conceptions of civility.[13] The ways that the literate male elites of these different phases of European civilization expressed and policed their collective and individual sense of salvation from the hell of barbarism and madness had important differences, but just as the Romans consciously derived many of their standards of civility from the Greeks, so the Christians derived many of theirs from both the Romans and the Greeks. The importance in Christianity of orthodox confessional practice, which later Protestants reified out as 'belief', might, from a methodological viewpoint, benefit from being re-embedded in the matrix of civilizing disciplines.

If *pietas* and *religio* in their Latin forms could be strongly linked to a concept of ritual observance, "a series of standardised acts", as W. C. Smith put it, or what I would also describe as disciplines of civility, then we would at least have a possibility of theorizing these terms in an anthropologically useful way, and avoid the modern reification of religion and religions, and their supposed essential difference from power, politics and economics.

Talking about 'ritual' in general and also more specifically referring to the Japanese context, Jan van Bremen writes:

> the bipartite division of society into sacred and secular domains is progressively being abandoned by anthropologists studying industrialised as well as non-industrialised societies ... There is no essential or qualitative shift between the categories and relations of the everyday world and those used in rites. Rites must not be taken as events which are essentially different in form, quality, and substance from those which constitute and inform the so-called routine of daily life. The study of ritual is not a search for the essential qualities of a peculiar and qualitatively different event; it is a way of examining how trivial elements of the social world can be elevated and transformed into symbols, categories, mechanisms, which, in certain contexts, allow the generation of a special or extraordinary event ... Rites, in other words, are an aspect of social ties, which explains the use made of ordinary articles ... such as fingers, rings, or even towels ... brooms ... and foodstuffs ...   (1995: 2–3)

This de-essentializing approach to the history of the category 'religion' cannot be defended in any detail here, but it can be taken to signal an intention to find other productive ways of deconstructing the reified religion–secular dichotomy.

This is not, of course, to claim that Roman '*religio*' and Christian '*religio*' amount to the same thing, for the discourses of their use need to be analysed historically.[14] Clearly the nuances of '*religio*' in Roman and medieval Latin were different, and the latter different from those of the English word 'religion' in the early modern period (Bossy 1982; 1985), and these changed again as part of the Enlightenment reconfiguration of European values. It is these acts of historicization that show us that a category has many nuances with significantly different outcomes, and that the meanings we take as given may conceal a history of alternative and even contradictory implications.

If we agree with the historians Despland and Vallée (1992) that the modern category of religion did have a "turning point", did have an "emergence", then we cannot assume that fifteenth-century Europe had 'religion' or was 'religious' in the modern sense. Religion was all-encompassing Christian Truth. No one would have described Christianity as "a religion" until fundamental changes in our ideological constructions of the world had occurred. As the quotation from the *Encyclopaedia Britannica* indicates, the expression 'religious', or rather 'the religious', along with 'the secular', referred to a status of persons and institutions within Christendom well into the nineteenth century. They were not simply and univocally standing in a mutually exclusive opposition as in religion:non-religion, and there are still many areas of Western cultures where this is still true.

In the medieval and early modern periods, secular courts, although organizationally distinct from ecclesiastical ones, were not 'non-religious' in the modern sense. (Who would ever have described the secular Thomas More as 'non-religious' in the modern sense?) These are not nit-picking points about mere semantics. They go to the heart of our modern confusions, where multivalent terms are used in simplistic ways by scholars in prestigious institutions, and beg important questions about how we construct and reconstruct our world order (or disorder) on the basis of such category mistakes.

When tracking the genealogy of religion, many historians fail to keep a consistent eye[15] on what is happening to those other categories without which we could not think of religion in the modern sense at all – 'the secular' as the 'non-religious' in various constructions such as: the secular nation state; secular politics and law; economics and markets; scientific naturalism and materialism. It is as though the ability to imagine these discursive spaces is merely a contingently related matter outside the vital focus of concern: 'religion' (but see Asad 1993; 2003). But what counts as 'religion' and what counts as 'the secular' are mutually delimiting and defining concepts, the distinction between them continually shifting depending on the context.

In this book we want to place these changes and processes in the context of the beginnings of capitalism with the search for American colonies from the fifteenth century. We wish to stress the importance of colonial sites and interests, their influence on the thinking within the metropolitan centres, and the connection between the flexible ideology of the religion–secular dichotomy and the development of a hegemonic world economic system that makes capital markets look like unavoidable natural occurrences, the highest point of rational exchange.

Thus one theoretical claim here is that 'religion' cannot be treated as a category in isolation, what McCutcheon has referred to as 'sui generis religion' (1997), but must be analysed in its historical emergence as part of a network of categories. The religion–secular dichotomy (in its various forms) is a fundamental part of this network, since it holds together, and is in turn sustained by, a number of other over-essentialized, shifting dichotomies, such as nature and supernature, body and soul, spirit and matter, private and public, and inner and outer.[16]

## THIS BOOK

The poignant essay by Anna Blume (Chapter 1), located in Guatemala at the Central American end of the colonial relationship, is in several ways an ideal introduction to some central themes of this volume. The first two parts of Blume's chapter deal with the history of the initial Spanish colonization, the biography and interventions of Bartolomé de las Casas and the debates that he engendered among his contemporaries and fellow Catholics. This is history based, in the European manner, on texts. The third part of Blume's essay is an ethnography of contemporary Mayan uses of the old colonial churches. Blume shows how these imported and planted symbols of foreign domination have become transformed into sites where local people remember their own history, renegotiate and make sense of the violence and the hierarchies that have been inflicted on them, and reconstruct their own identities and sense of continuity with the sufferings of their ancestors.

This essay reminds us not only of the violence involved in the very early colonization by the Spanish from 1498, but also of the recent violence perpetrated by the Protestant dictator Rios Montt, who in 1982 massacred Maya people in his desire to break up their indigenous forms of land-holding and production and to introduce modern capitalist values, markets and forms of production and consumption.

In these ways Blume's essay marks out the historical period of modern colonialism, and gives us a picture of the postcolonial continuity with the colonial past. The initial violence of the Spanish in the late fifteenth century was not the violence of 'religion' in the modern sense, that is, the violence frequently attributed to religion as contrasted with the rationality of the non-religious, secular state (see Chapter 12). The religion that hit the indigenous people of Central America in the late fifteenth century was itself a state, the pope himself also a prince; the Spanish Christian king required the pope's blessing for his colonization of the New World. This was all-encompassing Religion, Christian Truth (see Chapter 11). The early colonization was a confrontation between a previously unknown people and a feudal European polity that itself recognized no modern distinction between church and state, and whatever or whoever subsisted outside of its cognitive borders could not properly *exist* except as irrational barbarians, demons or savages, marginal beings arguably fit to be slaves (Pagden 1982).[17] It was Las Casas who, in shock and misery at the suffering inflicted by his own people upon the Amerindians, went into a monastery for eight years to seek solace from God, to emerge with the inspiration of *congregación*. While Las Casas praised the human attributes of the Indians highly, he also sought to make them dependent on the Roman Church, its rites, language and ideology of order. His organization of *congregación*, so well described by Blume, reproduced much of the Spanish feudal order. While personal devotion was a central part of Las Casas's practice and motivation, he was in the service of God, the pope and the king, as well as the Indians.

Trevor Stack (Chapter 2) focuses on the dichotomy of secular and religious knowledge. Specifically, he looks at histories told and written of a Catholic icon in twentieth-century west Mexico, the Virgin of Defence. He distinguishes between secular and non-secular histories of the Virgin and asks why some narrators chose to produce secular histories. He also finds different kinds of secular narrative and argues that there was no single reason for choosing secular narration. One of the reasons was that secular knowledge gave narrators a kind of higher ground: narrators claim to look in from the outside on the religious devotion of their narrative subjects. This higher ground gives them authority, although even this varies from one narrator to another. Stack focuses on the twentieth century, but he still places secular knowledge within a broader history that he terms "modern-colonial": just as people continue to be ranked in terms of race, civilization and so on, people who take a secular perspective are set above people judged incapable of this. He also finds that some secular histories are produced under the auspices of the Church and argues that secular knowledge was developed partly *within* the Church. He even suggests that Spanish missionaries had already sown the seeds of secular knowledge by the late sixteenth century.

James Cox (Chapter 3) is concerned with the direct impact of capitalism on the conceptual world of the indigenous people of Alaska, and on the cultural and economic effects that capitalist concepts of ownership have had on indigenous forms of life. He effectively brings out the subversive function of the ideological distinction between religion and the secular in this form of neo-colonialism. He succinctly argues that the Alaska Native Claims Settlement Act of 1971 "must be seen as the culmination of over a century of concerted ... US government efforts to assimilate the Alaskan natives". This policy of assimilation began in earnest with Sheldon Jackson, who was head both of the Protestant Mission and the US Government Education Agency at the end of the nineteenth and beginning of the twentieth centuries. As Cox indicates, Sheldon's aim was to completely change the traditional life and collective values of the indigenous people to produce American-style individualism. This included a policy of suppressing the native language and only allowing English to be used in the mission schools.

Jun'ichi Isomae (Chapter 4) discusses the impact of the threat of colonization on Japan, the imposition from the outside of an American-style constitution guaranteeing the separation of religion from politics, and the problems of translating these concepts into Japanese. He follows the vicissitudes of the public debates about how a Protestant Christian concept of religion, and its corollary 'religious freedom', could be made sense of in Japanese, and how this led to the reformulation of the Japanese state, with the cult of the Emperor's divinity at one stage being classified as the equivalent of *secular* morality, and at other times as state religion.

Thomas Pearson's essay (Chapter 5) focuses on the invasions and manipulations of the tribal 'Montagnard' in highland Vietnam by the US Central Intelligence Agency (CIA), missionaries and anthropologists. French colonialism in the early twentieth century led to the involvement of the American military and the Vietnam War. The people who belonged to different ethnic and linguistic groups were lumped together under the French rubric 'Montagnard'. The colonizing groups – missionaries, anthropologists and the military – all claimed their own distinctive roles, and while on the one hand they distinguished themselves by classifying their activities as either 'religious' or 'secular', in reality their activities overlapped to such an extent, and they aided and abetted each other in such a way, that the religion–secular distinction takes on an appearance of ideologically motivated rhetoric rather than substantial reality.

Will Sweetman (Chapter 6) locates his research in India, and on documents written in Tamil, German, French and English. He focuses on an important debate in Indology that includes a theoretical discussion of Nicholas Dirks, who has argued that it was the British colonialists who reified caste as a central Indian institution and that before India became a British colony caste was configured quite differently. The British classification of caste as a 'religious' rather than a 'political' institution was an instrument of colonial policy designed to strengthen the Brahmin castes at the expense of kings and princes. Sweetman discusses this in the context of German missionary documents and analyses the language of the missionaries. Sweetman shows that the nuance of terms such as 'religious' and 'civil' used by the missionaries changed over time, especially after around 1820.

John Zavos (Chapter 7), writing about nineteenth- and twentieth-century India, tries to get at (or "cut across") the colonial division of the religious and the political by thinking about modern 'politics' in India as *performance*. In a sense the invention of 'religion' is also the invention of 'politics', but in typical rhetoric they are placed in a relationship of mutual exclusion; religion is defined as being private and non-political, whereas politics is ideally defined as public and non-religious. Wherever these separated domains are brought into contact problems of an analytical and even a legal kind result. But the problem may be created by the assumption that these are distinct domains in the first place. Performance as an analytical category can be simultaneously 'religious' and 'political' and as such problematizes the distinction itself. Zavos looks at major examples of anti-colonial and postcolonial indigenous movements and suggests that the English-language word 'performance' can help us to get closer to an indigenous idea of meaningful collective action, which we tend to try to categorize as being either 'secular' or 'religious'.

David Chidester (Chapter 8), from his location in southern Africa, here develops and brilliantly crystallizes the important analysis of the colonial process of category formation of his famous work, *Savage Systems* (1996). On the basis of historical evidence Chidester focuses a high-powered lens on the way in which English-language categories such as 'religion' have been adjusted to suit different phases of imperial control and domination, particularly over the Zulu peoples. He points out how, according to the narrative needs of the moment, 'savages' who live in open spaces without boundaries or any 'civilization' did not have 'religion', but once subjugated as colonial subjects within externally imposed boundaries apparently did have 'religion' (or superstition) after all. 'Religion' or its absence thus becomes a classificatory term for control over different kinds of (primitive) social orders. He reveals the connections between local European 'experts' such as missionary ethnographer Henry Callaway, indigenous informants such as Mpengula Mbande, Anglican functionaries such as Bishop J. W. Colenso, colonial administrators such as Theophilus Shepstone, popular novelists such as H. Rider Haggard and John Buchanan and the metropolitan theory-makers who invented comparative religion such as F. Max Müller, E. B. Tylor and Andrew Lang. Chidester shows how supposedly objective 'knowledge' has been constructed that effectively elides the actual shifting conditions of power under which such knowledge originated in the first place, such that mistaken Europhone theories have been derived from thirdhand information wrongly translated and abstracted from the actual conditions of colonial power.

Abdulkader Ismail Tayob (Chapter 9) questions the classification of Islam as a 'religion'. He also questions W. C. Smith's distinction between the noun 'religion' and the adjective 'religious', in Smith's claim that, while the reification of 'religions' is invalid, personal 'religious' experience is a reality. Tayob examines the uses made of the English-language concepts of religion and religious within Islamic discourse, and then abandons them on the grounds that they do not represent clearly identifiable aspects of human life. In particular he studies the modernizing rhetoric of two important Muslim scholars, Sayyid Ahmad Khan and Jamal al-Din al-Afghani, both of whom played an influential role in the translation of 'religion' and the reinterpretation of Islam in the context of modern discourse.

Some of the essays presented here are concerned with the metropolitan end of the colonial relationship. In his seminal essay on Rudolf Otto (Chapter 10), Gregory Alles provocatively explores the relationship between German cultural colonialism and Otto's experience of the Holy, which has been a major influence in twentieth-century renditions of comparative religion. From a close reading of contemporary German texts, including Otto's correspondence, Alles brilliantly reveals the inventions and even mythical elements in the narrative of Otto's definitive 'religious experience', and the way its retelling has disengaged it from a context of colonial ambitions and relocated it as a pure mysticism guaranteeing a *sui generis* reality called 'religion' separated from power and politics.

Timothy Fitzgerald (Chapter 11) follows the emergence of modern discourses on religion, politics and other categories in English and North American historical documents since the sixteenth century. He argues that the dominant discourse on religion as Christian Truth, which was based on an organic analogy with the human body in which all stations in life are hierarchically included in an organic totality, became challenged and subverted in the developing context of new colonial interests by minority discourses that posited essentialized dichotomies between religion as private faith and an objective outer world of non-religious, objective rationality. The need to describe and control non-European peoples, the emergence of empirical science, and new demands for toleration by non-conformists, all combined to redefine the meaning of 'religion' as an essentially inner form of belief separated from the public rationality of the secular state, facilitating a new idea of 'politics' as a *sui generis* sphere of human activity. He shows how American Constitutionalism has emerged as a hegemonic representation of these new essentializing dichotomies, authorizing a higher ground of non-religious secular rationality in which the practices of Christians and non-Christians alike could be turned into voluntary 'religious' associations licensed by the state and available for 'scientific' research. These rhetorical constructions have gradually become transformed into a hegemonic ideology of universal rationality and civility against which indigenous forms of life of colonized peoples could be judged.

William Cavanaugh (Chapter 12) focuses on contemporary rhetorical constructions of the supposed threat to the benign and neutral secular state by the inherent fanaticism of 'religion'. He shows how this discourse, which is actively promoted by academics who present themselves as neutral and objective observers, proceeds in the first place on a number of myths. One is the myth of 'religion' as a distinct and universal agent in the world with an unstable and irrational tendency towards violence and terrorism. The other is the myth of the secular state as an essentially rational agent that is only reluctantly violent in the face of unreasonable fanaticism. In this powerfully argued and provocative critique of the widely held rhetorical convention that 'religions' cause violence, and that therefore the secular state had to be invented to keep the peace, Cavanaugh argues instead that 'religion' was invented as a by-product of the violent emergence of the nation state, which in turn was developed to allow princes to wage war in the newly competitive competition for lucrative colonies.

The topic is a vast one, and this book can only attempt to open up a line of enquiry that it is hoped other specialists in specific cultures and languages will develop in the same critical manner as we have tried to do here. We hope that this book will open up a wider debate, not about the definition of religion, which, if the arguments here are correct, is inherently circular and question-begging, but about the ideological function of the idea of religion and religions in the formation of an imagined domain of non-religious politics, economics and the liberal capitalist ideology generally. The topic demands interdisciplinarity, which invites dangers as well as gains. There is bound to be a degree of arbitrariness in the approaches that each individual author has taken within the broad theoretical parameters that I have outlined. But while the variety of subject matter, and the approach taken to it by each writer, may be to some extent arbitrary, I believe that most readers will clearly discern a common thread of theoretical cohesion that can be fruitfully applied to aspects of this huge topic not analysed here.

## NOTES

1. I have analysed a number of these in *The Ideology of Religious Studies* (2000).
2. Let me make one admission of failure. Although through sheer good fortune I have contributions from a range of outstanding scholars, I had always hoped for a larger participation from women and from people from non-Western cultures in general. There were a large number of women at the conference, but I have only been fortunate enough to get one contribution from them, from Anna Blume. Jun Isomae and Abdulkader Ismail Tayob are the only two non-Western scholars; the talented Chinese scholar Ivan Hon, who is a PhD candidate at the University of London's School of Oriental and African Studies (SOAS), contributed what will become important research on the nineteenth-century debates over the meaning of 'religion' in China, but unfortunately was unable to put it into shape for this book in time. However, what we have here are a number of outstanding individual contributions and a serious methodological proposal for the future of the study of 'religion'. It was never imagined that this could be anything more than a beginning, an attempt to open up a field of study concerning the many colonial sites in which the religion–secular dichotomy has been negotiated in a vast number of languages and addressing the problems of translation involved, the imposition of Western style constitutions, and the pressures placed on indigenous elites to re-represent their own traditions in ways that accommodated this essentialized dichotomy. The importance of this book we believe lies in the method and the approach: seeing 'religion' not as a *sine qua non*, a part of the furniture of the world, but as a category that has ideological work to do in the service of complex colonial interests.
3. In Purchas ([1613] 1626), 'religions' are usually an ironic reference to superstitions and barbaric practices. However, in many descriptive passages the irony is lost and we can see the emergence of a

descriptive neutral category. But it is highly ambiguous and the whole work is framed biblically and Christologically.

4. Although the words 'politics' and 'politicians' can be found earlier in English, for example, in Elizabethan drama, I argue that it is only since the late seventeenth century that such a modern discourse becomes explicit and powerful, and even then it has not definitely replaced the more dominant discourse of 'politic behaviour' as fundamentally encompassed by Christian Truth.

5. There were earlier editions, such as the first in 1757, but according to H. E. Root's notes on the text (Hume 1957) the 1777 edition was definitive.

6. S. N. Balagangadhara's "The Heathen in His Blindness" (1994) has many interesting arguments on the problems with 'religion' as a category, and deserves more attention than I can give it here. Various symposia have been held to critically discuss this important work.

7. I am grateful to an anonymous reader for pointing out the existence of The Invention of Religion: Rethinking Belief in Politics and History by Derek R. Peterson and Darren R. Walhof (2002), which I have not seen, and for pointing out that this book is close to the present volume in terms of its approach, its inter-disciplinarity, and its varied content deriving from studies of different colonial sites. The anonymous reader suggested that the book had not been well publicized. I therefore regret not being able to discuss it here.

8. I have only recently received a copy of Tomoko Masuzawa's valuable book, and my feelings about it are based on a very cursory reading. Clearly it deserves more than that, since it is full of interesting discussion and detailed information, and Masuzawa's style is subtle and inventive. However, while it is an important and informative new contribution to research on the origins and history of the field of religious studies, it is different in a number of ways from this book: it is single-authored, it is centred mainly on northern European intellectual developments, it is basically concerned with discourses on 'religion' and 'world religions' but not with the wider categorical context. Nor could I see much specific focus on the development of institutions and practices outside the immediate context of textuality and intellectual history. Methodologically, the book seems in the final analysis to be a fairly standard history of ideas.

9. I have discussed this volume in more detail in my essay "Playing Language Games and Performing Rituals: Religious Studies as Ideological State Apparatus" (2003).

10. Cf. Balagangadhara (1994: 46). This approach would also arguably be consistent with Pierre Bourdieu's (1977) fruitful idea of practice.

11. I do not think that it is a stretch from this to Bourdieu's (1977) notions of practice and habitus. Bourdieu uses these ideas in the sense of individual and collective practices that are learnt and passed on from one generation to another within given sets of relations, which mark out an identity and a living space, and from which observers, both indigenous and outsiders, can derive structure. The structures are embedded in the practices, and the practices organize and generate representations that are shared and understood by the collective, but that do not presuppose explicit beliefs or worldviews or sets of rules in the minds of those who do the practices.

12. Similarly, one might ask the same about ritualized representations of modern America, its Constitution, its founding myths, and its idea of "manifest destiny". These symbolic representations of American power and civility as against those unenlightened barbaric others who only know terror and violence might in this sense be taken as collective 'religio'.

13. See Jones (2003). I believe that this reading of religio would be compatible with Anthony Pagden's The Fall of Natural Man (1982.)

14. An interesting case in point that I mention not as conclusive proof of anything but as an indication of changing usages are the Richard Hakluyt translations (1599) from Latin into English of the travel diaries of two friars, Iohannes de Plano Carpini and William de Rubruqui, who were sent as emissaries by Pope Innocent IV and the French king Louis IX respectively in 1246 and 1253, to gather information about the Tartar/Mongol leadership and customs, to open diplomatic communications and ideally to convert to Christianity. Hakluyt has published the Latin original and his English translations side by side. These fascinating travel records are in many ways an attempt by the writers to record factual observations about virtually entirely unknown peoples, their customs and superstitions, in order

to enlighten their masters in Europe. And yet in neither of the Latin accounts could I find a single mention of *religio* (although *superstitio* does appear). On the other hand, in two places and two places only Hakluyt has translated from William de Rubruqui "the religion of Mahomet" (Hakluyt 1599: 94, 120). However, this is not a translation from *religio* but in both cases from "legem Machometi", which I believe would now be translated as 'the law of Mahomet'.

15. W. C. Smith was aware of this issue, and broached it, for example, in his 1983 presidential address to the American Academy of Religion, "The Modern West in the History of Religion" (1983).

16. This theoretical claim, namely, that it is an illusion to treat 'religion' as though it stands alone in a simple one-to-one relationship with things that exist in the world, was a basic part of the argument of my *The Ideology of Religious Studies* (2000), and can be found for example in the Preface, chapter 1 and subsequently in my criticisms of writers such as Juergensmeyer.

17. Pagden (1982) has shown with great interpretative skill how the application of the Aristotelian categories of 'barbarian' and 'natural slave' to the American Indians was debated by theologians in the sixteenth century as a way of legitimizing the *de facto* conquest and enslavement of the people. That these debates about the correct classification of the indigenous people may have been a source of 'secular' discourse would fit well with Stack's argument in Chapter 2.

## REFERENCES

Ambedkar, B. R. 1936. *Annihilation of Caste*. Allahabad: Bheem Patrika Publications.

Arnal, William. 1993. "Definition". In *The Guide to the Study of Religion*, eds Willie Braun and Russell McCutcheon, 21–34. London: Cassells Academic Press.

Asad, Talal. 1993. *Genealogies of Religion: Discipline and Reasons of Power in Christianity and Islam*. Baltimore, MD: Johns Hopkins University Press.

Asad, Talal. 2003. *Formations of the Secular: Christianity, Islam, Modernity*. Palo Alto, CA: Stanford University Press.

Balagangadhara, S. N. 1994. *"The Heathen in his Blindness": Asia, the West, and the Dynamic of Religion*. Leiden: E. J. Brill.

Berger, Peter, ed. 1999. *The Desecularization of the World: Resurgent Religion and World Politics*. Washington DC: Ethics and Public Policy Center & Wm. B. Eerdmans Publishing Company.

Biller, Peter. 1985. "Words and the Medieval Notion 'Religion'". *Journal of Ecclesiastical History* 36: 351–69.

Bossy, John. 1982. "Some Elementary Forms of Durkheim". *Past and Present* 95: 3–18.

Bossy, John. 1985. *Christianity in the West 1400–1700*. Oxford: OPUS.

Bourdieu, Pierre. 1977. *Outline of a Theory of Practice*. Trans. R. Nice. Cambridge: Cambridge University Press.

Breckenridge, Carol A. and Peter van der Veer, eds. 1993. *Orientalism and the Postcolonial Predicament: Perspectives on South Asia*. Philadelphia, PA: University of Pennsylvania Press.

Bremen, Jan van. 1995. *Ceremony and Ritual in Japan: Religious Practices in an Industrialised Society*. London: Routledge.

Cavanaugh, William T. 1995. "'A Fire Strong enough to Consume the House': The Wars of Religion and the Rise of the State". *Modern Theology* 11: 397–420.

Chatterjee, Partha. 1986. *Nationalist Thought and the Colonial World: A Derivative Discourse*. London: Zed Books.

Chatterjee, Partha, ed. 1995. *Texts of Power: Emerging Disciplines in Colonial Bengal*. Minneapolis, MN: University of Minneapolis Press.

Chidester, David. 1996. *Savage Systems: Colonialism and Comparative Religion in Southern Africa*. Charlottesville, VA: University of Virginia Press.

Comaroff, J. 1994. "Epilogue". In *Asian Visions of Authority: Religion and the Modern States of East and South East Asia*, eds C. F. Keyes, L. Kendall and H. Hardacre, 301–10. Honolulu, HI: University of Hawaii Press.

Despland, Michel and Gérard Vallée, eds. 1992. *Religion in History: The Word, the Idea, the Reality; La Religion dans l'histoire: Le Mot, l'idée, la réalité*. West Waterloo, Ontario: Wilfrid Laurier University Press.

Dubuisson, Daniel. 1998. *L'Occident et la religion: mythes, science et idéologie*. Brussels: Editions Complexe. Trans. William Sayers as *The Western Construction of Religion: Myths, Knowledge and Ideology* (Baltimore, MD: Johns Hopkins University Press, 2003).

Dumont, Louis. 1986. *Essays on Individualism*. Chicago, IL: Chicago University Press.

Easterling, P. E. and J. V. Muir, eds. 1985. *Greek Religion and Society*. Cambridge: Cambridge University Press.

Fitzgerald, T. 2000. *The Ideology of Religious Studies*. New York: Oxford University Press.

Fitzgerald, T. 2003. "Playing Language Games and Performing Rituals: Religious Studies as Ideological State Apparatus". *Method and Theory in the Study of Religion* 15(3): 209–54.

Fitzgerald, T. 2006. "Bruce Lincoln's Theses on Method: Antitheses". *Method and Theory in the Study of Religion* Fall (2006): 392–423.

Flood, Gavin. 1999. *Beyond Phenomenology: Rethinking the Study of Religion*. London: Cassell.

Gandhi, Mahatma. 1936. "A Vindication of Caste". *Harijan*, 11 July, 18 July, 15 Aug 1936. Reprinted in B. R. Ambedkar, *Annihilation of Caste* (Allahabad: Bheem Patrika Publications, 1982).

Gould, John. 1985. "Making Sense of Greek Religion". In *Greek Religion and Society*, eds P. E. Easterling and J. V. Muir, 1–33. Cambridge: Cambridge University Press.

Guha, Ranajit and Gayatri Spivak, eds. 1988. *Selected Subaltern Studies*. Delhi: Oxford University Press.

Hakluyt, Richard. 1599. *The Principal Navigations, Voyages, Traffiques, and Discoveries of the English Nation, made by Sea or Overland to the Remote and Furthest Distant Quarters of the Earth, at any Time within the Compass of these 1600 Yeres: Divided into Three Severall Volumes, According to the Position of the Regions, Whereunto they were Directed*. London.

Halliday, F. 2005. "A Matter of Power, not Religion". Interview by Adam Holm. *LSE Magazine* (Winter 2005): 6–7.

Hallisey, Charles. 1995. "Roads Taken and Not Taken in the Study of Theravāda Buddhism". In *Curators of the Buddha: The study of Buddhism under Colonialism*, ed. Donald Lopez Jr., 31–62. Chicago, IL: Chicago University Press.

Harrison, Peter. 1990. *Religion and the Religions in the English Enlightenment*. Cambridge: Cambridge University Press.

Hervieu-Léger, D. 2000. *Religion as a Chain of Memory*. Cambridge: Polity.

Hume, David. [1757, 1777] 1957. *The Natural History of Religion*. Ed. H. E. Root. Palo Alto, CA: Stanford University Press.

Jones, W. R. [1971] 2003. "The Image of the Barbarian in Medieval Europe". In *Facing Each Other: The World's Perception of Europe and Europe's Perception of the World*, ed. A. Pagden, 21–52. Aldershot: Variorum.

Juergensmeyer, Mark. 1993. *The New Cold War? Religious Nationalism Confronts the Secular State*. Berkeley, CA: University of California Press.

Juergensmeyer, Mark. 2000. *Terror in the Mind of God: The Global Rise of Religious Violence*. Berkeley, CA: University of California Press.

King, Richard. 1999. *Orientalism and Religion: Postcolonial Theory, India and the Mystic East*. London: Routledge.

Knott, Kim. 2005. *The Location of Religion: A Spatial Analysis*. London: Equinox.

Lincoln, Bruce. 1996. "Theses on Method". *Method and Theory in the Study of Religion* 8(3): 225–7.

Lincoln, Bruce. 2003. *Holy Terrors: Thinking about Religion after September 11*. Chicago, IL: University of Chicago Press.

Masuzawa, Tomoko. 2005. *The Invention of World Religions*. Chicago, IL: University of Chicago Press.

McCutcheon, Russell T. 1997. "The Category of Religion in Recent Scholarship". In *Manufacturing Religion: The Discourse on sui generis Religion and the Politics of Nostalgia*, ch. 5. New York: Oxford University Press.

Pagden, Anthony. 1982. *The Fall of Natural Man: The American Indian and the Origins of Comparative Ethnology*. Cambridge: Cambridge University Press.

Penn, William. 1680. *The Great Question to be Considered by the King, and this Approaching Parliament, Briefly*

*Proposed, and Modestly Discussed: (to wit) how far Religion is Concerned with in Polity or Civil Government, and Policy in Religion?* National Library of Scotland microfiche.

Peterson, Derek R. and Darren R. Walhof, eds. 2002. *The Invention of Religion: Rethinking Belief in Politics and History*. New Brunswick, NJ: Rutgers University Press.

Purchas, Samuel. [1613] 1626. *Purchas, his Pilgrimage; or, Relations of the World and the Religions Observed in all Ages*. London.

Said, Edward. 1978. *Orientalism*. New York: Vintage.

Smith, Adam. [1776] 1993. *An Inquiry into the Nature and Causes of the Wealth of Nations, a Selected Edition*. Ed. Kathryn Sutherland. Oxford: Oxford University Press.

Smith, Jonathan Z. 1982. *Imagining Religion: From Babylon to Jonestown*. Chicago, IL: University of Chicago Press.

Smith, Jonathan Z. 1998. "Religion, Religions, Religious". In *Critical Terms for Religious Studies*, ed. Mark C. Taylor, 269–84. Chicago, IL: University of Chicago Press.

Smith, W. C. [1962] 1978. *The Meaning and End of Religion: A Revolutionary Approach to the Great Religious Traditions*. London: SPCK.

Smith, W. C. 1983. "The Modern West in the History of Religion". Presidential Address to the Americal Academy of Religion Annual Meeting. *Journal of the American Academy of Religion* 52(1): 3–18.

Smith, W. C. 1992. "Retrospective Thoughts on the Meaning and End of Religion". In *Religion in History: The Word, the Idea, the Reality; La Religion dans l'histoire: Le Mot, l'idée, la réalité*, eds M. Despland and G. Valléem 13–22. West Waterloo, Ontario: Wilfrid Laurier University Press.

# 1
# Dialectics of conversion:
# Las Casas and Maya colonial *Congregación*[1]

## *Anna Blume*

## INTRODUCTION

The fifteenth-century arrival of Europeans along the coast and eventually inland into the American continents is mostly known to us through the writings of Europeans. This essay begins by recounting the story of one extraordinary Spaniard, Bartolomé de las Casas, an early colonist turned radical advocate of the Indians. Our sources are mostly his extensive autobiographical writings. Biographical or autobiographical narratives have a logic of their own that often seamlessly move into written histories. What we know directly from the Indians, they have written, so to speak, into the land or have left in the form of images that remain as ciphers for us to read. Writing the histories of these kinds of historical phenomena demands a different kind of looking and writing, an enthnohistorical approach through which we combine archeology, art history, oral stories and the markings of the land itself. Therefore, the second half of this essay shifts in tone, method and perspective, so that we may read land and decipher images in an attempt to write a dialectical history. Our focus will be on *congregación*: one of the strategies the Spanish adopted to convert Indians of the New World to Christianity. The origin of *congregación* begins with the thoughts of Las Casas, which he minutely records in written accounts. When it is implemented, however, conversion itself is fractured and redefined by the indigenous population it was meant to transform.

## PART I. STORY LEADING TO A PLAN: NARRATIVE – BIOGRAPHY[2]

In 1538, forty years after he had arrived in the New World, Bartolomé de las Casas finally won the right to attempt peacefully the conversion of Indians. When he first arrived in

1498, a member of Columbus's third voyage, he was a twenty-four-year-old educated entrepreneur curious and ready to begin the life of a Spanish gentlemen in the newly dominated colonies. He arrived on the island of Hispaniola (Dominican Republic) when Spanish conquistadores were infiltrating the neighbouring island of Cuba. In the village of Caonao in the central fertile provenance of Camaguey, Las Casas witnessed the everyday life of the indigenous people who were then brutally and treacherously massacred by his land-hungry unrestrained Spanish companions. This experience fundamentally changed his perceptions of both the Spanish and Indians and challenged him to find another way towards Spanish colonial rule.

After witnessing the Caonao massacre of 1514, Las Casas refused to accept a *repartimiento* (gift of land and Indian slaves from the Spanish crown) in Cuba and instead returned to Spain to plead his case before King Ferdinand and Cardinal Ximenes, two of the most powerful arbitrators in the affairs of the New World. Both king and cardinal were openly concerned by his report and in 1516 named Las Casas "Protector of the Indies", empowering him to impose sanctions on colonists in the New World who perpetrated such acts as the massacre at Caonao. Las Casas, however, went beyond condemning violent conquest to speak out against the *repartimiento* system itself, claiming that the natives of the New World could be peacefully converted to Christianity, and thus become rightful citizens of the growing Spanish empire.

Armed with his new title, Protector of the Indies, Las Casas returned in 1516 to Hispaniola for the second of what would be eleven voyages between the New World and Spain. In these early years, his plan to end the *repartimiento* system was a complete failure in practice. Neither the church nor the loose political infrastructure of the newly forming colonies had sufficient power over the acts of conquistadores or colonists; nor were they in agreement on the parameters that should govern Spanish treatment of Indians. Were Indians human? Could they be Christianized? Should they be enslaved? These were questions that remained unanswered deep into the sixteenth century.

Unable to stop the *repartimiento* system, Las Casas shifted his strategy. For the next six years he would plead for a portion of the New World in which he could carry out an experiment of peaceful conversion. If this experiment were to be successful he could offer it up as a blueprint to be followed in new territories in the Americas being explored and colonized each year. Like Plato before him, attempting to realize the Republic on the coast of Sicily, Las Casas desperately wanted to prove that, far away from economic ambitions and violence, a new kind of society could form.

One of the obstacles to his plan was that Spanish colonists did not want to be labourers in the New World. If they were to make this voyage and leave the comforts and familiarity of the Old World behind, the least they expected was to become *finceros* in the New World: landowners and entrepreneurs, a kind of new gentry. So who was to do the labour if the Indians were not to be enslaved and their land appropriated?

In 1518, in response to these questions of labour and land, Las Casas came up with his first specific pragmatic plan that was endorsed by Charles V, the young king of Spain, soon to become Holy Roman Emperor. This plan included the selection and transport of fifty

Spanish colonists who were given financial incentives and Africans as slaves to begin a community that would include the indigenous Indians as neighbours and collaborators in the formation of a colony in Cumaná, a region on the north-east coast of Venezuela.[3] These fifty colonists, Las Casas's private knights, so to speak, were to be dressed in white with large red embroidered crosses to signal to the indigenous population that they were different from the earlier wave of colonists that had been so violent and ruthless. With a rich agricultural base and access to pearl fishing on its coast, Cumaná was to potentially provide this brave new world of Spaniards, African slaves and Indians with the economic self-sufficiency they would need to be successful and live in harmony.

When the Cumaná experiment ended in disaster in 1522, due in part to the naivety of the plan and the unabated greed of the colonists, Las Casas returned to Hispaniola dejected and defeated. In 1530, after eight years of seclusion in a Dominican monastery, Las Casas, now an ordained monk, returned to his lifelong struggle as Protector of the Indies, a struggle he would continue until his death thirty-six years later. It was during this next period that he would begin to use writing as a tool to document and influence the colonization process.[4] His first published work of 1535, after this long period of seclusion, was *De Unico Vocationis Modo Omnium Infidelium ad Veram Religionem* [The Only Way to Call the Unfaithful to the One True Religion]. Here he clearly articulated his theory that the only way to convert anyone to the Christian faith, and to do this as a Christian, was to convert them through peaceful persuasion.

In 1538, three years after the publication of *De Unico*, Las Casas would finally have his opportunity to successfully implement this theory in highland Guatemala. He had arrived in Guatemala on his way to Peru to stem the already notorious violent conquests lead by Francisco Pizarro. While there he heard about a mountainous area called Tezulutlán, known to the Spanish as *La Tierra de Guerra* (Land of War), being the region where the Quiché Maya had been most resistant and difficult to subdue.[5] The warring resolve of the Maya combined with the steep mountain passes temporarily insulated this region from some of the worst, often repeated, abuses of the notorious Pedro de Alvarado. Alvarado had been a lieutenant under Hernán Cortés in the conquest of Mexico. Shortly afterwards, in 1524, he and his brother Jorge de Alvarado were given troops including Spanish soldiers and over 5,000 Nahua soldiers from Quauhquechollan to continue the conquest into southern Mexico and Guatemala, where he was eventually made governor.[6] When no gold was found in these regions, Perdro left the remainder of the offensive in Guatemala to his brother Jorge, and went to Peru. It was during these years that Las Casas first arrived in Guatemala.

Tezulutlán was thus an extraordinary region where the Maya maintained much of their pre-conquest lives separated from the direct effects of colonization by the very terrain they inhabited. On 2 May 1537, Alonzo Maldonado, the temporary governor of Guatemala, granted Las Casas sole jurisdiction over this region for a five-year period. During that time no other colonists, conquistadores or Spaniards of any kind, other than the governor himself, would be allowed in Tezulutlán. This gave Las Casas the opportunity to introduce Christianity through a new method devoid of the physical violence or overt economic motives that had characterized contact up to this point. This experiment in

Tezulutlán was to be fundamentally different from his attempt fifteen years earlier at Cumaná. Unlike Cumaná, with its easily accessible pearl fishing, Tezulutlán was isolated from the colonizing process, and, furthermore, Las Casas was seeking to engage directly with the indigenous Maya to transform them into a Christianized colony of Indians devoid of other Spaniards other than the Dominican monks who travelled with him.

With exclusive access to Tezulutlán, what specific strategies would Las Casas and his monks devise to Christianize and colonize the Quiché-speaking Maya inhabitants of the region? Maya merchants, who began trading European goods, such as scissors, mirrors and bells, were the primary liaisons between the Domenicans and the Maya of these mountainous regions of highland Guatemala. Knowing this, Las Casas and his monks, Luis Cancér, Pedro de Angulo and Rodrigo de Ladrada, decided to send along with these material goods a modified version of the central themes of Christian belief. They first wrote the story of Christ into *coplas* (rhyming Spanish couplets), and then translated these couplets into the Quiché language. Over a three-month period they taught the Quiché translation of the Passion of Christ to the Maya merchants, and set it to music using the indigenous drum and flute of the Guatemalan highlands.

The Christian ethos and message was thus packaged along with other European goods for the isolated Maya of Tezulutlán to consider at their own pace on their own terms. One of the Maya rulers from around the lake of Atitlán was particularly taken by these verses and the description of the monks by the travelling Maya merchants. These monks were distinctly different from other Spaniards, and this Christian story and mention of new gods, sung in their own Quiché language, made such an impression that the Maya ruler sent his own son back to Santiago de Guatemala with the merchants to meet Las Casas and the other Dominicans. With this began a new kind of contact, one that moved along trade lines and involved the slower process of language, translation and the space for curiosity. After a short visit with Las Casas and his monks, the ruler's son returned to Atitlán with the Dominican monk Luis Cancér who spoke the Quiché language. After several months of living in this Maya region Cancér had Christianized the ruler to such an extent that when Las Casas himself arrived there in October of 1537 they baptized him Don Juan and together oversaw the construction of a Christian church.

The experience with Don Juan emboldened Las Casas in the next phase of conversion that would take place in the Maya town called Rabinal, and this is where *congregación*[7] in the New World begins, in actuality. In Rabinal, Las Casas and the Dominicans introduced the Passion of Christ through the Quiché couplets set to music. They then expanded on this strategy to include medieval passion plays of the basic stories of the Old and New Testaments, to be performed by Maya inhabitants of Rabinal in the Quiché language.[8] After introducing this new set of religious stories, Las Casas persuaded the ruler of Rabinal, Don Juan, to move his people from the various mountaintop regions into a consolidated valley, where they built a Catholic church where one still stands today. Although they continued to work many of their agricultural fields, known as *milpas*, in the mountains they did move their homes around the newly constructed church. This city plan, medieval in its format, and classical in origin, provided Las Casas with two simultaneous and inextricably intertwined "successes". He was able to demonstrate that the Maya, and indigenous people of the Americas, could be peacefully converted into Christians (at least apparently so), and he could congregate them into small city units that would be monitored and taxed within the new expanding territories and logic of colonial Spain. We know this from the foundations of the city of Rabinal itself. This happened. We also know this from the extensive histories written by the Spanish about this moment, especially from Remesal's *Historia general de las Indias* (1620). What we do not know from these sources are the many inner stories of Don Juan and the Maya of Rabinal. What appeared to Las Casas and the Spanish as peaceful conversion has left its mark in the land where the Maya today still respond to the weight of this encounter.

The concept of *congregación* had been written into the Laws of Burgos of 1512, the earliest laws intended to structure the colonization of the New World; it would be later written and codified to the New Laws of 1542. As a lived strategy it began here in 1537 with the Maya of Rabinal, Las Casas and his monks, and would remain into the twenty-first century as the underpinnings of postcolonial life in highland Guatemala. What had been called the "Land of War" by Spanish soldiers would, by 1620, be renamed Verapaz (True Peace) by the Dominicans.[9]

What took place between 1537 and 1538 would become on several levels a blueprint for the colonization of indigenous peoples of the Americas under Spanish rule. This would include diverse territories and peoples from Mexico and the Caribbean south to the tip of Brazil. The plan and its implementation were a performance of sorts, orchestrated by Las Casas with his now forty years of experience in the Americas. It was a plan devised to convert systematically indigenous people, religiously and economically, through city planning as an alternative to the chaotic and brutal warfare that had marked the first half century of the Spanish invasion into the New World.

## PART II. COLONIAL DEBATES AND BOOKS: HISTORY – TEXT

In the first years of European contact with the Americas, Pope Alexander VI, in the Bull of 1493, granted Ferdinand and Isabella sovereignty over the newly encountered territories across the Atlantic, provided that they Christianized its inhabitants. How to Christianize the inhabitants and what this sovereignty actually meant, how it would be administered in terms of land and peoples found there, was not specified. One piece of this administrative challenge had to do with encouraging and compensating Spanish colonists, who were to be the first European settlers, a situation Las Casas had tried to address in 1522 with his colony at Cumaná. In the West Indies the Spanish crown granted these colonists land and Indian slaves. Originally, the legal term used for these land and labour grants was *repartimiento* (distribution).

With growing concern within the Catholic church and Spanish crown over the human status of Indians and the spiritual consequences of cruelty towards them, slavery was officially banned and new laws of conduct were drafted, known as the 1512 Laws of Burgos. These laws were meant to remedy ambiguities that may have lead to excessive violence and death of the natives in the New World. In these laws we can clearly see the Spanish legal and theological council struggling to write specific guidelines that would nurture the Christianization of the Indians, as well as assure economic growth.

According to the Laws of Burgos, the greatest obstacle to the religious and economic transformation of Indians into true citizens of Spain was that "their dwellings are remote from the settlements of the Spaniards ... Because of the distance and their own evil inclinations, they immediately forget what they have been taught and go back to their customary idleness and vice". To remedy this, the laws prescribe a distinctly feudal paradigm in which land and Indians would be given to colonists in what would then be called an *encomienda* rather than *repartimiento* grants. The very term *encomienda* was a historical term dating back to the fiefdoms of medieval Spain. This semantic shift from the use of the *rapartimiento* to *encomienda* was thus a distinct way for Old World Spain to indicate that in the New World they were not instituting slavery nor any kind of new system incompatible with Christine doctrine, but rather, at least in part, returning to an older method associated with the medieval estates. Under these new laws Indians were not to be enslaved, nor made into beasts of burden, but rather gathered around their new Spanish superiors, much like serfs around a feudal lord.

In section III of the Laws of Burgos we can see the writers awkwardly juggling diverse and disparate needs in the religious and economic conversion of the natives:

> [W]e order and command that the citizen to whom the said Indians are given in encomienda shall, upon the land that is assigned to him, be obliged to erect a structure to be used for a church ...; and in this said church he shall place an image of Our Lady and a bell with which to call the Indians to prayer; and the person who has them in encomienda shall be obliged to have them called by the bell at nightfall and go with them to the said church, and have them cross themselves and bless themselves, and together recite the Ave Maria, the Pate Noster, the Credo, and the Salve Regina, in such wise that all of them shall hear the said person, and the said person hear them, so that he may know who is performing well and who ill ...

In this section the writers further reveal their interest in how to teach the Indians daily the basic elements of Christian practice, prayer and church-going, within a highly structured labour schedule, with both regulated by the ringing of the church bell. These distinctly feudal arrangements on the one hand were meant to humanize the Indians, to socialize and Christianize them, but on the other hand they were meant to infantilize and subordinate them within a nascent capital economy. As Spain was extracting more and more raw materials including silver from the New World, thus growing Europe's potential domination of capitalistic global markets as far east as China, they were simultaneously resorting to feudal labour relations and feudal domestic and civic planning to contain, control and subdue the native populations of their new territories, marking this as a time of rapidly changing economic and social realities in which solutions were distinctly hybrid and anomalous.

The debate over the human and spiritual status of Indians began in the first decades of conquest, and continued for centuries. In the Laws of Burgos, the Crown, at least on paper, desperately sought to combat the dehumanizing reality of colonial domination. Indians had been so badly treated – forced to carry burdens that literally broke their backs, treated worse than animals – that one of the Laws of Burgos, Number 24, reads, "no one may beat or whip or call an Indian dog, or any other name unless it is his proper name".[10] Here we have a slight glimpse into the tangled web of brutal impulses and a court thousands of nautical miles away feebly attempting to define a better world. What does it mean to have a law against colonists calling their colonial subjects dogs?

The Laws of Burgos were a success only in that they established a theoretical plan that Las Casas would later implement as *congregación*. As to the Christianization and treatment of Indians, however, the laws were a miserable failure in the first decades of contact and colonization, so much so that word quickly travelled back to Spain that thousands if not millions of Indians were dying due to the un-enforced new laws and unchecked Spanish cruelty. In 1530, response to such reports, Spanish students in Bologna had begun to protest that all war, even in self-defence, was fundamentally contrary to the Catholic religion.[11]

* * *

In the colonial New World Las Casas was not alone in his defence of the Indians. Among Dominicans there were several who came before and after him, such as Antonio Montesimos, who spoke out against slavery of any kind, or Saint Louis Bertrand, who was canonized in part for his divinely inspired methods of converting Indians to Christianity. What set Las Casas apart was his extraordinary ability and willingness to confront the papal court and the Spanish Crown, to confound and challenge them both to formulate and carry out an Indian policy that recognized Indians as human subjects. His descriptive writing about the brutalities of conquest and colonization coupled with his activist, pragmatic suggestions changed the very nature of experience in the Spanish New World. One does not speak in a vacuum, especially not in his position amid the arguments of his contemporaries, whose greed and ruthless willing violence at times could circumvent his intentions. Nonetheless, his voice and perspective slowed the carnage and shaped a future markedly different from what it might have been.

Through his writings and public debates after the establishment of *congregación* in Rabinal, Las Casas became the central advocate for the humanity and protections of Indians. In his most widely read text of 1542, entitled *A Short Account of the Destruction of the Indies* (1992),[12] Las Casas passionately defended the Indians as true beings of God, and exposed the Spaniards as godless, cruel torturers. Throughout this text he stretches language as far as he can into a series of images through which he describes the horror of what he has witnessed; in doing so he also seeks to define the actions of the Spanish within what he calls the "eyes of God [and] the law". He wants to expose not only the civic and social crisis at the outset of Spanish and Indian relations, but also to look deeply into what he experiences as an excruciating spiritual crisis. The extremely vivid and specific nature of Las Casas's writing is best understood as a conscious rebuttal of earlier Spanish accounts of a savage Indian in need of a civilizing process. In direct contrast to this Las Casas defines the Indian as an innocent being brutalized by Spaniards in search of endless domination.

> [The Spaniards] forced their way into native settlements, slaughtering everyone they found there, including small children, old men, pregnant women, and even women who had just given birth. They hacked them to pieces, slicing open their bellies with their swords as though they were so many sheep herded into a pen. They even laid wagers on whether they could manage to slice a man in two at a stroke, or cut an individual's head from his body, or disembowel him with a single blow of their axes. They grabbed suckling infants by the feet and, ripping them from their mother' breasts, dashed them headlong against the rocks ... They spared no one, erecting especially wide gibbets on which they could string their victims up with their feet just off the ground and then burn them alive thirteen at a time, in honour of our Savior and the twelve Apostles. ([1542] 1992: 15)

For Las Casas it is the Indians who are lambs, sheep, noble while his fellow Spaniards have become wolves, tigers, savage lions, "not Christians", he would later write, "but only devils". Rhetorically Las Casas knows what he is doing here: intentionally inverting the often used image of the Indian as devil and infidel,[13] and instead characterizing his fellow Spaniards as the real devils prompted by greed and abandoned to violence, using fire to torture and destroy, audaciously doing so in honour, as Las Casas writes, "of Our Savior".

In *A Short Account of the Destruction of the Indies*, Las Casas does not only visually describe, he also begins to sketch a theory of the epistemological status of the Indian in terms of Christian theology, civic law and the laws of nature, in this case as they were defined by Aristotle. First he looked to the gospels, specifically to Matthew 28:19, after Christ has risen from his tomb when he says to his Apostles:

> Go ye therefore, and teach all nations, baptizing them in the name of the Father, and of the Son, and of the Holy Ghost:
> Teaching them to observe all things whatsoever I have commanded you: and, lo I am with you always, *even* unto the end of the world.

Las Casas must have felt that Christ was speaking to him through Matthew when he said, "Go ye therefore, and teach all nations". Certainly Las Casas was physically, so to speak, "at the end of the world", the known world that is, and these Indians, Las Casas deeply believed, were children of God who simply did not yet, but could, know the one and true God.

* * *

In direct opposition to Las Casas's argument, on 5 May 1544, the Dominican provincial Diego de la Cruz sent a letter to Charles V in which he vehemently argued against allowing Indians to preach or even study Christianity, claiming that Indians are not "stable persons ... nor is their language sufficient or copious enough as to be able to express our faith without great improprieties, which could lead easily to serious error" (DII, VII, 541). This extraordinary claim by de la Cruz that the Indian language itself was incompatible with Christianity was just one of hundreds of testimonies demeaning Indians, fuelled by religious and social claims of European superiority that were meant to guarantee full reign to Spanish domination over Indians as if they had no rights beyond that of a tree, a stream of water or a dog.

The debate on whether Indians could be Christianized, and how they and their lands should be handled, raged so vehemently within the court of Charles V, that on 16 April 1550 he suspended all acts of conquest in the New World until a proper debate could determine the manner in which these new lands should be occupied and the Indians treated. The ensuing debate took place in Valladolid, Spain, during the month of August 1550. The debate consisted of hundreds of pages of testimony with Las Casas in defence of the Indians and Juan Ginés de Sepúlveda in defence of Spanish superiority and the 'just causes' for war and Indian servitude.[14] In his argument, most of which is published in the 1550 text *Apología del libro de las justas causas de la Guerra contra los indios*, Sepúlveda proclaims against the Indians that: "In prudence, talent, virtue, and humanity they are as inferior to the Spaniards as children to adults, women to men, as the wild and cruel to the most meek, as the prodigiously intemperate to the continent and temperate, that I have almost said, as monkeys to men" (Sepúlveda 1951: 33). Again, as in the 1512 Laws of Burgos, Sepúlveda returns to this issue of Indians as animals. In this case, however, he wants without censor to return to the notion that Indians are animals, not people. He is careful to speak metaphorically, yet only in the most slightly veiled way, claiming that the Indian is a subhuman unable to receive the gospels or govern themselves. He exhaustively argues against the Christianization of Indians and further contests, based on theological and secular laws, that war against them is both necessary and just. For Sepúlveda, the Indian cannot be converted and thus the only way to properly proceed in the New World is to dominate, subjugate and colonize the new land along with their inhabitants.

In terms of secular law, Sepúlveda relies heavily on Aristotle's arguments in Book I of the *Politics*, in his distinction between those who were by nature born to rule, and those who were by nature born to be slaves. At the outset of the *Politics* Aristotle defines the natural-born ruler as one that can, "foresee by the exercise of mind", and the natural born slave as one that can only, "with its body give effect to such foresight" (*Politics*: Book I, 2). Aristotle goes on to support his social theory with an ontological analogy observing that "a living creature consists in the first place of soul and body, and of these two the one is by nature the ruler and the other the subject" (*Politics*: Book I, 6). The master is thus akin to the soul, which, when properly situated, rules over the body, its slave.

To combat specifically Sepúlveda's claim that the Indian is only a tool or body devoid of a mind or soul, and thus justly to be used or owned, Las Casas praises the Indians in terms of their own "governance, politics and customs", and even goes on to state that these Indians "exceed by no small measure the wisest of all these, such as the Greeks and Romans, in adherence to the rules of natural reason" ([c. 1559] 1967: I, 4). As to their ability to be Christianized, in one of his last and most articulate pleas, Las Casas would testify in these debates at Valladolid that:

> The Indians are our brothers, and Christ has given his life for them. Why, then, do we persecute them with such inhuman savagery when they do not deserve such treatment? ... [They] will embrace the teaching of the gospel, as I well know, for they are not stupid or barbarous but have a native sincerity and are simple, moderate, and meek, and finally, such that I do not know whether there is any people readier to receive the gospel. Once they have embraced it, it is marvelous with what piety, eagerness, faith, and charity they obey Christ's precepts and venerate the sacraments. For they are docile and clever, and in their diligence and fits of nature, they excel most people of the known world.                    ([c. 1551] 1974: 42–3)

In 1514 Las Casas had renounced his ownership of Indian slaves and land given to him as *repartimiento*, and had entered the bewildering worlds of Christianity and an expanding Europe as they redefined themselves within the context of conquest, capital expansion and human crisis. Over his lifetime he would testify in person and in writing, struggling to establish some way other than through violence and greed for humanity to recognize and encounter itself. His struggle did lead to a nominally less brutal conquest into the sixteenth and seventeenth centuries, with Indians free from the burden of slavery and endless war but, nonetheless, subordinated to a Western expansion that would abruptly relocate them into alien communities, forced to contend with a world newly defined by their dominators.

## PART III. POSTCOLONIAL MAYA: ETHNOHISTORY – IMAGE

According to the 1512 Laws of Burgos, and subsequently guided by decisions after the 1550 debate at Valladolid, Dominican and Franciscan friars used Las Casas's blueprint of *congregación* to relocate the Maya of Mexico and Guatemala who had survived devastating disease and the brutal violence of the first conquistadores and colonists. As Las Casas had done in Rabinal in 1538, these friars oversaw the building of a central church and the movement of Indian homes into its vicinity, a configuration that is still visible and still structures daily life for the Maya who today live in the Mexican state of Chiapas and the highlands of Guatemala. Equally important to the sixteenth-century friars as the building of churches was the conversion of these new subjects of Spain to Christianity. With *coplas* similar to the ones used by Luis Cancér to convert the ruler of Atitlán, the friars began to teach the Maya the basic Christian belief that human beings are fallen due to the transgression of Adam and Eve, that life is thus inevitably defined by sin and suffering, and that salvation through the martyrdom of Christ, the mortal son of God, would bring eternal life elsewhere.

Stories of violence and sacrifice to explain the predicament of human existence would have had efficacy for the Maya, would match certain elements of their cosmologies and meanings. For the Maya, the cosmos was made up of three realms: the upper, middle and lower worlds. The gods, as is told in the *Popol Vuh,* made blood sacrifices of themselves, mixed with cornmeal to create human beings, who in turn could to talk to the gods, count their days, and make sacrifices so that ongoing cycles of time would continue at infinitum.[15] To count the days the Maya created several different kinds of elaborate lunar, solar and Venus calendars and charts. The pre-conquest Maya preformed a range of sacrificial rituals, from the offering of food and self-mutilation to, at the far end, human sacrifice.

Christian concepts of sacrifice as a means of linking the human and divine realms would have appealed to the Maya. The Christian belief in one god, and a messianic concept of time, however, would have been alien and counter-intuitive to their understanding. Although the Maya did have cosmogonies, stories that tell of the origins of things, such as we find in the *Popol Vuh*; they did not believe in one overarching concept of time with one beginning and one ending, dependent on a single savoir.

In an attempt to gloss over the violent clash of cultures and beliefs, especially when constructing new colonial towns, the friars named the towns with a saint name combined with a Mayan name, for instance Santa Catarina Ixtahuacan, or San Juan Cotzal. This syncretism in naming, half-Mayan/half-Christian, half-familiar/half-foreign was not, however, so facilely reflected in how the Maya would interpret or use the concepts or images of the saint, the structure of the church or, for that matter, Christianity itself. In the Maya highlands of the sixteenth century the saints, their many numbers and their association with fragmentation and healing deeply appealed to the Maya. In embracing them they appeared on some level to have converted. In reality, however, the Maya were surreptitiously metabolizing Christianity, as they shaped and redefined their own concepts of themselves, transcendence, and the nature of time.

*Congregación*, although devised by the Spanish and implemented by Las Casas as a kinder means of colonization than the outright massacres of the first decades of conquest, was still a fundamentally violent assault on Maya social life and beliefs. As an agricultural society sustained by *milpa* farming of family-sized plots of corn and beans, the Maya had hundreds of years of deep and specific relations with their immediate landscape.[16] Corn itself was a gift of the gods, a gift that arrived each year only after dying at the end of the harvest. Sacrifices were performed on auspicious days before and after the harvest to ensure the continuation of this cycle necessary for the continuation of life. Each family had its own *milpa*, which allowed it to be self-sufficient. In addition, there were certain places in the landscape – mountains, caves, streams and other bodies of water – through which the Maya believed they had access to supernatural gods and forces, and a complex nexus of time that linked the living to those who had died. To be forcibly relocated away from their ideologically defined landmarks was as brutal an attack as the loss of their autonomy, lost with the arrival of the Spaniards.

In their new colonially defined feudal towns, the Maya re-established their practice of *milpa* farming, which slowly gave them at least subsistence level resources and the means to pay taxes in kind. They also found new places through which to access their concepts of the past and cosmic forces. Ironically, some of the places the Maya would go and continue to go for such access were the colonial churches, many of them build in the early decades of the sixteenth century.

## Concepción Sololá

In the very isolated town of Concepción Sololá in the Guatemalan highlands, four hundred years after Las Casas, the Maya still actively lay hands on the colonial church placed at the centre of their town (Figure 1). The filigreed stucco on its facade has recently been repaired and painted, as have the heraldic golden lions around its central window above the door. An iron cross with a weathervane still stands atop the structure with its bell and four saints secure in their right places. A parish priest from the larger town of Sololá comes into Concepción occasionally to say Mass or offer rites for the dead. Most of the time, however, the Maya of Concepción perform their own rites, independent of any official Christian hierarchy or observation. They diligently clean and repair the colonial church and hand-carved wooden altars. Most of the altars and niches are filled with poly-chromed saints, yet others are equally maintained as barren frames whose saint images have long been missing.

In one delicately arranged altar, Saint Dominic stands in the centre with a bible in one hand and ceremonial rattle in the other. Saint Dominic is dressed in brocaded ecclesiastical robes while Mary to his right and Joseph to his left are dressed in cloth that the Maya weave for themselves and wear in this highland town. Similarly, in Santa Catarina Zunil, Maya women take the cloth they weave for themselves and place it on their saints. In the cloth they weave a mark of where they are from, their specific geographic location within Guatemala.

Distinctions in weaving patterns and colours change from town to town; they change significantly enough so that you can distinguish a woman from Zunil from another woman who might live in the adjacent town. On the saint this woven cloth, which contains multiple elements of identity, becomes part of a composite image, a montage of cultures in which issues of difference and domination converge. What or who is being converted here becomes a question in the present. Imagine a Maya woman looking into the white face of this saint, who is draped in cloth that is of the same weaving as her own. There is no simple equation of mirroring or mimesis. What is being made present is the space between histories. Through this montage of sculpted saint and woven cloth the Maya evoke the unresolved incongruities of their postcolonial world as a way to enter or rather encounter the contingencies of such a world. The forced conversion of the Maya to Christianity was a process initiated within the early colonial history of Western domination. The infrastructure and artifacts of that process continue into the present as the Maya themselves

*Figure 1.* Apse and main altar in the church Concepción Sololá, Guatemala. (Photograph by Anna Blume, 1989)

still contend with the often violent economic and social domination reasserted from the West in the form of NAFTA or other foreign policies written for the benefit of first world global expansion at the expense of local economies and cultures.[17]

In the landscape of the mountainous regions of Mexico and Guatemala, the Maya continue to work out relations of domination and meaning within these colonial churches. In the centre of the church in Concepción, ten or fifteen feet towards the apse, is a series of stone tiles placed on the church floor perpendicular to the high altar (Figure 2). There are twenty tiles made up of two rows of ten. In front of the tiles and along the right-hand side are loose flower petals and over the entire surface you can see the debris of candles and stains from poured alcohol. As the Maya pray they are counting, twenty the number of tiles, twenty the number of day names in their Pre-Columbian 260-day calendar, which is part of an ongoing ritual of counting the days. The tiles are steps that lead beyond the visible. They are like the candle itself, which begins with wax and a wick. When lit, the candle extends to fire, then smoke, until eventually all material moves along a path to the invisible. The candle begins as mass, then it disappears, apparently consuming itself. Similarly, the tiles are the step-by-step material initiation into somewhere else which is entered through prayer and the sacrifice of materials. The transfer of materials into the invisible marks a pathway from this world to another. The Maya of Concepción enter the church and come to these tiles first. They lay down their flowers, drink and pour alcohol around them, and begin to talk. They talk as if to someone or something they know. They start slowly with a prescribed set of initial prayers in Spanish that may include fragments of the Our Father or Hail Mary intermixed with an address in their native language. A connection is made and they go further into the specifics of why they have come, usually pertaining to daily needs about land or loved ones. Here the conversation becomes very personal, sometimes extremely emotional. From the tiles they then move on to other areas of the church, where they make other contacts through disparate objects and images.

This is not a simple opiate, this drive to expend a significant portion of vital resources on counting the days of their ancient calendar or adorning saints. In the motions of prayer – the preparation, long walk and final communion – the church is transformed, and the self is saturated in a momentary dialogue with power and compassion. The saint images

*Figure 2.* Twenty tiles in the church Concepción Sololá, Guatemala. (Photograph by Anna Blume, 1989)

and the structure of the church, linked to a past and still continuous line of domination, are absorbed into an evolving Maya belief. Prayer to such objects, and inside such structures, is an act of interlocking with forces that are often ineffable, and as constant as the rising and setting sun. Saints, churches, woven cloth and crucifixes contain different meanings and forces that the Maya arrange and configure into a performance of speaking or exorcism of longing. Such acts of power are exercised precisely through the material leftovers of colonial and postcolonial history.

In the apse of the church in Concepción the pitch of such an aesthetic pushes to the edge of the material world. Here, through repetition and syncopation of form, the Maya take material to the threshold of sensation. At first, if you look down the centre of the church to the apse, editing out the side walls, it seems simple and serene; it could be a church in a rural town in Spain. The twenty stone tiles where the Maya of this town perform specific rites present only a slight fissure in the overall familiarity. Yet, when you pass the last pilasters before the apse, with a sense of shock you see over thirty different life-size crucifixes leaning up against the wall. The high altar, traditionally set to envelop the spectator in a singular contemplation of the host, is flooded with images of Christ. The Maya here disrupt the imported hierarchy of stressed authority, replacing it with syncopated, subtle multiplicity. Each sculpted figure is a Christ that, when looked at closely, is slightly different from the next. One's head is more severely tilted or arms extended longer; the other looks down and is shorter. With no single source of eminence, spirituality and hierarchy are fragmented and dispersed. Spirituality is visualized as a cacophony of ongoing sacrifices. This is not a sequential movement common in retablos or fresco cycles of the conception, birth, and death of Christ: an identifiable narrative. This conscious repetition of the image of the crucified Christ places the passion in motion, evoking the moment of the death of Christ as if he had not died yet or did not die once, as if the moment kept repeating itself out of the past into the present, over and over again. This kind of repetition of sacrifice is much more like the Maya's Pre-Columbian concept of the Maize God, God of Corn, who dies each year with the harvest and returns again each spring.

Amid and through material brought in by the Spanish and subsequently by international commerce, the Maya rearrange the artifacts of authoritarian rule into arrangements that echo elements of their own ancient beliefs, taking apart hierarchy, like removing a veil and replacing it at will, and in this movement making a place for themselves to intervene in history's course.

## San Juan Cotzal

In the town of San Juan Cotzal in the eastern portion of the Cuchematanes mountains, the Maya tell a story about the images of saints in their church. One day in 1983 a group of soldiers from the local base came in to hunt subversives. Not finding any, they began randomly to kill members of the town. Soldiers such as these were mostly Maya themselves forcibly recruited from one region of the country into a counter insurgency militia to oppress the Maya of another region of the country. This strategy of manipulating the Maya to participate in the mechanisms of their own oppression was mercilessly exploited by the dictator Rios Montt from 1982. Montt was a newly evangelized Protestant Christian with a desire to modernize and integrate Guatemala within global trade and economy. For him the obstacles to this end were the socialist legacy of the 1950s and leanings of the intelligentsia as well as the traditional lifestyle of the Maya, which included the syncretic Catholic indigenous religious practices and small-farm *milpa* agriculture. Montt systematically set out to isolate and eliminate both communities. During his dictatorship thousands of mostly middle-class educated resisters were either disappeared or killed and over 200,000 Maya were killed.[18]

On that particular day in Cotzal in 1983, when they could not find who they were looking for, the soldiers abruptly went into the church and there smashed altars and cut wooden limbs off the bodies of saint images. After the soldiers left, the people of Cotzal gathered the images of saints and placed them, like refugees, up against the wall, some with missing limbs exposed and others just standing there looking out over the pews. Other broken saints were placed back up by the main altar and covered with bits of old cloth wrapped around their broken bodies. The shattered or cracked panes of glass for altar boxes were left as they were

*Figure 3.* Battered saints in the Church of San Juan Cotzal, Guatemala. (Photograph by Anna Blume, 1989)

and saints with tattered limbs returned to them. It remained that way in 1988, five years after the violence. What might have been repaired was left as it was. In a particular way, the saints in this and many other instances had become part of the history of the place and the process of life. The Maya of Cotzal did not erase the violence done to their saints. Instead they left the danger there to loom conspicuously in their church, making it present not as a spectacle or catharsis, but as a place where the Maya of Cotzal come to negotiate the loss or terror that had been placed inside them. Saints had become their companions through time. In Cotzal, and throughout Maya villages since the colonial period, these imported Catholic images have become phantasmagorical sites of contested meaning that move out from the realm of religion into the brutal facts of everyday lives.

\* \* \*

At a site in the Cuchumatanes mountains in the early years of the sixteenth century, Spanish friars chose a particular plateau atop one range of mountains to congregate Maya families that lived or had recently fled high into this formidable region. Maybe because it was so beautiful there, nothing like they had ever seen in Spain, they decided not to give this town a particular patron saint, but rather all saints, naming this town, as it is known today, Todos Santos Cuchumetantes.

About 500 metres from the central church that the Maya built to the friars' specifications is a house made of mud and straw with white lime-painted walls on the outside, not unlike the homes the Maya live in throughout the highlands. Off the main road, this particular house sits inconspicuously in a field of corn, a *milpa*. Inside there are no images; there are simply two yellow boxes, one with a small wooden cross. Inside the boxes are bundles of very old papers and texts written in Spanish. The Maya of Todos Santo who come to this place do not read these books; they are mostly older members of the community who were never taught to read or write. They come here daily, however, to pray before these boxes. Only on special feast days do they take them out and process them through the town, as if they were sculpted images of saints or the Virgin. The caretaker of the box, named Don Pasquale, told me that all the animals, land and spirits of the living and the dead are in those books, all three realms of the earth, beneath the earth, and above the earth.

When I began to read the old Spanish, it became clear that these books and papers were actual land documents related to the initial *congregación* of this town, generated over the past four hundred years. From book to book, one could read the various negotiations that had taken place over land, some hostile, some fortuitous to the town. There were disputes between neighbours, and forced transfers of land parcels to the state or encroaching land owners. There were titles of ownership and titles to communal land intertwined and tied tight by a cord.

What mechanism or metabolic law within memory makes land documents into all saints, all beings, all things and all time? It is an idea older than the Spanish conquest that reads relations through land. When I told Don Pasquale that I thought the books were filled with land documents he told me, "Of course they are". I am sure people have told

*Figure 4.* Land documents from the Cofradia Box in Todos Santos Cuchumatanes, Guatemala. (Photograph by Anna Blume, 1989)

him many things. But he knows something I do not know. Something about land in the minds of people that moves across time and its contingencies, something about continuities out of history's debris. What Los Casas had initiated as *congregación* is here in Todos Santos retranslated out of writing by the Maya into an image of an ongoing dialectic.

## NOTES

1. I should like to thank Timothy Fitzgerald for his vision for the conference that led to this book and my writing of this essay, which was also improved by Kate Williams's careful edit of the English, Spanish, French and occasional Latin in the text and sources. I thank Alessandra Russo for her precise insights especially into the colonial material. And finally I thank the Maya of highland Guatemala who welcomed me into homes and churches and on to the land where they have placed their stories.
2. For a full and detailed account of the life of Las Casas in the Americas see Las Casas (]1561] 1951), Helps ([1873] 2003) and Antonio de Remesal (1620). All the incidents retold in this narrative are from these three sources.
3. In the sixteenth century, African slavery was an established norm to Las Casas, practised in Africa itself, especially in the Islamic territories just across the Strait of Gibraltar. Conversely, Indian slavery was repugnant to Las Casas because Indians were a new people to him that he believed were capable of being Christianized. Later in his life Las Casas would openly regret suggesting the use of African slavery in the New World. Throughout most of his time in Guatemala and Mexico, however, he was often carried in a chair over steep mountain passes and across rivers by a very tall African.
4. Although he began to write his magnum opus, *Historia de las Indias* [History of the Indies] in 1529, he did not complete or publish it until 1561.

5. In *Popol Vuh*, Goetz and Morley refer to Otto Stoll's hypothesis that Tezulutlán meant 'place of owl'. The word may have originated with the Quiché word *Tucur*, meaning owl, which in Náhuatl is *tecolotol*, which in Spanish was customarily pronounced Tezulutlán (1950: 112). Remesal vividly describes this region as utterly formidable, both as a place of incessant rain and "feroucous, barbarous people who were impossible to dominate or subjugate … and for these reasons the region is called 'place of war'" (1620: 182).

6. For a description and analysis of the Quauhquechollan collaboration with Jorge de Alvarado in the conquest of Guatemala see Asselbergs (2004: 13ff.). Asselbergs (2004) also publishes the little known *Lienzo Quauhquechollan*, an early indigenous map of Guatemala, with an accompanying visual narrative of the conquest of this region.

7. In the fifteenth and sixteenth centuries, and in the subsequent colonial literature, *congrecación* is also known as *reducción*. For description and analysis of the administration of *congregación* in the highlands of Guatemala, see "The Pursuit of Order: *Congregación* and the Administration of Empire" in Lovell (2005).

8. For an in-depth analysis of the specific use of theatrical models for the conversion of the Maya of Rabinal see Tedlock (2003).

9. In Remesal's first mention of Las Casas in this region of Guatemala, he tells us "La de Tzulultán o tierra de guerra que ahora se llama la Verapaz" (Tezulutlán or the land of war is now called True Peace) (1620: 165).

10. Laws of Burgos (1960: 32).

11. This student rebellion is noted by Losada (1970: 249).

12. Las Casas first published this text in Latin in 1542, entitled: *Narratio Regionvm Indicarvm per Hispanos qvosdam deuastatarum verissima*. The most populist and mass produced of these was the 1656 English edition entitled: *The Tears of the Indians: Being an Historical and True Account of the Cruel Massacres and Slaughter of Above Twenty Million Innocent People Committed by the Spanish* (1972). This long ideologically weighted title was meant to embolden the English to establish their own Protestant colonies in the new world according to their supposedly more compassionate Christianity.

13. See Elizabeth Boone's (1989) excellent essay on European concepts of Indian, especially Aztec gods, with a specific section on the assumption that certain Indian gods were incarnations of Satan himself.

14. In 1530, twenty years before the debate at Valladolid, the Pope had sent Sepúlvida to Bologna to stop the vehement protest by Spanish students against all wars. It thus fell to Sepúlvida very early in the colonial process to devise a Christian theory that could justify war against the New World 'infidels'. (Hanke 1974: 61–2).

15. The *Popol Vuh* was secretly written down in the sixteenth century in the Roman alphabet the Maya had been taught by Spanish priests. Ancient bark codices that the Maya had written in their own hieroglyphic writing were systematically burnt and otherwise destroyed by the Spanish, who wished to eradicate the extensive beliefs of their newly colonized subjects. For a history and translation of the *Popol Vuh* see Dennis Tedlock (1996).

16. *Milpa* agriculture consists of mostly corn crops with some additional vegetable farming, such as beans and squash. The Maya have subsisted on *milpa* farming for the past 3,000 years. Like weaving and language, *milpa* farming constitutes one of the three most significant continuities of Maya life in the isthmus.

17. For an in-depth account of the recent Maya struggle against NAFTA see Marcos (2002).

18. A full report of the violence that occurred in Guatemala during Rios Montt's dictatorship was published in *Guatemala, memory of silence = Tz'inil na'tab'al* (CEH 1998). As is stated in its introduction, "The CEH's Report is structured in accordance with the objectives and terms of the mandate entrusted to it by the Parties to the Guatemalan peace process as expressed in the Accord of Oslo, signed in Norway, on 23 June 1994".

# BIBLIOGRAPHY

Aristotle. [350 BCE] 1988. *The Politics*. Trans. Benjamin Jowett, ed. Stephen Everson. Cambridge: Cambridge University Press.

Asselbergs, Florine G. L. 2004. *Conquered Conquistadores: The* Lienzo de Quauhquechollan: *A Nahua Vision of the Conquest of Guatemala*. Leiden: CNWS Publications.

Borah, Woodrow. 1983. *Justice by Insurance: The General Indian Court of Colonial Mexico and the Legal Aides of the Half-Real*. Albany, NY: SUNY Press.

Borah, Woodrow. 1951. "New Spain's Century of Depression". *Ibero-Americana* 35: 2–42.

Borges, Jorge Luis. 1962. "Three Versions of Judas". In *Labyrinths*, trans. James E. Irby, 95–100. New York: New Directions.

Boucher, Bernadette. 1983. *Icon and Conquest: A Structural Analysis of the Illustrations of de Brey's Great Voyages*. Chicago, IL: University of Chicago Press.

Brown, Peter. 1981. *The Cult of the Saints*. Chicago, IL: University of Chicago Press.

Boone, Elizabeth H. 1989. "Incantations of the Aztec Supernatural: The Image of Huitzilopochtli in Mexico and Europe". *Transactions of the American Philosophical Society* 79(2): 1–107.

Carmack, Robert M., ed. 1988. *Harvest of Violence: The Mayan Indians and the Guatemalan Crisis*. Norman, OK: University of Oklahoma Press.

Carmack, Robert M. 1973. *Quichean Civilization: The Ethnohistoric, Ethnographic and Archeological Sources*. Berkeley, CA: University of California Press.

CEH. 1998. *Guatemala, Memory of Silence - Tz'inil na'tab'al: Report of the Commission for Historical Clarification, Conclusions and Recommendations*. Guatemala: Comisión para el Esclarecimiento Histórico.

DII. 1864-84. *Colección de documentos inédito relativos al descubrimiento, conquista y organizaciónde las antiguas posesiones espannñolas de América y Oceanía*, 42 vols. Ed. Joaquín F. Pacheco, Francisco de Cárdnas and Luis de Mendoza. Madrid.

Goetz, Delia and Sylvanus G. Morley. 1950. *Popol Vuh: The Sacred Book of the Ancient Quiché Maya*. Norman, OK: University of Oklahoma Press.

Gossen, Gary. 1994. "From Olmecs to Zapatistas: A Once and Future History of Souls". *American Anthropologist* 96: 553–70.

Hanke, Lewis. 1974. *All Mankind is One: A Study of the Disputation Between Bartolomé de las Casas and Juan Ginés de Sepúlveda on the Religious and Intellectual Capacity of the American Indians*. De Kalb, IL: Northern Illinois University Press.

Hanke, Lewis. 1959. *Aristotle and the American Indians: A Study in Race Prejudice in the Modern World*. Chicago, IL: Henry Regnery.

Helps, Arthur. 1897. *The Spanish Conquest in America, and its Relation to the History of Slavery and to the Government of Colonies*. New York: Harper & Brothers.

Helps, Arthur. [1873] 2003. *The Life of Las Casas: The Apostle of the Indies*. Honolulu, HA: University Press of the Pacific.

Las Casas, Bartolomé. [1535] 1951. *Del único modo de atraer a todos los pueblos a la verdadera religion*. Eds Agustín Millares Carlo and Lewis Hanke. Mexico: Fondo de Cultura Económica.

Las Casas, Bartolomé. [1561] 1951. *Historia de las Indias*, edicion de Agustín Millares Carlo; estudio preliminary de Lewis Hanke, 3 vols. Buenos Aires and Mexico: Fondo de Cultural Económica.

Las Casas, Bartolomé. [c.1559] 1967. *Apologética Historia Sumaria*. Ed. Edmundo O'Gorman. Mexico: Universidad Autónoma Nacional de Mexico.

Las Casas, Bartolomé. [trans. 1656] 1972. *The Tears of the Indians: Being an Historical and True Account of the Cruel Massacres and Slaughters of Above Twenty Million Innocent People Committed by the Spanish... .* Trans. John Phillips. New York: Oriole.

Las Casas, Bartolomé. [c. 1551] 1974. *In Defense of the Indians*. Trans. and ed. C. M. Stafford Poole. DeKalb: Northern Illinois University Press, (1551ca.) 1974.

Las Casas, Bartolomé. [1542] 1992. *A Short Account of the Destruction of the Indies*. Trans. and ed. Anthony Pagden. New York: Penguin.

Laws of Burgos. 1960. *The Laws of Burgos of 1512-1513: Royal Ordinances for the Good Government and Treatment of the Indians*, trans. and with an intro. and notes Lesley Byrd Simpson. Westport, CT: Greenwood Press.

Losada, Ángel. 1970. *Fray Bartolomé de Las Casas a la luz de la moderna crítica histórica*. Madrid: Editorial Teconos.

Lovell, W. George. 2005. *Conquest and Survival in Colonial Guatemala: A Historical Geography of the Cuchumatán Highlands*, 3rd edn. Montreal: McGill-Queens University Press.

Lovell, W. George. 1988. "Surviving Conquest: The Maya of Guatemala in Historical Perspective. *Latin American Research Review* 23(2): 25–57.

Lovell, W. George and Christopher H. Lutz. 1995. *Demography and Empire: A Guide to the Population History of Spanish Central America, 1500-1821*. Boulder, CO: Westview Press.

Marcos, Subcomandante. 2002. *Our Word is Our Weapon*. Trans. and ed. Juana Ponce de Leon. New York: Seven Stories Press.

Muro Orejón, Antonio. 1956. "Ordenanzas reales sobre los indios (las leyes de 1512–1513)". *Anuario de Estudios Americanso* (Seville) XIII: 417–71.

Remesal, Antonio de. 1620. *Historia general de las Indias ocidentales, y particvlar de la gouernacion de Chiapa, y Guatemala*. Madrid: Abraca.

Sepúlveda, Juan Ginés de. 1550. *Apologia del libro de las justas causas de la Guerra contra los indios*. Unpublished Spanish trans. by Ángel Losada of treatise printed in Rome in 1550.

Sepúlveda, Juan Ginés de. 1951. *Demócrates, Segundo o de las Justas causas de la Guerra conta los indios*. Ed. Ángel Losada. Madrid: Consejo Superior de Investigaciones Cientificas, Instituto Francisco de Vitoria.

Smith, Carol A., ed. 1990. *Guatemala and the State, 1540-1988*. Austin, TX: University of Texas Press.

Tedlock, Dennis. 1996. *Popol Vuh*. New York: Touchstone.

Tedlock, Dennis. 2003. "Under Spanish Rule". In *Rabinal Achi: A Mayan Drama of War and Sacrifice*, 187–206. Oxford: Oxford University Press

Todorov, Tzvetan. 1984. *The Conquest of America: The Question of the Other*. Norman, OK: University of Oklahoma Press.

# 2

# A higher ground: the secular knowledge of objects of religious devotion

## Trevor Stack

Fitzgerald argues in the Introduction that secularism is best understood as a way of circumscribing 'religion', of marking it off from other things that we do. In this chapter I argue, following the anthropologist Michael Lambek, that secularism does this by looking in on 'religion' as if from the outside (2003: 3). I propose not just one but several reasons why people choose to take this secular perspective, I note that there are different varieties of it and I observe that a wide range of people, including Catholic priests, take such a perspective. I focus on secular knowledge rather than the secular politics on which most of the other chapters focus, and I look in particular at the knowledge of history, which also happens to be the key genre of this volume. I end by placing secularism within the broader politics of knowledge that the literary critic Walter Mignolo has termed "modern/colonial" (2000: 22). By this I mean that the secular perspective has developed, possibly since the sixteenth century, as a way of marking the difference between peoples.

It is often said of history that it is a secular kind of knowledge. I had taken that claim to mean that history banished divine agency from its narratives, thus contesting the previously dominant narratives of the church and other religious authorities. There are of course histories that do this, some of which are frankly anti-clerical. However, other histories do find a place for divine agency and yet I still want to call them secular because divine agency is placed outside the main body of the narrative. This is different from narratives, such as the Book of Job, in which God happens not to intervene, but could do so at any moment. Narrators of secular histories consign divine agency not to the wings, but to roles outside the narrative itself. For example, narrators may be inspired by God or offer the narrative to God as an act of devotion, or they may focus on their protagonists' devotion to God rather than on God himself. I look in this chapter at several histories of a Catholic icon, the Virgin of Defence, in twentieth-century west Mexico. I describe as secular those histories of the Virgin that bracket her agency in the

*Figure 1.* Poster of the Virgin of Defence's annual visit to Tapalpa, 2004. Obviously the poster is focused on the parish church, and it does not show the whole town, but it still gives an indication of the church's imposing size.

*Figure 2.* The Virgin of Defence in procession from Juanacatlán to Tapalpa for her annual visit, 2005. Note the video camera.

main body of the narrative, focusing instead on the human agency of her devotees, even if some of these secular narrators find other places for the Virgin and for God.[1]

Having distinguished between secular and non-secular narration, I reflect on why these narrators chose to narrate the Virgin's history from a secular perspective. I suggest several reasons. One is that secular narrators could claim a special kind of higher ground: not a moral or religious higher ground, but instead a ground from which narrators could look in, as if from outside, on the devotion of their narrative subjects. Although not all west Mexicans chose to take this perspective, many accepted the possibility that others might do so, and conceded some authority to those who did. I use the term 'higher ground' (with obvious irony) to evoke this authority derived from secular narration. By contrast, the Guatemalans described by Anna Blume (Chapter 1) reject the secular perspective, perhaps seeing through the hierarchy embedded in it.

Some of these secular histories were produced under the auspices of the church. I focus on a history of the Virgin that was written by a prominent lay Catholic, and published by a local parish. The author made allusions to God and to the Virgin but, like other secular histories, he left them out of the main body of his narrative. This justifies my broader use of the term secular. It allows us to see that the secular perspective is not the preserve of nation states or of liberal academics. Indeed, I conclude by suggesting that secular narration was nurtured, possibly since the sixteenth century, within the church itself. I argue that secular narration allowed the church to renew the authority not just of its texts, but also of its ministers.

## SECULARISM AND RELIGIOUS DEVOTION IN WEST MEXICO

I went to west Mexico originally as a historian after completing an undergraduate degree in history at the University of Oxford. In 1992 I began research in small town called Tapalpa in the state of Jalisco with a population of about 6,000. Ethnic distinctions were common, but the only residents to self-identify as 'Indian' or 'indigenous' were the traders from the neighbouring state Michoacán. Tapalpa was the seat of the municipal government and, since the building of a tarmac road in 1961, only an hour-and-a-half's drive from Guadalajara, Mexico's second city. Many weekenders visited Tapalpa from Guadalajara, attracted by the beauty of the Sierra and the image of Tapalpa as a *pueblo típico* (quaintly rustic town or village). Some of these weekenders owned houses in the town or in the surrounding countryside. The lands of the region were mostly private property in the hands of wealthy Tapalpan families or, increasingly, tourism developers from elsewhere. Few people lived directly off the land other than a few cattle-ranchers. Many Tapalpans worked in California; this provided perhaps the most important income (Stack forthcoming).

Secularism as a political doctrine was alive and well in west Mexico. This seemed to me a paradox, since devotional practices, predominantly Catholic, permeated the lives of most Tapalpan residents.[2] On the one hand, politics in Tapalpa (as elsewhere in Mexico) had a strongly secularist flavour. Religious faith was not to be an issue, and the clergy was kept out of municipal politics. Education was also secular, although an order of nuns effectively ran one of the local private schools. On the other hand, people crossed themselves publicly, they wore badges of their faith including emblems of saints and virgins, and they talked about the objects of their devotion. Many of these practices were closely identified with the town as a whole. The parish church was visible from any point in the surrounding countryside and towered over the public plaza (see Figure 1). I was also woken constantly during religious festivities by the sound of rockets being fired at dawn and the passing of brass bands through the streets.[3]

Priests enjoyed considerable authority in Tapalpa, despite the secularism of politics. In Chapter 1 Blume describes the multiple crucifixes of the church in the Guatemalan town of Concepción Sololá, noting that there was "no single source of eminence" and concluding that residents had "rearrange[d] the artifacts of authoritarian rule ... taking apart hierarchy, like removing a veil and replacing it at will". This was not the case in Tapalpa. The parish church, built in the mid-twentieth century to replace the seventeenth-century church, was notable for its sparse, impeccable order. The authority of priests was also more evident than in Concepción. For example, I often heard people refer approvingly to what priests had said, whether in a sermon, at a meeting or in a discussion group.[4]

Many Tapalpans professed devotion to a local icon called the Virgen de la Defensa (Virgin of Defence) (see Figures 1 and 2). The Virgin spent most of the year in a nearby town, Juanacatlán, and also visited a third town, Atemajac. But she visited Tapalpa for two months each year, and her only rival in the devotion of many Tapalpans was the town's patron, the Virgin of Guadalupe. To describe the Virgin of Defence as an object of devotion is perhaps misleading, since she was anything but a passive object for her faithful. Blume describes her Guatemalan subjects in conversation with Catholic images, and many Tapalpans enjoyed a similarly intimate relationship with the Virgin, expressed in terms of trust, seduction and gift exchange. Tapalpans prayed to her for miracles and made her promises of all kinds, such as to walk with her from Juanacatlán to Tapalpa each year. There was much give and take between what Tapalpans did for her and what she did for them. Both depended, my landlady said, on "the faith you have for her".

## THE SECULAR KNOWLEDGE OF OBJECTS OF RELIGIOUS DEVOTION

I examine in this section a range of histories of the Virgin of Defence, and I argue that some of these were secular in the sense that I have introduced above. I also show that there were different kinds of secular narrative, and that some were produced under the auspices of the church. I then consider in the following section the different reasons for which people chose to narrate from a secular perspective.

In his study of narratives of saints and virgins in 1970s Colombia, Michael Taussig (1987) distinguishes between official and popular histories of the images. He shows, for example, that official histories tended to play up the Spanish role in discovering and looking after these images, whereas popular histories often played up the Indian role. Taussig describes the "heavy tone and mystical authority of the official voice of the past" in published histories of Niña María de Caloto and argues that this official "monologue" was:

> brought down to earth and familiarized with gentle and sometimes saucy wit [in oral narratives] … teasing, with their multiplicity and double epistemologies, the pretensions of a master language … Perhaps there is a secret life and a hidden Society of Saints and Virgins of which the Church is ignorant … In this society the saints seem more like us … a far cry from the impassive faces they stolidly present to the public …
> (*Ibid.*: 202–3)

In other words, official and popular histories were not just different versions in which, say, Indians and Spaniards played different roles in the Virgin's comings and goings. They were whole different genres of narration in which agency and authority were configured quite differently.[5]

Despite these differences, I would describe neither kind of history as secular. Taussig's "official histories" do not sound secular: their "heavy tone and mystical authority" derived from the divinely invested authority of clerical knowledge. Moreover, the clergy themselves exercised a mystical authority in these narratives. In the official history of the Virgin of Remedies in Cali, for example, the missionary conquers the malevolent jungle in his "wondrous journey" to find where the Indians had taken her (*ibid.*: 189–90). I had supposed initially that Taussig's popular narrators, on the other hand, were secularizing these "mystical monologues" by bringing them "down to earth". I realized later that this was not the case. His popular narrators were refusing to bracket the agency of saints and virgins, and to separate the divine from the human. They narrated a world in which the divine was immanent and not remote.

In Taussig's account, the only obviously secular account is his own. He does bracket divine agency and focus on the devotion of his protagonists. I argue in this section, by contrast, that there were several secular histories of the Virgin of Defence. I begin, however, with some histories of the Virgin that were no more secular than Taussig's examples.

## Non-secular narratives

### Intimate encounters

I heard many narratives of intimate encounters between the Virgin and her faithful that resembled Taussig's popular narratives. For example, when I asked Toni, a 20-year-old Tapalpan, for the history of the Virgin, he wondered whether I meant her healing, adding that the Virgin had healed many people through miracles. I explained that I meant how the Virgin came to the Sierra. He recalled that the catechists in Juanacatlán spoke of the Virgin's history and of a booklet that they had written. Toni could not remember exactly what they had said, but he knew it had something to do with a plague and also oppression. The catechists had promised to send the booklet to the Tapalpa group, but they never did.

These were not secular narratives in the sense that I have outlined, any more than the popular narratives described by Taussig. Note that Toni's first response was to assume that I meant the Virgin's miracles. I have mentioned that people sometimes talked of miracles, which ranged from healing to passing exams. A Tapalpan lady, Francisca, explained that miracles depended on faith. She told me that she had once prayed to the Virgin of Defence when she was leaving Tapalpa for Juanacatlán, asking her to intercede before God to reunite her son with his wife. That same week, Francisca said, the couple got back together. The Virgin is a protagonist of these narratives, as much as the faithful who seek and welcome her intervention. Moreover, both Toni and Francisca clearly identify with the faithful, and offer their narrative as testimony to the Virgin's grace.

Accounts of the Virgin's origins were often no more secular. I was also sent to talk to a 95-year-old lady, Josefina, in the third town visited by the Virgin, Atemajac:

> Here the poor suffered a lot. Two persons from here [Atemajac] and two from Juanacatlán decided to go to visit a bishop – I don't remember his name. He took this image, and said: "This is going to be your Defence". Then the four of them brought the Sacred Virgin. The two from Juanacatlán decided to take it to Juanacatlán. That is the history of the Virgin. But guess what? Four years ago, the Sacred Virgin must have wanted to stay here – she didn't fit in any of the niches. The priest shed tears, saying that "we only brought you on a visit". Then she allowed herself to enter into her niche. We have an immense faith. She's going to arrive here [at a chapel close to her home] on the 6th, and then she'll go to the parish church. What do you think about that? Many people come on Sundays to visit her. There used to be many drunks and mariachi music. Now there's none of that, just religion. Having seen the Sacred Virgin, he [the parish priest] said to them: "do you want the Virgin or alcohol?"

The first part of Josefina's narrative, focused on the Virgin's origin, might seem secular because the Virgin does not act in her own right. Rather than finding her own way to Juanacatlán, for example, the Virgin is given by the bishop to the four individuals, who bring her back to Juanacatlán. I argue, however, that Josefina is making the Virgin wait in the wings. Note how easily Josefina moves from the Virgin's origins to her miraculous reluctance to leave Juanacatlán. Josefina tells the origins of the Virgin as a prelude to the Virgin's present-day miracles.[6] Her account is, in other words, no more secular than the Book of Job.

### Mystical monologues

I also found narratives that resembled Taussig's official histories. These were no more secular, but narrators of these histories gave more emphasis to the role of the clergy, and stressed their privileged relationship to the Virgin.

One example was a chapter on the Virgin that appeared in a book published in 1954 with the title *Marian Iconography of the Archdiocese of Guadalajara* (Orozco 1954: 209–18). The author was a priest of the archdiocese; the history was published by a Catholic press and was intended, no doubt, for the priesthood within and beyond the archdiocese, and for other learned Catholics of the archdiocese. Father Orozco focuses much of his chapter on the Indians' journey to Puebla, on the generosity of the bishop who gave them the Virgin, and on the priests who later sponsored the building of the church (*ibid.*: 212–16). However, like Taussig's clerical authors, Father Orozco brings the Virgin out of the wings when he can cite documentary testimony of her acts. He narrates, for example, the 'favours' granted by the Virgin to her first owner, the seventeenth-century hermit Juan Bautista, before she was acquired by the Bishop of Puebla (*ibid.*: 212–13). Father Orozco also describes the 1920 coronation of the Virgin by the Archbishop of Guadalajara as a 'favour' granted by the Virgin (*ibid.*: 215–16). At several points, he uses 'miraculous' as an epithet for the Virgin.

Josefina, like many elderly residents of the Sierra, gave the parish priest a prominent role in her narrative; Father Orozco plays up still further the role of the clergy. Just as Taussig's 'official' historian narrates the missionary's 'wondrous journey' to take back the Virgin of Remedies from the Indians, Father Orozco not only highlights the 'favours' performed for clergy, but also narrates their struggle to guide and correct the wayward Indians of the Sierra. He gives pride of place to the bishop who gave the image to the Indians, and to the priests who encouraged her cult. For example, he includes the names and titles of all the clergy present at the Virgin's coronation in 1920 (*ibid.*). In another section, Father Orozco notes approvingly that one parish priest had banned an Indian festival for "irreverence to the Virgin" (*ibid.*: 214–15). He also writes that the people of Juanacatlán had accused another parish priest of making a copy of the Virgin so he could keep the original for himself. Their accusation only proved, he concludes, the qualities "so unique to the indigenous race ... lazy, materialistic, and stubborn" (*ibid.*: 216).

## Secular narratives

Although Taussig's is the only secular narrative in his account, I found several secular histories of the Virgin of Defence. Some narrators did narrate the human devotion of their human subjects as if from the outside. I note, in fact, that a wide range of people took this perspective, and that there were different variants of it, including some histories produced under the auspices of the church.

### A section of Tapalpa's history

Some secular histories were produced within a secularist context, such as in government documents. One example was a history written in the 1980s by the Tapalpa library staff with the help of the municipal president, in a short, typed document called *Monograph of Tapalpa* (Nava López *et al.* 1985). The *Monograph* was often consulted by visitors to

Tapalpa's library, including schoolchildren who had been set projects about local history and bureaucrats who needed a section on Tapalpa's history for municipal reports. It began with three one-page sections on "Historical Data", "Civic Status" and "Spiritual Conquest", followed by a section entitled "Our Lady of Defence of Tapalpa". This section was followed in turn by a list of municipal presidents, a map, a list of illustrious sons of the town and socioeconomic information.

Why was a section on the Virgin included in a document produced and kept within the secularist context of a municipal library? The librarian explained in an interview in 2004 that the authors were all devotees of the Virgin, and that they considered the Virgin important to the town and the Sierra. The librarian had not thought twice about this, although she did see the objection when I raised it. But I argue that the authors had another reason for including the section on the Virgin. They had lifted the historical sections of the *Monograph* from Father Orozco's chapter on the Virgin; he had provided a useful historical background, and they reproduced it, almost word for word. Father Orozco's chapter was one of the only written sources available at that time, and his whole chapter led up to the section on the Virgin of Defence, which would therefore have been difficult to cut.

In any case, the *Monograph* authors had secularized Father Orozco's narrative. They cut the sections that referred to the 'favours' performed by the Virgin and to the 'irreverence' of the Indians. The authors kept their distance from the 'Indians' who, together with the clergy, were the protagonists of the history. I have said that very few people in the Sierra considered themselves to be Indians in the 1990s. They did not attempt to bring the history up to the present day: to claim that Tapalpa was still a Catholic town, for example. The "Our" in the section title might hint at their devotion, but this was the Virgin's official title and it was also the title of Father Orozco's chapter.[7] Moreover, the authors turned Orozco's chapter in a book on Catholic icons into one section of an overwhelmingly secular monograph. There is some allusion to Catholic faith in other sections: the preceding section focuses on the "Spiritual Conquest", the only event listed under "Festivities" is the Virgin of Guadalupe's festival, and a poem is included, by a Tapalpan poet, on religious devotion (pitting the poet's spontaneous devotion against his wife's prayer-book devotion). But the *Monograph* as a whole presents a township that was legally founded – recognized by a secular state - and that has 'progressed' since then, although without losing its 'traditions'. The Virgin is encompassed within that secular context; she is presented as just one aspect or episode of the township's history and tradition.[8]

## *History without devotion?*

Other secular histories were produced by narrators who did not share the devotion of their narrative subjects. I was the only one to write this kind of history, but I argue, crucially, that others accepted the validity of such a history.

The history that I wrote (Stack 1994) was, in fact, not of the Virgin of Defence, but of a Tapalpan church dedicated to another Virgin, the Virgin of Mercedes. I published this history to raise funds for the restoration of that church. The Virgin does not act in her

*Figure 3.* Presentation of Martín González's history in the ex-parish church, now municipal cultural forum. At the table from left to right are the municipal chronicler, José Fajardo; the parish priest; Martín González; a chronicler from a nearby town, and an unknown person. The speaker is a priest born in Tapalpa but with a parish in Ciudad Guzmán.

own right in my narrative and nor does God. I did not rule out the involvement of God and the Virgin, but I still chose to bracket their agency in my narrative. What I gave was a narrative, sufficient in itself, of the human work that went into building that church. For example, I argued that the person who sponsored the building of the church, did so because of his devotion to the Virgin of Mercedes, rather than arguing that the Virgin had moved him to build the church.

A prologue and an epilogue were added to my text by Escoto, the wife of one of the members of the restoration committee. I read a draft of the prologue and asked for the religious referents to be removed. When the printed copies appeared, however, her prologue was full again of saints and martyrs devoted to the Virgin. Moreover, Escoto had added an epilogue that was a prayer to the Virgin. I felt that she had compromised my text with her prologue and epilogue. Escoto's prologue implied that I was also motivated by love for the Virgin, while her epilogue turned my history into an act of devotion rather than of fund-raising.

Later I decided that I had overestimated the difference between Escoto's perspective and mine. This is a critical point and serves to illustrate how I have revised my preconceptions. I began with a narrow conception of the secular, one that excluded any mention of divine agency; in this reading, she clearly subverted the secular tone of my text.

Significantly, however, Escoto made few if any changes to the main body of my text. Why did she not do so? One reason was that she felt that a piece of secular narration made a perfectly good act of devotion to the Virgin. This fits the broader model of secular narration that I have proposed. Divine agency (and thus one's own devotion) is bracketed in the main body of the narrative, but there are plenty of other places to put devotion: in this case, the prologue and epilogue.

Others also accepted the possibility of a secular history of the Virgin, even if they did not take this perspective themselves. Indeed, they accepted that someone like me could narrate the Virgin's history even without sharing their devotion. The church restoration committee, for example, was aware that I was not myself one of the faithful, but they still accepted my offer to write a history of the church. On many other occasions, people referred to my history of the Virgin without worrying about my own devotion or lack thereof. People raised quibbles about the historical detail of my narrative but not, as far as I know, about my suitability as an author.[9]

### Secular histories of liberation

I found other secular histories produced under the auspices of the church. The narrators of these histories stressed the human struggle for social justice, rather than the Virgin's miraculous favours. One of these was written by Martín González (2002), who lived in Ciudad Guzmán, the regional capital of southern Jalisco and seat of the diocese (see Figure 3). Like my own history of the Tapalpan church, there are no miracles in his narrative. I asked about this in an interview, and he explained:

> I don't mention any of the miracles. There's one meaning of the Virgin that I want to recover. This has to do with her origin: The Virgin of Defence is 'defender of the peripheral and marginalised'. There are two other meanings: one is almost mystical, which is 'defender of little birds' [birds sheltered in the hermit's image in Father Orozco's account], and I think that miracles are involved in this meaning. There is another meaning that is 'defender of ecclesiastical authority' and '[defender] of projects of conquest' for powerful groups.[10] I leave aside these two meanings. I am interested in the meaning that has historical transcendence – that has real historical repercussion.

Note that González appears to attribute agency to the Virgin as an active "defender of the peripheral and marginalised". However, when I asked him about this, he replied: "She is the justification of many of the events. She doesn't have human functions and produce things. It's the social nuclei around her [that produce things]".[11] González's reply resonates with a point made by Taussig:

> I have said 'image' when I could just as well have said 'the community of persons among whom the image exists, the community of persons doing the imagining and therewith bringing the image to life over and over again'. It is of course fetishistic

to endow the image per se with the active role in what is a reciprocating relation
between viewer and viewed.                                    (Taussig 1987: 198)

This is, I propose, classically secular narrative. González and Taussig, even though playing
rhetorically with divine agency, both leave that agency outside the main flow of the narrative. They both retell what might otherwise be a narrative of miraculous intervention,
in purely human terms.

Note that González was as closely connected to the church as Escoto, although his
brand of Catholicism was different from hers. González had rewritten the Virgin's history
in the spirit of liberation theology. Liberation theology emphasizes human responsibility
in a this-worldly struggle; it does so, in a sense, by bracketing the next world (although
not of course excluding it). Rather than featuring the miracles featured in most talk about
the Virgin, González focused on the struggle for social justice of the "peripheral and the
marginalised". Unusually for Mexico, the bishop of Ciudad Guzmán had promoted liberation theology since the founding of the diocese in 1972, and González explained in the
interview that he intended his history to help revive that movement in the diocese (cf.
Vázquez 1997: 84–90). This helps to explain the clergy's support for his history, which was
published by the Atemajac parish.


CHOOSING SECULAR NARRATION

I have explained what I mean by the secular perspective, and I have said that I was only
one of those taking a secular perspective in west Mexico in the 1990s. In fact, I have identified different secular perspectives, and noted that these were taken by a wide range of
people. In this section, I examine people's motives for choosing to take this perspective.
Some of these motives were specific to the Sierra de Tapalpa or to individuals such as
Martín González, while others were common throughout Mexico or even the modern
world. I explain how and why narrators such as González produced their narratives under
the auspices of the church. I then focus on one motive: narrators could gain authority by
claiming the 'higher ground' of secular knowledge.


## Hegemony of the secular

One reason for taking a secular approach was the hegemony of the secular. By the 1990s
people in west Mexico had become used to the idea that there was a secular 'outside' to
religion. They were not surprised, as a result, that I would have something to say about
the objects of their devotion. This was no doubt partly because the Mexican state had
successfully carved out a 'secular' arena of politics that encompassed the ecclesiastical
arena. For example, the parish priest had to seek permission for religious processions,

and this was occasionally denied.[12] Economic practices were also secularized. James Cox argues in this volume (Chapter 3) that the US government, through the Alaska Native Claims Settlement Act, secularized lands in Alaska by commoditizing them; in order to render the lands alienable, US officials redefined indigenous practices embedded in the land, as 'cultural traditions' separable from the land. This was achieved long before in the Sierra de Tapalpa, where lands were mainly commoditized by the early twentieth century and, by the 1990s, were bought and sold with some frequency through the tourist industry.[13] Land ownership and other economic practices were one thing; religion was another. Tapalpans were also used to the secular gaze of tourists' video cameras on their processions, and migrants on return visits from California had begun to film the Virgin too (see Figure 2).

But it was not just that people accepted the possibility of secular knowledge. There were more positive reasons for choosing secular narration in west Mexico in the 1990s. To begin with, it allowed narrators to identify with their devout subjects in certain respects, while remaining "outside" in other respects. Narrators such as the authors of the *Monograph* could thus write of religious devotion within a secular context. They identified with their narrative subjects as residents of the Sierra but not, at least explicitly, as fellow devotees of the Virgin. There were other variations on this theme. For example, the municipal chronicler José Fajardo wrote several articles about the Virgin of Defence in his column in a regional newspaper: he used poetic language to aestheticize Tapalpans' devotion to the Virgin and to evoke his sympathy for their devotion, but he did not make explicit his own devotion to the Virgin in that secular context. Nor did he celebrate her miracles, any more than I did in my booklet on the Tapalpan church (e.g. Fajardo Villalvazo 1995). In a similar vein, he pleaded in another article that "it would be a lack of *historical sensibility* for memory to forget the celebration of San Antonio [the former patron saint of Tapalpa]" (Fajardo Villalvazo 1994, emphasis added).

## Under the auspices of the church

We have seen that narrators such as Martín González (and I) chose secular narration even when writing under the auspices of the church. If the 'secular' is understood as the exclusion of divine agency, it is difficult to see why the church would give its seal of approval. For that reason, I have proposed a broader concept of secular knowledge, one that embraces all narration that brackets divine agency even if it finds other places for it. To narrate in a 'secular' way is not necessarily, in these terms, to narrate in a 'profane' way. I would use the term 'profane' for narration that focuses on objects that are not considered 'sacred', or that treats such objects as if they were not 'sacred'. Some secular narration could be taken to profane the sacred, but I suggest that there are many uses of secular narration that are not really profane in this sense. Indeed, what is peculiar to the secular is that it need *not* profane the sacred. One can, for example, simply put one's own devotion on hold and view religion "from a position that is ostensibly outside it" (Lambek 2003: 3).

This helps to explain *how* it is possible to produce secular narratives under the auspices of the church. It does not explain *why* they are produced. I propose three possible reasons. First, secular narration fits particularly well with one kind of Catholicism, liberation theology. Secondly and more broadly, secular narration allowed narrators to reach a wider audience. For example, González explained in his interview that he was concerned to reach a wider audience than just the Virgin's faithful. In particular, he was anxious to draw the attention of politicians to the injustices of life in the Sierra de Tapalpa. Thirdly, those educated in church seminary schools were in a strong position to produce and gain authority from secular knowledge. González himself took up employment in a secular university after thirteen years of seminary education. At the same time, his friendship with priests gave him access to their parish archives, which were the principal source for his history. Secular knowledge was something that clerics (and those with clerical education) could do well and benefit from.

### A higher ground

I want to stress in this chapter another reason for choosing a secular perspective. These narrators were able to claim a special kind of 'higher ground', one that lay 'outside' the world of their narrative subjects, and from which they could look in on their narrative subjects. This allowed narrators to do various things. One was to demystify others' claims of access to the divine. On one occasion, a friend said that people used to take the Virgin of Defence to visit hacienda owners who had threatened to take their lands; the hacienda owners would then forget their threats, and even join the processions. Another friend, Alfonso, replied that "this didn't work for them either", presumably since everyone knew that the hacienda owners had ended up with all the lands. Perhaps because he was not a practising Catholic, Alfonso effectively ironized the people's devotion. He portrayed the devoted as mistaken or misled.

Academic historians often claim this kind of higher ground.[14] One example is an article by the Mexican sociologist Jesús Tapia (1986), on the cult of the Virgin of the Purest Conception in the town of Zamora, Michoacán. Zamorans said that the Virgin had saved them from plague in the nineteenth century. Tapia, then based at a research centre in Zamora, argued that the Virgin's cult had been sponsored by Zamora's conservative bourgeoisie, as a response to liberal anti-clericalism. In other words, rather like Martín González, Tapia retold the Virgin's history in social terms. A Zamoran schoolteacher, Rafael, had read the article and asked what I thought. I thought it was very good. He agreed, but added that "you can't take the people's faith away". Rafael was a devout Catholic but was also a high-school teacher with a bookish knowledge, often disdainful of popular beliefs and practices. On this occasion, though, even as he recognized the value of secular history, he seemed to sympathize with popular devotion, asserting its immunity to secular history.[15]

I argue, however, that this secular higher ground was not simply anti-Catholic. In fact, the sociologist Tapia was also known to be a practising Catholic.[16] Again, I am using the term 'secular' for all histories that make a point of bracketing 'divine' agency from the main frame of the narrative, even if they find another place for it. Alfonso finds no place for it, except in the deluded heads of the Indians who took the Virgin to win back their lands. Tapia leaves divine agency out of his narrative entirely, but speaks of divine agency in other contexts. Escoto writes divine agency into her prologue and epilogue, but is happy for me to leave it out of my narrative. González does something still more complex. In his interview, he claims, on the one hand, to champion 'popular devotion' in the face of 'ecclesiastical authority'. On the other hand, he distances himself from certain aspects of their devotion, arguing in particular that "a mystical, individualist devotion is not enough ... it is important to sustain more and more the social meaning".

Of course, for a ground to be higher, others must recognize that ground as higher, while only some people should actually take that higher ground. It must look, in other words, as if only the select few are able and willing to take that perspective. I have shown that this was the case in the Sierra de Tapalpa. Many recognized that history offered a worthwhile perspective on the Virgin, but did not take this ground themselves. Toni allowed that the catechists of Juanacatlán (and I) might produce a history of the Virgin's origins, but again had little to say about this himself. Rafael in Zamora agreed that Tapia's history was "very good", but showed little inclination to follow suit. Just as there were several reasons for taking a secular perspective, there were also several reasons for not taking one. It may be that some people were still not used to this perspective, while others were not confident enough to narrate history. Still others seemed to feel that it was harmless enough and perhaps of some value, but not worth the kind of energy involved in, say, processing with the Virgin all the way from Juanacatlán to Tapalpa. I do not recall anyone actually objecting to the idea of a history of the Virgin, however.

## HISTORY OF SECULAR NARRATION

History itself has a history, as does secular narration in general. In this final section, following other chapters in this book, I situate secular narration within colonial and postcolonial history. I argue that secular narration has been one way of marking the difference between peoples. I then conclude by discussing the place of the church in this history of secular knowledge.

### Modern/colonial secular knowledge

This higher ground has its place in the broader politics of knowledge that Mignolo (2000: 22) terms "modern/colonial". Mignolo uses that term to highlight the persistence of certain ways of ranking people, from the fifteenth century to the present day. He notes, however, that new modes of distinction have emerged during this period. For example:

In the sixteenth century, Spanish missionaries judged and ranked human intelligence and civilization by whether the people were in possession of alphabetic writing... the colonial difference was situated in space. Toward the end of the eighteenth and the beginning of the nineteenth century, the measuring stick was history and no longer writing. 'People without history' were located in a time 'before' the 'present'. People with history could write the history of those people without.

(*Ibid.*: 3)

Mignolo goes on to argue that: "At the beginning of the twentieth century, Max Weber transformed this ... into a celebration of the possession of true knowledge, an Occidental achievement of universal value ... Weber was blind to the colonial difference and to the subalternization of knowledge built into it" (*Ibid.*: 3–4). In Mignolo's view, this is just another way of ranking some groups of people over others: we claim to fit other peoples into our universal framework. Bernard McGrane (1989) suggests a twist on this in his book *Beyond Anthropology: Society and the Other*:

One of the basic values of our culture [in the twentieth-century West] is that it and its basic values are relative ... Our culture *knows* that it is one-among-many ... and further, it *values* this knowledge ... it locates inferiority (ignorance) in ignorance of this relativity ... The Other becomes *an occasion for seeing the strength of custom*. He manifests, above all, his own imprisonment within culture ...

(*Ibid.*: 120–21, emphasis added)

In other words, not only can we look in on the culture in which others are imprisoned, but we can even step outside our own culture. This makes us feel superior. Anthropologists specialize in this, of course, and claim to achieve this perspective through 'culture shock' and 'reverse culture shock'.

The secular perspective is a variant of this, since it looks in on religion as anthropology looks in on culture. This is where the modern/colonial perspectives of González and Taussig most resemble each other: they share that same higher ground. Both authors imply that their narrative subjects are, in a sense, imprisoned within their religion. They seal their subjects off into worlds of religious devotion, while they themselves presume to slip in and out of those worlds with ease. They may sympathize and even identify with the devotion of their subjects, while choosing their moment to step outside that devotion and peer in on it.[17]

It is possible that this perspective was developed, as Mignolo suggests, during the nineteenth and twentieth centuries. But Michel de Certeau has argued that seventeenth-century France already saw the rise of sciences such as history:

of which religious life will be more and more the object and less and less the principle. Science imposes its criteria upon everyone; one's belief or unbelief is of no importance here. It places religious facts outside of scientific process; religious facts are either before science as an *object*, or behind it, with the status of an interior *motivation* (the learned man's 'pious intention') or of a place in society (the scholar is Christian only in living in the style of a 'solitary' or as a monk) ...     (1988: 133)

This sounds like a step in the direction of the secular perspective that I have outlined in this chapter. Narrators bracket divine agency in the main body of the narrative ("scientific process"), even if they find other places for it. In fact, I suggest below that the secular perspective was already emerging in the sixteenth century.

In the Sierra de Tapalpa in the 1990s, people ranked themselves and others in various ways, some of which fitted Mignolo's account of the modern/colonial. People often accused each other, for example, of lacking '*cultura*'. By this, they meant that they lacked the ability to apprehend that which lay beyond the immediate. Those found lacking in *cultura* included peasants who sold their land for short-term gain, citizens who traded their vote for promised favours, and politicians who were corrupted by personal, familiar or partisan interests. People also used time as a measuring stick: Tapalpa's neighbour Atacco was considered an older place, one that had been left behind. Tapalpans often ethnicized these distinctions too: for example, they described the people of Atacco as 'Indians' (Stack 2004). They ranked people, moreover, in terms of knowledge: Atacco might be a place of which history was known, by virtue of being older, but it was not considered a place in which history was known (Stack 2006). Together with these distinctions, some people in the Sierra – as different as Escoto, González, Alfonso and me – could claim the higher ground of secular knowledge. I argue that to take a secular perspective was, indeed, to show *cultura*. It was a sign that narrators were not trapped in their devotion, but could step outside it.[18]

The Guatemalan state may have made fewer inroads in Concepción Sololá and Todos Santos Cuchumetantes than the Mexican state in the Sierra de Tapalpa, but both Guatemalan towns had obviously been exposed for centuries to the modern/colonial order. It is unlikely that anthropologists were the only outsiders to look in on their culture and on their religion. However, it is possible that residents of those Guatemalan towns had avoided ranking *each other* in these modern/colonial terms. They may have realized that hierarchy was embedded in the secular perspective, and preferred to abstain from it. They may also have resisted the secular gaze of others: hence, perhaps, the cryptic answer given to Blume's question about the books kept in Todos Santos.

## Under the auspices of the church?

I have said that some narrators took a secular perspective even when writing under the auspices of the church. In the rest of this chapter, I argue that there was a modern/colonial dimension to this. Secular narration allowed the church to look in, as if from outside, on the devotion of different groups of people. This helped the church to renew the authority not just of its texts, but of its ministers.

## Renewing the authority of texts

Scholars have offered various explanations for the use of secular knowledge within the church over the centuries. Briefly, some have argued that the church has submitted to the hegemony of secular knowledge, just as to the hegemony of political secularism. Secularism as a political doctrine implies the existence of a 'religious' arena that is defined and delimited from a secular 'outside', in the form of the state. Similarly, Certeau argues that:

> [contemporary] historians spontaneously take their task to be the need to determine what a field delineated as 'religious' can teach them about a society ... The very [social] questions that [early modern historians] had to explain through a truth (God, Providence, etc.) have become what makes their explanations intelligible to us. Between their time and ours, the signifier and the signified have castled ...
>
> (1988: 138)

Hence, Tapia and González examine the 'religious' narratives of miracle-working Virgins for clues about the struggle between social classes; this 'social' explanation allows us to make sense of these narratives. By the eighteenth century, moreover, "[a]n 'iconographical repression' excluded nudity, animals, representations which did not conform to 'historical truth' – in a word, everything prompting 'derision'; that is, *what did not conform to the taste of the intelligentsia which was a model for these clerics*" (ibid.: 189, emphasis added). This implies that the church accepted secular accounts of its 'religious' truths because of pressure from the secular establishment.

However, secular narration may also have developed under the auspices of the Church itself. For example, Asad has noted that: "it was Christian doubt and anxiety [particularly about the divine revelation of Scriptures] ... that drove biblical scholars to develop textual techniques that have since become part of the foundation of modern, secular historiography" (2003: 42). He cites Butterfield: "the truth of religion was so momentous an issue, and the controversies about it so intense, that the critical methods were developing in ecclesiastical research before anybody thought of transposing them" (1955: 15–16).

Given this, we should not be surprised to find among the documents of the Second Vatican Council (1962), arguments such as the following: "Hence the exegete must look for that meaning which the sacred writer, in a determined situation and given the circumstances of his time and culture, intended to express and did in fact express, through the medium of a contemporary literary form" (Vatican Council II 1975: 757).

The church used literary, sociological and historical criticism to give credence to (as well as to rationalize) its canon of knowledge. Secular narration offered, in other words, a way for the church to renew the authority of its sacred texts.

## Renewing the authority of ministers

I argue that secular narration also allowed the church to renew the authority of its ministers. To begin with, some sixteenth-century Spanish missionaries were already marking off a 'religious' sphere of practices. Blume begins her chapter (Chapter 1) by describing the attempts of sixteenth-century Spanish missionaries to convert the American peoples. This 'conversion' was designed to transform an entire way of life rather than the private 'beliefs' of individuals. But missionaries such as Las Casas did consider some pre-Hispanic practices worth preserving, even as they decided that other practices were inspired by the devil. Later in the century, the Jesuit missionary José de Acosta ([1590] 2002) sharpened this distinction in his classic work *Natural and Moral History of the Indies*. He praised in one chapter the pre-Hispanic practices that he considered evidence of the natives' civilization and thus of their aptitude for Christianity. He had focused the previous chapter, however, on pre-Hispanic 'religion', arguing that it was inspired by the devil and should be rooted out in its entirety (cf. Cervantes 1991). Acosta was effectively circumscribing pre-Hispanic 'religion', marking it off from other practices that he did not consider 'religious'. Perhaps this was an initial step toward the fully fledged secular perspective that I have described in this chapter. It is often observed, of course, that sixteenth-century missionary accounts of the American peoples read rather like twentieth-century ethnographic accounts.

Why would sixteenth-century missionaries do this? And what about the twentieth-century church? Briefly, indigenous American peoples often developed an intimate relationship with the Catholic icons brought by the Spaniards. The attitude of Catholic clergy has, then and now, been ambivalent. On the one hand, the clergy have encouraged the cult of these icons: Mexican clergy did so, for example, after the church–state conflicts of the 1920s and 1930s. On the other hand, the clergy have tried to keep hold of these cults, which have often, as Taussig (1987: 202–3) shows, slipped out of the clergy's grasp.[19]

The clergy keeps hold of the cult of these icons, first, by insisting that devotional practices stay within the limits of orthodoxy. Hence, Father Orozco complained in 1954 of the unruly practices of the Indians, which he contrasted to clerical devotion to the Virgin. The Colombian priests described by Taussig (1987: 189–93) did something similar in the 1970s. Secondly, however, the church asserts its authority by *authorizing* a degree of deviance from that orthodoxy. This is one way of reading Acosta: he was distinguishing in 1590 between a domain of 'non-religious' pre-Hispanic practices that he could tolerate, and a 'religious' domain that he would not. The Second Vatican Council took this further:

> Even in the liturgy the Church does not wish to impose a rigid uniformity in matters which do not involve the faith or the good of the whole community. Rather does she respect and foster the qualities and talents of the various races and nations. Anything in these people's ways of life which is not indissolubly bound up with superstition and error she studies with sympathy, and, if possible, preserves intact. She sometimes even admits such things into the liturgy itself, provided they harmonize with its true and authentic spirit.                    (Vatican Council II 1975: 13)

The church now 'studies' not just to tolerate, but even to 'foster' the peculiar devotion of different peoples. It allows a generous margin of error, of deviance from orthodoxy, even if it continues to police the 'superstition and error' on the boundaries of popular devotion.[20]

Note how close this is to the modern/colonial perspective identified by Mignolo and McGrane: the church is looking in, as if from outside, on the objects of others' devotion. This allows the church to do more than just keep hold of the cult of its icons. It claims a higher ground, beyond those of mystical authority and of dogmatic expertise. The church's ministers take a perspective that most of their faithful, trapped in their peculiar devotion, are unable or unwilling to take for themselves. By sealing people off into 'different' worlds of popular devotion, the Church opens a space for itself on the outside of those worlds; it looks in, knowingly.

I often heard priests in the Sierra take this perspective, perhaps because the diocese was keen to implement the Vatican Council's reforms.[21] For example, I suggested to one priest that the Catholic Church was, paradoxically, both hierarchical and also plural in the cult of its many icons. He replied by arguing that religion had progressed from the polytheistic worship of primitives who used objects to reach God, to the fully evolved worship of those no longer in need of such objects. He went on to talk sympathetically, however, of devotion in the Sierra as a 'tradition' in which he was not yet fully 'immersed': "I can understand it with my head and they live it with their body". That notion of immersion (familiar to anthropologists) is obviously akin to the modern/colonial notion of being trapped within devotion. But the priest also saw his role as guiding that popular devotion: to encourage people to perform traditional dances in religious festivals, for example, when they were not doing so. In order to do this, he explained, he needed local knowledge, so as not to "put his foot in it", like another priest he knew, who had processed with one image while the people were processing with another.

The parish priest of Tapalpa also noted that priests gradually acquire knowledge of popular devotion: "One enters bit by bit in the culture, in the way of being of each parish". He felt, too, that the faithful needed guiding, and he wanted to steer them away from dependence on the Virgin's miracles. He complained, for example, that people talked about the Virgin doing things for them, when they should be talking about the Virgin motivating them to do things in their lives. In saying this, the parish priest did not go quite as far as González, for whom the Virgin was simply 'justification' for popular activism. But he was still taking the Virgin out of the cut-and-thrust of events: the Virgin moves people to do things, rather than doing things in her own right. Again, he expressed his tolerance and sympathy for popular devotion, he marked its limits and deficiencies and, in passing, he staked out the higher ground from which he did all this.

The Second Vatican Council also played up the role of lay men and women, but I found that these lay leaders often viewed popular devotion in a similar way to priests. According to the Council, lay Catholics had a role to play in guiding the church, but they would do this to different degrees: "By reason of the knowledge, competence or pre-eminence which they have the laity are empowered – indeed sometimes obliged – to manifest their opinion on those things which pertain to the good of the Church" (Vatican Council II 1975: 394). González was a prominent lay member of the diocese, bringing to bear his knowledge and abilities. Indeed, he made a point of criticizing, in his history, the account given by the parish priest in 1920 of the Virgin's coronation, which was also cited by Father Orozco. Both priests had failed, he argued, to give popular devotion its rightful place in their account of the ceremonies conducted that day (González 2002: 80–82). Some traditionalist Tapalpans objected to González's criticism of those priests, but the parish priest of Atemajac still published his history. As a lay leader, González could get away with that criticism but, in any case, the current priests may well have agreed with him. Although González did champion popular devotion over 'ecclesiastical authority', he also distanced himself from that popular devotion, just like the priests, complaining about the prevalence of "mystical, individualist devotion".[22]

I argued at the beginning of this chapter that priests enjoyed considerable authority in the Sierra de Tapalpa, unlike in Todos Santos Cuchumetantes and Concepción Sololá. They enjoyed this authority in spite of the fact that the church had been outflanked by the state: People had come to accept that there was a secular 'outside' to religion in politics and education, even though religious devotion still permeated much of their lives. Priests maintained their authority partly through their sacramental role and through personal charisma, as well as through less obvious means such as church architecture and design. But both priests and their lay associates in the Sierra could themselves lay some claim to the secular. They could take the higher ground of secular knowledge, and they were in a strong position to do so. This could, indeed, help them to recover some of the authority that had been lost to secular politics.

## ACKNOWLEDGEMENTS

Versions of this article were presented to both the Religious Studies and Hispanic Studies seminar series at the University of Aberdeen, as well as to the Latin American Cultures seminar series at the University of Manchester, and to a seminar at El Colegio de Michoacán. I am grateful for the comments that I received on those occasions, as well as for feedback on written drafts from Anna Blume, Matthew Butler, Tim Fitzgerald, Michael Lambek, Andrew Roth Seneff, Matt Tomlinson and Kristina Wirtz. Grants for fieldwork were provided by the British Academy, Royal Anthropological Institute and the Carnegie Trust.

## NOTES

1. By secular narrators, I mean people who choose at a particular moment to narrate from a secular perspective; I do not mean that these individuals are inherently secular. Narratives are not inherently secular either; I give examples of narrators retelling non-secular narratives from a secular perspective.
2. At least, this was a paradox in the context of a British-style secularism in which the separation of church and state is found together with a decline in religious devotion (cf. Bruce 2002).
3. There were also converts to Protestantism. For example, a group of Jehovah's Witnesses was building a church on the outskirts of Tapalpa.

4. Some Tapalpans did disagree with or even challenge priests, sometimes in public. I heard Tapalpans complain that priests were too authoritarian, while older Tapalpans remembered that priests used to wield still greater authority and tended to have greater respect for present-day priests.

5. Taussig (1987: 190) also suggests, interestingly, that these 'contradictory histories' served to fuel the cult of these images.

6. I did find some disjuncture between talk of miracles and talk of origins, although I have not discussed this here. Talk about miracles was generally personal and fragmentary. Each person recounted his or her own experience, and there was little attempt to catalogue the Virgin's miracles. By contrast, people often drew on a shared narrative of origins. They sometimes attributed this shared narrative to priests, and priests did promote knowledge of the Virgin's history. In Juanacatlán, for example, the parish priest had incorporated the Virgin's history into the catechism for children. (Toni was unsure in 1998 of the Virgin's origins, even though he was well educated and an active participant in Catholic groups, but by 2004 I noticed that Tapalpans narrated her origins more readily, usually citing a leaflet printed in 1992 by the parish priest.)

7. As other authors in this volume stress, however, the boundary between the secular and the non-secular is blurred. Just as the *Monograph* gives hints of a non-secular perspective, Father Orozco's chapter may have secular elements. This may help to explain the ease with which the library staff lifted sections of Father Orozco's history into their *Monograph*. It could be argued, to begin with, that Father Orozco (and the priests described by Taussig) plays up the distance of the divine from the human. Following Peter Berger's (1969: 105–25) discussion of the secular, this may provide another way for priests to assert control over popular devotion. By distancing the divine from the human, priests narrow access to the divine, and can challenge popular claims to access through local icons.

8. I note below that the municipal chronicler in his newspaper articles also presented the cult of local icons as a 'tradition' that Tapalpans should preserve.

9. I pitched my history as the history of a church, rather than as the history of a Virgin; this might explain why they accepted my history. However, most people referred to it as a "history of the Virgin".

10. As I discuss below, González (2002: 80–82) critiques in his history the account given by the parish priest in 1920 of the Virgin's coronation in that year. He argues that the parish priest's account reflected the alliance of the church with elite groups in the Sierra in that period.

11. At the same time, González allowed in his interview that "the symbol also has a certain autonomy ... it convokes and congregates; eventually the original subjects disappear and it becomes an attraction in itself".

12. The parish priest also told me in 1999 that the municipal president had harangued him after the priest had criticized the municipal government in an interview with journalists.

13. Elderly residents of Tapalpa's neighbour Atacco recall that a 'book of Atacco' was once kept in the chapel. It seems that this book, like the papers kept in the outhouse in Todos Santos Cuchumetantes, contained the community's colonial land titles. They were apparently removed from the chapel during the Mexican Revolution, and remained buried in family papers until the 1980s.

14. I do not use quotation marks for 'higher ground' in the rest of the chapter, but I have explained in my introduction that the ground is 'higher' (just as it lies 'outside') from the perspective of narrators and their audiences. I am not endorsing this as an inherently higher ground. I would, of course, say the same of other higher grounds, such as those of mystical authority and of dogmatic expertise.

15. Matt Tomlinson has pointed out to me that Rafael is echoing Kierkagaard's argument that Christianity "does not lend itself to objective observation, precisely because it proposes to intensify subjectivity to the utmost" (Kierkegaard 1941: 55). This allows Rafael to accept the validity of both Tapia's perspective and that of 'the people'.

16. Tapia (1986) himself, unlike Alfonso, avoids ironizing popular devotion; instead, like González, he plays up the role of the clergy in alliance with powerful groups. Tapia is also reluctant to criticize the church as a whole; his criticisms are confined to the nineteenth-century clergy. In fact, rather as Rafael finds a place for both academic history and popular devotion, Tapia puts the theology of miracles on an equal footing with his "sociology of miracles". Although the article was published by

the research centre, a state-funded institution, it almost feels as if it were written under the auspices of the church. Tapia even concludes that "nothing impedes [*nihil obstat?*] a sociology of miracles" (*ibid.*: 50).

17. Anthropology is a fine example of secular narration (cf. Stewart 2001). I began this chapter with the claim that history is a secular kind of knowledge, but it may be that anthropology is still more acutely secular, at least in the terms of this chapter. Lambek (2003: 2) notes that this makes it difficult for anthropologists to write about the secular.

18. Devotion itself was compatible with *cultura* and, indeed, priests were sometimes said to have *cultura*. When I confessed to the Zamoran schoolteacher, Rafael, that I was an atheist, he replied that I still had a lot to learn. He was not referring, I suggest, to mere academic learning but to *cultura*, which people did not generally feel was learned in schools.

19. Matthew Butler has pointed out to me that, after the Cristero rebellion of the 1920s, the clergy needed to reassert control over a militant laity that had fought to defend clerical privilege. Among other things, they needed to reassert clerical control of the cult of icons. Specifically, they were keen to promote and control Marian cults, in order to offset the cult of Cristo Rey (Christ the King) that had flourished in the 1920s and given its name to the Cristero movement (cf. Butler 2005). Hence, no doubt, the publication in 1954 of Father Orozco's book on Marian iconography.

20. Tolerance does not always come naturally to priests. One priest ripped the mask off a man doing a traditional dance during a religious festival in Atacco. That priest was thereafter known as 'Thousand Masks', presumably in allusion to his two-faced switch from generous tolerance to despotic censure.

21. My anthropology, unlike my history, was not produced under the auspices of the church. But I found the priests in Tapalpa supportive of my project, and I learned much from my conversations with them. One of the priests was also happy to get this chapter translated.

22. Traditionalist Catholics disputed the authority of lay leaders like Martín González, especially when those lay leaders dared to question or challenge those priests. For priests, there were also dangers in sharing the higher ground with lay leaders. I have noted that the clergy, for much of the twentieth century, were keen to assert control over lay Catholics. But when I asked Francisca in Tapalpa whether priests approved of the Virgin's cult, she replied that they had to do what the *pueblo* (people or town) wanted. I was also told that lay leaders had effectively driven one priest from Tapalpa during the 1990s. Nevertheless, I suggest that lay leaders did help the clergy to contain popular devotion.

## BIBLIOGRAPHY

Acosta, Jose de. [1590] 2002. *Natural and Moral History of the Indies*. Ed. Jane E. Mangan, with an introduction and commentary by Walter D. Mignolo, trans. Frances López-Morillas. Durham, NC: Duke University Press.

Asad, Talal. 2003. *Formations of the Secular: Christianity, Islam, Modernity*. Palo Alto, CA: Stanford University Press.

Berger, Peter. 1969. *The Sacred Canopy*. New York: Doubleday.

Bruce, Steve. 2002. *God is Dead: Secularization in the West*. Oxford: Blackwell.

Butler, Matthew. 2005. *Popular Piety and Political Identity in Mexico's Cristero Rebellion: Michoacán, 1927-29*. Oxford: Oxford University Press for British Academy.

Butterfield, Herbert. 1955. *Man on his Past: The Study of the History of Historical Scholarship*. Cambridge: Cambridge University Press.

Certeau, Michel de. 1988. *The Writing of History*, trans. Tom Conley. New York: Columbia University Press.

Cervantes, Fernando. 1991. *The Idea of the Devil and the Problem of the Indian*. London: Institute of Latin American Studies, University of London.

Fajardo Villalvazo, José. 1994. "Memoria sobre la devoción de San Antonio de Padua". In *El Informador*, 11 June.

Fajardo Villalvazo, José. 1995. "La Virgen de la Defensa". In *El Informador, Suplemento Cultural,* 17 December: 2–3.

González, Martín. 2002. *Defensora sin institución: una interpretación histórica de la Virgen de la Defensa*. Atemajac de Brizuela, Jalisco, Mexico: Parroquia de San Bartolomé Apóstol.

Kierkegaard, Søren. 1941. *Kierkegaard's Concluding Unscientific Postscript*. Trans. David F. Swenson. London: Humphrey Milford and Oxford University Press.

Lambek, Michael. 2003. "On Standing 'Outside' Religion: A View from the Pre-Alps". Paper presented at American Anthropological Association annual meeting.

McGrane, Bernard. 1989. *Beyond Anthropology: Society and the Other*. New York: Columbia University Press.

Mignolo, Walter. 2000. *Local Histories/Global Designs: Coloniality, Subaltern Knowledges, and Border Thinking*. Princeton, NJ: Princeton University Press.

Nava López, J. Guadalupe, *et al.* 1985. *Monografía de Tapalpa, Jal.* Tapalpa, Mexico: Biblioteca Pública Municipal de Tapalpa, Jalisco.

Orozco, Luis Enrique. 1954. *Iconografía Mariana de la Arquidiócesis de Guadalajara*, Tomo 1. Guadalajara: Arzobispado de Guadalajara.

Stack, Trevor. 1994. *Historia del Templo de la Merced de Tapalpa, Jalisco*. Guadalajara, Jal.: Imprenta Nueva Galicia.

Stack, Trevor. 2004. "The Time of Place in West Mexico". In *The Qualities of Time: Anthropological Approaches*, eds W. James and D. Mills, 55–69. London: Berg.

Stack, Trevor. 2006. "The Skewing of History in Mexico". *American Ethnologist* 33(3): 427–43.

Stack, Trevor. forthcoming. "Rooting and *Cultura* in West Mexico". *Bulletin of Latin American Research*.

Stewart, Charles. 2001. "Secularism as an Impediment to Anthropological Research". *Social Anthropology* 9(3): 325–8.

Tapia Santamaria, Jesús. 1986. "Identidad social y religión en el Bajío Zamorano 1850–1900. El culto a la Purísima, un mito de fundación". *Relaciones: Estudios de Historia y Sociedad* 7(27): 43–71.

Taussig, Michael. 1987. *Shamanism, Colonialism, and the Wild Man: A Study in Terror and Healing*. Chicago, IL: University of Chicago Press.

Vatican Council II. 1975. *Vatican Council II: The Conciliar and Post Conciliar Documents*. Wilmington: Scholarly Resources.

Vázquez, Lourdes Celina. 1997. *Identidad, Cultura y Religión en el Sur de Jalisco*. Guadalajara: El Colegio de Jalisco.

# 3

# Secularizing the land: the impact of the Alaska Native Claims Settlement Act on indigenous understandings of land

## James L. Cox

The Annual Report for 2002 of the Cook Inlet Region, Inc. (CIRI), an Alaska Native regional corporation created by the Alaska Native Claims Settlement Act of 1971, lists among its investments: the Westin Kierland Resort and Spa in Scottsdale Arizona; partnership in VoiceStream Wireless Corporation and BellSouth Corporation (a communications system operating in major US cities); ownership of multi-tenant business parks in Anchorage and other locations in the lower 48 states (including Miami, Florida and Kent, Washington); venture interests in Peak Oilfield Service Company; partnership in the Ritz-Carlton, Lake Las Vegas luxury resort hotel and full ownership of the Casino MonteLago, which is attached to the Ritz-Carlton Hotel (Cook Inlet Region, Inc. 2003: 11–15). These capital ventures run and operated by a major Alaska Native regional corporation paint a far different picture of the indigenous peoples of the Arctic and sub-Arctic regions of Alaska than are depicted in popularly held stereotypical images, such as those outlined by the Alaskan anthropologist, Wendell Oswalt:

> Eskimos are for many reasons the most exotic people in the world. After all, what is more demanding than living in a land where it is nearly always cold? What is more unprecedented than a diet of meat or a house built from snow? What could be kinder than never punishing children or more pacific than being ignorant of war? What is more bizarre than killing one's children or aged parents without showing emotion? What is more daring than hunting great whales from frail skin-covered boats or facing a polar bear when protected by nothing more than a spear backed by bravery? (1999: 1)

Of course, these characterizations of indigenous life in the Arctic regions are presented by Oswalt to underscore what he calls the "overstated qualities" found in customary images of Eskimos.[1] Another Alaskan anthropologist, Ann Fienup-Riordan, in a somewhat more sophisticated manner than Oswalt, suggests that the indigenous peoples of Alaska in particular have been depicted quite misleadingly "as conservationists practicing waste-free management and consumption of scarce and limited resources; as being peaceful and nonaggressive; as living free from law in a state of 'contained anarchy'; and as lacking the concepts of leadership, territory, and landownership" (1990: xii). She calls these "half truths", which have resulted in part from the tendency of Arctic scholars to lose themselves in the "minutiae of their own field" and thus leave such popular characterizations of Eskimos "to the generalists" (ibid.).

It would be easy, therefore, following conventional notions, to suggest that the changes that occurred in 1971 following approval by the US Congress of the Alaska Native Claims Settlement Act (referred to throughout Alaska simply as ANCSA) created a radical change of direction among Alaska Natives away from traditional life towards an American, free-market, capitalist culture. In fact, the history is much more complex than this. It would be more correct to see the enshrinement of Native[2] land in corporate shares as an innovative attempt finally to achieve the longstanding aim of the US government to assimilate Native peoples into the lifestyle and culture of mainstream America. Initial efforts at Native assimilation were undertaken by Sheldon Jackson, the architect of the Protestant Mission in Alaska and the US Government's General Agent for Education in Alaska from 1885 to 1907. Under Jackson's leadership, schools and mission stations were established throughout Alaska with the aims of changing the indigenous way of life in virtually every aspect, including replacing subsistence and communal living with an individualized cash economy by teaching indigenous peoples how to work, live in single family units and, in Jackson's words, "how to make more money in order to live better, and how to utilize the resources of the country in order to make more money" (Cox 1991: 27).

The Alaska Native Claims Settlement Act of 1971, therefore, must be seen as the culmination of over a century of concerted but at times sporadic and uneven US government efforts to assimilate the Alaska Natives. ANCSA implemented a policy that affected every Native (born by the date the law was enacted) by providing each with shares in village and regional corporations in exchange for any future indigenous claims to the land. I shall argue in this chapter that ANCSA had the effect of secularizing the land, which in traditional society was understood in terms of a 'religious' relationship (as I define it below) to the animals, sea mammals and fish that lived on the land and within the adjacent seas. By redefining land as ownership of corporate shares, the US government sought to ensure that any sense of a spiritual connection to the land held by the Native population at last was eliminated in favour of making profits and increasing personal wealth.

## DISTINGUISHING RELIGION FROM THE SECULAR

The distinction between the religious and the secular is pivotal for understanding the progressive colonization of Alaska Native lands from the time the United States 'purchased' the territory from Russia in 1867 until ANCSA was enacted. It is important, therefore, at the outset to clarify in what ways I am using the terms 'religion' and 'secular'. I am helped in this by the French sociologist Danièle Hervieu-Léger in a book first published in French in 1993, with the English version appearing recently under the title *Religion as a Chain of Memory* (2000).

According to Hervieu-Léger, sociologists in the tradition of Durkheim have defined religion substantively by referring to spiritual entities or to a 'sacred' understood as "a tangible reality, a subject which can be identified by its properties and that is generally to be found in every religion" (*ibid.*: 48–9).[3] Properties of the sacred include "mysterious power, total separation between a sacred and profane world and an ambivalence which renders the sacred an object at once of fascination and revulsion" (*ibid.*: 49). Hervieu-Léger contends that this way of thinking transforms the concept of sacredness from an adjective into a noun, and thereby renders the sacred the unique subject matter of all religions. This means, in the words of François-André Isambert, that the sacred "in a rather confused way" denotes "the relationship in subject matter between all religions, indeed between all beliefs and between all religious feelings" (cited *ibid.*).

Hervieu-Léger argues that the French sociologist Henri Desroche has demonstrated conclusively that Durkheim defined religion in terms of a primary experience of the sacred, which is then transposed into institutional forms or a social order so that religion becomes "the administration of the sacred" (*ibid.*: 52).[4] On this reading of Durkheim, at a primary level, religion is constituted by an experience of what Hervieu-Léger calls "emotional contact with the divine principle", but at a secondary level, this experience is "socialized and rationalized, by being differentiated into beliefs and into offices and rites". This has the effect of distinguishing between what might be called an experience of the sacred – "a pure religious core" – and its institutional expressions (*ibid.*: 53). The sacred thus becomes the unique social reality behind "the multiplicity of religious expression in humanity" (*ibid.*: 49). In this way, religious practices are understood as converging into the concept of the singular sacred (a homogenous social entity rather than an ontological reality), characterized in modernity "by the individualization and the subjectivization of systems of meaning" (*ibid.*).

Because in modern, secular societies religion is expressed widely in intensely individualistic and non-institutional ways, the term 'sacred' has been substituted for religion, and used to identify the uniquely religious elements hidden within the symbolic expressions of modernity. However, this approach, according to Hervieu-Léger, has produced just the opposite effect: "The notion of the sacred is bound to reintroduce surreptitiously the very thing it was supposed to eliminate, namely the preponderance of the Christian model in thinking about religion" (*ibid.*: 51). Hervieu-Léger thus challenges us to rethink the usefulness of Durkheimian interpretations of the religion–secular dichotomy, which outline a primary experience of the sacred and a secondary institutionalization of the experience. She asks if religion really can be understood best in contemporary society as referring to "this first intense experience of the sacred" (*ibid.*: 52), rather than the way it is administered through institutions.

In order to answer this, she employs the example of sport, initially by drawing attention to the primary emotional experience of individual athletic achievements, such as those attained in mountaineering, surfing or canyoning, so-called high-risk sports. These all share a sense of danger that pushes participants towards an experience that can be likened to religious mysticism (*ibid.*: 54). The institutionalization of individual achievement, however, is best exemplified in spectator sports that draw huge crowds into a state of high excitement, during which they collectively create a "shared sacred" (*ibid.*: 55). It is here that the Durkheimian analysis becomes most evident: "Across the emotive intensity which makes the crowd one, society affirms itself" (*ibid.*: 56). Sport thus contains the primary and secondary elements, which in Durkheim's analysis constitute religion, by combining its experiential and social components. In Hervieu-Léger's words, "It would appear that, in modern societies, sport fulfils the social function of self-affirmation which in traditional societies belonged to religion" (*ibid.*). The example of sport, moreover, can be illustrated in many other collective activities that bind people together in modern society on the basis of an elementary emotional experience, such as rock concerts or political rallies. On this account it would appear that, since the primary experience of the sacred can be expressed in numerous institutional forms, it provides an effective analytical model for understanding religion in secular terms.

Although she finds this argument intellectually compelling, Hervieu-Léger rejects it, suggesting that the emotional experience of the sacred, rather than confirming the persistence of religion in modern society, actually signals its demise. This is because 'sacredness' and 'religion' cannot be equated; they "refer to two types of distinct experience". Although the two types usually run in tandem with each other, they can and do at times stand in firm opposition to one another (*ibid.*: 58). For example, the growth of charismatic movements around the world, with their overwhelming emphasis on emotion, reflects a modern rebellion against the institutionalization and bureaucratization of religion. Hervieu-Léger theorizes that Pentecostalism, on one level, because it insists on speaking in "unknown tongues" (glossolalia), represents a new language for those most deprived of a voice in society. On another level, the phenomenon of glossolalia demonstrates that in modern society belief has been so eroded that the only avenue for expression for many is found in that which is inexpressible, quite literally (*ibid.*: 58–9). Rather than providing evidence that religion is being renewed in contemporary society by what Hervieu-Léger calls "the definitive fantastication of religious utterance", emotional experiences as fostered within the charismatic movements expose a thorough alienation in modernity from rational belief itself (*ibid.*: 60). For Hervieu-Léger, therefore, the bond between the experience of the sacred and religion must be disconnected so we can identify "what is specific to the experience of both the one and the other" (*ibid.*).

It is important to note that Hervieu-Léger's analysis thus far has in part served the purpose of exposing the essentialist and Christian assumptions beneath many prior attempts to analyse the relationships between the sacred and religion in modernity. She explicitly rejects the idea that the sociologist should employ ontological definitions of religion by arguing that that the aim of the sociologist is "to comprehend changes in the sphere of religion, considered by way of its tangible socio-historical manifestations" (*ibid*.: 69). For this reason, any definition of religion must be operational or instrumental, aimed at assisting the scholar to describe and understand socio-religious change. Moreover, if traditional or historical religions and so-called secular religions share certain characteristics, these should not be assumed to reflect identical beliefs. There are many differences, for example, between a Marxist eschatology and an Islamic one. Religion, therefore, needs to be understood in its own socio-cultural and historical contexts.

For Hervieu-Léger, the meaning conveyed to individuals by religion is connected inextricably with institutions that transmit authority. This leads her to identify religion as existing whenever "the authority of tradition" has been invoked "in support of the act of believing" (*ibid*.: 76). She explains: "Seen thus, one would describe any form of believing as religious which sees its commitment to a chain of belief it adopts as all-absorbing" (*ibid*.: 81). In other words, there is no religion without the explicit, semi-explicit, or entirely implicit invocation of the authority of a tradition, an invocation that serves as support for the act of believing. "*As our fathers believed, and because they believed, we too believe*" (*ibid*.: 81).

The emphasis on believing is central to understanding Hervieu-Léger's reconstruction of religion in the modern world. For her, changes in the context of believing define fundamentally the transformations that are occurring in contemporary society. She deliberately refers to believing as opposed to beliefs because she wants to underscore the dynamic process that is occurring. By believing, she means: "the body of convictions – both individual and collective – which are not susceptible to verification, to experimentation and, more broadly, to the modes of recognition and control that characterize knowledge, but owe their validity to the meaning and coherence they give to the subjective experience of those who hold them" (*ibid*.: 72). Acts of believing play a major role in social processes in modernity because they construct meanings for individuals and for society. Although scientific rationality has in some sense eroded traditional meanings, this does not lead us to conclude that the human need for meaning is thereby diminished. On the contrary, what it indicates is that meaning is "no longer fixed and stable ... but unpredictable and unprotected, where change and innovation have become the norm" (*ibid*.: 73). It is precisely within the field of meaning-making that believing interacts with social processes. What scholars of religion need to develop, therefore, are methods that investigate the key elements of religion, which, for Hervieu-Léger, include expressions of believing, memory of continuity and the legitimizing reference to an authorized version of such memory (*ibid*.: 97).

Religion thus is best defined as "an ideological, practical and symbolic system through which consciousness, both individual and collective, of belonging to a particular chain of belief is constituted, maintained, developed and controlled" (*ibid*.: 82). This definition implies that religion cannot be equated with the 'sacred', which is experienced in multiform ways and in numerous manners of intensity. Religion denotes institutions of society, which bind adherents together through a shared allegiance to an overwhelming, authoritative tradition, which provides meaning for individual adherents. Many people in contemporary society, of course, testify to profound 'religious' experiences, even though these are not connected to an authoritative tradition. Hervieu-Léger calls such testimonies evidence of experiences of sacredness, understood not ontologically, but as emotional responses to particular socio-cultural contexts, including sporting events, political rallies, rock concerts and gatherings dominated by speaking in tongues (glossolalia).

## THE PROCESS OF SECULARIZATION

Hervieu-Léger's definition of religion in modernity leads us naturally to consider how this relates to theories of secularization. In particular, her perspective forces us to ask if the individualistic and atomized experiences of sacredness, so common in contemporary society, foster the decline of religion, understood, in Hervieu-Léger's terms, as an authoritative 'chain of memory'.

The term 'secularization' is often used synonymously with activities that can be labelled 'irreligious'.[5] This is the way, for example, Jan Platvoet uses secularization to describe the rapid change in Dutch society away from what he calls "a fairly monochromatic ... Christian scene" during the first half of the twentieth century "to one of dazzling diversity, tolerance and religious indifference" in the second half (2002: 83). This occurred, according to Platvoet owing to the "rapid rate of disaffiliation from the Dutch mainline churches, ... which turned Dutch society from the 'most Christian' nation of Europe in 1950, to, most probably, the most secularised and irreligious one in 2000" (*ibid.*). If we follow Platvoet, we would classify as 'religious' those who maintain allegiance to a unitary tradition that is passed on authoritatively, and often dogmatically, from generation to generation. Secularism, on the other hand, is marked by a 'disaffiliation' from organized religion, which results in widespread indifference to the authoritative tradition. Hervieu-Léger refers to this as "the crumbling memory of modern societies" (2000: 127).

The process of secularization, however, involves more than people in modern Western societies rejecting the authority of a tradition that had for previous generations been all-consuming. It includes processes at work that, under the influence of increasing globalizing forces, create an overarching homogeneity of power, resulting, according to Hervieu-Léger, "from the eclipse of the idiosyncrasies rooted in the collective memory of differentiated concrete groups" (*ibid.*: 128). For example, as Platvoet notes, despite the overall domination of Christianity in the Netherlands up until the middle of the twentieth century, the distinctive expressions of Christianity in the Netherlands "were heavily polarised and segmented" (2002: 83). Dutch religion, although derived from the authority of an allegedly single revelatory tradition, found its allegiances devolved into quite distinct and historically defined religious groupings. The homogeneity of modern society, by contrast, differs markedly from Platvoet's "monochromatic Christian scene" because secularization aligns all social life, in Hervieu-Léger's words, with "the sphere of production" (2000: 128). This, accompanied by mass and almost instant communication, has produced a collective memory that is far different from the religious memory; secularized memory is "surface memory, dull memory, whose normative, creative capacity" has been dissolved (*ibid.*). This process is embodied today in the dominating and total power of world capitalism, which coerces all differentiated societies with their various collective memories into one mould, defined and exploited by market forces.

The very factors that create a homogeneous economic system lead at the same time to a radical fragmentation of what Hervieu-Léger calls the "individual and group memory" (*ibid.*: 129). In modern societies, individuals belong to numerous, specialized and atomized groups. Although each operates within a general framework dictated by market forces, none is able to sustain a singular commitment to an all-consuming authority. In other words, individuals in modern societies are unable to coalesce around a unified memory. Because modern institutions are fragmented in space and time, individuals relate to them in a piecemeal fashion. No real central, organizing tradition can be sustained. As soon as a bit of memory is established, it is nearly always immediately destroyed. For Hervieu-Léger, "the collective memory of modern societies is composed of bits and pieces" (*ibid.*). The secular, as opposed to religion, therefore, is best defined as the homogenization in the contemporary global society of a surface memory, promulgated under the guise of the world economic system, which in turn is accompanied by a radical fragmentation of all collective memories.

## RELIGION, TRADITION AND SECULARIZATION IN ALASKA

I am suggesting in this chapter that 'religion' in the Alaskan context corresponds to traditional ways of relating to the land and the life that the land and surrounding seas and waterways sustain. The tradition, moreover, depends on an authority that the people acknowledge by respecting socially constructed boundaries and rules, and that they experience through the oral transmission of stories, ritual performances and particularly through the mediation of the shaman, who acts as a boundary-crosser between the seen and the unseen worlds (Fienup-Riordan 1994: 305–10). I acknowledge that no equivalent word for the Western term 'religion' existed among indigenous Alaskan groups, but they nevertheless passed on their traditions and customs authoritatively from generation to generation, and adhered to them closely in order to ensure communal well-being and to avoid calamities and misfortunes. This is why they referred to themselves, as I note below, through variations of the term 'Inuit', meaning the 'real' or 'authentic' people, which I interpret as referring to the ways in which their authoritative traditions were preserved in the collective memory.

The 'Inuit way of life', therefore, defines the best term in this context to indicate what I mean by the Western category 'religion', since for such a way of life to persist depended on the authoritative transmission of tradition. Moreover, this 'way of life' can be contrasted sharply with what I am calling the secularizing forces of Americanization, which not only challenged traditional authority, but systematically sought to displace it with a different kind of authority, rooted in a postulated and invented homogeneous

American cultural model. At the time of Jackson, this contrived Americanization emphasized hygiene, a cash economy, wooden-framed houses, classroom education, marriage
according to American law, nuclear and patrilineal families, permanent settlements, a
church building at the centre of the permanent settlement, a Protestant clergyman with
responsibility for the permanent settlement, and the exclusive use of the English language. By calling the Americanization of Alaska Natives a process of secularization, I am
suggesting that the authority on which the imposition of American values was based was
alien to the tradition that for Alaska Natives was all-consuming and that demanded full
and total allegiance. The Americanization perpetrated on Alaska Natives was based on
an ideology of power aimed at subduing and controlling Alaska Natives by making them
subservient to the new American political and social systems.

It is true that Jackson postulated an 'American way of life', which he and his selected
missionary teachers enforced in Alaska. This, however, did not conform to a unified
'American' system of beliefs, since no such singular way of life ever existed. Americans,
even at the end of the nineteenth century, did not all reside in permanent settlements;
they did not all participate in classroom education; they did not all live in wooden houses;
they certainly were not all Protestants; family life was never free from strife and divorce;
they did not even all speak English. The authority demanded of the Alaska Native by the
US government after 1867, therefore, was rooted in political expediency, not the authoritative transmission of a tradition, and thus, can rightly be called 'secular' (void of a collective memory) as opposed to 'religious' (where the collective memory is passed on
authoritatively from generation to generation).

It should be emphasized that the Americanization of Alaska, which began in the late
nineteenth century, can be understood as the gradual unfolding of a strategy of assimilation. The American missionary teachers who began arriving in increasing numbers
after 1880 could not have envisaged the methods that would be employed eighty years
later finally to eradicate indigenous traditions. Nevertheless, they began a process that
flowed naturally into land policies that would be controlled by the dictates of the market
economy and global capitalism. Hervieu-Léger's "dull" memory thus was already beginning to replace the traditional memory in ways that would have devastating consequences
for indigenous ways of life in Alaska. As I shall try to explain in the remainder of this
chapter, by 1971, when the land was transferred to Native Corporations, a whole new class
of individual shareholders was created. The homogenizing power structure of the free
market had at last fragmented the collective, deeply rooted and authoritative memory
of Alaska Native traditions.

SOME PRELIMINARY LIMITATIONS AND CLARIFICATIONS

Before discussing in detail the secularizing effects of ANCSA on traditional understandings of the land, I need to identify the context about which I am writing and define some

basic terms. It should be noted at the outset that Alaska extends over 533,000 square miles, crossing nearly 20 degrees of latitude. Within this wide area, numerous indigenous peoples reside, including: the Aleuts, who inhabit the chain of islands extending into the Pacific Ocean in the direction of Asia; the Alutiiq or Pacific Eskimos who are found along the Gulf of Alaska; the Yupiit, comprising the Yup'ik speakers in southwest and central Alaska (often referred to simply as the Yup'ik Eskimos); the Inupiat, whom Ernest Burch calls the "Inuit-Eskimo speaking inhabitants of the northern part of Alaska and extreme northwestern Canada" (1998: 3); the Athabascans, an Indian group living in the interior regions; and the Southeast Coastal Indians, primarily the Haida and Tlingit. The anthropologist Steve Langdon explains that "these groupings are based on broad cultural and linguistic similarities", but in a strict sense they "do not represent political or tribal units" (2002: 4). Since I am attempting in this chapter not to write an exhaustive description of Alaskan indigenous peoples, but instead to identify some key components within the traditional patterns of life that confirm the secularizing impact of ANCSA on these patterns, I shall restrict my discussion to the Yupiit, about whom Ann Fienup-Riordan (1990; 1994; 2000) has written extensively, and the Inupiat, with whom I have some limited personal experience (Cox 1991). For my purposes, sufficient similarities exist between Yupiit and Inupiat peoples to reach conclusions about the consequences of ANCSA for contemporary expressions of traditional Alaskan culture.

Since terminology in these cases can be confusing, I shall use the terms Yupiit and Inupiat (both plural forms), following Langdon (2002: 48–77), but it should be noted that these often are designated, as has been done by Oswalt (1999: 5), under the broad general categories of Yuit and Inuit. Oswalt's basic classifications denote the connections between the Alaskan Yupiit and Siberian Yup'ik speakers, and between the Inupiat and Inuit groups stretching from northern Alaska across Canada and into Greenland, all of whom speak similar dialects of Inupiaq. The Yup'ik and Inupiaq languages have common roots, but they are likened by Langdon (2002: 11) to the differences between German and English and thus they are mutually unintelligible. The terms 'Yuit' and 'Inuit', or their derivatives, translate into English as 'the real people' or, as Burch suggests (1998: 3), 'authentic' or 'special' human beings. Scholars today persist in lumping Yupiit, Inupiat and Alutiik Alaskan indigenous peoples under the generic term 'Eskimo', which Oswalt (1999: 5) contends originally had a derogatory meaning since it was derived from the Algonkian-speaking Indians of Eastern Canada who referred to the Canadian Inuit as "eaters of raw flesh". I should add, moreover, that the term Native (note with an uppercase N) is used widely today by all indigenous peoples of Alaska to designate themselves collectively, particularly in the context of land claims and indigenous rights.

Fienup-Riordan explains that the Yupiit are members of the larger family of Inuit cultures that extend from Prince William Sound on the Pacific Coast of Alaska to the Siberian and Alaskan sides of the Bering Sea and from there thousands of miles north and east along Canada's Arctic coast and into Labrador and Greenland. Both Yupiit and Inupiat peoples claim a common ancestry in Eastern Siberia and Asia, probably appearing on the west coast of Alaska in relatively recent times, perhaps just over 2400 years ago

(Fienup-Riordan 2000: 9). According to Oswalt, the Yupiit and Inupiat were characterized by the manufacture of "harpoons, tailor-made skin clothing, oil-burning lamps, and skin-covered boats known as kayaks or *umiaks*" (1999: 6). They became sea-mammal hunters along the coasts of the Bering and Chukchi Seas or, in more inland regions, they hunted caribou or fished the rivers and streams.

Despite their common origins with other Inuit peoples, the Yupiit and Inupiat of Alaska varied in significant ways from related groups, particularly those living in Canada and Greenland. Oswalt notes that the economies of the Alaskan Inuits were more diversified than their Canadian, Greenlandic or Polar counterparts since they "did not base their livelihood on hunting seals at breathing holes" as those in Canada did, nor did they "concentrate on open-water sealing" as was done in East Greenland (*ibid.*: 203). Snowhouses were rarely constructed in Alaska, but instead semi-underground dwellings insulated with sod were built. Moreover, unlike Inuits living in Canada or Greenland, the Yupiit and Inupiat of Alaska developed well-established centres for trading that were accompanied by elaborate ceremonies aimed at reinforcing relationships with neighbouring groups. Numerous complex rituals were observed at various levels in which, according to Oswalt, "all the members of a village participated and great wealth might be redistributed" (*ibid.*). Often the rituals included dramatic dancing, which was enhanced by the use of masks symbolizing the spirits of animals, birds or sea mammals. These peculiar characteristics of Alaskan Yupiit and Inupiat peoples make research on both groups relevant to understanding indigenous Alaskan patterns of subsistence and concepts of the land.

## TRADITIONAL CONCEPTS OF THE LAND

Patterns of life among the Yupiit and Inupiat peoples traditionally have centred on subsistence activities. A Canadian judge, Thomas Berger, who in the early 1980s conducted an extensive survey of Alaska Native experiences of ANCSA on behalf of the Inuit Circumpolar Conference (to which I shall return in detail later), quotes an old woman who testified at one of the over-sixty village meetings he conducted as saying, "Subsistence to us is ... our spiritual way of life, our culture" (Berger 1985: 47–8). Berger explains this comment by referring to the tradition of whale hunting in north and northeast Alaska: "For thousands of years, Inupiat Eskimos have lived and taken bowhead whales .... The Inupiat believe that these great whales give themselves to their hunters, if they have been hunted by Inupiat rules that govern the relationship between the people and the whales" (*ibid.*: 48). Berger notes that throughout Alaska the traditional economy is based on similar activities to those he found among whaling communities. Success in hunting and fishing depended on observing rules in relation to the natural environment. Berger calls these "cultural values", which include "mutual respect, sharing, resourcefulness, and an understanding that is both conscious and mystical of the intricate interrelationships that link humans, animals, and the environment" (ibid.: 51).

Further south along the coast of the Bering Sea, where the Yupiit live, the waters are too shallow for hunting bowhead whale. Instead, the people traditionally hunted seals, beluga whales and sea lions. The region stretching inland from the sea is crossed by numerous streams and rivers that yield abundant supplies of salmon, trout, northern pike, several species of whitefish, burbot, blackfish and stickleback. In addition to sea mammals and fish, a variety of birds, including geese, ducks and swans supplement food sources (Fienup-Riordan 1990: 8–9). Among both Yupiit and Inupiat peoples, Caribou herds were hunted as they moved through the inland mountain passes to the coasts. In addition, mountain sheep, polar bears, grizzly bears and moose provided sources of food for those living in inland areas. Various types of berries, which are also abundant throughout Alaska, were harvested annually. In some regions, these were mixed with seal fat and preserved.

Despite the abundance of natural resources available to the Yupiit and Inupiat, owing to the extreme climate and, in many places, the barrenness of the land, a certain fragile relationship with nature existed. The people had little control over the environment and depended on their own skill and ingenuity in hunting and fishing to ensure adequate supplies of food and materials needed for survival. This tenuous relationship to the land explains why in the traditional worldview life, spirit or soul (inua or personhood) was attributed to the animals and fish that provided the primary sources for sustenance (Dupre 1975: 207). Spirits were thought also to inhabit the instruments used in hunting and fishing, and to be connected to the weather, particularly the winds blowing from the cardinal directions, which brought quite distinct climatic conditions (Fienup-Riordan 1994: 317). The spirits, which were necessary for survival, could be influenced in rituals, or even controlled by shamans, but mostly they could be counted on to respond favourably to the needs of the people if the rules of the society were followed.

An example of the spiritual sense in which animals were regarded is demonstrated by the traditional annual bladder festival, in which the bladders of the seals killed in the seasonal hunt were inflated and hung in the traditional men's house (Qasgiq in Yup'ik).[6] The bladders, representing the inua of the seals, were 'entertained' for five days before being released through holes in the ice ready to return for the next cycle of hunting. The seals would not offer themselves to be killed if they were not respected in this way. Fienup-Riordan suggests that seals had the ability to ascertain both the merits and intentions of the hunter. If the hunter is "awake to the rules of the proper relationship between humans and animals, and between humans and humans, then the seal will allow the hunter's harpoon or bullet to kill it" (1990: 45).

Subsistence, therefore, quite correctly must be linked to tradition in Alaska, since survival depended on adhering strictly to a way of life that had been passed on authoritatively from generation to generation. Fienup-Riordan asserts that the people "are not simply surviving off the resources of their environment but are living in a highly structured relationship to them. This relationship is important to comprehend, not as an exercise in Eskimo esoterica, but as a key to why they act and feel the way they do" (ibid.: 47).

Subsistence is also related directly to the land, since it is on the land and adjacent seas and waterways that the animals and fish live in their cycles of birth, death and rebirth. As has been implied in Fienup-Riordan's research, traditional concepts of the land defined how resources were shared, dictated trading practices and constituted the proper rules governing social relationships.

In his report developed for the Inuit Circumpolar Conference on ANCSA, Berger argued that the issue of land stands at the centre of the cultural divide between Alaska Native peoples and Western society. He calls land "inalienable" for Alaska Natives and asserts that "every member of the community in succeeding generations acquires an interest in the land as a birthright". He cites Paul Ongtooguk from Kotzebue, an Inupiat town located on the northeast coast, as saying in a village meeting: "I believe that if people, if the vast majority of Alaska Natives, were given the opportunity to either kill or die for their land, that most of them would do just that – if it was that simple" (Berger 1985: 173). On the same issue, Jimmy Stotts of Barrow on the far northern coast of Alaska, testified: "The single biggest fear that we Inupiat have ... is the fear of losing control over our own lands, which we need for subsistence purposes" (*ibid.*).

That land and subsistence are connected to traditional social relations and under-standings of shared ownership is demonstrated by the annual whaling festivals among the northern Inupiat, which, unlike the seal bladder rituals described by Fienup-Riordan, still occur, although in modified forms. In the tradition of the coastal Inupiat, prelimi-nary preparations for the whaling season began in early March when the whaling equipment was cleaned and the crew were given new sets of clothing. The captain of a whaling crew, called an *umelik*, was one who, according to Oswalt, had earned respect in the community, had acquired wealth and commanded the loyalty of his men. During the early spring preparations, the *umelik*'s wife supervised making a new cover for the boat and just before the hunt began prepared a special meal for those about to embark. During the time of preparations, prohibitions against sexual intercourse were observed. The sea was watched carefully to ensure that the exact timing for beginning the hunt coincided with the break-up of the ice. For this reason, a shaman, acting as a clairvoyant, was consulted to 'see' into the precise moment when the whale hunt should commence (Oswalt 1999: 213).

The whaling season lasted from two to six weeks, usually beginning in late April, depending on weather conditions. The *umelik* and his crew observed food taboos during the hunt while those remaining in the village followed ritual prohibitions. The *umelik* carried with him in a wooden box a small carved figure of a whale, which certainly represented the life, spirit or *inua* of the whale being hunted. Capturing a bowhead whale required exact skill and close cooperation among the crew, since the animal usually extends to around 33 feet and weighs over 30 tons. It also required the cooperation of the spirit of the whale that was being hunted. The harvest was shared equally among the members of the crew. Following the hunting season, the residents of the village held what Oswalt calls a "victory celebration", *nulukatuk*, "to let the whale know we are happy". Games and feasting occurred, including demonstrations of strength or endurance. Members of the various fishing teams shared *muktuk*, the black skin of the whale, considered to be a delicacy, among the entire community. This sharing was a sign of generosity and thanksgiving for the successful whaling season and helped to bind the community together (ibid.: 213–18).

Fienup-Riordan describes a similar village event among the Yupiit called a "seal party", which was held when "the men and boys of the village brought home the first seals of the season" (1990: 39–43). During her early research trips in the 1970s to Nelson Island, just off the west coast of central Alaska, Fienup-Riordan describes how she was sitting in her room having a cup of tea when she heard noise from the neighbouring house, which indicated the beginning of a series of events associated with seal parties. She went out to witness "a woman standing on her porch throwing Pampers and packs of gum into the waiting hands of a large group of women". She followed the group to the next house where the same sharing of goods occurred, although the group did not comprise the same women. Fienup-Riordan records: "By this time I was extremely excited. Here was a distribution of goods through which social relations were articulated", since sisters, mothers, mothers-in-law and parallel cousins were excluded from a particular seal party. During any seal party, the hostess allowed an older woman, usually the mother of the hostess's cousin, to select a special person from the group to receive a gift of raw meat. The next day after these series of seal parties had been completed, dances occurred in the community hall (the modern replacement for the *Qasgiq*) in which the women carried in, literally 'danced in', gifts for the men of the village. That evening the men 'danced in' gifts to the women in a manner similar to the way the women had done for them. Fienup-Riordan observes: "The entire sequence of dances and gift-giving takes hours and hours, as everyone in the community has a turn on the dance floor". Through this elaborate arrangement of dances and gifts, the Yupiit "world view, their whole cultural mode of being, has ... been put on stage along with the dancers, acted out, and so re-established and reaffirmed". It begins with the harvesting of the first seals of the season and culminates with rituals of sharing, confirming that, in Fienup-Riordan's view, "living off the land is still the preferred pattern" (*ibid.*).

These examples, taken largely from ethnographic accounts and anthropological studies from the early to late twentieth century, suggest that the Yupiit and Inupiat traditions for centuries had been connected closely to the land and the subsistence patterns they had spawned. The concept of spirits, the communal and social relations that were welded together by the spirits, the rules of respect that were strictly adhered to and the elaborate rituals and festivals were all associated with subsistence activities and were legitimized by reference to ancient authoritative traditions. Moreover, Berger's hearings on ANCSA, conducted during the early 1980s, revealed that the land and its related subsistence way of life were referred to repeatedly by rural Alaska Natives as being under threat, thereby confirming that the traditional understanding of the land persisted widely among Alaska Natives late into the twentieth century and well over ten years after the ANCSA had been ratified. It is to ANCSA and its implications for the indigenous way of life that I now turn.

## THE PROVISIONS OF THE ALASKA NATIVE CLAIMS SETTLEMENT ACT

The Alaska Native Claims Settlement Act of 1971 extinguished all indigenous claims to the land in exchange for 44 million acres of land, which is approximately 10 per cent of the state's territory, plus $962.5 million in compensation for the 321 million acres of land, or 90 per cent of the state's territory, that was appropriated by the State of Alaska and the US federal government. All US citizens with one-fourth or more Alaska Indian, Eskimo or Aleut blood who were living when the settlement bill was enacted were qualified to participate. Natives would receive their settlement through twelve regional corporations and more than 200 village corporations created by ANCSA (Berger 1985: 24). As the volume entitled *Alaska Native Land Claims*, edited by Robert D. Arnold, and published by the Alaska Native Foundation as a basic guide to the law for use in schools, explains: "Benefits under the settlement act would accrue to Natives not through clans, families or other traditional groupings, but, instead, through the modern form of business organization, called a corporation. All eligible Natives were to become stockholders – part owners – of such corporations" (Arnold 1976: 146).

To take advantage of the settlement, the first step was for a Native to register as a permanent resident in a particular village and region. The new stockholder would then be given 100 shares of stock in one of the twelve regional corporations and in most cases 100 shares of stock in a village corporation. Natives who did not live in a village were given shares in regional corporations and became known as at-large stockholders. Those who did not reside permanently in Alaska were not excluded from receiving benefits, but were also permitted to register in one of the regional corporations or a thirteenth corporation, which was created for non-resident Natives and based in Seattle, Washington. The thirteenth corporation was not granted land, but received a portion of the $962.5 million compensation package on a pro rata basis. Since there was only one issue of shares, no one born after 18 December 1971, the day President Nixon signed the Bill into law, received shares (Berger 1985: 24–5).[7]

The village corporations, which were granted 22 million of the 44 million acres of land, received only surface rights to the land, meaning that their ownership would not extend to minerals below the ground. The rights to the minerals would belong to the regional corporations so that "the subsurface estate of lands selected by village corporations would go to regional corporations" (Arnold 1976: 151). Village corporations were given the option of registering as non-profit entities, but all chose to become profit-making organizations. Each regional corporation was required to distribute 70 per cent of the income it earned from the sale of timber and mineral rights among the other regional corporations "to balance regional disparities in natural resources" (Berger 1985: 25). To protect the land, the law instituted a time restriction that forbade any Native corporate shares to be sold to non-Natives for twenty years, that is until 1991, when all such restrictions would be removed. In addition, the corporations would be exempt from state taxation until 1991.

These main provisions of ANCSA indicate that the law was extremely complex, but one outcome is indisputable: in the words of Norman Chance, it "forever transformed the relationship between the Native peoples of Alaska and the land" (1990: 165). The words of the Act itself are explicit in this regard:

> All claims against the United States, the State, and all other persons that are based on claims of aboriginal right, title, use or occupancy of land or water areas in Alaska, or that are based on any statute or treaty of the United States relating to Native use and occupancy, or that are based on the laws of any other nation, including any such claims that are pending before any Federal or State court or the Indian Claims Commission are hereby extinguished.      (cited in Case & Voluck 2002: 58)

## ANCSA AND THE LAND

As 1991 approached, it became apparent that village and regional corporations could be taken over by large non-Native interests, such as multinational corporations and oil companies. In response to this threat, the Inuit Circumpolar Conference, an international organization of Inuit peoples from Alaska, Canada and Greenland, appointed British Columbia Supreme Court Justice Thomas Berger to head the Alaska Native Review Commission to ascertain Native attitudes towards ANCSA. The study was co-sponsored by the World Council of Indigenous Peoples. Berger was selected because he had made a significant contribution to Canadian indigenous land rights when he had been appointed in the mid-1970s by the Canadian government to conduct the Mackenzie Valley Pipeline Inquiry. Berger's new assignment for the Inuit Circumpolar Conference took him, in his own words, "to Native villages all over Alaska to hear the evidence of Alaska Natives" (1985: vii). His findings are reported in the 1985 publication *Village Journey: The Report of the Alaska Native Review Commission*. In the sections above in which I outline traditional subsistence patterns among the Yupiit and Inupiat peoples, I have already made extensive use of this book, but I have not yet explored the most influential result of Berger's report: that which underscored the risk ANCSA posed to Native land rights.

According to the original provisions of ANCSA, precisely twenty years after the law came into effect, on 18 December 1991, all Native corporations, both village and regional, were required to call in their shares and issue new shares that would be entirely unrestricted. As Berger explains, "After 1991, shareholders will be free to sell all or any portion of their shares, to pledge them as collateral, or to use or dispose of them in any other way" (*ibid.*: 96). Individual shareholders thus could sell their shares in any way that they chose, even if such choices were opposed by other shareholders or by the majority of those who held stock in the relevant corporation. The threat was clear: "The Native corporations can then become targets for takeover" (*ibid.*). The possibility of government confiscation of the land also loomed in 1991, since state and local authorities could then levy taxes on the land, whether it was developed or undeveloped. This second threat meant that if a village or regional corporation could not afford to pay the taxes, the land could be claimed by government authorities. In his extensive hearings conducted throughout Alaska, Berger found the same fear repeated: "Alaska Natives expressed fear that their ancestral lands will be lost after 1991" (*ibid*.). The importance of this concern cannot be minimized, primarily because it demonstrates that for Native peoples, in rural regions at least, the law linking corporations to the land had not transformed the traditional subsistence culture. The success or failure of the village and regional corporations was not the crucial issue; retaining the land and the tradition of subsistence was paramount.

Berger found just this concern voiced over and over again. For example, Dean George from Angoon in southeast Alaska is reported by Berger as testifying: "The biggest issue that I see before me now is 1991, and I don't believe it is a stock issue. For me, it is the land issue because the people who do hold stock hold title to the land, when that stock is sold, traded, or revested back to the corporation, so does their right to the land" (*ibid*.: 96–7). A similar concern was voiced by Alice Tucker, a Yup'ik from Emmonak: "After 1991, when we are able to sell our shares ... and perhaps have our land taxed, what little we have left, we may never have anymore" (*ibid*.: 97–8). Sam Demientieff, at a hearing conducted by Berger in the city of Fairbanks, underscored the connection between land and Native culture: "One hundred shares represents the past life of the Native people, it represents the culture, the land, lifestyle, village living. And this portion, this hundred shares, is something that's going to become available for sale to the public in 1991" (*ibid*.: 98).

Another threat to community life that occurred with ANCSA is not quite so obvious. This relates to excluded Natives who were born after 18 December 1971. The Act granted shares only to those who were alive on that date. Thus, a child born on 18 December 1971 was a shareholder, but one born on 19 December 1971 was not. As the children of the same generation grew older, this created wide disparities in the community, when some of almost the exact age owned 200 shares in village and regional corporations and others owned none. Of course, inheritance laws applied, meaning that when shareholders died, they could leave their shares to their children. Yet this also created the possibility of increasing inequity, disharmony and competitiveness. For example, if one shareholder had two children, these might receive 100 shares each in inheritance, but if another had four children, these would receive 50 shares each. As the generations succeeded, the inequities would increase. Thus, what began as an absolutely equitable distribution among Alaska Natives would become over time highly disparate with the long-term effect, in Berger's words, that "increasingly smaller divisions of the shares will reduce dividends, already trivial, to insignificance" (*ibid*.: 106–7). The subsistence culture of sharing and community involvement, as demonstrated in the whaling festivals and the seal parties I described earlier, thus would be eroded into an individualistic and competitive system in which shareholders sought ways to overcome the problems of diminishing return, often at the expense of one's fellow shareholder.

Berger's findings demonstrated that at the time he conducted his hearings, despite having lived under the village and regional corporate structure for over ten years, for rural Alaskans subsistence remained the fundamental way of life. The land may have been connected legally to market performance, but for day-to-day living, fishing, hunting and whaling continued as normal. However, if the corporations could be taken over by non-Native commercial interests, the land could also be taken away from the people and could thereby divest them of their ancestral heritage and radically change their traditional patterns of life. The potential effects of ANCSA, therefore, were shown by the Berger Commission to undermine and eventually destroy the Alaska Native subsistence culture by transforming the concept of land into a system of shareholding within a corporate structure. Alaska Natives, who had relinquished all rights to the land, eventually would have no recourse but to assimilate into the patterns of life imposed by the dominant Western society.

Those who conceived this solution to Alaska Native claims were not unaware of the social consequences entailed in the legislation. In their review of the history of Alaska Natives and American laws, David Case and David Voluck assert that "the intent of ANCSA, as initially enacted, was pretty clearly to incorporate the Alaska Natives into the mainstream of the American free market economy and its values" (2002: 176). They cite the testimony of Douglas Jones at a roundtable discussion organized in 1984 in Anchorage (Alaska's largest city) by Berger's Alaska Native Review Commission. Jones had been a member of Alaska's US Senate staff at the time ANCSA was first considered and participated in the various stages leading up to its passage by the US Congress. Jones testified at the Anchorage roundtable that the concerns voiced by Alaska Natives to Berger throughout rural Alaska about the possibility of corporate takeovers "was exactly the possibility that we had in mind". Jones explained that the intention of ANCSA was to instil "normalcy" within Alaska Natives, which he defined as "normal commercial behaviour, a movement toward business as usual. He added: "It's got nothing to do with ... cultural traditions ... but in part of one's life, it's important to be like everyone else". Jones concluded his testimony by admitting that the "mechanisms" of ANCSA, "how the land was allotted and the money provided", were chosen "to accomplish ... social engineering" (*ibid.*: 176–7).

In the report of the Alaska Native Review Commission, Berger sought to reverse the assimilating impact of ANCSA on Native people, as articulated by Jones, primarily by recommending that ANCSA's provisions relating to land be revoked in favour of laws recognizing tribal sovereignty (1985: 155–72). These included retribalization of the land, Native self-government and Native jurisdiction over fish and wildlife. Berger was aware that the land could not simply be transferred to tribal governments, since ANCSA had made the land the private property of Native corporations. However, he suggested that this could be accomplished by shareholders themselves: "I recommend that the shareholders of village corporations who are concerned that their land may be lost should transfer their land to tribal governments to keep the land in Native ownership" (*ibid.*: 167). In order to achieve this, Berger argued that the US Congress should pass legislation that would enable tribal governments to "claim sovereignty with respect to the land" by facilitating "the transfer of land by the village corporations to tribal governments without regard for dissenter's rights" (*ibid.*). Village and regional corporations could still exist, since Berger's recommendations related only to the land, and primarily to village life. The corporations could retain their business assets, but without the land, he conceded, it would be most likely that village corporations would dissolve (*ibid*.: 168). The regional corporations, which own the subsurface of village lands, should transfer these rights to the village tribal governments (*ibid*.). In this way, tribal governments would obtain full legal jurisdiction over the original functions of village corporations and maintain ownership of both surface and subsurface land. Moreover, under Berger's recommendations, no Natives would be excluded, since each Native resident within particular villages would be members of the tribe, regardless of his or her date of birth. Berger concluded his recommendations by insisting that Congress "must fully acknowledge that ... Native governments are legitimate political institutions, and that they have a right to retain ancestral lands in perpetuity" (*ibid*.: 161).

## ANCSA IN THE POST-1991 SITUATION

There can be little doubt that the Alaska Native Review Commission exercised a powerful effect by raising consciousness about the threats posed by ANCSA to traditional Native culture and subsistence patterns. Berger's recommendations that effectively would have destroyed village corporations by transferring them to tribal governments, however, were not implemented. Rather, Congress passed in 1987 several crucial amendments to the law. The most vital was to alter the conditions of the automatic termination of restrictions on the sale of Native shares scheduled for 18 December 1991. The prohibition against selling individual shares was extended indefinitely, or until "a majority of all the outstanding shares in any particular corporation voted to eliminate them" (Case & Voluck 2002: 177). The result was that after 1991 individuals could sell their shares only by collective, or at least by majority, consent.

A second critical amendment allowed the shareholders of Native corporations to issue stock to those born after 18 December 1971. In the opinion of Case and Voluck, this appeared to give priority to kinship relationships of the shareholders over "ANCSA's original goal of fostering 'normal commercial behaviour'" (*ibid*.). This was not entirely the result, however, since between 1988 and 1998 only six Native corporations, three regional and three village, voted to issue shares to the children of the original shareholders, and these on different conditions. Unlike the original shareholders, the children received "life estate" stock that lasted only for the lifetime of the particular shareholder, and thus it could not be inherited but reverted back to the corporation at the death of the shareholder. Two corporations set no limits on the issuing of life estate shares to children of shareholders, whereas some issued shares only for those born between 19 December 1971 and 31 December 1992. This meant that, throughout Alaska, disparity increased among shareholders in village and regional corporations with some experiencing increasingly diluted value of their shares as more children were issued stock, as had been predicted by Berger.

A third amendment to the original act altered the law regarding taxation, allowing taxes to be levied only on developed land. Native corporations were further protected against claims from creditors, court judgements and bankruptcy (*ibid*.: 184–5). These provisions were clearly responses to fears that, as business ventures, the failure of Native corporations would dispossess the people of their land. By protecting against the consequences of serious financial losses, Congress eased concerns that unsuccessful commercial ventures by Native corporations would lead to corporate takeovers. Case and Voluck observe that these provisions make Native corporations "unique", since they are protected from loss and are exempt from many regulations that affect "normal" corporations. They conclude: "The Alaska Native Claims Settlement Act is an experiment that is still evolving" (*ibid*.: 185).

The issue of tribal sovereignty in Alaska that was raised by the Berger Commission, however, has been addressed in part by the US Congress. Although this is a complicated issue, it is clear that at the time Berger wrote his report, Alaska Natives were being treated differently from other Native groups in the lower 48 states that had been recognized as tribes with sovereignty over reservation areas. Since there were no reservations in Alaska, this had not been applied to indigenous groups there. In their detailed discussion of this issue, Case and Voluck observe that Native sovereignty in Alaska was confused for many years. Now, however, they argue, "the federal government recognizes Alaska Native tribes with the same status as tribes in the lower forty-eight states" (*ibid*.: 427–8). This means that Alaska Native villages must "be treated as sovereign tribes with the same rights, responsibilities, and immunities as tribes in the rest of the nation". Alaska Natives, however, operate under different conditions with respect to the land. Because of ANCSA, the US Supreme Court has ruled that ANCSA lands, the precise land that was offered to the Natives of Alaska in the 1971 settlement, do not qualify as so-called Indian country. As Case and Voluck note, this leaves "Alaska Native tribal governments as sovereigns without territorial reach" (*ibid*.: 428).

## CONCLUSIONS

Despite changes in the law since its original enactment, in my view ANCSA persists as a tool of social engineering aimed at assimilating the Native peoples of Alaska into the mainstream American free market and competitive culture, and as such operates as an instrument of power. As I noted at the beginning of this article, this has become translated into business ventures that in many cases are very far removed from the culture of subsistence and its connection to the land. A regional corporation, such as CIRI, can invest widely in projects that have no relevance to the indigenous way of life, including, as we have seen, in a major hotel and casino in Las Vegas. Although in rural Alaska subsistence lifestyles endure and progress has been made towards Native sovereignty, the land, which I have argued is crucial to self-identity and cultural awareness, has been dissected from its concrete relation to the people and to its role in the collective memory and placed into the abstract notion of shares in stocks. Property-owners and shareholders are now identical. This has not been altered by the protections set in place by the government against financial failure.

This leads to my conclusion that the land in traditional Alaska, which was viewed as the locus of traditional ways of life, has been secularized by ANCSA. I have argued that the land was traditionally linked with the forms of life that provided the means of subsistence for the people who lived on it (the 'real people'). These forms of life were perceived by the people as possessing souls or spirits (*inua*), which in turn fostered a reciprocal relationship between human beings and the natural environment. All life, both natural and human, was understood as enveloped by cycles of birth, death and rebirth. Although, again as I noted at the outset, it would be easy to romanticize the indigenous world view and to present Alaska Natives in quite exotic terms or, as Fienup-Riordan calls it, in 'half-truths', it is clear that the indigenous people traditionally maintained a religious relationship with the land, in the sense that I have defined it following Hervieu-Léger. The rules governing their relationship to the land, particularly the animals, fish and sea mammals that dwelt on or near it, were translated into well-defined social regulations aimed at ensuring survival and well-being in an often harsh environment.

These dimensions of indigenous Alaskan culture, which had been passed on authoritatively for generations, can be contrasted starkly with the atomization of life in Western capitalist society, which is based on maximizing profits in a competitive economic market. The transformation of the traditional concept of land thus pinpoints decisively the secularizing effect of ANCSA, precisely because it disrupts the authoritative transmission of tradition in Alaska Native communities by fragmenting communal life through private shareholding. Indeed, after one hundred years, it could be said that the Americans have fully secularized Native Alaskans according to Jackson's original formula: "to make more money in order to live better … and to utilize the resources of the country in order to make more money".

Thomas Berger concluded his landmark report for the Alaska Native Review Commission by commenting that when ANCSA was adopted by the US Congress, it "shone as a beacon of hope" for indigenous peoples in other parts of the world. Ironically, he added, it was rejected as a model for indigenous land rights. Instead, indigenous peoples in other parts of the world "have reaffirmed their conviction that Native lands should be passed intact from one generation to the next" (1985: 182). Although Berger's recommendations were not implemented in the form he envisaged, his call for Native control over the land can be understood fully only in the light of a traditional way of life and its opposition to what I am calling the secularizing impact of ANCSA. Berger's penultimate words in *Village Journey* sound very much like a rallying cry to return to an authoritative transmission of tradition: "Indian country must remain Indian Country, Eskimo Country must remain Eskimo country, Aleut country must remain Aleut Country" (*ibid.*: 187). Whether Berger's vision is fulfilled or not very much depends on widespread acceptance of the claim that a fundamental contradiction exists between the core of traditional Alaskan culture and the secularizing intentions of ANCSA.

## NOTES

1. I am employing the word 'Eskimo' from the sources I am citing, but it is important to note that this is not accepted as a term of self-designation among Inuit peoples generally. I shall clarify use of terminology later in the chapter.
2. 'Native' here refers to 'Native Alaskan', a term generally accepted by the indigenous people of Alaska, but always capitalized.
3. Hervieu-Léger refers the reader to the work of the French sociologist, François-André Isambert, who in his 1982 publication, *Le Sens du Sacré*, traces the history of the notion of the sacred in the Durkheimian tradition.
4. The discussion of Desroche is derived from Desroche & Séguy (1970). According to Hervieu-Léger (2000: 52), the term 'administration of the sacred' was coined by the French Durkheimian anthropologist Henri Hubert, who is noted in the English-speaking world for his classic book, *The Rise of the Celts* (1934).
5. For example, see, Bruce (2002: 3). Bruce asserts: "I will show ways in which the declining social significance of religion causes a decline in the number of religious peoples and the extent to which people are religious".
6. For a discussion of the *Qasgiq*, see Fienup-Riordan (1994: 283–92) and Cox (1991: 11–13).
7. See also Mitchell (2001: 492–3).

## BIBLIOGRAPHY

Arnold, Robert D., ed. 1976. *Alaska Native Land Claims*. Anchorage: The Alaska Native Foundation.

Berger, Thomas R. 1985. *Village Journey: The Report of the Alaska Native Review Commission*. New York: Hill and Wang.

Bruce, Steve. 2002. *God is Dead: Secularization in the West*. Oxford: Blackwell.

Burch, Ernest S., Jr. 1998. *The Inupiaq Eskimo Nations of Northwest Alaska*. Fairbanks, AK: University of Alaska Press.

Case, David S. and David A. Voluck. 2002. *Alaska Natives and American Laws*, 2nd edn. Fairbanks, AK: University of Alaska Press.

Chance, Norman A. 1990. *The Inupiat and Arctic Alaska: An Ethnography of Development*. Chicago, IL: Holt, Rinehart and Winston.

Cook Inlet Region, Inc. 2003. *Annual Report 2002*. Anchorage, AK: CIRI.

Cox, James L. 1991. *The Impact of Christian Missions on Indigenous Cultures: The "Real People" and the Unreal Gospel*. Lewiston, NY: Edwin Mellen Press.

Cox, James L. 1999. "Intuiting Religion: A Case for Preliminary Definitions". In *The Pragmatics of Defining Religion: Contexts, Concepts and Contests*, eds J. G. Platvoet and A. L. Molendijk, 267–84. Leiden: E. J. Brill.

Desroche, H. and J. Séguy. 1970. *Introduction aux Science Humaines des Religions*. Paris: Cujas.

Dupre, Wilhelm. 1975. *Religion in Primitive Cultures*. The Hague: Mouton.

Fienup-Riordan, Ann. 1990. *Eskimo Essays: Yup'ik Lives and How We See Them*. New Brunswick, NJ: Rutgers University Press.

Fienup-Riordan, Ann. 1994. *Boundaries and Passages: Rule and Ritual in Yup'ik Eskimo Oral Tradition*. Norman, OK: University of Oklahoma Press.

Fienup-Riordan, Ann. 2000. *Hunting Tradition in a Changing World: Yup'ik Lives in Alaska Today*. New Brunswick, NJ: Rutgers University Press.

Hubert, Henri. 1934. *The Rise of the Celts*. London: Kegan Paul, Trench, Trubner.

Isambert, François-André. 1982. *Le Sens du sacré: fête et religion populaire*. Paris: Les Éditions de minuit.

Langdon, Steve J. 2002. *The Native People of Alaska: Traditional Living in a Northern Land*. Anchorage, AK: Greatland Graphics.

Hervieu-Léger, D. 2000. *Religion as a Chain of Memory*. Cambridge: Polity.

Mitchell, Donald Craig. 2001. *Take My Land, Take My Life: The Story of Congress's Historic Settlement of Alaska Native Land Claims, 1960–1971*. Fairbanks, AK: University of Alaska Press.

Oswalt, Wendell H. 1999. *Eskimos and Explorers*, 2nd edn. Lincoln, NE: University of Nebraska Press.

Platvoet, Jan. 2002. "Pillars, Pluralism and Secularisation: A Social History of Dutch Sciences of Religions". In *Modern Societies and the Science of Religions*, ed. G. Wiegers, 83–148. Leiden: E. J. Brill.

# 4

# The formative process of State Shinto in relation to the Westernization of Japan: the concept of 'religion' and 'Shinto'

*Jun'ichi Isomae*

*Translated by Michael S. Wood*

## STATE SHINTO WITHIN THE LARGER PROCESS OF WESTERNIZATION

Accompanying the overseas advancement of various Western nation states, Christianity and even more so the very concept of 'religion' fundamentally based on Christianity came to proliferate throughout the world. Japan and other nations that were at least nominally politically independent came under the encroaching cultural dominance of the West. With the opening of the country to the West, mid-nineteenth-century Japan's status as a sovereign nation state remained elusive owing to unfair treaties established with Western countries. Whether Japan was to be acknowledged as an independent nation state, or instead follow the path of a colonial state depended on how well the country could adapt to a Western-style nation state model. Essential conditions to be achieved included the establishment of a constitution and recognition of Christianity. The recognition of Christianity took place in 1873, at which time a specific concept of religion began to spread throughout society primarily through intellectuals. This new concept of *shûkyô* or 'religion' was based on the central characteristics of Christianity but was also embraced as a larger category that included various other non-Christian practices and social formations that appeared in some respects analogous to Christianity.[1]

Closely related to this new concept 'religion' were the ideas of 'religious freedom' and separation of church and state that came to proliferate. Following the principles of Western-style enlightenment, 'religion' (*shûkyô*) was entrusted to the sphere of the individual's interior freedom, while the 'secular' sphere of morality (*dôtoku*) was determined to be a national, and thus public, issue. With a clear differentiation between the religious and moral categories being made along the private–public dichotomy, Western modernity came to be comprehended in terms of a dual structure. From the beginning the very notion of an individual with an interiority was for the first time made possible as a form of self-understanding only through the transplantation of Christianity and the related concept of religion.[2]

What ran parallel to the process of establishing the conceptual categories of 'religion' and a 'secular' realm of the nation state are the prewar Japanese shrine policies known as State Shinto (*kokka shintô*) and the institutional indoctrination of state subjects into an emperor-based nationalism through shrine worship. The reformulation of Shinto native beliefs in terms of imperial nationalism was an ambivalent double gesture. On the one hand, this transformation emphasized the existence of a traditional body in opposition to Christianity, while on the other hand it advocated a universal aspect of this traditional body in compliance with the logic of a church–state dichotomy and the nation state inherited from the West.

The existence of a State Shinto with these particular characteristics suggests that the importation of this Western concept of religion in Japan was not simply a superficial reaction allowing for the possibility of Christianity. Even more so, the the process of State Shinto development affected the very policies of traditionalism surrounding an indigenous Shinto that otherwise had no direct relationship to Christianity. In dividing the process into three historical stages, we shall elucidate just how the framework of State Shinto was established based on an oppositional relation to this Western concept of religion.

## THE PROCESS OF FORMATION OF STATE SHINTO

In retrospect we can point to three historical stages that were passed through before a recognizable form of State Shinto emerged. The first stage ultimately leading up to the establishment of State Shinto is the period of Shinto national indoctrination policies (*Shintô kokkyôka seisaku*). This period roughly began with the proclamation of the *Jingikan*[3] in 1868 (Keiô 4)[4] and continued until 1882 (Meiji 15) with the formal end of indoctrination and responsibilities being shared between shrines and the government. As "National Teaching", or more precisely "Great Teachings" (*taikyô*), the government attempted to establish Shinto as a pillar of emperor-centered nationalism. The period is further divided into the following two sub-phases: the first was the *Jingikan/Jingishô* period,[5] which focused primarily on ritual and ceremonies; the second might be called the Education Ministry period, since the propagation of *Sanjô kyôken* (three standards of instruction) became paramount. At this point, the notion of separation of church and state based on the concept of 'freedom of religious belief' had not yet taken root in society. Based on pre-modern notions of local gods and their respective teachings, this first sub-phase can be thought of as a time when uniform indoctrination of the masses was pursued while opposing Christianity.[6] Christianity was repudiated and served as a recognized threat to indigenous forms of practice. In this light, the governing structure of Japan embraced the idea of pre-modern teachings that did not distinguish between morality and religion in order to counter this particularly Western concept of religion. We can see fundamental differences in the foundational logic of Christianity (which held morality to be a private concern of the individual) and these oppositional policies of the state (which hoped to project a public component to morality in the service of the state).

With various Western nations requesting an end to the ban against Christianity and, furthermore, with the succession of the True Pure Land Buddhist sect from the official organization in charge of national indoctrination (*Daikyôin*), these policies of Shinto national indoctrination (*Shintô kokkyôka seisaku*) eventually led to a collapse owing to the rising demands for religious freedom by both domestic and foreign forces. With the wave of Westernization, as long as Japan had to focus on the goal of establishing a modern nation state, fixing the axis of a consolidated national subject in early modern teachings was prone to structural difficulties. Jeopardized by the demands for 'religious freedom' both domestically and externally, the Japanese ruling regime became keenly aware of the essential need to establish a governing structure that fully incorporated a Western concept of religion.

In this context, shrines became cut off from their earlier characteristics as they underwent various reforms such as *Shinbutsu bunri rei* of 1868 (Meiji 1), a policy to separate shrines from temples and purge Shinto practices from Buddhist influence. Prohibitions against the inheritance of shrine management and priestly positions, which soon followed in 1871 (Meiji 4), resulted in an even greater discontinuity between earlier shrine practice and an emerging notion of standardized Shinto.[7] In place of the older system of organization, an official hierarchy that divided shrines into the categories of national, prefectural and local institutions (*Shakaku taikei*) was established and came to serve as the foundation for the ensuing State Shinto system. In the name of "National Ancestral Worship", shrines came under the unitary control of an imperially sanctioned state. With developments such as the change in name from *Tôkyô Shôkonsha* to Yasukuni Shrine in 1879 (Meiji 12), the basic skeletal hierarchy of shrines came to be established. Indoctrination of the masses at this time differed from the conditions that we see a bit later when shrines gain their greatest stronghold as sites of public ritual. It was promoted through public officials[8] as they worked to encourage congregational solidarity as the object of their pedagogical efforts (Fujii 1943; Nakajima 1972). In these terms we can see the difference between the position of shrines in this first stage and the view of a modern established Shrine Shinto, which only appears in the third and final stage, to be addressed later.[9] The full realization of the political and cultural function of what is referred to as State Shinto had to first wait for a meaningful reorganization of the shrine hierarchy. Certain conditions that did not take place until the second stage were first necessary, such as the establishment of a distinction between church and state and other political reforms.

The second stage of this process occurred at a time when the concept of 'religious freedom' took root in Japan. The public realm of the people's moral duty and the private realm in which religion is left to the discretion of the individual comes to be clearly distinguished for the first time according to the official education system, which accompanied the abolition of the *kyôdôshoku* system in 1884 and the Imperial Japanese constitution promulgated in 1889. From this point Shinto came to be divided between "denominational Shinto" (privatized religion) and "Shrine Shinto" (public national morality). Accompanying this, shrines divorced from teaching became exclusive proprietors of national ritual, while losing those attributes of indigenous practice that had been seen as analogous to Christian 'religion'.

However, as sites of homage from which to worship *kami* (usually translated as 'gods'), shrines of course could still be classified as 'religion' in the generic English-language sense proposed by modernity and derived from Christianity. Despite the government's assertions of Shrine Shinto as civic morality, it tended to attract the epitaph 'religious'. Therefore we cannot say that the regime at this time actively used shrines as ideological devices for purposes of indoctrinating the masses; they fell into somewhat of a gray zone. But with an entrenched shrine hierarchy in which Ise Shrine occupied the apex, they instead chose a policy of decreasing or completely cutting off financial support for most shrines in order to regulate the role of these institutions (Nakajima 1977; Sakamoto 1994; Yamaguchi 1999).

Imbued with the shades of the now passé early modern era (*kinsei*), the regime withdrew their Shinto national indoctrination policies of the first phase and instead promoted policies based on the separation of church and state in line with the enlightenment of Western modernity. For this purpose, emphasis was placed on a 'secular' curriculum as a means of indoctrination into imperial nationalism through policies such as the Imperial Rescript on Education (*Kyôiku chokugo*), distribution of the Emperor's photograph to schools (*Goshinei no haifu*) and the teaching of non-mythic history (Taki 1988; Yamamoto & Konno 1973). The only examples of active shrine policies at this time are limited to events marked by their overt connections to the nation state. They include the expansion and reconstruction of Yasukuni Shrine and the foundation of shrines dedicated to loyal retainers and patriots (*sôken jinja*), which differed from typical shrines in that they were intended to pacify the souls of historical personages constituting a pantheon of nationalist heroes. This was in line with the ideas of enforcing loyalty to the nation demanded by the Imperial Rescript on Education (Murakami 1974; Tsubouchi 1999).

By 1889 (Meiji 22), with the delineation of imperial graves (*Tennô ryô no jitei*) nearly set, and the posthumous bestowal of rank on historic national heroes of the Restoration being carried out, the loyal were not only recognized, but also the history of the imperial family becomes visible as an object of devotion for the masses.[10] However, at this point the guarantee of religious freedom for the private individual was strictly limited since the duty of maintaining national morality imposed on the national subject took priority. Symbolizing this was the incident of imperial irreverence that took place with the Christian thinker Uchimura Kanzô refusing to recognize the Imperial Rescript on Education in 1890. With the storm of criticism generated in Japan regarding the Uchimura affair, religious freedom in Japan came to be seen as dependent on the approval of the secular authority of the imperial system (Ozawa 1961). Furthermore, despite the conservative backlash surrounding Kume Kunitake's essay, "The Archaic Traditions of Shintô Ceremony" (*Shintô ha saiten no kozoku*) in 1892 (Meiji 25), we can see that although this was a time when Enlightenment policies were in full force, rational interpretations of Shinto remained limited (Ôkubo 1991). Recently some scholars maintain that there was actually a space for freedom of religion since the network of indoctrination for imperial nationalism was not based in shrines, but instead in the realm of education, where taboos against interfering with freedom of religion were already established. To this end, the government developed educational curriculums for the subjects of 'religion' and 'morality' based on categories of Western modernity that articulated a clear distinction between church and state. However, in the name of cultivating imperial ideology, the emperor himself was defined outside these two categories, instead considered to have an unlimited existence as a living god exceeding morality and religion. Thus, the status of both the emperor and the imperial family as being beyond the realm of either state morality or personal religion allowed politicians to appropriate the subjects of 'religion' and 'morality' quite freely in order to legitimize education and indoctrination policies. Realizing the rivalries among various Shinto sects based on *kami* that they each enshrined, in 1880 politicians chose to leave the specific content of the imperial system vague and did not impose any regulations on it (Fujii 1977). Thus they managed to tailor it to serve as a contrivance capable of adapting to various projections from the masses. The imperial system actively employed the characteristics of pre-modern teachings, not as some pre-modern remainder unaffected by the West, but instead understood as something transcending the categories of Western modernity. This also served as one strategy to resist Westernization and appease anti-Western sentiments.[11]

During the third and final phase of State Shinto development, the state actively pursued national indoctrination policies (*Kokumin kyôka seisaku*) through the use of shrines and a rigid institutional form of State Shinto came to spread. This stage was initiated around 1906 (Meiji 39) with the enforcement of a system in which national shrines came to be financed directly by government (*Kankokuheisha kokugun gushinkin*) and the earnest consolidation of shrines began. It continued until 1945 (Meiji 20) with Japan's defeat in the Fifteen Year War.[12] During this time the government came to further develop the secular shrine argument, insisting that shrine worship was not religion, but instead the secular responsibility of the national subject. Seen as the institutional framework of national morality, shrines came to be regarded as the local strongholds of mass indoctrination and the focus of regional improvement policies (Akazawa 1985; Morioka 1987). However, shrines at this time were not just sites from which to propagate the teachings of the state on to the people that we see at the time of Shinto national indoctrination policies of the first phase (*Shintô kokkyôka seisaku*). Instead their meaning was being transformed into sites for sacrificial ritual conduct on the part of the people by which they honoured the imperial ancestors. Shrines, just like the imperial system itself, avoided maintaining any specific doctrine, instead being made to appear capable of various projections from the people themselves. However unlike the system of imperial worship (*Tennôsei*), which was maintained through educational rescripts and government directives, the absence of doctrine challenged the significance of shrines, making the ambitions of shrine worship all the more imperceptible to the people.

The Ministry of Home Affairs (*Naimushô*) held the Conference for Three Teachings (*Sankyô kaidô*) in 1912 (Meiji 45) in order to measure just how well religious institutions could serve as the network of indoctrination for imperial nationalism. Following this, in 1920 (Taishô 9), the Ministry of Education (*Monbushô*), in reforming the national history curriculum, for the first time included mythic stories of pre-historical *kami* (Doi 1967; Kaigo 1969). These events should be distinguished from State Shinto policy, but they mark the end of the 'morality' education promoted in the previous phase and were the means of attaining the indoctrination of the public while also exceeding the bounds of rational moral education. The State Shinto policies corresponding to this encouraged shrine worship.

During the first decade of the Taisho era (1912–1922) the 'secular' shrine category came to be debated and, in attempting to regulate the meaning of 'religion', those shrines that possessed qualities analogous to Christianity and Buddhism tended to be reclassified as 'religious'. In concert with this movement, the Investigative Committee for Religious Institutions (*Shûkyô seido chôsa kai*) of 1926 (Taishô 15) and the Shrine System Investigation Committee (*Jinja seido chôsa kai*) of 1929 (Shôwa 4) began to serve as consultation agencies to the governing regime. With the initiation of a new academic discourse of Shinto studies on the part of the conservative camp, 'things Shinto' were categorized as part of neither religion nor morality. Rather, they were seen as part of an all-encompassing concept in which the national body (*kokutai*), and its closely related system of emperor worship, came to be emphasized (Isomae 2000). Furthermore, with the dawn of the Shôwa era (1926–89) and the transition to a martial social structure, the masses were blatantly forced into shrine worship even while various incidents such as the problem of Sophia University students refusing to visit Yasukuni Shrine in 1932 (Shôwa 7) took place. With the Fifteen Year War being waged, the State Shinto system of the third phase achieved its apex with the introduction of the shrine system for the protection of the nation (*Gokoku jinja sei*). This took hold through the proliferation of branch shrines of Yasukuni Shrine in 1939, and then in 1940, commemorating the 2600 year of imperial reign, with the formation of a *Jingiin* (Office of Ritual) independent of the Ministry of Home Affairs (*Naimushô*).

As pointed out, the fully fledged development of a State Shinto system can, strictly speaking, only be thought of as beginning from this third phase. However, the basis for this State Shinto depended on previously implemented strategies. Not until shrines became sites of state worship through the establishment of an institutional hierarchy during the first phase could the foundations of the system be realized. Furthermore, developments achieved in the second phase, such as the establishment of imperial rule based on a distinction between church and state and elements of national thought (*Chûkun shisô*) such as the foundation of patriotic shrines dedicated to loyal retainers, patriots and national heroes (*sôken jinja*), imbued certain shrines with a nationalist flavor. In other words, while repeatedly responding to the looming threat of Westernization in a flexible manner, the institution of State Shinto that we find in the third phase was produced by taking in and adapting to policies established in preceding historical phases.

Current research clearly delineates just how this Western concept of religion, which was a presupposition for the construction of the State Shinto system, was imported into

Japan.[13] As a subject for further consideration, it has to be resolved just how the transformation to this third phase actually took place in relation to the invention of a category known as 'religion' and the fundamental concepts such as 'Shinto' and 'shrine' on which State Shinto rested.

Ultimately, State Shinto was an ambiguous system, clearly classifiable as neither 'religion' nor 'secular', born out of trial and error and adopted as a means by the native elite in Japan to unify the people in a response to the wave of Westernization. The most distinctive feature was that it sought to establish a native Shinto system that perceived shrines as non-religious or secular while also fully exploiting the Western idea of religious freedom. That is, not only were shrines considered to be part of the realm of public morality (as opposed to that of private religion), but they had no relation whatsoever to an individual's religious principles based on Christianity, Buddhism or popular religions. Shinto was instead founded on a logic that placed it in a transcendental dimension beyond the Western category of religion. This means that even though the Japanese regime was forced to participate in a world that embraced a concept of 'religion' based on Western modernity, by undermining this very logic, they endeavoured to deviate towards a non-religious realm in which Shinto became the axis on which the people were unified. Thus Shinto was able to successfully avoid any direct competition with Christianity for the time being, while also appearing politically to dominate those practices that were now defined as 'religious'. However, while it was politically protected, actually State Shinto policies could not totally free Shinto from the cultural hegemony imposed by a Christian concept of religion. The price to be paid for not placing Shinto in the realm of religion necessitated a transformation in the very qualities of shrines and even more so Shinto itself. This resulted in a significant blow to the charismatic allure among Japanese citizens that the regime anticipated. Following Japan's defeat in 1945 in the Second World War and the subsequent dismantling of the State Shinto system by Allied forces, qualities and provisions unique to this type of Shinto began to unravel. From this point, it is essential that we expand the discussion to also consider just how the State Shinto system that was instituted came to influence shrines, popular religion and thought that was generally disseminated throughout Japanese society.[14] This would prove useful, even if it meant re-evaluating the manner in which a systemized separation of church and state were innovated in Japan under the American-led Allied forces during the post-war period. State Shinto research that engages issues of the concept of 'religion' and related topics is just now getting under way. Making clear the exact relationship between the concept of 'religion' and the concept of 'Shinto' will certainly contribute to our understanding of how the religious–secular dichotomy that originated in Western societies was articulated in Japanese society, and furthermore provide an important case study for challenging the axiomatic status of the religious–secular division common to modern Western societies.

## NOTES

1. This was taking place at roughly the same time as the notion of world religions was being established. For mid- to late-nineteenth-century Japan the problem became one of having Japanese indigenous practice recognized as a unique, yet not inferior, manifestation of culture. [Translator's note.]

2. The 'discovery' of interiority (*naimensei*) being equated with modernity (*kindaika*) has held powerful sway in Japanese historiography and cultural studies since the 1980 publication of Karatani Kôjin's *Nihon kindai bungaku no kigen* (The origins of modern Japanese literature). Karatani and those who have followed him consider the formation of modern literary characters with a developed sense of interiority, its relationship to new forms of writing and other related 'discoveries' such as landscape, children's literature and so on. To the best of my knowledge, the author is the first to argue that the historicity of interiority is directly linked to a modern category of 'religion'. For a translation of Karatani's work see, Karatani (1993). [Translator's note.]

3. Established in the fourth leap month of 1868, the *Jingikan* was a government office overseeing the regulation of ritual and indigenous religious practice. In 1871 the *Jingikan* was renamed the *Jingishô*. [Translator's note.]

4. Throughout this chapter some dates have been given in both the Gregorian calendar and the Japanese era calendar scheme, which identifies a year with both an era name and the year number within the era.

5. The author here treats the *Jingikan* and the *Jingishô* as both characterizing the first half of this first stage of his tripartite development of State Shinto. [Translator's note.]

6. The primary research concerning this period includes: Yasumaru (1979), Miyachi (1981) and Haga (1994a).

7. With the *Shinbutsu bunri rei* in place, the Meiji government for the first time clearly distinguished between the institutions of Buddhism and Shinto. Until 1871 shrines were often inherited from one generation to the next. Known as the *shinkan seshûsei*, this practice is another early example of how indigenous practices came to be regulated and homogenized under the power of the state. [Translator's note.]

8. According to the author, these officials, known as *senkyôshi* and *kyôdôshoku*, served as official propagators of National Teaching and were responsible for propaganda for the state. *Senkyôshi* was the term used for those 'educators' serving under the *Jingishô*, while *kyôdôshoku* was used for those employees working for the office of the *Kyôbushô*, which succeeded the *Jingishô* in 1872. [Translator's note.]

9. Concerning shrines at this time see Hatakama (1992).

10. With the formation of the modern nation state the emperor was elevated to stand for a living *kami* and representative of the nation. While examples of reverence to the emperor can be found from before this time, it was not until the masses could understand themselves as national subjects that the emperor became the object of national devotion. [Translator's note.] See Takeda *et al.* (2001).

11. In other words, the existence of an ostensibly unbroken imperial line going back more than two thousand years and the divine status of the living emperor became 'proof' that Japan was superior to other nations. The origins of this ideology can be found in the emergence of "Divine Nation" or *Shinkoku* thought developed by nationalist scholars (*Kokugakusha*) of the eighteenth and nineteenth centuries. [Translator's note.]

12. What is commonly known to English reading audiences as the Second World War is also referred to by some East Asian historians as the Fifteen Year War, in order to emphasize the continuity of events beginning in 1930 and ending in 1945. [Translator's note.]

13. Previous research dealing with this topic includes: Tsuda (1964); Kuroda (1990); Inoue (2001); and Haga (1994b).

14. Earlier research includes: Murakami (1970); Yasumaru (1979); Miyachi (1981); Akazawa (1985); Morioka (1987); and Shimazono (2002).

# BIBLIOGRAPHY

Akazawa Shirô. 1985. *Kindai Nihon no shisô dôin to shûkyô tôsei*. Tokyo: Azekura Shobô.

Doi Akio. 1967. "Sankyô kaidô". *Kirisutokyô shakai mondai kenkyû* 11: 14–15.

Fujii Sadafumi. 1943. "Senkyôshi no kenkyû". *Kokugakuin zasshi* 49: 5–6.

Fujii Sadafumi. 1977. *Meiji kokugaku hassei shi no kenkyû*. Tokyo: Yoshikawa Kôbunkan.

Haga Shôji. 1994a. *Meiji ishin to shûkyô*. Tokyo: Chikuma Shobô.

Haga Shôji. 1994b. "Jinja to kinenseki". In *Meiji ishin to shûkyô*, ed. Shoji Haga, 326–52. Tokyo: Chikuma Shobô.

Hatakama Kazuhiro. 1992. "Yamato koku ni okeru jinja seido no tenkai". *Shintô shûkyô* 148: 60–95.

Inoue Hiroshi. 2001. *"Jinja" no seiritsu*. Memoirs of the Osaka Institute of Technology, Series B, 46: 1.

Isomae Junichi. 2000. "Tanaka Yoshito and the Beginnings of Shintô-gaku". In *Shintô in History: Ways of the Kami*, eds J. Breen and M. Teeuwen, 318–39. Richmond: Curzon Press.

Kaigo Tokiomi. 1969. *Rekishi kyôiku no rekishi*. Tokyo: Tôkyô Daigaku Shuppankai.

Karatani Kôjin. 1980. *Nihon kindai bungaku no kigen*. Tokyo: Kôdansha.

Karatani Kôjin. 1993. *The Origins of Modern Japanese Literature*. Durham, NC: Duke University Press.

Kuroda Toshio. 1990. "Chûsei shûkyô shi ni okeru shintô no ichi". In *Nihon chûsei no shakai to shûkyô*, ed. Toshio Kuroda, 35–62. Tokyo: Iwanami Shoten.

Miyachi Masato. 1981. *Tennôsei no seiji shiteki kenkyû*. Tokyo: Azekura Shobô.

Morioka Kiyomi. 1987. *Kindai no shûraku jinja to kokka tôsei*. Tokyo: Yoshikawa Kôbunkan.

Murakami Shigeyoshi. 1970. *Kokka shintô*. Tokyo: Iwanami Shoten.

Murakami Shigeyoshi. 1974. *Irei to shôkon: Yasukuni no shisô*. Tokyo: Iwanami Shoten.

Nakajima Michio. 1972. "Daikyô senpu undô to saijin ronsô". *Nihonshi kenkyû* 126: 26–67.

Nakajima Michio. 1977. "'Meiji kenpô taisei' no kakuritsu to kokka ideorogii seisaku". *Nihonshi kenkyû* 176: 166–91.

Ôkubo Toshikane, ed. 1991. *Kume Kunitake no kenkyû*. Tokyo: Yoshikawa Kôbunkan.

Ozawa Saburô. 1961. *Uchimura Kanzô fukei jiken*. Tokyo: Shinkyô Shuppan.

Sakamoto Koremaru. 1994. *Kokka shintô keisei katei no kenkyû*. Tokyo: Iwanami Shoten.

Shimazono Susumu. 2002. "19 seiki Nihon no shûkyô kôzô no henyô". In *Iwanami kôza kindai Nihon no bunka shi*, vol. 2, ed. Susumu Shimazono, 1–53. Tokyo: Iwanami Shoten.

Takeda Hideaki, Kunikazu Yamada, Satoshi Tanaka *et al.* 2001. *Rekishi kenshô Tennô ryô*. Tokyo: Shinjinbutsu Ôraisha.

Taki Kôji. 1988. *Tennô no shôzô*. Tokyo: Iwanami Shoten.

Tsubouchi Yûzô. 1999. *Yasukuni*. Tokyo: Shinchôsha.

Tsuda Sôkichi. 1964. *Tsuda Sôkichi zenshû, vol. 9: Nihon no shintô*. Tokyo: Iwanami Shoten.

Yamaguchi Teruomi. 1999. *Meiji kokka to shûkyô*. Tokyo: Tôkyô daigaku shuppankai.

Yamamoto Nobuyoshi and Konno Toshihiko 1973. *Kindai kyôiku no tennôsei ideorogii: Meiji ki gakkô gyôji no kôsatsu*. Tokyo: Shinsensha.

Yasumaru Yoshio. 1979. *Kamigami no Meiji ishin*. Tokyo: Iwanami Shoten.

# 5
# Religious and secular in the Vietnam War: the emergence of highland ethno-nationalism

## Thomas Pearson

The people living in the central highlands of southern Vietnam spoke dozens of languages, had no political or social organization above the level of the village, and no sense of themselves as 'a people' until French colonial administrators began to arrive in force in the early twentieth century. French imperial policy gathered the disparate highlanders under the label "*Montagnard*" (French for "mountain people" or "highlander") and began codifying the differences between the highland "savages" and the lowland Vietnamese people (considered 'civilized' in the orbit of the great Chinese tradition). French ethnographies contrasted the densely populated Vietnamese society (described as based on wet rice paddy cultivation, a Confucian social system and rich Buddhist monasteries) to what they characterized as the Montagnards' "primitive" swidden agriculture, "isolated" and "crude" villages, and no written language. The image of highland men in loincloths and women dressed in wraparound skirts, naked above the waist, only reinforced the clarity of the French classification system that placed the highland people as "proto-indochinese"-primitives living naturally off the rich plant and animal resources of the jungle.[1]

The category of 'religion' was central to French ethnographic analysis of Montagnard culture. Highlanders often spoke of *yang* (translated into French as "spirits") that resided in distinctive natural landmarks, powerful animals and the forces of nature. Highlanders said that *yang* control people's fate and influence human and natural events. They referenced *yang* in their consumption of rice and rice wine, and the ceremonial killing of chickens, pigs and water buffalo. For the French, the highlanders' references to *yang* constituted their "primitive" religious system, which, they said, played a central determining role in Montagnards' lives:

> Their religion is based on the belief in a multitude of spirits that are believed to have created the world and continue to govern it. The spirits are also the rulers of the world, and the maintainers of the socio-religious system. Any violation of this social

organization is an attack on these spirits, and requires a reparation. These spirits occupy a primary place in their view of the world; nothing is done before consulting them for fear of punishment. For the people do not believe that the supernatural is separate; it constantly intervenes in the economy, customs, morals, and in all of society. (LaFont 1963: 12, my translation)

This paragraph exemplifies the great axiom of mid-twentieth-century anthropological analysis: 'religion' is at the heart of primitive culture; and yet primitive cultures do not have a distinct realm of the religious because religion permeates all aspects of primitive life and primitives do not distinguish between the natural world and the supernatural realm of the spirits.

My point here is not to determine whether highlanders truly conceived of the *yang* as 'spirits', whether Montagnards thought *yang* inhabited this or some other world, or whether the ceremonies and social systems that referenced the *yang* constituted 'Montagnard religion' – nor even whether this religious system permeated all of highland life and customs and thus played a central determining role in highland society. The only sources to answer such questions would be the French ethnographic accounts that are already completely imbued with the category of 'religion' that is in dispute. Rather than try to recover the lost original understanding of the *yang* and how or whether it conforms to or undermines the common Western distinction between religious and secular realms, this chapter analyses how the identification of 'the religious' has been crucial in Westerners' representations of highland people. I argue that Westerners have emphatically asserted a clear discursive distinction between the religious and the secular realms in their dealings in the highlands, *precisely because* the actual strategies of Western encounters with highlanders continuously breached this religion–secular distinction. Western representations of the highland people have been structured by this religion–secular divide, even while this divide has been incessantly breached in practice. What is more, this structuring trope of representation has been appropriated by the highland people themselves. The religion–secular divide is central to Montagnard strategic self-representations today, and the instability of this dichotomous trope in the colonial theatre continues to be manifest. Today it is Christianity that is said to animate the religious heart of Montagnard society. And yet even while the Montagnards are deeply invested in the distinction they assert between the Christian (religious) Montagnards and the atheistic (secular) Vietnamese, their representations of native highland culture are dependent on (secular) cultural-relativist anthropological discourses that would seem to contradict their universalist Christian claims. The unstable assertion and breach of the religion–secular divide continues to infuse representations of traditional highland culture.

I start by briefly reviewing how Western discourses in the highlands anxiously asserted the religion–secular divide, even though – or really, *because* – their actual colonialist practices violated that divide. Then I consider the work of a Montagnard leader in exile that disturbs that categorical distinction in interesting ways.

\* \* \*

The American military entered the highlands in the late 1950s to organize the local population to forestall a communist guerrilla insurgency emanating from North Vietnam. They contracted with anthropologists to study the highland people for purposes of political control and manipulation. But the most knowledgeable Westerners on highland customs, languages and traditions were Christian missionaries: French Catholic missionaries who had established the first Western presence in the highlands in the mid-nineteenth century, and members of the Christian and Missionary Alliance (CMA), a large Canadian-American missionary organization in the conservative Evangelical-Holiness tradition that had entered the highlands in the 1930s. Area Studies and military training pamphlets frequently cite missionaries as primary sources in the footnotes. Anthropologists and their military patrons relied on the Wycliffe Bible Translators for knowledge of the many non-written languages in the highlands, and in a subsequent account of the historical period the American anthropologist Gerald Hickey depicts himself as frequently consulting with American and Catholic missionaries.[2]

But if missionaries appear with regularity in the footnotes, the actual ethnographic descriptions in these Area Studies completely erase the presence of missionaries among the Montagnards and the possibility of religious conversion and Christian identity among the highlanders. Instead these texts repeat the French ethnographic analysis that the Montagnards' worship of the *yang* "plays a dominant role" in the lives of these "primitive people" (United States Army Special Warfare School 1964). While it is difficult to gauge how widespread Christianity was in the highlands in the 1960s (the historical record indicates that at least several, and perhaps many, of the most prominent Montagnard leaders identified themselves as Christians; Hickey 1982: 304–7), it is clear that the omission of Christianity from these texts is in keeping with anthropology's long tradition of textual ambivalence toward Christian missionaries (see Herbert 1991). Classically, anthropologists were preoccupied with documenting cultures before they were corrupted by outside influences. This led them actively to omit changes introduced by colonialism, and especially by missionaries. In the mid-century anthropological paradigm in which these military ethnographies were produced, missionaries were not part of the data to be collected and analysed. Christianity was not part of 'Montagnard culture'.[3]

The omission can also be read as betraying the need of anthropologists and the military to define themselves on the secular side of the religion–secular divide. Anthropologists share with missionaries the space of cross-cultural encounter out in the field, trying to understand cultural difference. For that very reason anthropologists must emphatically assert their difference from religious missionaries. Anthropologists do not seek conversions; they do not seek to change the native cultures they study. Except, in this case the anthropologists' job was quite explicitly to inform and assist the military's own peculiar project of conversion: a project that the military described as "winning the hearts and minds" of the highlanders in support of the American war effort and the free world.

The missionary nature of American military intervention in the highlands is a curious and complicated tale (see Pearson 2001). The military's phrase "winning the hearts and minds" would seem to mimic the missionary project designed to persuade (or proselytize) that mysterious entity: the non-material self (or soul) that animates the physical materiality of the body. The American military pursued this missionary project to convert the (interior, non-material) hearts and minds of the highlanders by tending to the ailments of their (exterior and physical) bodies: the diseases, and malnutrition of inadequate economic development that made them prey to a rival conversion to communism.

This might seem to contrast military/humanitarian proselytizing with the evangelical variety, except that CMA missionaries similarly sought to influence highlanders' interior souls by ministering to their exterior bodily needs. Missionary texts from this period dwell on the physical ailments of the body, particularly the highlanders' poor health and nutrition that were caused, missionaries argued, by the savages' reliance on the worship of demons through animal sacrifice. These were outward signs of Montagnards' sinful distance from Christ's cleansing salvation. Accounts of missionary doctors wilfully cross back and forth between biomedical and spiritual cures for sick Montagnard bodies:

> The doctor is able to minister to hundreds of sick tribespeople. His medicine and good professional care replace the hideous old superstitions and horrible practices of torturing and slaying poor animals and sprinkling their blood over doorposts, gongs, drums and the sick persons.
>
> There is a terrifying amount of sickness through the valley-children with distended stomachs and rickety limbs; scaly eyes, with trachoma, is rife. There are ugly ulcers and much tuberculosis, with awful racking coughs …. But Dr. Haverson is a seasoned missionary-doctor and he comes to grips with these diseases and prays the sick ones through to deliverance, as well as helping them with pills. He preaches the Gospel to each patient. (Smith 1965: 226–7)[4]

Missionary texts from the highlands obfuscate the role of biomedicine in healing Montagnard bodies and souls, not only because providing medicine was an effective strategy to gain a hearing of the gospel, but also because of a complicated theology that constructed conversion as a kind of healing as well as the way in which the missionaries understood the highlanders' rival religious tradition to be essentially the rites and rituals of animal sacrifice, and these were often focused on healing. Both missionaries and military presumed that healing Montagnard bodies would produce a conversion: would "win their hearts and minds".

Despite their similarities, both evangelical and military 'missionaries' were deeply invested in maintaining the difference between their two projects by distinguishing between the humanitarian treatment of physical bodies and the evangelical transformation of non-material souls. However, this difference was more often nervously asserted than actually evident. The evangelicals and military shared a rhetoric and a common conceptualization of their projects that belies the religion–secular dichotomy they both sought to maintain.

They shared real material relations as well, which both groups were also anxious to deny. CMA missionaries followed American troops into pacified areas and often relied on military transportation, protection and surplus materials. The military was reticent to admit that it was using missionary informants, for fear, it claimed, that the missionaries would then be seen as combatants by Viet Cong guerrillas. And in fact, Viet Cong did occasionally target missionaries, and often called them CIA spies, a charge that shocked the missionaries who protested that they were "only there to help the people". This project to "help the people" inserted them within a vast humanitarian missionary project – funded, encouraged, directed and spearheaded by the military – to minister to the physical needs of Montagnards through relief programmes and developmental aid. CMA missionaries disavowed their participation in this secular project to "win the hearts and minds" of the Montagnards. Their missionary tracts incessantly assert that they are not "mere humanitarians" but are in the highlands "to save souls for Christ" (see e.g. Haverson 1968; Smith 1965).

Another example of how the line between the secular and the religious was rhetorically asserted and maintained through its violation in practice can be found in Protestant missionaries' suspicion towards the upstart "atheistic science" of anthropology, which intruded on their mission field, condemned their evangelical project and claimed a more authoritative representation of the people they worked with. But beginning in the 1950s, some evangelical missionaries began to make their peace with academic anthropology and sought to put anthropological methods and insights to use for Christian missions. An early proponent of this was Gordon Smith, the pioneering CMA missionary to the highlands. On furlough back in the United States during the Second World War, he researched and wrote two books that sought to apply anthropological principles to the missionary project (Smith 1945; 1947). Smith writes somewhat defensively in an attempt to persuade evangelicals: "in its place, anthropology can become a sharp tool, cutting through superstition and ignorance, and rendering [sic] the veils that hide poor lost humanity from our all too clumsy efforts to reach them with the gospel" (1945: 5). This explicitly strategic use of anthropological knowledge and methods mimics the strategic use of anthropology by French and American colonial authorities in the highlands, and was just as controversial in evangelical circles as the military appropriation of anthropology was in academic circles.

The missionary group known as the Wycliffe Bible Translators offers an intriguing example of the disavowals and anxieties that maintained, through violation, the religion–secular dichotomy in which Montagnards encountered the Western colonizing regime. Founded in the 1930s to translate the Bible into every known language, this organization of academically trained ethno-linguists has obscured its evangelical purpose among academics and governments by operating overseas under the name of the Summer Institute of Linguistics.[5] They convinced the South Vietnamese president to invite them into the highlands in 1956 to prepare literacy materials for the vernacular languages in the highlands. Raising money among evangelicals to translate the Bible (under their Wycliffe Bible Translators name), and entering countries to prepare literacy materials (under the name of the Summer Institute of Linguistics), the two faces of this organization maintained the religion–secular dichotomy duplicitously. It engaged the secular task of studying the languages of the highlands, served as a conduit for ethnographic information about the Montagnards for the military (as well as the missionaries) and prepared evangelical materials and Bible translations for evangelization. The Wycliffe Bible Translators/Summer Institute of Linguistics is a religious missionary organization that has trained itself in the skills of, and learned to represent itself effectively within, a secular world of linguistic science and international development. The organization breaches the religion–secular dichotomy, but must deceitfully and assiduously maintain that dichotomy, in order to satisfy its patrons on both sides of the divide: both have vested interests in maintaining the categorical distinction even while they contravene it for their own strategic reasons.

No one better epitomizes evangelicals' mid-twentieth-century use of anthropology – and the enabling tension of the religion–secular dichotomy – than Eugene Nida. His seminal work, *Customs and Cultures* (1954), was radical new reading in the sorts of Bible schools that CMA missionaries attended on their way to the highlands. Drawing widely on the work of Ruth Benedict, Clyde Kluckhohn, Melville Herskovits and A. L. Kroeber, Nida's book gives easy and repeated articulation to the central thesis of mid-twentieth-century anthropology: cultural–relativistic functionalism premised on the conceptualization of culture as a "complex whole".[6] Nida writes: "Not only are the patterns of culture complex, but they reveal interpretation and interdependence of the various divisions of culture .... No part of life exists in and of itself. It is all a part of the large whole and is only understandable in terms of that wider frame of reference" (1954: 46). Nida frequently repeats the then common anthropological understanding that religion plays a central and determining role in this cultural whole, especially in primitive cultures. He then reinscribes anthropology's paradoxical assertion and denial of the religion–secular divide by asserting that religion is both central to, and undifferentiated from, primitive culture. This paradox becomes even more complicated and unstable because Nida's anthropology is in service to his missiology: a theory of how to *change* a culture's religion. But what would that "religion" be in relation to the "culture", if religion permeates every aspect of primitive culture? On the one hand Nida promotes an anthropological cultural relativism that would vindicate – not critique or find wanting – any primitive culture because it is a "functioning whole". But when necessary he falls back on the missionary's absolutist critique of any non-Christian culture by asserting the imperative to *change* that culture by changing its religious beliefs and practices. And although he argues that these religious beliefs are at the "heart" of the culture (pervasive throughout the culture), he somehow claims that this evangelical project does not thereby constitute an "imposition" of Western culture or "ethnocentric chauvinism". (These are the terms he uses.) He rarely addresses this apparent contradiction head on. When he writes for fellow evangelists, not fellow linguists – just like the Summer Institute of Linguistics/Wycliffe Bible Translators, Nida had two distinct audiences – he marshals his arguments to overcome their assumed cultural chauvinism and their suspicions of, if not hostility towards, the secular project of anthropology. In these texts he feels no need to justify evangelism, only the need to temper it (or really, to sharpen it) by applying the insights of scientific ethnography. For example, he writes:

> No one must imagine ... that cultural anthropology is the answer to the problems of Christian missions, but it can aid very materially in the process by which the missionary endeavors to communicate to others the significance of the new way of life made possible through the vicarious death of the Son of God. If a person is no longer hampered by his cultural pride and by failure to identify himself completely with those to whom he goes with the words of life, he can more fully carry out his divinely ordained mission. ... Christian missions ... must permit the Holy Spirit to work out in the lives of the people those forms of Christian expression which are in accordance with their distinctive qualities.                    (Nida 1954: 22–3)

In this passage Nida has reduced his usually strident cultural relativism to simply the missionary's ability to "identify himself completely with those to whom he goes with the words of life". Christian missions, correctly informed by the cultural relativism of anthropology, should "permit the Holy Spirit to work out" the proper forms of Christian expression for each culture. He seems to leave it to the Holy Spirit to resolve the tension between cultural relativism and the Christian claims to universal truth.

To summarize, in the mid-twentieth-century colonial encounter in the central highlands of Vietnam, anthropologists relied on evangelical missionary informants but wrote them out of their ethnographic accounts. Evangelicals openly sided with and benefited from the American military presence, even while they proclaimed their neutrality. Missionaries were important contributors to the American government's military–humanitarian project to "win the hearts and minds" of the Montagnards, all the while insisting that they were neutral in the conflict and were certainly not "mere humanitarians" but had a religious purpose in the highlands to "save souls for Christ". The military used anthropology to help them influence (and combat) highlanders, which worried anthropologists. And missionaries used anthropology to sharpen their evangelism by appreciating the culturally relative context in which religion is expressed, which worried evangelicals. Evangelicals sought signs of a sincere internal religious conversion in the transformations of Montagnards' external bodily practices of healing through animal sacrifice. Similarly, the military's civic action programme sought to intuit Montagnards' sincere internal political allegiance through their participation in the material practices of economic development projects.

All of these overlapping and mutually dependent Western discourses and practices had strong interests in not fully disclosing the ways in which their respective projects violated the religion–secular dichotomy that is sacred (so to speak) to the modern West's understanding of society. They all had a large stake in affirming and staying on the right side of that divide. Their denials made their projects more effective and made them all the more invested in the categorical distinction. The anxiously asserted difference between the religious and the secular was a primary means of cross-cultural contact in the highlands.

\* \* \*

It is in this colonial context of disavowal and anxiety regarding the rhetorical maintenance of the religion–secular dichotomy that leaders emerged in the highlands to assert a collective ethnonationalist identity under the French-invented moniker "Montagnard".[7] This pan-highland Montagnard identity drew from and amalgamated the various authoritative discourses and practices through which highlanders had encountered the West and become aware of themselves as a single people. Montagnard collective identity was fashioned precisely on the unstable categorical divide between the religious and the secular that characterized the Western discourses of colonial contact. Both missionaries and military sought to "win their hearts and minds". Highland leaders were convinced that American (missionary, anthropological and military) interest and aid signified American support for their ethnonationalist movement, and Montagnards remained largely loyal to their American benefactors and thus the South Vietnamese state during the war.

When the Americans cut their losses and withdrew from Indochina in 1974, a Montagnard guerrilla resistance movement took up arms against the victorious Socialist Republic of Vietnam. They were decimated. Then, ten years later in 1986, a group of about 200 Montagnards, representing the leadership of this guerrilla resistance movement, suddenly emerged from the jungle border region between Cambodia and Thailand and sought United Nations refugee status. Two things were remarkable about this group as they were airlifted for resettlement in the United States: that they existed at all (no one in the outside world had any idea that there was still a group fighting the Vietnam War) and that they were all devout Christians. As one Montaagnard told me, "Our belief in God brought us through so we survived. We believed very strong that God help for us. In the jungle, we prayed and prayed every day, all the time. We believe very hard. God help Montagnard people, a lot".[8] Judging by the rhetoric of their leadership and innumerable personal accounts gathered in interviews and conversations, the Christian faith is central to this refugee group's collective identity, just as, ironically, their "primitive religious system" was described by French ethnographic discourse as central to their primitive society in the highlands. But their expression of ethnonationalist collective identity is also dependent on the ethnographic discourses that established – and valued – their cultural, and therefore essential, difference from the Vietnamese. And, as the quote above indicates, the universalist moral imperative that undergirds their right to exist as a people is voiced in a mixed genre that combines a religious language of God's action in the world with a secular language of human rights. Montagnards have developed ways to assert their cultural particularity within a Christian universalist framework. They have fused the categorical opposites of the religion–secular dichotomy so nervously asserted, and surreptitiously violated, in the colonialist discursive practices through which they encountered the West and formed a collective identity.

Living in refugee exile since 1986, Montagnards have learned to represent themselves and their history and to articulate their demands using the rhetorics and systems of documentation that draw on, and creatively amalgamate, the colonialist discursive traditions of missionaries, anthropologists and military strategists: discourses that are simultaneously maintained and troubled by the religion–secular dichotomy. Montagnards consistently contrast their Christian faith with the atheistic non-faith of the communist Vietnamese. In these accounts, the absolute universals of Christian faith mingle nervously with a cultural relativism promoted by anthropologically informed veneration of Montagnard cultural difference. Both (religious) Christian universals and (secular) anthropological cultural relativism are used to justify Montagnard difference from and resistance to the Vietnamese.

As an example, I shall highlight a writing project of one particular Montagnard refugee community leader with whom I have worked extensively and whom I have got to know quite well. One day, in his North Carolina home, Hip K'Sor was passionately explaining to me why it was so important that he write a book about "Montagnard culture", as he called it. "The Montagnard need a book", he said, "or they will not know who they are. They will become Vietnamese". He pulled an American high-school textbook off his shelf and showed me the chapters on the civilization of ancient Greece. "See, all the other people have a book. They have it written down, who they are and what they have done. But the Montagnard don't know this. They don't know who they are." Then he told me that the French had been good to the Montagnards, and that they had recognized and supported Montagnard culture. "Here", he said, and grabbed from a huge stack of papers a xeroxed copy of a French-language ethnography he had brought with him from Vietnam. "The French made this book. They love the Montagnards. Here we can look in this book and learn all about our people. The Vietnamese do not like this book. They do not want us to know that we have our own way. They want to tell us that we are Vietnamese."

Then Hip showed me a small handwritten notebook, worn and mouldy on the edges, crammed with descriptions of highland traditions, transcriptions of "prayers" and summaries of old stories. He asked me to help him translate this text into English. His goal, he said, was to correct and improve the French ethnographic account and to make it accessible to Montagnards, those in exile as well as those in Vietnam. Recognizing that the younger generation of Montagnard refugees cannot read their native language, he described for me a side-by-side English translation of his text that he hopes will help teach the next generation of children their native language.

Raised in the 1950s and 1960s, as his society was undergoing tremendous stress and change in the midst of a war zone, Hip did not participate in these native customs as an adult. His account is explicitly dependent on French ethnographic conventions and the French representation of the Montagnards, which codified highland cultural difference for the purposes of colonial control. Hip's writing project is a celebration of, and a strategic ethnographic representation of, Montagnard cultural difference, in order to create and maintain a collective ethnic identity in opposition to Vietnamese state-building in the highlands.

But Hip's book is also *theological* in its ethnographic celebration of Montagnard cultural difference. It is a very careful amalgamation of the universal claims of the Christian faith (as learned from his Christian missionaries) with the particularities of Montagnard traditional religion (as conceptualized by Western anthropological discourses). Hip's text bridges the religion–secular divide to promote the cultural and political integrity of the Montagnards against the communist Vietnamese state.

Hip's frayed notebook announces the religious nature of his project immediately on the first page, where he has carefully drawn a rendering of the future book's cover and title page (Figures 1 and 2). Translated, the text reads:

| | |
|---|---|
| Outline of the System | THE DAY OF |
| of Genies | THE LORD |
| of the MONTAGNARD PEOPLE | Sing and Praise |
| OF THE ENTIRE | the Lord |
| CHEO-REO | God |
| REGION | THE LORD SENDS ME |
| | – I go |

Apparently assuming that "genie" has the same connotation in English as it does in French, Hip has resisted my suggestions that he use the term "spirit" to translate "*yang*", as is the common practice in English translations from the French and highland languages. It would seem that he is accustomed to using the word "genies" when speaking in what might be called his "ethnographic voice", learned from French, the language in which he knows and represents his own native culture.

The next page of his notebook provides a complicated diagram that serves to organize his text and became the basis of his table of contents (Figure 3). The convoluted drawing encapsulates the theological purpose of his writing project. The diagram has three columns. Column A is labelled "No Genies". He divides Column B, "Too Many Genies (sacrifices achieve nothing)", into five sub-categories, providing a taxonomy of the pantheon of "genies" that inhabit the Montagnard world. This taxonomy is rendered in the diagram as a staircase that leads up to column C: "Following the Way of the Christ (One Single Genie)". Thus, the first step, "the genies that make us covet", leads to the second step, "the lying genies" (in which he groups the various systems of divination), followed by "the frightful genies" a step higher, and then the "healthful genies" (involved with healing rituals) and finally "the creator and protector genies". Across the top of the diagram, over a bold arrow pointing down to the staircase of genies in column B, Hip has written "Oi Adai" ("Grandfather the Sky") the missionaries' name for God (favoured over *Yang Jesus*, used sparingly early on). In Hip's diagram, the Montagnard genies anticipate Christ, culminate in Christ and approach Christ, the true God, like ascending a staircase that in effect discards distracting and inappropriate genies as they reduce to the few and most exalted "protector and creator genies" and then finally to the single genie, Christ.

It is not that the genies are false or not real, Hip explained to me; his text gives repeated credence to their existence. It is just that the genies are *partial*. Hip believes that Montagnards in their ignorance and fear failed to acknowledge the true creator God who

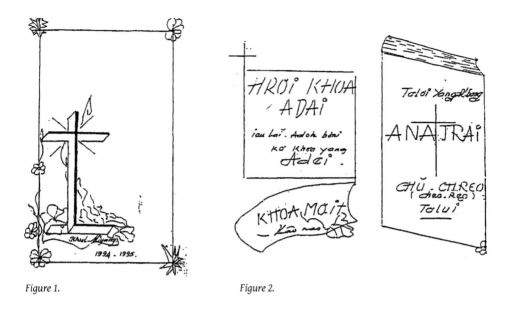

Figure 1.

Figure 2.

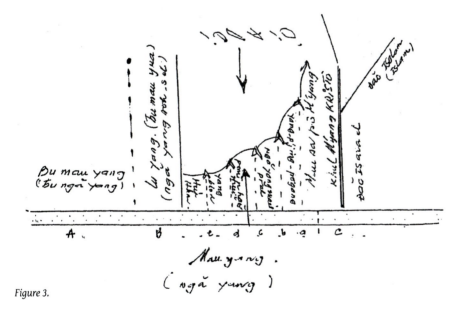

Figure 3.

is revealed in Christ. The power that Montagnards attribute to the genies actually comes from God. So if Hip's diagram juxtaposes "too many genies" with the true God revealed in Christ, his text also makes it clear that the genies do actually exist as a part of God's creation (although sometimes his text refers to the creator as "the genies and God").[9] In the following passage, Hip makes a self-conscious attempt to clarify this matter:

All of these things come from the genies who created the ancestors. If we think hard about these statements and ask ourselves who are the genies of the ancestors, we see and feel inside ourselves that the genie who created our ancestors is God [Oi-Adai], because all of the things in this world are not made by people but by the hand of God who creates them and takes care of them. He himself gives us our destiny however he desires. (K'Sor n.d.: 44)[10]

Hip told me that his ethnography "is like the Old Testament". The real opposition for Hip is not between belief in the genies and belief in God, but between belief in "God or the genies" and belief in no genies at all, which, Hip's text explains, is the condition of the Godless communist Vietnamese regime. Hip writes:

The communist government of the people does not have any genies. This government does not believe in the genies or the God who created mankind and everything on the earth. Therefore, they do not take seriously the power and glory of God. The people's communist government does not care about the life of the people. They consider the people to be like animals. They treat them like they don't have a soul. This is because they don't believe in God who is the creator of all people and all the world. (*Ibid.*: 1)

In Hip's analysis, atheism is at the root of the communists' ill-treatment of the Montagnard people. Hip explains that the Montagnards thus have a special spiritual mission to bring the gospel of Christian brotherhood to the communist Vietnamese. "We bring our heart. Just send the Bible", he told me. "That's the way to make the Vietnamese people open their eyes. When they believe, they will change. Love of God will change everything."

Hip's ethnographic theology operates within the tension produced by valorizing Montagnard cultural difference while simultaneously assuming and promoting Christianity as a universalistic absolute. Hip's project celebrates and seeks to salvage the anthropological–relativist difference existent in Montagnard culture, in the name of a universalist–Christian faith. He does not want to encourage Montagnard animal sacrifices. But the traditions of animal sacrifice must be remembered and venerated, lest the Montagnard "not know who they are". If "the Montagnards need a book", then the specific book they need is this Montagnard Old Testament. If Montagnards "know who they are" – and who they are is Christians (as revealed in this ethnographic Old Testament) – then they can bring the gospel to the atheist Vietnamese, who will then see the injustice in their repression of traditional Montagnard culture. The Vietnamese will respect the cultural (secular/anthropological) particularity of Montagnard tradition through the ethical religious universality of the Christian gospel. Once again, the religion–secular divide has been reinscribed as it is simultaneously violated.

\* \* \*

Montagnard refugees' representations of the traditional culture of the highlands constitute a complicated appropriation of the missionary, military and ethnographic discourses
that were productive of colonial power in the central highlands of Vietnam through the
unstable categorical opposition of the secular and the religious. French and American
ethnographies – drawn on by both missionaries and the military – define Montagnard
cultural difference by placing the anthropological category of animism at its centre. They
also venerate that culture through the doctrine of cultural relativism. Yet Montagnard
refugees' representations of the culturally relative traditions of the highlands mingle
with Christian discourses of the universal truth and necessity of Christ. Montagnard
representations have displaced animism from its position purportedly shaping all of
Montagnard traditional culture. "Traditional culture" remains, but the "animism" by
which the Westerners understood this culture has been converted to Christianity. For Hip
K'Sor, the genies are fulfilled, or collapsed into, (the Christian) God.

Creative Montagnard appropriation of both missionary and ethnographic discourses
(and these discourses' relationship to each other and to the exercise of colonial power)
produces a new way by which highland people – now refugees and Christians – can
assert the essential value and worth of their particular, culturally relative, traditions
(learned from their anthropologists) by simultaneously asserting the universal truth of
their religious faith (learned from their missionaries). And 'religion' is still held (as the
anthropologists would expect) at the core of their cultural expression. Religious/Christian
Montagnard makes an essential contrast with secular/atheist Vietnamese, reinscribing
the colonialist distinction between the secular and the religious. But Montagnard self-representations also contest that distinction by fusing the cultural relativism learned from
anthropological discourses (understood here as a 'secular' ideology) with the Christian
universalism learned from their missionaries (constituting the 'religious' alternative to
secular cultural relativism). And that has been the pattern throughout: representations
of "the Montagnards" assert and simultaneously transcend the religion–secular divide
that helped authorize colonial power in the highland.

## NOTES

1. Oscar Salemink (2002) provides a contemporary critical analysis of this French ethnographic
   tradition.
2. See, for example, United States Army Special Warfare School (1964), American University Cultural
   Information Analysis Center (1966) and Mole (1970). Overviews of the work and activities of the
   Wycliffe Bible Translators can be found in Pike (1977) and Stoll (1982). Gerald Hickey's accounts are in
   Hickey (1982: 30, 63, 130).
3. Written in the style of "the ethnographic present", the omission of highland Christianity reflects
   the then prevailing perception that "primitive cultures" are stagnant and unchanging. See Fabian
   (1983).
4. Dr Haverson, in fact, wrote his own account of his mission to Vietnam (Haverson 1968).
5. For a withering critique of this organization, see Stoll (1982).

6. For an intriguing analysis of "the culture concept" see Herbert (1991).
7. The best history of this period is Hickey (1982).
8. The author conducted anonymous interviews in North Carolina from 1995 to 2000.
9. In Hip's text, the genies and God are often interchangeable, written in a serial manner. For example: "Mankind cannot refuse the destiny that God or the genies have fixed for us. However they fix our destiny, that is how we should live" (K'Sor n.d.: 16).
10. The translation is difficult to render because the Jarai language does not signify the plural form of nouns (or verbs). Thus "*yang*" could be translated as either "genie" or "genies". Hip consistently uses the plural form as he speaks, until he hits a sentence like this one that must shift from "who are the genies of the ancestors" to "the genie who created our ancestors is God [Oi-Adai]".

# BIBLIOGRAPHY

American University Cultural Information Analysis Center. 1966. *Minority Groups In The Republic of Vietnam.* Washington DC: American University Cultural Information Analysis Center.

Fabian, Johannes. 1983. *Time and the Other: How Anthropology Makes its Object.* New York: Columbia University Press.

Haverson, Stuart. 1968. *Doctor in Vietnam.* Westwood, NJ: Fleming H. Revell.

Herbert, Christopher. 1991. *Culture And Anomie: Ethnographic Imagination in the Nineteenth Century.* Chicago, IL: University of Chicago Press.

Hickey, Gerald. 1982. *Free In The Forest: Ethnohistory of the Vietnamese Central Highlands, 1954-1976.* New Haven, CT: Yale University Press.

K'Sor, Hip. unpublished manuscript. *Outline Of A System Of Genies.*

LaFont, Pierre Bernard. 1963. *Toloi Djuat: Coutumier de la Tribu Jarai.* Paris: Ecole Francaise d'Extrême-Orient.

Mole, Robert L. 1970. *The Montagnards of South Vietnam: A Study of Nine Tribes.* Rutland, VT: Charles E. Tuttle.

Nida, Eugene. 1954. *Customs and Cultures.* New York: Harper & Brothers.

Pearson, Thomas. 2001. "Missions And Conversions: Creating the Montagnard-Dega Refugee Community". PhD dissertation. University of North Carolina.

Pike, Kenneth L. 1977. *The Summer Institute of Linguistics: Its Works and Contributions.* The Hague: Mouton.

Salemink, Oscar. 2002. *The Ethnography of Vietnam's Central Highlanders: A Historical Contextualization, 1850–1990.* Honolulu, HI: University of Hawaii Press.

Smith, Gordon Hedderly, B. D. 1945. *The Missionary and Anthropology: An Introduction to the Study of Primitive Man for Missionaries.* Chicago, IL: Moody Press, 1945.

Smith, Gordon Hedderly, B. D. 1947. *The Missionary and Primitive Man: An Introduction to the Study of his Mental Characteristics and his Religion.* Chicago, IL: Van Kamper Press.

Smith, Mrs. Gordon H. [Laura]. 1965. *Victory in Viet Nam.* Grand Rapids, MI: Zondervan Publishing House.

Stoll, David. 1982. *Fishers of Men or Founders of Empire? The Wycliffe Bible Translators in Latin America.* London: Zed Press.

United States Army Special Warfare School. 1964. *Montagnard Tribal Groups of the Republic of South Viet-Nam.* Fort Bragg, NC.

# 6

# Colonialism all the way down? Religion and the secular in early modern writing on south India[1]

## Will Sweetman

Recent historiography of colonialism has emphasized that the colonial encounter was not merely an arena in which ideas originating in the European metropolis were projected and forcibly imposed on the colonized, but rather a process in which those ideas took their modern shape through the actions of both colonizer and colonized. Although scholars have begun to attend to the colonial context in which the category 'religion', and its corollary, the 'secular', acquired their modern sense, the significance of colonialism for the production and deployment of the categorial distinction is more often asserted than demonstrated. One colonial context where the religion–secular distinction was explicitly invoked as an element of policy on the part of a colonial power was in India, where the East India Company, and later the British Crown, maintained a policy of non-intervention in the religious affairs of its colonial subjects that was predicated upon the distinction. The policy was extensively debated in the early nineteenth century in relation to issues such as the banning of *sati* and the toleration of Christian missions in Company territory. Arguably the most consequential deployment of the religion–secular distinction during the colonial period in India, however, was in relation to caste.

In his recent work on caste Nicholas Dirks has advanced an important argument that suggests that the analysis of caste as a religious, rather than a political, institution was not merely convenient for the British but a necessary instrument of the very specific form of indirect rule that the British exercised in India. For Dirks, indirect rule meant not only the apparatus of residents installed at the courts of nominally independent princely states but, more generally, "the mechanisms that were used both to buttress and to displace colonial authority" (Dirks 2001: 14–15). One such mechanism was the elaborate ceremonial display that the British promoted in the Indian princely states, which covered the fiction of independence, disguising where true power lay, and thus enabling indirect rule.[2] For Dirks, the representation of caste as religious functioned analogously. Throughout British India, "caste could take over many of the functions of colonial rule" (*ibid.*: 80), just as the Indian princes did in the states subject to indirect rule: "Because of caste, and the colonial ethnology that constructed it as the centerpiece of Indian society, the British could rule *all* of India indirectly, as it were" (*ibid.*). The importance of the religion–secular distinction here is that this construction of caste as religious enabled the displacement of kingly authority by the "transcendental spiritual authority" of the Brahman at the apex of the caste system. By separating religious and political authority in this manner, the British were able to arrogate political power to themselves, leaving India, with its supposed "fundamental civilizational disregard for the political" (*ibid.*), to occupy itself with religion. Caste:

> was refigured as a religious system, organizing society in a context where politics and religion had never before been distinct domains of social action. The religious confinement of caste enabled colonial procedures of rule through the characterization of India as essentially about spiritual harmony and liberation; when the state had existed in India, it was despotic and epiphenomenal, extractive but fundamentally irrelevant.                                    (Dirks 1993: xxvii)[3]

This refiguration was only partially successful for, as Dirks argues, "caste never succumbed to an analytical dualism that allowed the easy separation of the social and the religious" (2001: 40). This was not, as has been supposed, because of the intractable nature of caste, or the inherent conservatism of Indian society. Rather, according to Dirks, the religious was not easily separated from the social or political:

> in part because the ideological underpinnings of separate religious and social (or political) domains had only developed – however uncertainly – in Europe from the middle of the eighteenth century, and were still imposed in ways that made little sense in Indian society, let alone in the colonial contexts that such deliberations inherently took place.                                                    (*Ibid.*)

Although, as Fitzgerald argues (in the Introduction), the demarcation of a domain of the religious over against the secular was already underway by the end of the seventeenth century, the second half of the eighteenth century saw important shifts in the British colonial enterprise, with the loss of the American colonies and the development of the East India Company into a territorial power in India. In this context, the debates over whether or not caste was to be seen as religious are significant for understanding religion "as a category that has ideological work to do in the service of complex colonial interests" (Introduction: n2).

Writing about 'culture', a term that has provoked among anthropologists a debate that in many respects resembles the debate over 'religion', Dirks argues that: "colonialism was not just a historical stage and an epistemological problem but the crucible in which the category of 'culture' itself had been formed. To paraphrase Geertz's story about turtles and the wisdom of the east, it was colonialism all the way down" (1993: xvii).[4] As the other chapters in this book suggest, 'religion' and its various supposed opposites were also forged in the crucible of colonialism. Building on Dirks's important claims about the significance of the interpretation of caste as religious for the exercise of colonial authority in the nineteenth century, the origins of the idea of caste as a specifically religious ordering of society will be traced here in order to determine whether in the deployment of the religion–secular distinction in relation to caste, it really is a case of colonialism all the way down.

## THE ROLE OF MISSIONARIES

For Dirks the roots of the colonial reconfiguration of caste as religious are to be found in the works of Christian missionaries. Not only did missionaries write "far more about caste and other social matters than did any others during the first half of the nineteenth century" – they were, says Dirks, "obsessed with caste" – but the barrier that caste posed to conversion meant that "missionaries came to hold a special contempt for caste; their ascription to it of a totalizing power was not seen in other contemporaneous British writings" (2001: 27–8). Dirks argues that the view that caste was religious: "became missionary orthodoxy by 1850, when the Madras Missionary Conference put forward a minute in which it was held that 'Caste ... is one of the greatest obstacles to the progress of the Gospel in India ... whatever it may have been in its origin, it is now adopted as an essential part of the Hindu religion'" (ibid. 131).

After the events of 1857 missionaries attempted to exploit the idea that the rebellion had been sparked off by caste practices incompatible with military discipline to spur the government to act against caste. In fact the view that carried the day was that the rebellion had been inspired not so much by caste practices themselves as by the perceived threat to them. Thus in 1858 Queen Victoria reaffirmed in strong terms the policy of non-interference, predicated on the religion–secular distinction, charging her representatives in India to "abstain from all interference with the religious belief and worship of any of subjects on pain of our highest displeasure" (ibid.: 130). Dirks argues that although missionary concerns with conversion were not important to a colonial state with an explicit policy of non-interference in the religious lives of its Indian subjects, nevertheless the influence of missionary accounts of caste persisted and drove the development of colonial ethnography. Missionary writing on caste:

> came to be of special interest for the state during the years after the Great Revolt, as the colonial state realized that a simple policy of non-intervention was insufficient. Missionary concerns about conversion were dropped, of course, even as missionary interests in the relationship between religious and civil domains of social life were incorporated. The policy of nonintervention was based upon the specification of autonomous religious domains that could be preserved with particular sensitivity

only if the delineation of customary practice and social disposition could proceed at a much accelerated pace. The colonial state believed that the reasons behind the revolt were less political than they were anthropological, and that the primary basis of its rule had now to be found in a comprehensive ethnographic knowledge of custom, religion, caste and character. Caste was converted into a primary concern of the colonial state, even as missionary discourse dropped out of both the colonial and nationalist registers.                                        (*Ibid.*: 148)

The missionary obsession with caste was, then, the model for the later colonial preoccupation. Not only did the missionaries bequeath to the state a concern with caste as the central feature of Indian civilization, but their extensive writings on it prefigured the colonial ethnography that did so much to reify caste structures. Dirks stresses that it was missionary interests in the relationship between religious and civil domains of social life that were incorporated in the colonial state's refiguring of caste as a distinctly religious system, which, in turn, enabled colonial procedures of rule. "In doubting the ultimate possibility of the conversion of native interiority into genuine Christian subjectivity, missionaries acted out the deepest contradications of the colonial state" (*ibid.*: 147), that is, the promise of independence always deferred by the inability of India to escape "tradition" (caste).

As "the first extensive, and in the early years of the nineteenth century the most influential, European account of caste" (*ibid.*: 21), Dirks singles out a work entitled *Description of the Character, Manners, and Customs of the People of India, and of their Institutions, Religious and Civil*, which was first published in 1817 under the name of the Abbé J. A. Dubois, a secular French priest of the Missions Étrangères. Dirks immediately indicates that he is aware that this work is largely based on a manuscript written by another French missionary, the Jesuit Gaston-Laurent Cœurdoux, in the 1770s. Nevertheless Dirks treats the work throughout as that of Dubois,[5] whom he identifies as a Jesuit (*ibid.*: 22).[6] Dirks writes that in general "Dubois's writings attained extraordinary authority for the British rulers" (*ibid.*: 26)[7] and, significant for our purposes here, suggests that it was Dubois who was responsible for introducing "a separation between caste as a kind of civil institution and Hinduism as the religious basis of it" (*ibid.*: 25).

## THE DUBIOUS DUBOIS

Dirks writes that Dubois, despite being extremely critical of the Brahmans:

had nothing but admiration for the great early seventeenth-century Jesuit missionary Roberto de Nobili, who took on Brahman customs and modes of life, and managed to convert a number of upper-caste Hindus to Christianity, in part because he did not insist, as many other missionaries did, that they break caste mores. But once the Catholic Church challenged this form of conversion, leading to the famous controversy about the so-called 'Malabar Rites,' the Jesuits had to fall in line with stated Church policy that religious conversion should lead to social conversion, as well.

(Dirks 2001: 25)

Dirks does not comment here on an obvious corollary of Nobili's taking on of Brahmanic customs: if he thought they were legitimate for a Christian missionary, he cannot have taken them to be an essential part of Hindu religion.[8] Moreover the Catholic Church intially ruled *in favour* of Nobili (in the 1623 bull of Gregory XV, *Romanae Sedis Antistes*) and did not finally rule against 'adaptation' or 'accommodation' to Brahmanic customs (as Nobili's strategy became known) until well into the eighteenth century.[9] Among the last defenders of the strategy were the mainly French Jesuits of the South Indian missions, including the actual author of the text published under Dubois's name, Gaston-Laurent Cœurdoux (Murr 1987, II: 60). Commenting on his reasons for writing the work, Sylvia Murr, whose research identified the text as substantially Cœurdoux's, states that:

Le projet individuel du P. Cœurdoux s'identifie pour une large part aux intérêts de la Compagnie de Jésus, et plus particulièrement à ceux des Missions de l'Inde. Rappelons qu'il était Supérieur de ces Missions pendent la période qui suivit immédiatement la condamnation par le Saint-Siège, en 1739, des méthodes de propagande religieuse sur lesquelles étaient fondées les institutions missionaires des Jésuites en Inde ... Ces méthodes consistaient à s'adapter pour s'implanter dans les hautes castes, quitte à faire des concessions aux mœurs locales et, dans le cas de l'Inde, a tolérer la ségrégation des castes.

[Fr. Cœurdoux's individual project is for the most part to be identified with the interests of the Society of Jesus, and more particularly with those of the Indian missions. It should not be forgotten that he was Superior of these missions during the period that immediately followed the Holy See's condemnation, in 1739, of the methods of religious propaganda on which the missionary institutions of the Jesuits in India were founded ... these methods consisted of adapting in order to establish themselves among the high castes, even if that meant making concessions to local manners and, in the case of India, tolerating caste segregation.]　　(*Ibid.*: 58)

Murr notes also the extent to which Cœurdoux drew on the work of other French Jesuits in the south Indian missions (*ibid.*: 70), among whom were several of the most active polemicists in the rites debate, in particular Jean-Venant Bouchet, the probable author of a work in defence of adaptation, the *Relation des erreurs qui se trouvent dans la religion des gentils malabars de la Coste Coromandelle* (Dharampal 1982: 233–9), and Pierre Martin, who went to Rome in 1716 on behalf of the missions to argue the case for adaptation. By the 1770s, Murr points out, the Jesuits who remained in India had seen French defeat in India, the expulsion of the Jesuits from France and the suppression of the Society by the Pope, and were in no position to press their case on the rites debate. Yet even if Cœurdoux's work is, as Murr suggests, best understood as an attempt to prove the indispensability of experienced priests to train the new missionaries of the Missions Étrangères (Murr 1987, II: 58), and not a final salvo in the battle over the Malabar rites, the account of caste that he presents is entirely consistent with that which informed the Jesuit position in the rites debate.

Cœurdoux presents caste as an ancient institution, comparable to the division of the French into three estates, and not peculiar to India but found also among the Israelites, where it was established by Moses, at God's command, by adapting and perfecting "le Système politique de l'Egypte et de l'Arabie" (Murr 1987, I: 14).[10] Although Cœurdoux reports what he calls the "legendary origin" of the castes, their emergence from the different parts of Brahmā's body, and says that it is known to all the Indians (*ibid.*), he suggests that the true basis for caste is the need for order in society:

> C'est que plus on établit de Classes et de distinction dans un état; plus il y a d'ordre et d'arrangement, de facilité à le conduire et à y conserver les bonnes mœurs. *C'est effectivement ce que produisent Les Castes Indiennes: Le déshonneur qu'attireroient à un corps les fautes d'un particulier, l'engage à en faire lui-même Justice, pour venger son honneur et retenir dans le devoir tous les membres qui le composent*; Car les Castes ont leurs loix particulieres, ou plutôt leurs coùtumes suivant lesquelles, à l'exemple des anciens Patriarches, elles exercent quelquefois une justice bien Sévére Sur les Coupables.
> [The more one establishes classes and distinction in a state, the more order and accord there is that enables direction of the state and preservation of good manners within it. This is what the Indian castes in fact produced: the dishonour that the faults of the individual attracted to the group, which itself carried out justice to defend its honour and to keep to their duty all the members of which the group was composed. For the castes have their own laws, or rather their own customs, according to which, following the example of the ancient patriachs, they sometimes mete out justice quite severely on the guilty.] (*Ibid.*: 8)

I have already quoted Dirks's claim that "Dubois made a separation between caste as a kind of civil institution and Hinduism as the religious basis of it" (2001: 25). And, indeed, in his version[11] of Cœurdoux's second chapter, on the "Advantages of Caste", he argues that the ancient law-givers of the Hindus, recognizing both the value of caste for producing order, and the "indolent", "careless" nature and "propensity to be apathetic" of the people:

> saw no surer way of attaining their object than by combining in an unmistakable manner those two great foundations of orderly government, religion and politics. Accordingly there is not one of their ancient usages, not one of their observances, which has not some religious principle or object attached to it ... Nothing is left to chance; everything is laid down by rule, and the foundation of all their customs is purely and simply religion. It is for this reason that the Hindus hold all their customs and usages to be inviolable, for, being essentially religious, they consider them as sacred as religion itself. (Dubois 1906: 30–31)

There is, however, no parallel passage in Cœurdoux's text; it is most likely that this is entirely Dubois's addition. Cœurdoux makes no statement about the indolence, careless-ness or apathy of the Hindus. On the contrary he stresses their attachment to caste: "On ne Sera plus étonne après ce que je viens de dire, que les Indiens soient autant ou plus attachés à leurs Castes, qui font leur noblesse, que nos Gentilshommes à le leur" (One should no longer be astonished when I venture to say that the Indians are as much or more attached to their castes, which are their nobility, than our gentlemen are to theirs) (Murr 1987, I: 12). For Cœurdoux, then, there is no requirement for a religious sanction for caste and the absence of any assertion about a religious basis of caste in his text is exactly what we would expect from him as an inheritor of the Jesuit tradition of adapta-tion begun by Nobili. If there is a distinction in Dubois's text between "caste as a kind of civil institution and Hinduism as the religious basis of it", it is best understood as the fault line between Cœurdoux's presentation of caste as a civil institution, common to the Indians, the Egyptians, the Israelites and even the French, and Dubois's perception that the foundation of all the Hindus' customs is "purely and simply religion".

In conflating Cœurdoux and Dubois, and treating the former's text as straightforwardly that of the latter, Dirks elides the difference between the view of caste that predomi-nated among missionaries in the eighteenth century, and that which came to predomi-nate among missionaries and those they influenced in the nineteenth century. Further evidence of a significant change in attitude to caste may be found in the works emanating from the Protestant missions.

## PROTESTANT MISSIONS

At the height of the rites controversy, in the same year that the Vatican confirmed Tournon's decree condemning sixteen of the Jesuits' adaptationist practices and Bouchet arrived in Rome to contest it, a new chapter in the history of Christian missions in India opened quietly with the arrival in Tranquebar in July 1706 of the first Protestant mission-aries in India, Bartholomäus Ziegenbalg and Heinrich Plütschau. Although commissioned by the king of Denmark, and sent to Tranquebar, a small coastal town controlled by the Danish East India Company, during the course of the eighteenth century virtually all of the missionaries were Germans who took their spiritual direction from the Pietist August Hermann Francke and his successors in Halle. As Protestants the Danish-Halle missionar-ies had no precedents in India to draw on and while their methods attracted criticism in Europe from the beginning, they were not subject to the same degree of oversight as their Catholic counterparts. In many respects they pioneered what became a distinctively Protestant missionary strategy, including translating the Bible into Indian languages and running schools. Even their tolerance of caste distinctions among former Hindus who converted to Christianity was, as will be shown, shared to a greater or lesser degree by many Protestant missions until the 1820s.

Ziegenbalg is one of the outstanding early European scholars of Hinduism, his achievement matched only by some of the Jesuits mentioned above.[12] Although his two main works on Hinduism were not published until many decades after his death, they remain important sources for our knowledge of South Indian Hinduism in the early eighteenth century, especially the minor deities of popular village Hinduism. Far from being "obsessed with caste", Ziegenbalg, as the author of one recent work on him writes, "never set himself up as an implacable enemy of the caste system, or sought to destroy it, or indeed even paid much attention to it" (Singh 1999: 56). One reason may have been that he did not regard the caste system as a major hindrance to conversion; the degenerate lifestyle of the supposedly Christian European traders in India was much more often cited by him, and the Hindus whose views he reports, as the main reason why Hindus saw no reason to convert. In spite of the length and detail of his works, as Gita Dharampal-Frick comments, "[i]n comparison to later works on India, it is remarkable how relatively little attention Ziegenbalg devotes to a description of Tamil social groups, in fact a mere five pages of his first book, *Malabarisches Heidenthum*, numbering more than 250 pages" (1995: 92). The chapter in question (Ziegenbalg 1926: 195–9) is entitled "Von ihren vielfältigen Geschlechtern oder Zünften", which Dharampal-Frick translates as "About Their Manifold Families or Guilds". In his writings Ziegenbalg uses *Geschlecht*, which can mean 'family', rather loosely, using it within the space of a few pages not only to translate *varṇa, jāti* and *gotra*,[13] but also as an explicit synonym for the European term 'caste', and even as a term for the whole of humanity.[14] The semantic range of *Geschlecht* in Ziegenbalg is perhaps best captured in English by 'kind'. Although Ziegenbalg notes that the *Geschlechte* differ from one another in food and marriage rituals, in clothing, rank and in many other things, in his list of 71 Śūdra *jāti*s he comments only on their occupation, sometimes noting where their actual occupation differs from their traditional role. He notes also the flexibility afforded in cases of exceptional talent or need. While exogamous marriage and conversion to Christianity are briefly mentioned as causes of a loss of *Geschlecht*, in its emphasis on occupation as the basis of caste difference Ziegenbalg's account is thus, as Dharampal-Frick suggests, typical of early works in which the "religious connotations of caste" were not as prominent as they were in later European accounts (Dharampal-Frick 1995: 86–7).

Another, briefer, account of caste appears in the annotations to a series of letters from Hindus received by the mission and published in German as the "Malabarian Correspondence". While the emphasis remains on occupation, the missionaries also mention endogamy, commensality and ritual differences:

These heathens establish among themselves 96 different *Geschlechte*. And even though these are actually only differentiated from one another in their arts, positions, professions and roles, nevertheless they observe among themselves a superstitious difference, such that one may not marry out of his *Geschlecht* into another, nor may eat with people from another *Geschlecht*. Each *Geschlecht* has its special names, its special ceremonies, its special customs and its special way of eating and kitchenware. Should one go against these, he has thereby lost his *Geschlecht* and is regarded as the most depised of men.          (Gründler & Ziegenbalg 1998: 54)

The acknowledgement of a "superstitious" (*abergläubisch*) dimension to caste is reinforced in the next annotation to the same letter:

When one of these heathens enters our Christian religion, he must give up such superstitions. For we permit no such difference, rather teach that they are all one in Christ and herein no-one is to be preferred before another. Therefore we also have them marry among themselves, not according to the *Geschlecht*, but rather as they wish, where they otherwise without restriction can be trusted in Christian ways.

(*Ibid.*: 55)

The result, according to a further annotation is:

From the abovementioned superstition, it seems very strange to these heathens when they see that those who enter the Christian religion sit together in one church, marry one another without respect of persons, live, eat and drink with one another and abolish all previous distinction. In other matters concerning *Dignitatem officii*, we do not abolish these differences, but rather see to it that all good order is maintained among our people.          (*Ibid.*)

On the basis of these and other similar passages, Daniel Jeyaraj describes Ziegenbalg as "a resolute opponent of caste", who "permitted no caste difference in the church" (1996: 227). Nevertheless, he adds that "in connection with the mission to the non-Christians, Ziegenbalg tolerated caste. Through 'Dignitatem officii', that is, through 'externals' of dress and food, Ziegenbalg wanted to make possible communication with non-Christians" (*ibid.*: 228). It is clear from other sources that at least some elements of the mission practice were influenced by considerations of caste. The most noticeable of these was that Śūdras and Paraiyars sat separately in the church, and Wilhelm Germann suggests that it is possible the church was deliberately designed to facilitate this (Germann 1868: 287).[15] It is also possible that separate cups were used for communion.[16] Caste considerations also influenced the selection of the mission's servants for positions where caste might be important, such as cook and churchwarden.

Although loss of caste as a result of conversion to Christianity is often mentioned in the reports from the mission, this is usually in the context of an appeal for funds to allow the mission to support converts thus excluded from their normal sources of support. It does not appear that exclusion from caste arose as the result of any particularly stringent insistence on the part of the missionaries that converts renounce caste. Germann cites a number of instances where Ziegenbalg tells potential converts that they will not be required to live like Europeans in "outward things" such as clothing, food and drink but will be free to live "in the manner of your country": "For we demand of you no alteration in such outward and physical things, rather an alteration of your heart and mind, wherein true conversion consists" (*ibid.:* 292). This was consistent with the Pietist understanding of conversion as a profound transformation of the heart that would lead to a change in outward behaviour without the need for enforcement by external rules. Dennis Hudson writes:

> Following Luther, [the missionaries] taught their Tranquebar congregation that if faith were genuine, the Word of God working in their hearts would transform their everyday life; once they recognized sin, they would renounce it voluntarily ... Outside the basic discipline required by baptism into the Danish Lutheran Church, the Pietist German Lutheran missionaries made no effort, as did later German and British 'Calvinists', to legislate an ideal social relationship between believers in the New Jerusalem Church. In particular, they did not employ external authority or force to erase caste distinctions in the matter of 'sitting together separately' during worship. Whatever changes in caste observance that might emerge among the congregation, they believed, should come from an inward 'rebirth' of the heart, not from an external application of law. (2000: 37)

Thus the evidence from the early years of the mission does not seem to support the strong claim Jeyaraj makes for Ziegenbalg as a resolute opponent of caste. Rather, as the comments of Singh (1999: 56) and Dharamapal-Frick (1995: 92), cited above, and Sharpe (1998: 127), cited below, suggest, there seems to have been no decisive position taken on caste in the early years of the mission in part because the missionaries shared the distinction made by John Locke and William Penn[17] in the late seventeenth century between an 'inner' religious sphere and an 'outward' worldly sphere, and relegated caste distinctions to the latter.

In 1726, seven years after Ziegenbalg's death, the missionaries reported that although they had to make some concessions to caste "in *politicis*", this did not happen at all "in *ecclesiasticis*".[18] Just over a year later, however, they admitted that as a concession to the weakness of the converts, they had allowed the practice of the Paraiyars sitting one stride apart from the śūdras in the church; only in regard to the sacraments was no difference acknowledged.[19] Gensichen notes that the significance of their introduction of a distinction between the "civil" (*bürgerlich*) and "religious" (*religiös*) spheres, can "hardly be overestimated" (1975: 174). While the distinction was to become increasingly important in the mission's later defence of its practice in relation to caste, as Gensichen suggests, there remains the question of "where, in relation to the caste question, does the political end, and where does the ecclesiastical begin?" (*ibid.:* 174). This question was never debated as intensively in the Protestant missions of the eighteenth century as it was in the contemporary Catholic missions, perhaps because of the relative newness of the former. While Protestant writers were certainly aware of the Catholic debate,[20] Eric Sharpe suggests that in the eighteenth century it had not yet become a central issue for the missionaries themselves:

> It seems clear that the Danish-Halle missionaries in the eighteenth century were content to regard caste as no more than a local pattern of social organization, some-times a nuisance, but otherwise worthy of attention only as an element of that arch-enemy of the Pietists, 'the world.' They neither exaggerated nor minimized its importance, nor did they have any preconceived notions about its character; they were however prepared to deal with its effects as they arose.          (1998: 127)

While this brief discussion of the Jesuit and Danish-Halle missions by no means exhausts the evidence on missionary views of caste in the eighteenth century, it does at least sug-gest that in the eighteenth century there was no 'missionary orthodoxy' that held caste to be an essentially religious institution. The debate over the nature of caste by no means came to an end with the papal ruling on the Malabar rites debate in 1744, and the works of the Jesuits – and, through them, Dubois – continued to be informed by a different view of caste. Moreover the issue was to be reopened following the restoration of the Jesuits,[21] and was yet to come to a head in the Protestant missions.

## THE *MINUTE ON CASTE* AND THE EMERGENCE OF A
## MISSIONARY ORTHODOXY ON CASTE

Toward the end of the eighteenth century the Danish-Halle mission founded by Ziegenbalg entered a period of decline, to which both a more rationalist mood in the German church of the *Aufklärung* and irregular support from Denmark contributed. In 1825 the mission came under the effective control of the Anglican Society for the Propagation of the Gospel (SPG), and later suffered the indignity of its Lutheran clergy (whose orders were not recognized by the Church of England) being required to be reordained. The same period saw the first Protestant missions in the north of India established. Although at first missionaries there were "willing to tolerate a degree of caste distinction both in their schools and among their converts" (Forrester 1980: 25), in the early decades of the nineteenth century they began to take a much stricter line against caste. Despite this developing Protestant intolerance of caste in the north, the SPG permitted the formerly Lutheran missions to continue their practice of tolerating caste on the basis that the spiritual equality of believers in Christ was "in no way incompatible with the various distinctions of rank and degrees in society which are recognised in the Gospel itself" (*ibid.*: 34). In the 1840s the newly established, and pas-sionately Lutheran, Leipzig Missionary Society began to reclaim the territory and the tradi-tion of the old Danish-Halle mission. Like the founders of the Danish-Halle mission, the new Leipzig missionaries, and especially Heinrich Cordes, the first of the Leipzig missionaries, and Karl Graul, Missiondirektor from 1844, took a flexible approach to the issue of caste.[22]

Graul wrote that the Leipzig missionaries "view Caste among the Native Christians in the light of a national institution, devoid of its superadded heathenish basis" (quoted in Sharpe 1998: 132), and argued that caste practices when carried out by Indian Christians did not have the same significance as the same practices carried out by Hindus. As Sharpe points out, Graul was deeply influenced by German Romanticism, which not only emphasized the distinctive identity of different *Völker* – each with its own *Kultur* based on, among other things, a shared language, religion and form of social organization – but was also profoundly Indophilic: "in the Romantic scale of values, no non-Western culture stood higher than that of India in respect of natural virtue" (*ibid.*: 135). This predisposition to a sympathetic view of caste was further reinforced by what Sharpe characterizes as a "hierarchical and bitterly anti-democratic" social theory. The Leipzig missionaries were nourished by a 'neo-Lutheran' movement, whose "vision of society was ... least of all egalitarian; rather it presupposed something not altogether different from a caste system of *Amt* and *Stand*" (*ibid.*: 128). Thus their tolerance of caste was more than just an expression of their self-understanding as the true inheritors of the Danish-Halle tradition, although it was that too.[23]

From 1849, largely because of their position on caste, the Leipzig churches began to receive 'fugitives' from other Protestant missions. The extent of the threat this posed to other missions is clear from the fact that, as Sharpe reports "by 1856, the Leipzig Mission had become the third largest Protestant agency in South India" (*ibid.*: 134). It was this threat, keenly perceived by other missions, that prompted the 1850 *Minute on Caste* of the Madras Missionary Conference,[24] cited by Dirks as expressing "what became missionary orthodoxy by 1850"; namely, that caste "is in its nature, essentially a religious institution and not a mere civil distinction" (quoted in Dirks 2001: 131–2).

There was thus a substantial change in Protestant missionary views of caste from the beginning of the nineteenth century, when few missionaries viewed caste as an essentially religious institution, to mid-century when the Leipzig missionaries were the only body of missionaries officially to maintain this view. The history of the emergence of this "Protestant consensus on caste" has largely been written from the point of view of the missionaries themselves, on the basis of their letters and published statements on caste.[25] There also exist, however, sources that enable us to trace the history of this change from the point of view of those most immediately and substantially affected by it; namely, Indian converts to Christianity. The sources consist mostly of petitions protesting the change to a stricter policy on caste written by high status Śūdra Christians.[26] The most prolific, and probably the most influential, of these was Vedanāyakam Piḷḷai (1774–1864), better known by his title Vedanāyakam Sastri (*cāstiri*). For 35 years Vedanāyakam was headmaster of the seminary in Tanjore established by Christian Friedrich Schwartz of the Danish-Halle mission. In 1829, as a result of the dispute over caste, he resigned his position, and was appointed court poet to Serfoji II of Tanjore. Over a period of three decades, Vedanāyakam produced a series of works in defence of the earlier Protestant missionaries' policy on caste, which saw high and low caste converts "sitting together separately" in church and high caste converts receiving the sacrament of the Lord's Supper before those of lower caste. In 1824 Vedanāyakam wrote a "Dialogue on the Difference of Caste" (*cātiyācāracampāvinai*), the preface of which was included in a larger collection of documents entitled "The Foolishness of Amending Caste" (*cātitiruttalin payittiyam*) compiled in 1828 as the dispute over caste, which had begun in congregations near Madras, gathered force and spread to Tanjore.[27] In 1854, his 80th year, Vedanāyakam wrote an "Afflictive Letter" in response to a tract by George Uglow Pope critical of the Lutheran mission's policy on caste.[28] Vedanāyakam is also probably responsible for a response to the Madras Conference *Minute on Caste* produced by the Lutheran congregations. The document, in Tamil with partial English translation, is dated 1851 and has two parts, the first entitled "Refutation against the Minute on Caste" (*cāti-t-tīrmāṉa-āṭcēpam*) and the second "The Petition of Tamil Christians" (*tamiḻ-k-kiristavarkaḷiṉ viṇṇa[ppa]pattiram*).[29] The Refutation is addressed to Cordes, the first of the Leipzig Society's missionaries, and to his colleague J. M. N. Schwartz; the Petition is addressed only to "the Revd. Recent Missionaries who came to preach the Gospel in India". The language, in both Tamil and English, is strong and the tone is sharp, at points extremely so. Although the authors of the text are identified only as the "Tamil Protestant Christians", or the "poor Tamil Christians", the intent and language of the text is very similar to that of Vedanāyakam's other works, and the wording is at times identical to that of another 1851 petition by him addressed to the Secretary of the SPG in Madras, A. R. Symonds.[30] Two of many arguments advanced in the "Refutation" and "Petition" against the *Minute*'s position on caste are of interest here. The first is that the changes were an innovation, introduced by new generation of missionaries in the space of the past twenty or thirty years.[31] Their practice is repeatedly contrasted with that of "the former missionaries", among whom in addition to "the Venerable Ziegenbalg", Vedanāyakam's "Guru" Schwartz and close friend John Caspar Kohlhoff are mentioned by name.[32] The second argument relies on the religion–secular distinction to claim that caste is a "civil privilege" and the "urbanity of the country", essentially similar to "the rank of Europeans" and therefore "neither sin nor heathenism".[33] The evidence of Vedanāyakam's "Refutation" and "Petition" demonstrates that until the 1820s Lutheran missionaries continued to tolerate some elements of caste among their congregations, and did so on the basis of an articulation of the religion–secular distinction. Together with Vedanāyakam's other writings, it also shows that from that time a new generation of missionaries in the south began to regard caste as essentially religious and hence incompatible with Christianity. It also indicates the depth of resistance that the new missionary orthodoxy on caste was to provoke in the south.

## CONCLUSION

Dirks identifies missionaries as the source of both the colonial state's concern with caste as the central feature of Indian civilization, and the "religious confinement of caste" on the basis of the modern distinction between the religious and the secular, which, as he demonstrates, functioned to enable the particular form of indirect rule that the British exercised in India. We have seen, however, that despite the papal ruling against them in the rites debate, the Jesuits of the later eighteenth century continued to present caste as a civil institution and thus something not incompatible with the practice of Christianity.

A distinction between the 'political' and the 'ecclesiastical' significance of caste is evident, although not elaborated, in Protestant missionary writings from at least the 1720s. Caste was not constructed as something primarily religious, and thus essentially incompatible with the practice of Christianity, until the debate over caste in the 1820s and the following decades. In his final version of Cœurdoux's text, and in his *Letters on the State of Christianity in India*, Dubois anticipated by a few years the growing tendency to a different view of caste among Protestants that culminated in the Madras Conference's emphatic declaration that caste was "essentially a religious institution".[34] It is open to question to what extent these changes in missionary views are themselves attributable to changes in the colonial context. The third and fourth decades of the nineteenth century were a time of significant change in the colonial enterprise, particularly under the reformist rule of Lord William Bentinck, Governor-General from 1828. The same period saw a marked increase in antipathy for both Hinduism and caste. Katharine Prior *et al.* note that the "official sanctioning of caste prejudices was particularly abhorrent" (2001: 94) to Charles Trevelyan, whom they understand as representative of a new generation of East India Company servants in the 1820s, which formed the bulk of the Anglicist party in the education debates of the 1830s. Other factors were also at work, however, which may have influenced missionary views of caste. Antony Copley argues that the years between 1830 and 1880 represent "a distinctive phase in the history of Protestant Mission in India" (1997a: 3). He identifies a mood of confidence among Evangelicals that gave rise to "an almost apocalyptic faith that Indian religions were in terminal decline" (*ibid.*: 14). When the expected conversions were not forthcoming, the missionaries "rather than admit that [their] millenarian belief in the superiority of Christianity over India's religions was ill-founded, scapegoated caste" (*ibid.*: 256). While Hudson takes the immediate cause of the debate over caste in the Lutheran congregations in the 1820s to be the result of an influx of a new generation of missionaries less sympathetic to Tamil culture, he suggests that ultimately the changes are to be explained by the fact that an "international Protestant mission operated within and through a developing colonial enterprise that had its own intellectual impact", transcending that of confessional differences:

> At the beginning of the nineteenth century, Protestant Malabarians had to face Enlightenment thought and values that had developed in the eighteenth century, ideas and values that had developed in the context of the international economy that had created Tranquebar itself. Europe had produced among its intellectual elite the idea of autonomous personhood in which the human body encodes individual 'rights' and 'duties' rather than the collective 'rights' and 'duties' of the holistic family, class or caste. It was that newly developing notion of personhood that had led the 'Junior Missionaries' in Tranquebar and Tanjore forcibly to change the mats in the church. (Hudson 2000: 185)[35]

The evidence presented here of missionary views of caste in the early stages of British colonial rule in the later eighteenth and early nineteenth century demonstrates that most missionaries, Catholic and Protestant, did not regard caste as incompatible with Christianity, and that it was not until the 1820s that it began to be widely regarded as an essential part of Hinduism, and thus of religious rather than merely social or civil significance. There appears, therefore, to be no straightforward relationship between colonialism and a view of caste as religious. This itself is in keeping with Dirks's statement that colonialism, both in itself and in its effect upon culture "was neither monolithic nor unchanging through history", but rather "a congeries of activities and a conjunction of outcomes that, though related and at times coordinated, were usually diffuse, disorganized and even contradictory" (1992: 7). This is not to deny that missionaries were significant agents for propagating the idea that caste was a religious institution, or even that the idea of caste as a religious institution later functioned to enable the indirect rule of the British in the way that Dirks suggests. However, British colonial rule in the second half of the eighteenth century does not appear to have relied on the construction of caste as religious. It may, therefore, be not so much a question of colonialism all the way down, as what sort of colonialism, and when.

## NOTES

1. I am grateful to the Alexander von Humboldt Foundation for the award of an Alexander von Humboldt Research Fellowship, during the tenure of which research for this paper was carried out.
2. See the influential work of Bernard Cohn (1983) and Dirks's own study of Pudukottai (1993).
3. Cf. Dirks (2001: 12).
4. The story (Geertz 1973: 28–9), appears in European writing on India as early as the seventeenth century (cf. Henrich 1963).
5. He writes, for example, "Dubois began *his* book by describing the 'caste system' in India, referring to the varna system as outlined in the *Dharma Sastras*" (Dirks 2001: 24, emphasis added). Cœurdoux's text begins in this way; see Murr (1987, I: 5ff.).
6. Although personally on good terms with the Jesuits, Dubois was "a respected member of the *Missions Étrangères*, a body traditionally hostile to the Jesuits" (Ballhatchet 1998: 3).
7. Later he seems to refer specifically to the *Description of the Character, Manners, and Customs of the People of India*, when he writes of "the continued prominence of Dubois's antiquated text" (Dirks 2001: 118).
8. In one of his works arising from the rites controversy Nobili states explicitly a further presupposition that underlies his practice, that "there is a norm by which we can distinguish between social actions and the purely religious" (Nobili 1971: 154–5). On the debate, and its influence on Jesuit conceptions of Hinduism, see Sweetman (2003).
9. Although the papal legate commissioned to decide the matter, Charles de Tournon, came down against 'adaptation' in 1704, Jesuits of the Indian missions continued to argue their case, and to maintain their practices, until the final bull, *Omnium Sollicitudinum*, of Benedict XIV in 1744.
10. Although the text published by Murr is not what she calls "l'Ur-manuscrit Cœurdoux", which is lost, but a version prepared by N. J. Desvaulx, she concludes that the changes made to Cœurdoux's manuscript consist for the most part in partial updating of the text and a reduction in its length (see Murr 1987, II: 56).
11. Dirks's account of Dubois is based on the third edition (1906) of Beauchamp's 1897 translation of the French edition of 1825, which is also cited here. This version differs considerably from the English translation, published in 1817, of the manuscript Dubois first offered to the East India Company in 1806. Beauchamp states that the work "was completely altered, recast and enlarged, until it bore

hardly more resemblance to the original work than a rough outline sketch does to a finished picture" (Dubois 1906: xvii). The corresponding chapter in the 1817 edition makes the same claims about the natural indolence of the Hindus, and the need for a religious sanction for all their customs and observances, but somewhat less emphatically. Later editions presumably reflect more closely Dubois's own views, perhaps as they developed, but in both editions there is a clear contrast with Cœurdoux's views, at least in so far as these are preserved in the manuscript of Desvaulx.

12. On Ziegenbalg's considerable contribution to the early development of Indological scholarship see Sweetman (2005).

13. Cf. Ziegenbalg (1926: 192–5).

14. Cf. *ibid.*, 199.

15. Cf. Gensichen (1975: 173).

16. Germann (1868: 285) denies this, but without citing any source; Arno Lehmann (1956: 99) concludes that we have no evidence either way for the earliest missionaries, but notes (1956: 105) that on arrival in Tranquebar in 1777 a new missionary reported to Halle that two cups were in use and Grafe (1990: 98–9) adds that this may again have been the case in 1799.

17. See Fitzgerald, Chapter 11.

18. *Der Königl. Dänischen Missionarien aus Ost-Indien eingesandter Ausführlichen Berichte. Anderer Theil, von der XIII. bis XXIV. Continuation.* Contin. XXII, 862.

19. *Ibid.* Contin. XXV, 39.

20. Cf. La Croze's comment on the Jesuits' justification for their adoption of *vipūti*, or *tiruniṟu* (ashes of cow dung): "Ces Missionaires pretendent que c'est un signe de noblesse, comme en effect c'en est un, mais de noblesse superstitieuse & fondée sur l'Idolatrie" (These missionaries make out that it is a sign of nobility, and in effect it is one, but one of a nobility that is superstitious and founded on idolatry) (La Croze 1724: 448).

21. Cf. Grafe (1990: 109). On the issue in other Catholic missions see also Ballhatchet (1998).

22. On the history of the Danish-Halle/Leipzig mission in the nineteenth century, and its position on caste, see Sharpe (1998) (from where much of the information given here is derived) and Bergunder (2000). Neill (1985: 407) prefers to emphasize Graul's acceptance that caste should eventually, if only slowly, be eliminated from the church.

23. Sharpe describes this as the "first, and perhaps the most important of the Leipzig missionaries' convictions" (1998: 127). Cf. Bergunder (2000: 33).

24. Sharpe quotes a later document from the Madras conference that "mentioned that at the root of the controversy had been the Dresden/Leipzig reception of fugitives from 'the Right communion of the Church of England' on the ground of caste" (1998: 132).

25. See, for example, Forrester (1980: 23–47).

26. Examples of these petitions are held in the Tamil Nadu Archives (cf. Frykenberg 2003: 14–15; Grafe 1990: 100), the British Library (cf. Hudson 2000: 140), United Theological College, Bangalore (cf. Copley 1997b: 198, 224) and the Evangelisch-Lutherisches Missionswerk Leipzig (see further below).

27. For details see Hudson (2000: 140–41).

28. *The Lutheran Aggression: A Letter to the Tranquebar Missionaries, regarding "Their position, their proceedings and their doctrine"* (Madras: Printed for the author at the American Mission Press, 1853). Cf. Copley (1997b: 198–200).

29. The manuscript is in the archive of the Evangelisch-Lutherisches Missionswerk Leipzig (LMW), shelfmark E225 (Tamil text of the "Refutation" and "Petition", and English text of the Petition) and E226 (English text of the first seven (of ten) chapters of the Refutation). Quotations are from the English translation, except where dates have been corrected by comparison with the Tamil, which is internally more consistent. I am grateful to the Rev. J. Chellappa for drawing my attention to the manuscript and for discussing it with me.

30. Discussed by Copley (1997b: 198–9).

31. In the Preface to the Refutation the practice of Ziegenbalg and Schwartz is contrasted with that of "the recent Missionaries who came from 1830" and their agents among the congregations (LMW E226, ix). Elsewhere the change is said to have occurred in "the time of the late Revd. Rhenius" and a "space

of 30 years" is mentioned (LMW E226, 72–3). Rhenius, a resolute opponent of caste, was active in the churches founded by the Danish-Halle mission from 1820, which would coincide with the period of 30 years given in the "Refutation".
32. E.g. LMW E226, v–vi, xi, 8, 27, 28, 32, 36, 51, 66, 72, 77. Cf. LMW E225, 1–2, 11–12.
33. LMW E226, viii, xii, 6.
34. Dubois's *Letters on the State of Christianity in India* was first published in 1823, but the letters are dated 1815 and 1816. His final version of Cœurdoux's text was first published in French in 1825 (see note 11 above).
35. The mats had previously marked the sitting areas for different castes in the church.

## BIBLIOGRAPHY

Ballhatchet, Kenneth. 1998. *Caste, Class and Catholicism in India 1789-1914*. London: Curzon.

Bergunder, Michael. 2000. "Geschichte der Leipziger Mission". In *Quellenbestände der Indienmission 1700-1918 in Archiven des deutschsprachigen Raums*, eds E. Pabst and T. Müller-Bahlke, 32–4. Halle: Verlag der Franckeschen Stiftungen zu Halle.

Cohn, Bernard S. 1983. "Representing Authority in Victorian India". In *The Invention of Tradition*, eds Eric Hobsbawm and Terence Ranger, 165–209. Cambridge: Cambridge University Press.

Copley, Antony. 1997a. *Religions in Conflict: Ideology, Cultural Contact and Conversion in Late Colonial India*. Delhi: Oxford University Press.

Copley, Antony. 1997b. "George Uglow Pope contra Vedanayagam Sastriar: a case-study in the clash of 'new' and 'old' mission". In *Religious Conversion Movements in South Asia: Continuities and Change, 1800-1900*, ed. Geoffrey Oddie, 173–228. London: Curzon.

Dharampal, Gita. 1982. *La religion des Malabars: Tessier de Quéralay et la contribution des missionnaires Européens a la naissance de l'indianisme*. Immensee: Nouvelle Revue de Science Missionnaire.

Dharampal-Frick, Gita. 1995. "Shifting Categories in the Discourse on Caste: Some Historical Observations". In *Representing Hinduism: The Construction of Religious Traditions and National Identity*, eds Vasudha Dalmia and Heinrich von Stietencron, 82–98. London: Sage.

Dharampal-Frick, Gita. 1999. "Malabarisches Heidenthum: Bartolomäus Ziegenbalg über Religion und Gesellschaft der Tamilen". In *Missionsberichte aus Indien in 18. Jahrhundert*, ed. M. Bergunder, 126–52. Halle: Verlag der Franckeschen Stiftungen zu Halle.

Dirks, Nicholas B. 1992. "Introduction: Colonialism and Culture". In *Colonialism and Culture*, ed. N. B. Dirks, 1–25. Ann Arbor, MI: University of Michigan Press.

Dirks, Nicholas B. 1993. *The Hollow Crown*, 2nd edn. Ann Arbor, MI: University of Michigan Press. (Originally published Cambridge: Cambridge University Press, 1987.)

Dirks, Nicholas B. 2001. *Castes of Mind: Colonialism and the Making of Modern India*. Princeton, NJ: Princeton University Press.

Dubois, J. A. 1823. *Letters on the State of Christianity in India; in which the conversion of the Hindoos is considered as impracticable, to which is added a vindication of the Hindoos, male and female, in answer to a severe attack made upon both by the Reverend \*\*\*\*\**. London: Longman, Hurst, Rees, Orme, Brown and Green.

Dubois, J. A. 1906. *Hindu Manners, Customs and Ceremonies*. Trans. and ed. H. K. Beauchamp. Oxford: Clarendon.

Forrester, Duncan B. 1980. *Caste and Christianity: Attitudes and Policies on Caste of Anglo-Saxon Missions in India*. London: Curzon.

Frykenberg, Robert Eric. 2003. "Introduction: Dealing with Contested Definitions and Controversial Perspectives". In *Christians and Missionaries in India: Cross-Cultural Communications since 1500*, ed. Robert Eric Frykenberg. London: RoutledgeCurzon.

Geertz, Clifford. 1973. "Thick Description: Toward an Interpretive Theory of Culture". In *The Interpretation of Cultures: Selected Essays*, ed. Clifford Geertz, 3–30. New York: Basic Books.

Gensichen, Hans-Werner. 1975. "'Dienst der Seelen' und 'Dienst des Leibes' in der frühen pietistischen Mission". In *Der Pietismus in Gestalten und Wirkungen*, eds H. Bornkamm, F. Heyer and A. Schindler, 155–78. Bielefeld: Luther-Verlag.

Germann, Wilhelm. 1883. "Bartholomäus Ziegenbalg als Bahnbrecher der lutherischen Mission". *Allgemeine Missions-Zeitschrift* 10: 481–97, 529–39.

Germann, Wilhelm. 1868. *Ziegenbalg und Plütschau: Die Gründungsjahre der Trankebarschen Mission. Ein Beitrag zur Geschichte des Pietismus nach handschriftlichen Quellen und ältesten Drucken*, 2 vols. Erlangen: Verlag von Andreas Deichert.

Grafe, Hugald. 1990. *History of Christianity in India; Vol. 4, Pt 2. The History of Christianity in Tamilnadu from 1800 to 1975*. Erlangen: Verlag der Ev.-Luth. Mission.

Gründler, Johann Ernst, and Bartholomäus Ziegenbalg. 1998. *Die malabarische Korrespondenz: tamilische Briefe an deutsche Missionare; eine Auswahl*. Ed. K. Liebau. Sigmaringen: Thorbecke.

Henrich, Dieter. 1963. "Die 'wahrhafte Schildkröte'". *Hegel-Studien* 2: 281–91.

Hudson, D. Dennis. 2000. *Protestant Origins in India: Tamil Evangelical Christians, 1706-1835*. Richmond: Curzon.

Jeyaraj, Daniel. 1996. *Inkulturation in Tranquebar: Der Beitrag der frühen dänisch-halleschen Mission zum Werden einer indisch-einheimischen Kirche (1706-1730)*. Erlangen: Verlad der Ev.-Luth. Mission.

La Croze, Mathurin Veyssière de. 1724. *Histoire du christianisme des Indes*. La Haye: Frères Vaillant & N. Prevost.

Lehmann, Arno. 1956. *Es begann in Tranquebar: Die Geschichte der ersten evangelischen Kirche in Indien*, 2nd edn. Berlin: Evangelische Verlagsanstalt.

Murr, Sylvia. 1987. *L'Inde philosophique entre Bousset et Voltaire*, 2 vols. Vol. I. Mœurs et coutumes des Indiens (1777) Vol. II. L'indologie du Père Cœurdoux. Paris: École française d'Extrême Orient.

Neill, Stephen. 1985. *A History of Christianity in India. Vol. II. 1707-1858*. Cambridge: Cambridge University Press.

Nobili, Roberto. [1619] 1971. *Narratio Fundamentorum quibus Madurensis Missionis Institutum caeptum est et hucusque consisit*. Trans. J. Pujo, ed. S. Rajamanickam. Palayamkottai: De Nobili Research Institute.

Prior, Katherine, Lance Brennan and Robin Haines. 2001. "Bad Language: The Role of English, Persian and other Esoteric Tongues in the Dismissal of Sir Edward Colebrooke as Resident of Delhi in 1829". *Modern Asian Studies* 35: 75–112.

Sharpe, Eric. 1998. "'Patience with the Weak': Leipzig Lutherans and the Caste Question in Nineteenth-Century South India". In *Religious Traditions in South Asia: Interaction and Change*, ed. G. A. Oddie, 125–37. Richmond: Curzon.

Singh, Brijraj. 1999. *The First Protestant Missionary to India: Bartholomaeus Ziegenbalg, 1683-1719*. New Delhi: Oxford University Press.

Sweetman, Will. 2003. *Mapping Hinduism: "Hinduism" and the study of Indian Religions, 1600-1776*. Halle: Verlag der Franckeschen Stiftungen zu Halle.

Sweetman, Will. 2005. "The Prehistory of Orientalism: Colonialism and the Textual Basis for Bartholomäus Ziegenbalg's account of Hinduism". *New Zealand Journal of Asian Studies* 6: 12–38.

Ziegenbalg, Bartholomäus. 1926. *Ziegenbalg's Malabarisches Heidenthum*. Ed. W. Caland. Amsterdam: Uitgave van Koninklijke Akademie.

# 7

# Understanding politics through performance in colonial and postcolonial India

## John Zavos

Religion has always been a looming presence in understandings of Indian politics in the colonial and postcolonial periods. Much scholarly time and trouble has been spent examining the way religion operates, and what its presence means for the development of Indian political structures. The classic dichotomy between the religious and the secular spheres underpins this concern. This is particularly so, of course, in recent times, as the polity has come to be dominated increasingly by forces claiming to represent specific religious identities. The state election result in Gujarat late in 2002, for example, was proclaimed a victory for Hindutva, for 'Hindu-ness' and the 'Hindu community' as it has been invoked by the Bharatiya Janata Party (BJP) and its allies. It was another nail in the coffin of the secular polity.

Ironically this development is occurring precisely at a time when the idea of religion is being questioned as a viable, discrete category for understanding certain cultural systems, particularly in a non-Western framework. In his recent book *The Ideology of Religious Studies* (2000), Tim Fitzgerald has argued that the category 'religion' developed in the particular context of post-Enlightenment Europe as a facet of capitalist development. The emergence of the rational, secular public marketplace invoked the idea of a mystical, private sphere of religion. Our understanding of the dichotomy between the religious and the secular is configured by this development. As a result, using the category 'religion' to understand the operation of non-Western systems is not only a misrepresentation, it is the continuation of a historic oppression. Rather like some arguments for the eradication of the concept of 'race' (see Miles 1993), therefore, Fitzgerald dispenses with the category of religion, and instead uses concepts such as ritual, soteriology and politics to understand and interpret, for example, the emergence of Ambedkarite Buddhism (Fitzgerald 2000: 128–32).

If we reflect on work concerned with the construction of Indian social categories, there is a degree of resonance to this argument. In particular, categories such as

'Hinduism' and 'caste' have long been understood as implicated in the development of colonial knowledge (Frykenberg 1993; Inden 1990). Yet despite this, political analysis has consistently implemented such categories as unproblematic. Nowhere is this more evident than in the analysis of election data on the basis of the so-called aggregationist model. This model understands voting behaviour as configured by community identity. People vote according to the interests of their community unit, and so it is the values of that community, normally defined in terms of either religion or caste, that are politically significant. As the anthropologist Thomas Hansen comments, this model has made the assumption that "communities (are) imputed collective wills, intelligence and rationalities" (2004: 19). Analysts have traditionally sought to understand Indian politics on the basis of these imputed community characteristics. Most major political parties in India take a similar approach. If you want to win an election in a particular area, you set about establishing an aggregate of different community votes, aligning yourself with an array of 'community interests', which will outweigh the aggregate established by your opponents. To a remarkable degree, then, this model has dominated the approach of both practitioners and theorists to the Indian voting public and the mechanics of political action.

Hansen has pointed out rather mischievously that if political parties were accurate in their assumptions that people will vote along community lines in this way, they would be able to win elections on a fairly regular basis, rather than, as he says, losing them "most of the time" (2004: 19). Given this point, the propensity of analysts to rely on a similar model for understanding Indian politics appears rather shaky. Indeed, he notes that a good deal of political analysis in India is given over to the explanation of apparent disjunctures between people's imputed identities and the way that they have voted – why, for example, should low-caste groups vote for self-evident high-caste parties such as the BJP, when this does not appear to serve their interests? If social and political identities are aligned in the uncomplicated way that the aggregationist model suggests, this does not make sense. His point is that this model cannot adequately encompass the complexity either of political action or of political identities in India. We might add, referring back to Fitzgerald, that the categories used to construct these identities – religion and caste – are themselves problematic. Indeed if we follow the logic of Fitzgerald's argument, we should dispense with them altogether, as they will only serve to mystify, rather than explain, the social and political relations they purport to describe.

How, then, is one to interpret Indian politics more accurately, with the hope of a better understanding? With an anthropologist's gaze, Hansen's solution is to foreground the idea of developing "public moods and sentiments", and the "production of authority" on local levels (2004: 20). Here, he says, the dynamics of politics are crafted. How political parties work with such dynamics is a key element in their ability to gain support and so win power. Foregrounding such ephemeral criteria enables Hansen to focus on what he has identified through ethnography as the key element in the success of the Shiv Sena in Mumbai politics: its "presence" in localities, established through a continual cycle of spectacles or performances that represent – "or better still ... express and create" – the locality (*ibid.*: 22). These performances constitute a style that encapsulates the worldview of the Sena, and its resonance within localities.

This identification of performance or spectacle as a means of understanding political culture again brings us back to Fitzgerald's arguments, because it presents itself as an analytical tool that cuts across the boundaries between the religious and the secular. The anthropologist Catherine Bell has usefully identified three aspects of performance that act as sites for the production of meaning. It is, she says, a multisensory experience that affects people's perceptions and interpretations; it "frames" activities (either at the time or subsequently), marking them out as "different", and therefore producing a form of "meta-communication"; and it has an "emergent" or transformative quality, it constructs, as Bell says, a new reality by virtue of its own dynamism (Bell 1997: 74–5). These points appear to echo Hansen's comments about the presence of the Sena in localities, the focus on public moods and sentiments, and in particular the expression and creation of communities. Bell's wider purpose is to investigate the social location of ritual, and her analysis of performance is one way in which she demonstrates the multiple contexts in which ritual has meaning, contexts that may otherwise be identified as discretely religious or secular. Of course, any performance has to rely on a range of ritual and symbolic forms in order to give it meaning within a given cultural and social context. Bell's analysis, focused on the sites for the production of meaning outlined here, shows that these forms are not constrained by categories of religion and secularity; they frequently cut across this imputed boundary, such that it is difficult to make the distinction between a ritual performance that is nominally religious and one that is not. As such, will the concept of performance help us to compare and understand a variety of political practices that might otherwise be constrained by the dichotomy between these two categories? In this chapter I shall investigate this issue through a comparison of performative politics in the colonial and postcolonial periods.

An investigation across history is salient because of an added dimension introduced by Hansen. He links the idea of performance to the actual form of democratic politics in the modern world. Drawing on the work of Claude Lefort, he pursues an argument that goes something like this: democracy is founded on the principle of representation – representation, that is, of itself (i.e. the democratic polity, or the abstract notion of 'the people'). At the same time, democratic politics creates the space for the articulation of diversity and opposition, which naturally leads to contestation over the principle of representation. This paradox means that representations of 'the people' find themselves in a continual cycle of struggle, as political society "is constantly in search of its own foundations" (Hansen 2004: 24). Performance and spectacle have a vital role to play, as they provide the most effective way to produce representations in this ever shifting arena; they become "generative political moments par excellence ... the heart of political society" (*ibid.*). Performance, then, emerges as an integral feature of the form of democratic politics.

Democracy, of course, is not an exclusively Indian trope. As such, this notion of political performance is potentially significant in multiple contexts across the modern world.

Nevertheless, Hansen says, it has a particular resonance in India, because here the idea has had an "extraordinarily rich and varied history" (*ibid.*). The key element here is the national movement, and in particular the development of strategies designed to induce mass involvement over the late nineteenth and early twentieth centuries. These strategies produced "a vast repertoire of spectacular representations and styles of mobilization" (*ibid.*), which have since been used to sustain and deepen the position of performance at the heart of Indian democracy.

At first sight this connection appears to be self-evident, a point emphasized by the fact that Hansen simply refers to it here, rather than exploring it in any depth. In addition, other authors have examined performative aspects of the national movement (see e.g. Gooptu 2001; Masselos 1987). A key problem with respect to this element of Hansen's analysis, however, remains how these pre-Independence performative moments relate to postcolonial performative moments, if the latter are so clearly generated as an aspect of democratic politics. This is because the operation of politics in the pre-Independence period is significantly problematized by the lack of an overarching framework of democracy. In this period, the locus of power is not so much the abstract notion of 'the people', but the rather more clearly identifiable edifice of the colonial state: a set of institutions that were, in the final analysis, quite antithetical to democracy. This is not to say, however, that issues of representation were not significant in the pre-Independence period, as I shall endeavour to demonstrate. But the question remains as to what precisely the contextual dynamic was that sustained these earlier performative moments, if they did not have what Lefort might cite as the critical dynamic of representation in a democratic framework. And how has the transition from a non-democratic to a democratic framework affected the political meaning and value of performance? What changes have occurred in the articulation of performance as political authority?

These are questions that I shall explore in this chapter, by examining first the character of performance as a feature of the anti-colonial nationalist movement, and then the implications of this character for postcolonial politics. My argument will be that a central performative idiom emerged in the earlier period inscribed with a very particular sense of moral authority. This idiom and its inscribed authority developed into a major discursive tool in postcolonial politics. In making this connection, I shall demonstrate a continuity not just between pre- and post-Independence political action, but also between political action that we might otherwise perceive as 'secular' and 'religious' (and therefore of a different type). Performance becomes a means of understanding politics that cuts across this problematic dichotomy. But as well as continuity, there has been change; particularly, as noted at the beginning of this paper, the increasingly intense focus on religious and caste identities in national- and state-level politics. By understanding politics through performance, I shall suggest that rather than being indicative of a drift away from secularism in the polity, this change is a development in the substantive quality of democracy in the post-Independence state.

## PRE-INDEPENDENCE: THE CONTOURS OF NATIONALIST PERFORMANCE

In the first instance, then, let us look at the emergence of nationalist performative politics. Even if we look at the early period of nationalist development, we can see that a distinctive relationship between performance and representation is apparent. The so-called 'moderate' political discourse of people such as G. K. Gokhale and Surendranath Banerjea was directed towards the construction and maintenance of a dialogue with the state. This dialogue occurred through petitions to state bodies, through the development of personal networks, and through institutional participation made possible by the limited constitutional concessions released by the state. These actions were initiated by organizations such as the early Congress, which had no real democratic infrastructure. Nevertheless these early leaders and organizations were articulated as representative of 'the nation'. What is striking is that this articulation consistently implemented the language of parliamentary democracy, despite the complete autocracy of the state (see Zavos 2000a: 69–70). A public space was emerging in which the performance of representative politics – what one might term 'quasi-democracy' – was constituted as legitimate, despite the lack of any mechanisms of representation.[1] Significantly, this form of discourse began to be projected by the colonial government as a form of 'loyal opposition', particularly as more radical nationalist strategies were established in the early twentieth century (see *ibid.*: 104–5). What I am suggesting is that the performance of representative politics during this period was part of the state's construction of power, in a similar way to its construction of power in relation to princely states through Durbars and other elaborate, orientalist rituals (see Cohn 1992). The performative elements of moderate nationalism, then, may be perceived as part of a broader, governmental performance. In effect, the government could be said to be developing a strategy designed to institute quasi-democracy as a feature of the colonial polity.

One interesting feature of this form of politics was its ability to conceptualize some very broad constituencies in a relatively unproblematic fashion. Because the idea of representation was quasi-democratic, it was easy to invoke the idea of the people or the nation as a constituency. Equally, this discourse allowed for the invocation of religious communities as political constituencies. Undoubtedly the state encouraged this particular form of identity politics, projecting the image of 'the Hindus' and 'the Muslims' as fixed identities, which required separate representation. This idea was institutionalized in the notion of separate electorates, which were introduced in 1909 as part of the Morley–Minto constitutional reform package, a package that was wholeheartedly supported by the moderate Congress. The idea was, of course, to have a profound impact on the development of democratic politics in India, but it is important to remember that it emerged in the peculiarly colonial discursive arena of quasi-democracy, where the concept of large, homogeneous communities could be floated with relative impunity.

Just as these putative ideas of Hindu and Muslim constituencies were beginning to establish themselves in early-twentieth-century political life in India, the form of politics within which they were articulated was becoming increasingly undermined. New strategies of nationalist action emerged from the 1890s onwards, which were directed not so much at the state, as at the idea of 'the people'. Elite nationalists such as B. G. Tilak and Aurobindo Ghosh were concerned to legitimize their representative claims by actively expanding the nationalist constituency. Richard Cashman (1975) and, more recently, Raminder Kaur (2004) have demonstrated how in the 1890s in Bombay Presidency, performance emerged as a key element in the development of this new approach. Both authors focus on the Ganapati festival, which was transformed during this period from a festival "confined primarily to the temple and the house" (Kaur 2004: 44) into extravagant public celebrations, including procession and immersion of large Ganapati *murtis* (images) accompanied by strident *mela* (singing) parties singing songs with a clear political content (Cashman 1975: 77–8). Kaur demonstrates how in Pune public celebration of the Ganapati festival was inspired by the Bhau Rangari Ganapati Mandal, which from 1892 promoted a public procession and immersion. The *murti* depicted the deity in the act of killing a *rakshasa* (demon) "as a personification of action and even violence" (*Maharashtra Herald*, 17 December 1990, quoted in Kaur 2004: 45). Kaur further notes that "as the remover of obstacles (*vighna*) in the way of national justice and self-determination, [Ganapati] is vividly recruited for the world of performative politics" (*ibid.*: 47).

Traditionally, this development in late-nineteenth-century Maharashtra has been identified as problematic because of its 'introduction' of religion into politics (Cashman 1975), an inappropriate and unfortunate incursion into a secular realm. Examining the same development using performance as a tool brings a rather different set of issues to the fore. The performance of moderate politics, with its gaze firmly fixed on the legitimizing authority of the colonial state, had employed a set of ritual and symbolic forms with meaning within that particular context; namely, the ritual and symbolic forms of parliamentary democracy. Extremist politics emerged with a very different audience – a prototypical vision of the Indian 'people' – and employed a set of ritual and symbolic forms within *that* particular context. The particular ritual and symbolic forms employed indicate the cultural context of the actors and their imagined constituency: a context of martial, *kshatriya* action as embodied in a developing Maratha identity (Kaur 2004: 46; see also O'Hanlon 1985: 15–49, 295–6). A reference to Bell's model enables us to see how these forms worked to produce specific meanings through performance. First, the new form of the festival emphasized the involvement of people in politics, not just as actors but also as audiences, audiences that are directly invoked as critical by the new public nature of the celebration; secondly, the symbolism associated with particular *murtis* and the didactic quality of the *melas* actively worked to frame the festival with specific meanings related to nationalism and *kshatriya* action; these meanings and the invocation of the public worked to construct a new reality, to "express and create" a new community of (dynamic, martial) nationalists. Ganapati may be understood, then, as indicative of the self-conscious desire of some nationalist politicians and other local leaders to underline their representativeness in the undemocratic context of the colonial public space. These desires are mediated by cultural signifiers that underline the power of the nationalist elite, both in the arena of colonial politics and in the arena of social relations.

One important point to be drawn from this example is that even the more radical wing of the Congress was constrained by the limitations of what I have termed quasi-democracy. Performance emerges as a means of articulating images of representation precisely in a political context that lacks representational structures. At the same time, the didactic quality of symbolic images and *mela* songs emphasizes the concern of elite nationalists to maintain control over their emergent constituency. This kind of control was, of course, more easily maintained in a context that lacked such structures. The pattern may be seen in more detail by looking at the development of nationalist politics in the post-First World War era. As it came out of the war, the government committed itself to an extension of constitutional reforms that undoubtedly increased the level of Indian involvement in the mechanisms of government, as well as the representative quality of this involvement. This was still a very limited form of democratic process, but it did emphasize the issue of representation across the political spectrum. M. K. Gandhi emerged as a key political figure in this context. He worked with ideas of representation that pushed at, and frequently transgressed, the boundaries of political acceptability (see below, and also Zavos 2000a: 128–9). At the same time, he used the limitations of the democratic space to retain a very particular sense of control over the development of nationalist action. The implications of this paradox are demonstrated by examining Gandhi's approach to political action, first in direct relation to representation and then through an understanding of his approach to performance.

It is no coincidence that the first real national Satyagraha campaign, the Non-cooperation movement of 1920–22, was incorporated with a movement of primarily Muslim concern: the Khilafat movement. Gandhi stated in 1920 that not protesting against British post-war actions that impacted on the future of the caliphate in Turkey would amount to an admission of "slavery"; not only for Muslims but for all Indians (speech at Idgah, Karachi, in Gandhi 1965–7, vol. 18: 80). From the point of view of the development of ideas of representation, this political programme cut clearly across the lines of responsibility articulated by the state. Through separate electorates, the state had sent out the message that Muslims formed a discrete group within society, and that Congress and other non-Muslim organizations were unlikely to be able to represent their concerns; this was doubly so, of course, when the concern was apparently religious. The incorporation of the Khilafat movement with Non-cooperation challenged this model, both in terms of the representative claims of Congress, and in terms of the blending of apparently religious and non-religious concerns. At the same time, the campaign did not challenge the concepts of Hindu and Muslim as political entities, those entities that had emerged in the context of moderate nationalism/quasi-democracy. Gandhi repeatedly referred to support for the Khilafat movement as a case of Hindus helping Muslims "in this time of trouble" (*ibid.*; see also *ibid.*: 204, 265). It was a case of the Hindus, as a political force, assisting the Muslims, another political force. These separate forces remained a key element in his thinking about the realization of an independent India. Again in 1920 he stated that independence would be "a partnership between equals, each respecting the religion of the other" (*Young India* 6 October 1920; Gandhi 1965–7, vol. 18: 326–7). Similarly, in 1929 in a speech at Aligarh Muslim University he invoked Hindus and Muslims as "the two eyes of Mother India" (*ibid.*, vol. 42: 368). It is clear from this evidence that he saw notions of Hindu and Muslim as legitimate political identities, constituting building blocks for a broader political identity, that of Indian.

In the Non-cooperation/Khilafat campaign, then, Gandhi pushed at the boundaries of recognized political discourse. But it was, nevertheless, a push within particular limits. To an extent, this reflects the peculiarities of the quasi-democratic space opened up by the colonial state, as Gandhi operated in conjunction with Muslim politicians who saw themselves as representing 'Muslim opinion' in India, and his approach, as indicated above, reflected an awareness of the need to respect these claims, despite the lack of any democratic mandate. In effect, what this indicates for us is the fact that even though the image of democratic sanction was significant in the post-war period, the polity still lacked meaningful democratic structures. As a result, the colonial middle-class elites who had always dominated nationalist politics retained control, and were able to fashion the movement in their own image (see Guha 1993). Given the connection noted by Hansen between performance and democracy, this may be seen as having profound implications for the form of performative politics that emerged in the late colonial period. Nothing demonstrates this more clearly than Gandhi's key political strategy: Satyagraha.

In fact Satyagraha is perhaps better described as a framework rather than a strategy, as it provided the overall rationale for a series of strategies of direct action, such as economic, political and institutional boycott, and non-payment of taxes. Much like Ganapati, this rationale was embedded in a specific cultural context; action is again emphasized, but this is action inspired by a particular combination of Vaishnavite bhakti and renouncer traditions drawn from the cultural contours of Gujarat, and overlaid with the classic turn of the century Hindu middle-class concern with the spiritual degeneration of India. The rationale had an explicit objective: it aimed to demonstrate truth (*satya*). By a progressive demonstration of truth through non-violent action (*ahimsa*), Gandhi envisioned a purification of the spirit (*atmashuddhi*) of India, a complete moral regeneration – a form of liberation, then, which was way beyond the expulsion of the colonial oppressor. Gandhi's vision of politics was, as he explained in a letter in 1919, to "touch the vital being of India almost at every point" (letter to Arundale, 4 August 1919, in Iyer 1991: 110) in order to effect regeneration.

Touching the vital being of India necessarily meant mass involvement, but not just involvement; this had to be involvement that would further the project of *atmashuddhi*, spirit purification. The satyagrahi's objective, Gandhi stated in 1924, "must be absolutely pure ... like milk in its whiteness" (Gandhi 1965–7, vol. 24: 21). And this point is critical, because it meant that Satyagraha, as a framing rationale, had to be learnt. It necessitated a pedagogic approach in which a vanguard of "ideal satyagrahis", Congress volunteers, would demonstrate through their conduct how the search for truth should be conducted. In issuing instructions to volunteers during the Kheda Satyagraha in 1918, he stated that "the volunteers must remember that this is a holy war. We embarked upon it because, had we not, we would have failed in our dharma. And so all the rules which are essential for living a religious life must be observed" (*ibid.*, vol. 14: 350). Volunteers, then, were to observe "all the rules" of a "religious life", and in doing so they would inspire the peasants to do the same, and so advance nearer to truth, and the realization of the Indian nation. In this formula it can be seen that the idea of performance was critical to the development of Gandhian nationalism: performance laced with a grandiose moral vision of the future. Nationalist performance emerges as a powerful form of morality play, directed towards the "expression and creation" (with the emphasis very much on creation) of a purified Indian nation.

The didactic quality of Satyagraha as performance is evident in the Salt March of 1930. The march of seventy-eight satyagrahis from Gandhi's ashram near Ahmedabad to Dandi, some 240 miles away on the Gujarati coast, in order to make salt and so defy the so-called 'salt laws', was a carefully choreographed and quite masterly performative act. Although taking some three and a half weeks, each stage was planned in advance and the arrival at Dandi was timed to coincide with the annual nationalist commemoration of the Jallianwalabagh massacre of 1919, as was pointed out by Gandhi in his statement to the press on the evening before reaching Dandi (*ibid.*, vol. 43; 179). Gandhi recalled the dramatic moment of the departure of the march from the ashram in his Gujarati journal *Navajivan*:

> We walked on between rows of people who had come to see us set out, the rows extending to as far as the Chandola lake. I can never forget the scene. ... Both the rich and the poor were present in proportion to their numbers in the population. If the spectacle has any meaning, it is this, ... that all the people want freedom and they want it through peaceful means. (*Ibid.*: 83–4)

The significance of the audience to the "meaning" of the spectacle is evident here. Gandhi's curiously pedantic reference to the rich and poor being present "in proportion to their numbers in the population" reinforces the idea that the audience is symbolic of the watching nation. This idea is indeed expanded in the course of the march, as Gandhi reminded the press that "hundreds of thousands will follow this batch of seventy-eight in whatever they do", noting that "if the satyagrahis follow truth in carrying on this struggle, they will show not merely to India but to the whole world, that ours is a holy war" (*ibid.*: 73). And on performing the act of making salt once reaching Dandi, Gandhi noted that "India's self-respect, in fact her all, is symbolised as it were in a handful of salt in a satyagrahi's hand" (*ibid.*: 215).

The Salt March, then, may be viewed as a paradigmatic nationalist performance. The elements of Bell's model of performative meaning are clearly evident: the audience is integral to the significance of the event; the progress of the satyagrahis is framed as indicating the righteousness of the struggle; and the making of salt symbolizes the emergence, the self-realization, of the nation. Embedded in this cycle of meaning is the idea of Satyagraha – invoking the objective of *atmashuddhi* as a form of morality with specific cultural allusions.

This form of performative politics increasingly assumed the status of a template for nationalist activity, in which the moral allusions of Gandhi's approach were invoked by performative association, in what may be seen as a ritualized fashion. As Nandini Gooptu states, for example, in relation to nationalist campaigns in the 1930s, a "repertoire of powerful oppositional political rituals" was developed, which were deployed in "theatres of nationalist action" (2001: 325–6). Jim Masselos has examined the beginning of the Civil Disobedience campaign in Bombay in 1930 from the perspective of the "interrelationships between audience and actors" (1987: 71). He charts the development of a formulaic "pattern of protest" over a period of several weeks in the city, in which Gandhi's stipulated acts were to be implemented: *hartal*, parade and procession, manufacturing of salt, and the acceptance of *lathi* charges by the police. Masselos explains in detail how the audience was an integral feature of the performance, to the extent that very often the police directed their violent attacks on these performances as much at the audience as at the actors (1987: 79). This is a rather drastic illustration of Bell's idea of ritual-like performance as a multisensory experience. The audience, as she says, are "cognitively and emotionally pulled into a complex sensory experience that can also communicate a variety of messages" (1997: 160). Similarly, Gooptu highlights official concern about the presence of crowds observing the actions of nationalist volunteers. She cites the Commissioner of the Allahabad Division in 1931 as commenting on a gathering in Kanpur: "by far the most dangerous element is provided by the large crowds collected, which call out revolutionary cries and jaunt and jeer at the police and provide at the same time the most obvious and adequate symbol of a contempt of Government authority" (cited in Gooptu 2001: 329).

One interesting point to note is that the nature of audience participation did not always conform to the expectations of the Congress actors. For example the initial processions that were taken out to make salt in Bombay led to some occurrences of members of the audience spontaneously collecting foreign caps and other items of foreign cloth and making bonfires of them. This was a reference back to the earlier campaign of non-cooperation in 1920–22. It was not, however, a feature of the Congress-led campaign in 1930, and led the Provincial Congress Committee to issue a plea for caps not to be collected, although they could be "voluntarily offered ... for later disposal" by the Congress "authorities" (Masselos 1987: 73). This, of course, devalues the whole exercise, as it removes the performative resonance of public destruction. As such it demonstrates again the idea of framing in nationalist performance. Performance frames action as different, enabling it to be understood as "something other than routine reality" (Bell 1997: 160). That other is often a "mock-totality, an interpretive appropriation of some greater if elusive totality" (*ibid.*). In the context of Satyagraha, we can recognize this totality as *atmashuddhi*: the purification of the nation's spirit.

Congress in the 1920s and 1930s, then, used ritual performance to express its moral authority as the representative of a particular community: the community of Indians. The grammar of nationalist performance – non-violence, discipline, transgression, the assumption of a moral high ground in relation to institutional authority – was persistently directed towards the objective of *atmashuddhi*, the "expression and creation" of a purified nation. Congress performance at this stage, then, was very much a morality play based on some specific, high-caste, middle-class ideas of what constituted purity and righteousness; the grammar of that performance reflected this inflection.

As a means of making politics meaningful in the late colonial period, this grammar came to be implemented in a whole host of contexts that were not directly related to the cause of Congress nationalism. It was implemented, for example, in a campaign to insist on the right to play music before mosques in Nagpur in 1924 (see Zavos 2000a: 138–42). It is also evident in the early development of the Rashtriya Swayamsevak Sangh (RSS) after it was founded by K. B. Hedgewar in 1925, also in Nagpur. Hedgewar was an ex-Congress volunteer who had taken a significant role in the organization of the Nagpur Congress of 1920 (see *ibid.*: 189). Despite his growing antipathy during the 1920s towards Gandhian ideals such as *ahimsa*, Hedgewar's vision for his new organization was precisely to develop a core group of volunteers who would be able to demonstrate to the wider public what Hinduism really meant, and how it should be perceived, much like the Gandhian notion of developing a core group of satyagrahis who could demonstrate the meanings of the nation. Hedgewar's letters demonstrate his concern with the need for his volunteers to present a disciplined image, in the same manner as Gandhi was concerned with the discipline of Congress volunteers, as an expression of the moral regeneration of the nation (see Guha 1993). This was particularly important during public festivals, when the Sangh was very much on display.[2] The Sangh's performance at such festivals was exemplary, in the sense that it sought to set an example that represented its vision of the Hindu nation.

My argument so far has been that in the thirty years or so leading up to independence in India, a form of political expression was established that brought to the foreground the idea of performance as a means of representing constituencies in the limited public space of colonial politics. The characteristic quality of this form of political expression was its reliance on ritualized signifiers of a very particular kind of moral authority, associated with the Gandhian Congress movement. This moral authority was directed at the purification of the nation, and it was delivered through what may be called the ritual 'grammar' of nationalist performance: non-violence, transgression or defiance, discipline (particularly of a core group – a kind of moral vanguard), and the assumption of a moral high ground in relation to institutional authority. Elements of this grammar were used by a variety of organizations to practise politics in a variety of contexts – imputing a form of moral righteousness to their actions in the process. The dominant performative politics of the pre-Independence period, then, held a very particular significance in relation to the idea of representation and democracy. Yes, people were to be represented, but they were to be represented in a manner that was, as it were, morally good for them.

## POST-INDEPENDENCE: THE RESONANCE AND RUPTURE OF NATIONALIST PERFORMANCE

How does this idea of performative politics, with its ritualized inflections, translate into the fully democratic (i.e. as opposed to quasi-democratic) context of post-Independence India? Indian politics is littered with echoes of Gandhi's approach to politics. The hunger strike, the courting of arrest and the non-violent *dharna* are all commonplace examples of the implementation of aspects of the grammar of nationalist performance in the multiple arenas of Indian politics, from school and college politics to the Lok Sabha.

Understanding politics through performance can demonstrate the implications of this legacy. This is particularly so when one considers perhaps the most significant implementation of performative models in the post-Independence era: that by the Hindu nationalist Sangh Parivar. Jackie Assayag has focused on the ways in which this performative approach to politics developed in the Sangh Parivar in the 1980s and 90s. He demonstrates how, through "reiterated ritual actions ... integral India has begun to exist as a site par excellence for the ideological construction of Hindu nationalism" (Assayag 1998: 127): what Hansen might refer to as the "expression and creation" of a constituency. Assayag turns to the litany of processions during this period, from the Ekatmata Yajna to the Rath Yatra, to demonstrate his point most forcefully. He argues that this use of processions is strongly based on the invocation and manipulation of some traditional, mostly Brahmanic ideas, specifically worship (*puja*), sacrifice (*yajna*), initiation (*diksa*), circumambulation (*pradaksina*) and pilgrimage (*yatra*) (*ibid.*: 141). The use of such ideas in the context of politics, he continues, is indicative of "a century-old elaboration of reformist neo-Hinduism" which has produced a "restructuring of both political practices and discourse" (*ibid.*: 127).

This analysis, then, places a rather heavy emphasis on the idea of "reformist neo-Hinduism" as an explanatory framework; here is a form of religious ideology which has (inappropriately?) entered the political arena, restructuring practices and discourse. Assayag's approach identifies Hindu nationalism as developing through, and being able to capitalize on, the way in which religion has had an impact on the 'secular' world of politics. It is an approach, then, that uses religion as an analytical tool, in the manner problematized by Fitzgerald. It also projects Hindu nationalism as a direct development from "reform" movements of the late nineteenth century, such as the Arya Samaj, an idea that, as I have argued elsewhere (Zavos 2000b), tends to distort the rather complex, multiple processes that produced this ideology. By foregrounding performance as an analytical tool, a different perspective may be produced. It has already been suggested that the early RSS drew on notions of nationalist performance when articulating their position in the public sphere in the late 1920s and early 1930s. I think it may also be useful to read developments in the 1980s and 1990s through the performative elements of nationalist strategy described above. The processions described by Assayag, I would argue, echo classic nationalist performances such as the Salt March. The Rath Yatra of 1990 is a case in point.

The Rath Yatra was undertaken by L. K. Advani, the then president of the BJP, during October 1990. The idea was to cover some 10,000 kilometres during this month, starting from the famous Somnath temple in Gujarat and ending up in Ayodhya on a specified date, 30 October, when the *kar sevaks*, Hindu volunteers, would commence building the disputed temple to Ram on the site of the Babri Masjid. Advani travelled in an air-conditioned Toyota minibus that was elaborately decorated to resemble the chariot of Ram (*rath*), and his entourage stopped at numerous points each day, whence Advani would deliver speeches on the Ram Janmabhoomi campaign and its wider significance. The Yatra was carefully organized – a somewhat euphemistic form of crowd control was handled by the Sangh Parivar youth organization the Bajrang Dal – and conscious of a broad India-wide audience. Each day would commence and end with a media conference. The starting-point of the Yatra, the Somnath temple, was carefully chosen. This temple had been partially destroyed by the army of Mahmud of Ghazni in the eleventh century. It was also sited in the princely state of Junagadh at the time of independence. This state was ruled by a Muslim Nawab, who announced his intention to accede to Pakistan, only to be overrun by the Indian army late in 1947. In the wake of this occupation, Sardar Patel announced that the temple would be rebuilt at the cost of the government, noting that "the restoration of the idols would be a point of honour and sentiment with the Hindu public" (Jaffrelot 1996: 84). In the context of the Ayodhya dispute, then, this was a site replete with symbolism. As Balasaheb Deoras, the RSS *Sarsanghchalak* (leader), noted at the time the Yatra commenced, "it is appropriate especially because it is starting from Somnath. By this *the country can be told* that immediately after independence, with Sardar Patel's initiative and the Central Government's support, this temple was rebuilt" (*Frontline*, 13–26 October 1990, emphasis added). Note here the element of pedagogy that we saw earlier in relation to the Salt March. Throughout, this pedagogic element recurs, as Advani and other senior Sangh Parivar figures point out the meaning of the Rath Yatra. The BJP MP Pramod Mahajan, for example, stated that the Yatra "symbolises the sentiment, the purpose. One goes towards the site in Ayodhya, victorious even in the belief itself, on a chariot of success" (*ibid.*). Advani claimed, rather improbably, that the Yatra would "ensure and preserve the old symbols of unity, communal amity and cultural oneness" (*ibid.*), and that "Rama was a unifying figure in Indian society" (reported in *Frontline*, 10–23 November 1990). As the Yatra progressed towards Ayodhya, the political heat was turned up, and the talk of Advani's arrest was constant. At the same time, his supporters courted arrest by attempting to gather in Ayodhya for the action on 30 October, many chanting "Jail for Rama" as they were carted off to makeshift detention centres in Lucknow and other areas of Uttar Pradesh state.

The parallels with the Salt March are marked. Precisely the same elements of actors and audience, moving inexorably across the country towards dénouement, are evident. As the narrative unfolds, it is punctuated by elements of the grammar of nationalist performance noted above: the transgression of laws, the focus on a vanguard, and the assumption of moral high ground in relation to authority are all apparent. Most significantly, the morality of the Yatra is presented as a higher meaning, which needs to be conveyed to the Hindu public in order to make them aware of themselves: in order to make them realize the significance of their Hinduness. Symbolic and ritual forms associated with Brahmanic practice are certainly evident, as Assayag points out; this is indicative of the concern of Hindu nationalists to "express and create" their constituency in their own image, a high-caste, middle-class image of the nation of Hindus. In a sense, this replicates the concern to "express and create" the high-caste, middle-class image of the nation of Indians invoked through Satyagraha and *atmashuddhi*. What I am suggesting, then, is that the Rath Yatra is indicative of the Sangh Parivar's use of performative techniques fashioned by the Gandhian Congress. Audiences and their participation, didactic framing and controlled emergence are all evident, and all geared towards the expression of wider moral meaning. In this case it is the meaning of Hinduness; in the case of the Salt March, the meaning of Indianness.

Reflecting on the ideological contours of elite-led Indian and Hindu nationalism can put the similarities apparent here in perspective. This is because there is a high degree of proximity between these ideologies (Zavos 2000a; Bhatt 2001), which is demonstrated particularly by the insistence on the process of identity-building at the heart of their respective projects. Just as elite-led Indian nationalism is all about the making of the Indian nation, so Hindu nationalism is all about the making of the Hindu nation. That is why the moral element of the performative grammar is so significant: because both elite-led Indian and Hindu nationalism are, at heart, didactic projects. The value of ritual-like performance, to return to Bell, is its ability to exemplify the core values of the movement; as performances, both the Salt March and the Rath Yatra are notable for their insistence on articulating just these kinds of core values.

In the late twentieth and early twenty-first centuries, however, we can detect a shift in the quality of national politics in India. This shift may be identified as what Emma Mawdsley has called a "third era" of politics, after the Nehru/domination of Congress and Indira/decline of Congress eras (2003: 36). This new era is characterized by the regionalization or fragmentation of national politics, and the emergence of issues of culture and identity as central to political mobilization. Hindu nationalism is unquestionably a key feature of this turn, but in the context of this paper we need to ask how far the regional actors who have become so critical to the articulation of politics at a national level – such as Shiv Sena, the Bahujan Samaj Party and the Samajwadi party – use the historically defined grammar of performative politics as identified here.

My contention is that what we see with this turn in Indian politics is a movement away from the morally loaded elements of this grammar. Performance is still central, because the form of democratic politics is still geared towards "expressing and creating" communities, but the didactic morality of Gandhian performance is no longer so significant, because the identities that parties seek to "express and create" are not high-caste, middle-class ideological projects in the same 'nation-in-making' sense that is evident in both Indian and Hindu nationalism.

Hansen charts something like this shift in his repeated reference to the difference between the Shiv Sena and the wider Hindu nationalist movement. The Sena, he writes:

> does not harbour any project of social transformation, of creating a different society … rather (its) programme has been and remains centred around creating a certain public attitude among Maharashtrians and Hindus in general: an attitude of assertiveness and self-confidence toward authority and toward forces perceived as "antinational".
> (2001: 195)

Such attitudes are fostered precisely through dramatic spectacle that indicates assertiveness *as it is*. Hansen's contention is that this programme effectively works to "purge the everyday world of its ambiguous, syncretic meanings and replace these with more manageable symbols, namely good versus bad, pure versus impure, Muslims versus Hindus" (*ibid.*: 108).

This point is demonstrated by the Sena's so-called Maha Aartis, first deployed during the dark days of January 1993, when communal rioting in the wake of the destruction of the Babri Masjid ripped through Bombay city, and thereafter an established feature of Sena practice. The Maha (grand) Aartis were an adaptation of the *aarti* ceremony, in which light, usually in the form of a flame, is offered to devotees. This rite of worship is usually performed in Hindu temples or homes, at sunset or in relation to particular significant events, and is important in giving individuals a sense of identification with a particular deity (Fuller 1992: 73). The Sena fashioned *aarti* as a mass congregational ceremony during December 1992 and January 1993, and they can be seen quite clearly, and indeed provocatively, as modelled on mosque-based *namaz*, particularly Friday *namaz*. The Sena's Marathi newspaper *Saamna* published detailed schedules of where and when such Maha Aartis would take place (*Frontline*, 30 January–12 February 1993), and they became springboards for the launching of communal attacks, "physical gathering points and emotional rallying spaces" (Masselos 1996: 116). At the same time, the symbolic content of the Aartis appears to have been minimal, and the Sena did not impute any broad meanings to the ceremony beyond Hindu solidarity. As such, the Aartis can be seen to work towards the propagation of assertiveness and self-confidence, without the pedagogic guidance associated with our earlier examples, the Salt March and the Rath Yatra.

This kind of fixed, identitarian approach to performative politics is also to be found in other parties. The Bahujan Samaj Party (BSP) provides a key example. This party was formed in the early 1980s as a Dalit party, a fighter for the rights of the downtrodden in the mould of Ambedkar's Republican Party of India (RPI). Some commentators, however, have pointed out that whereas the RPI focused on the alleviation of economic deprivation and the creation of a cultural identity related to this deprivation, the BSP has "appealed to those dalits who were already asserting their cultural identity" and "did not take up the question of land reform" (Singh 1998: 2616). In recent work on the rise of the BSP in Hoshiarpur, a BSP worker is recorded as stating that "our people are mental slaves ... this form of slavery is much more dangerous than economic slavery" (Chandra 2000: 37).

In this context, BSP strategy has often focused on the promotion of an established sense of Dalit identity, rather than the formation of new identities crystallized around the idea of dalitness. This is reflected in the approach of the party to election ticket and post allocation. As Chandra records:

> ethnic identity is the sole criterion for the distribution of posts and the allotment of tickets. And for the BSP ... this criterion is openly and systematically implemented. The party office routinely releases an ethnic profile of its candidates before each election. *Bahujan Sangarthak*, the party newspaper, routinely publishes lists of the caste identity of each office bearer in party and government, the immediate and long-term targets in caste representation, and the extent to which these targets have been achieved.
> (Chandra 2000: 40)

These announcements and published lists are themselves a form of performance, designed to assert the self-confidence of Dalit communities.

A similar approach is evident in the regular attempts by the BSP in power to rename districts and institutions after Dalit icons. In 1997 in Uttar Pradesh, the BSP had a tenuous power sharing arrangement with the Hindu Nationalist BJP: in ideological terms, a party that the BSP could only really oppose. The BSP chief minister Mayawati attempted to rename four districts of Uttar Pradesh after social reformers. One, for example, was to be Gautam Buddha Nagar, another Jyotiba Phule Nagar. The latter was said at the time to be critical to the party's strategy to develop its power base in western India, Phule being, of course, a Maharashtrian hero (*Frontline*, 31 May–13 June 1997). This demonstrates the potential of a performative act such as naming. It becomes a signifier of representation: our ability to establish spatial identity in your name is the reason you should vote for us. As Hansen states, naming "is a performative process that seeks retroactively to fix and stabilize identities, to invent constituencies and audiences" (2001: 232). As such it has become a key site of political contestation.

What I am trying to demonstrate is that a different form of performative politics is emerging in the current era of post-Independence politics. On the basis of evidence presented here, we might see this as an indication of democratization of the polity in India. The study of pre-Independence performative strategies employed by the national movement demonstrates that the development of a democratic approach was significant, in as much as it challenged the attempt to institute what I have called quasi-democracy as a feature of the colonial polity. In this context, performative politics emerged as a means of demonstrating the democratic credentials of the national movement. But this was still politics controlled by a high caste, middle class elite, who were not constrained by any very demanding structures of democracy, simply because these were not in place under the colonial regime. The type of performative politics which emerged, then, was geared towards the concerns of this elite, as it tried to fashion a nation in its own image. Satyagraha as performance was about representing the people to themselves, in order to persuade them to be the nation in a particular way. It is because of this that I have talked about nationalist performance as a kind of morality play. This structure of elite control has carried through to the post-Independence period, and this is reflected in the continuing significance of such morality plays in Indian politics. The Rath Yatra, I have argued, is an example of this.

What we have detected in recent years, however, perhaps reflects a turning away from this traditional elite control, as new forces emerge in the polity, asserting their right to democratic representation. What we have seen is that currently, this turn has been signified by a form of performative politics in which fixed identities are predominant, and the grand developmental designs of Indian or Hindu nationalists (what might be termed a 'nation-in-making' discourse) are less so. As one campaigning Samajwadi Party member of the Legislative Assembly asserted in the run up to the local municipal elections in Mumbai in 1997, as part of a strategy to capture Muslim votes, "our demand is simple – we want identity" (Hansen 2001: 182). This self-confident demand is indicative of the desire of newly empowered groups to assert their presence in political localities. Performance is a means of representing this presence. We are, of course, back to a confluence between community identity and political interests here. But by understanding politics through performance, I hope it may be possible to see the dynamic quality of this confluence in contemporary politics. This is not a case of "imputing collective wills, intelligence and rationalities" to communities as in the aggregationist model. As Indian democracy deepens, community identities emerge in local contexts, on the basis of local contestations of power, and expressed through the dynamism of performative politics. The certainties of imputed social and political alignment lose their clarity in this environment, in terms of both political practice and analysis.

This conclusion reinforces the idea that interpreting politics in terms of 'religious' identity is unhelpful, because it relies precisely on an idea of imputed wills, intelligence and rationalities. Indeed, I have tried to show that such interpretations can lead to the mystification of political practice. Focusing on performance, on the other hand, has enabled the recognition of historical continuities in such practice that cut across the presumed division between religious and secular identities. By the same token, it has enabled the recognition of a significant rupture in political practice, which signifies the coming to power of previously unheard voices in the polity.

## NOTES

1. On the idea of the public space in colonial India, see Zavos (2000a: 12–13).
2. See letter to Totade, 8 March 1932 (Hedgewar n.d.), emphasizing the need to present an orderly image at the Ramnaumi festival at Ramtek; also, a circular of 1 September 1932 (*ibid.*) to all shakhas asking them to prepare for Dussehra, when the Sangh would be "evaluated" by the public.

## BIBLIOGRAPHY

Assayag, Jackie. 1998. "Ritual Action or Political Reaction? The Invention of Hindu Nationalist Processions in India During the 1980s". *South Asia Research* 18(2): 125–48.

Bell, Catherine. 1997. *Ritual: Perspectives and Dimensions*. Oxford: Oxford University Press.

Bhatt, Chetan. 2001 *Hindu Nationalism: Origins, Ideologies and Modern Myths*. Oxford: Berg.

Cashman, Richard. 1975. *The Myth of the Lokamanya: Tilak and Mass Politics in Maharashtra*. Berkeley, CA: University of California Press.

Chandra, Kanchan. 2000. "Transformation of Ethnic Politics in India: the Decline of Congress and the Rise of the Bahujan Samaj Party in Hoshiarpur". *Journal of Asian Studies* 59(1): 26–61.

Cohn, Bernard. 1992. "Representing Authority in Victorian India". In *The Invention of Tradition*, eds E. Hobsbawm and T. Ranger, 165–209. Cambridge: Cambridge University Press.

Fitzgerald, Timothy. 2000. *The Ideology of Religious Studies*. Oxford: Oxford University Press.

Frykenberg, R. E. 1993. "Constructions of Hinduism at the nexus of History and Religion". *Journal of Interdisciplinary History* 23(3): 523–50.

Fuller, Christopher. 1992. *The Camphor Flame: Popular Hinduism and Society in India*. Princeton, NJ: Princeton University Press.

Gandhi, Mohandas K. 1965–7. *Collected Works of Mahatma Gandhi*, vols 17, 18, 24, 42, 43. Delhi: Government of India.

Geertz, Clifford. 1980. *Negara: The Theater State in Nineteenth Century Bali*. Princeton, NJ: Princeton University Press.

Gooptu, Nandini. 2001. *The Politics of the Urban Poor in Early Twentieth-Century India*. Cambridge: Cambridge University Press.

Guha, Ranajit. 1993. "Discipline and Mobilize". In *Subaltern Studies VII*, eds P. Chatterjee and G. Pandey, 69–120. New Delhi: Oxford University Press.

Hansen, Thomas. 2001. *Wages of Violence: Naming and Identity in Postcolonial Bombay*. Princeton, NJ: Princeton University Press.

Hansen, Thomas. 2004. "Politics as Permanent Performance: The Production of Political Authority in the Locality". In *Politics of Cultural Mobilisation in India*, eds J. Zavos, A. Wyatt and V. Hewitt, 19–36. New Delhi: Oxford University Press.

Hedgewar, Kashirav B. n.d. Unpublished Letters, held at Hedgewar Bhavan, Nagpur.

Inden, Ronald. 1990. *Imagining India*. Oxford: Blackwell.

Iyer, Raghavan, ed. 1991. *The Essential Writings of Mahatma Gandhi*. New Delhi: Oxford University Press.

Jaffrelot, Christophe. 1996. *The Hindu Nationalist Movement in India*. London: Hurst.

Jaffrelot, Christophe. 1998. "The Politics of Processions and Hindu-Muslim Riots". In *Community Conflicts and the State in India*, eds A. Basu and A. Kohli, 58–92. New Delhi: Oxford University Press.

Kaur, Raminder. 2004. "Fire in the Belly: the Politicisation of the Ganapati Festival in Maharashtra". In *Politics of Cultural Mobilisation in India*, eds J. Zavos, A. Wyatt and V. Hewitt, 37–70. New Delhi: Oxford University Press.

Masselos, Jim. 1987. "Audience, Actors and Congress Dramas: Crowd Events in Bombay City in 1930". In *Struggling and Ruling: The Indian National Congress 1885-1985*, ed. J. Masselos, 71–86. London: Oriental University Press.

Masselos, Jim. 1996. "The Bombay Riots of January 1993: The Politics of Urban Conflagration". In *Politics of Violence: From Ayodhya to Behrampada*, eds J. McGuire, P. Reeves and H. Brasted, 111–26. New Delhi: Sage.

Mawdsley, Emma. 2003. "Redrawing the Body Politic: Federalism, Regionalism and the Creation of New States in India". In *Decentring the Indian Nation*, eds A. Wyatt and J. Zavos, 34–54. London: Frank Cass.

Miles, Robert. 1993. *Racism after 'Race Relations'*. London: Routledge.

O'Hanlon, Rosalind. 1985. *Caste, Conflict and Ideology: Mahatma Jotirao Phule and Low Caste Protest in Nineteenth Century Western India*. Cambridge: Cambridge University Press.

Singh, Jagpal. 1998. "Ambedkarisation and Assertion of Dalit Identity: Socio-cultural Protest in Meerut District of Western Uttar Pradesh". *Economic and Political Weekly* 33(40) (9 October 1998): 2611–18.

Zavos, John. 2000a. *The Emergence of Hindu Nationalism in India*. New Delhi: Oxford University Press.

Zavos, John. 2000b. "The Arya Samaj and the Antecedents of Hindu Nationalism: An Analysis with Reference to the Concept of Reform in Nineteenth Century Hinduism". *International Journal of Hindu Studies* 3(1): 57–81.

# 8

# Real and imagined: imperial inventions of religion in colonial southern Africa

## David Chidester

As many analysts have recognized, conventional distinctions between the secular and the religious have often smuggled into cultural studies the ideological division between a modern Western 'Us' and a primitive, savage, barbarian or exotic 'Them'. While the West is supposedly secular, the alien is rendered as essentially religious. In his recent book, *Imperial Encounters* (2001), Peter van der Veer has neatly formulated this conventional opposition with respect to religion and modernity in nineteenth-century India and Britain. "India is a deeply religious, traditional society, whereas Britain is a deeply secular, modern society" (*ibid.*: ix). In this dichotomy, the metropolitan centre is secular, modernizing and making history, while the colonized periphery persists in traditional forms of religious life, perhaps since time immemorial, which can only be changed, supposedly for the better, by outside interventions. In the course of colonial history in India, this dichotomy between the secular and the religious has not merely been imposed from the outside but has also been appropriated and mobilized by Indian nationalists as a way of actively engaging the interventions by the West. The West might excel materially, as the Hindu philosopher Sarvapalli Radhakrishnan maintained, but the East excelled spiritually (Scharf 1998: 103).

Like the 'exotic' religion of the East, the 'savage' religion of Africa has often been represented in terms of this colonial opposition between the modern, secular West and an Africa that is traditional and, in the words of John S. Mbiti, "notoriously religious" (1969: 1). While the West was advancing, according to modernization theory, by means of a sustained 'disenchantment of the world', Africa remained enchanted by traditional religion. The West became secular through a broad social transformation in which religious authority was gradually separated from political power, economic exchange and scientific knowledge. Factored out of public institutions, religion was circumscribed within the 'private' sphere, thus leading to a decline in the impact of religion on Western societies (see Casanova 1994). According to Mbiti, however, traditional religion pervades every aspect of African life.

Wherever the African is, there is his religion: he carries it to the fields where he is sowing seeds or harvesting a new crop; he takes it with him to the beer party or to attend a funeral ceremony; and if he is educated, he takes religion with him to the examination room at school or in the university; if he is a politician he takes it to the house of parliament.                                                 (Mbiti 1969: 2)

In every public sphere of economic, social, and political activity, Africans, according to Mbiti, are essentially religious. "Although many African languages do not have a word for religion as such", Mbiti admitted, "it nevertheless accompanies the individual from long before his birth to long after his physical death" (*ibid.*: 2).[1]

In the anthropology of African religion, analysts have resisted this dichotomy of the religious and secular by means of three strategies, arguing that both sides are mixed, both sides are 'scientific' or both sides are 'magical'.

Following the advice of anthropologist Mary Douglas, we could reject this imposition that the West is secular while Africa is "notoriously religious" by arguing that both sides of the colonial divide display a mixture of religious and secular attitudes. "When we look more closely at our information we find plenty of secular savages", Douglas observed. When we look at Western civilization, modernization and science, we find that "God is not suddenly dead". If we were ever theoretically inclined to oppose religious 'others' to the secular West, we should resist, Douglas urged, "this particular fantasy about the difference between Us and Them" (1975: 73).

In his comparative analysis of African and Western thought, Robin Horton (1997) argued that African religion, magic and witchcraft beliefs were essentially "scientific" procedures for gaining theoretical knowledge, with predictive power, and practical control over the environment. More recently, Jean Comaroff and John L. Comaroff (1999) have found that Western capitalism, with its own "magical" aura, has generated "occult economies" in Africa that are both shadow and substance of the globalizing market economy. So, these are our alternatives: everyone is religious (or magical); everyone is secular (or scientific); or everyone is all mixed up.

All of this, of course, is not entirely helpful, because we are uncertain about the meaning of these terms, religious and secular. They do not appear to be stable terms of analysis. We notice the constant shifting and recurring slippage in their usage. As a result, we are denied the opportunity to choose among these three options because the very terms out of which they have been constructed – religious and secular – do not necessarily make sense. In his recent book, *Formations of the Secular* (2003), Talal Asad has implicitly challenged all three of these options for making sense out of the religious and the secular. The secular is not merely a transposition, into a different key, of religion; the religious is not merely the functional equivalent of the secular; and neither the religious nor the secular are stable terms for distinguishing between the sacred and the profane.

Locating my discussion in this contingency, I do not pretend to be able to stabilize the terms religious and secular. Rather, I want to begin with the historical conditions of possibility for the imposition of a dichotomy between the religious and the secular in nineteenth-century southern Africa. In the first instance, this opposition was negotiated on contested colonial frontiers. According to all European reports, at the beginning of the nineteenth century Africans lacked any trace of religion. Following a century of warfare, conquest and colonization, again according to all reports, Africans were all religious. By situating the dilemma of the secular and the religious in this particular colonial history, as I argued in *Savage Systems: Colonialism and Comparative Religion in Southern Africa* (1996), we might uncover some of the contours of a study of religion that can only be discerned from the colonized periphery.

Taking that colonial history as background, I want to move between the colonized periphery and the metropolitan centre of theory production of an imperial comparative religion in Britain in order to examine the ways in which a secular study of religion derived its evidence from "notoriously religious" Africans. Although claiming scientific status, theorists of religion such as F. Max Müller, E. B. Tylor and Andrew Lang developed their theories in large measure on the basis of evidence derived from reports about indigenous people in colonial situations. Certainly, these theorists operated with different working definitions of religion. For Max Müller, religion was a sense of the infinite that was mediated through language. For Tylor, religion was the cognitive propensity for believing in supernatural or spiritual beings. For Lang, religion was the cultural creativity of myths and rituals shared by all human beings. Here I want to consider how these theorists built their definitions and elaborations of the religious on evidence derived from indigenous beliefs and practices of southern Africa. For all their differences, as Bruce Lincoln has observed, their "discourses constructed a sharp discontinuity between two sorts of people: one associated with a European 'us' and the other with a lesser, alien 'them'" (1999: 70).

I take that as given. But other commonalities will appear: theorists of an imperial comparative religion, in developing a 'secular' science of religion, were engaged in distinguishing between the real and the imagined, distinguishing between the 'reality' of empire and the 'imaginary' world of people subjected to the military force, economic exploitation and social dislocation of colonization. An imperial science of religion explored and explained the imaginary world of colonized people all over the world. In the process, imperial theorists defined their imaginary world under the rubric 'religion' as a "disease of language", as "primordial stupidity" or as "primitive survivals" from human prehistory that should have long ago disappeared in the advance of modernity.

As a result of this imperial comparative religion, we grew accustomed to seeing these dichotomies – religious and secular, enchanted and disenchanted – as the basic terms in a temporal progression from a pre-modern past to a modern, secular present. British imperial theorists of religion proposed this temporal progression; Max Weber confirmed it; we still live with it.

In this chapter, I want to go back through the historical relations between imperial centre and colonized periphery in order to replace everyone involved in the production of these categories back in the same time zone. I am not doing anything new in doing this. From Johannes Fabian's (1983) insistence on co-temporality or "coevalness", through Edward Said's (1993) "contrapuntal reading", to Van der Veer's (2001) "interactive history", many others have sought to analyse colonial relations as relations of mutual formation, as a "shared history", in Ashis Nandy's (1983) terms, mutually constituting the identities of colonizers and colonized, both reciprocally and antagonistically.

My focus on the category 'religion', therefore, will be situated primarily in the context of colonial dreams and colonial adventures in southern Africa. For the imperial comparative religion that emerged in Great Britain following the inaugural lectures by F. Max Müller in 1870, these dreams and adventures were crucial to its formation. The other theorists I consider in this chapter, Tylor and Lang, developed theories of religion based on colonial dreams and colonial adventures. As a result, their theories were directly related – as co-temporal, contrapuntal and interactive – to the colonial situations in which indigenous people and alien intruders, Christian missionaries and adventure novelists, and a host of others, were also involved in the process of producing knowledge about religion for a secular science of religion.

## FRONTIER ZONES

As deep background, from a southern African perspective, we need to remember that our subject of study, 'religion', was a term of reference that did not come from Greco-Roman antiquity or the European Enlightenment. It came from the sea in ships. Beginning around 1600, the word 'religion' was consistently deployed by European navigators and explorers, travellers and missionaries, settlers and colonial administrators, as a term of denial. Coming to the Cape during the first half of the seventeenth century, European observers, whether Dutch, English, French, German, Spanish or Portuguese, found people living at the southern tip of Africa who supposedly had no religion at all. Although this denial of religion might have simply marked an absence of Christianity, it increasingly revealed that religion was emerging as a generic term, with different species, because the absence of religion was often linked with the alleged absence of other generic terms, such as language or politics, which even as early as 1600 were recognized by Europeans as having different species. This discovery of an absence of religion was repeated on every southern African frontier, configuring a discourse of denial that dismissed the full humanity of the indigenous people of southern Africa, who were represented as being no different than the "beasts that perish" because they lacked religion (Chidester 1996: 11–16).

This failure to recognize religion in local beliefs, myths and rituals, in other words, to recognize indigenous forms of religious life in southern Africa, was not merely a mistake, as if it were an unfortunate consequence of limited opportunities for participant observation, the unfamiliarity of strange customs, the incomprehension of local languages, the intrusion of Christian theological prejudices or some other failure of method. Instead, the denial of an African religion was itself the method: a method for entering contested frontiers and representing them as if they were empty spaces for conquest and colonization.

The nineteenth-century European discovery of indigenous African religions was just as problematic as their denial. In the eastern Cape, for example, the existence of any kind of indigenous Xhosa religion was consistently denied by travellers, missionaries and magistrates. Although they were credited with an abundance of superstition, a term that operated as the defining opposite of religion, the amaXhosa of the eastern Cape alleg-edly had no semblance of religious beliefs or practices. With the imposition of a colonial administrative system for native control, surveillance and tax collection in 1858, however, the amaXhosa were discovered to have a religion, even a religious system, as its discov-erer, the colonial magistrate J. C. Warner, insisted, that counted as a religion because it fulfilled the two basic functions of any religious system by providing a sense of psycho-logical security and reinforcing social stability. According to this proto-functionalist in the eastern Cape, therefore, the amaXhosa had a religious system that could be reduced to these psychological and social functions – security and stability – that oddly duplicated the aims of the colonial administrative system in keeping people in place. Rather than representing an advance in human recognition, however, this discovery of an indigenous religious system was a strategy of colonial containment that mirrored the structure of the magisterial system, location system, or reserve system (Warner 1858; Chidester 1996: 73–115).

In the British Colony of Natal, which was annexed in 1843, over 100,000 Africans were placed under the jurisdiction of the location system designed by the Secretary for Native Affairs, Theophilus Shepstone. This colonial system of indirect rule, which was governed by a system of white 'native magistrates', required expert knowledge about Zulu culture and social practices. "As secretary for native affairs under the system he had put in place", historian Carolyn Hamilton has observed:

> Shepstone, assisted on a day-to-day level by a network of 'native magistrates' – that is, white magistrates with jurisdiction over Africans – who dispensed justice by using their 'knowledge of the customs of the natives', became the primary inter-locutor between the African and European communities for much of the nineteenth century.
> (1998: 89)

This local mediation between settlers and indigenous people "depended on knowledge of African ways of thinking and acting: the system thus placed a high premium on 'that native expert', and Shepstone himself was widely recognized as the most 'expert' of all" (*ibid.*).

With respect to African ways of thinking and acting, other experts emerged in Natal and Zululand. Arriving in 1854, the Anglican Bishop J. W. Colenso, the linguist W. H. I. Bleek, and the missionary-ethnographer Henry Callaway conducted extensive research into the beliefs and practices of the Zulu (Chidester 1996: 129–72). At first glance, their research can be separated into religious and secular interests in gaining knowledge about African ways of thinking and acting. In trying to establish a Zulu name for God that could be used by Christian missions, Bishop Colenso's research was primarily driven by his interests in Christian proselytism and the objectives of his Christian mission (Colenso 1855). In tracing religious formations to linguistic structures, from a comparative perspective, Bleek (1857; 1862) developed a philology of religion in conversation with recent academic developments in Europe in a secular study of religion. In the case of Henry Callaway, medical doctor and missionary, ethnographer and scholar of comparative religion, religious and secular interests mixed and merged (Etherington 1987; Hexham 1996). His classic text, *The Religious System of the Amazulu* ([1868–70] 1970), was a detailed profile of Zulu beliefs in deity, ancestors, diviners, witchcraft and other ways of thinking and acting that comprised, as his title suggested, a coherent religious system. Presented in both Zulu and English, *The Religious System of the Amazulu* provided direct access to knowledge about the "customs of the natives" collected by a local expert.

This expert knowledge, however, was entangled in the violent conflicts of a colonial situation. In that context, Henry Callaway's text provided evidence of intercultural mediations not only between Europeans and Africans on the colonial frontier but also among Africans trying to understand the impact of colonial war, conquest, displacement and containment. Callaway's principal Zulu informant, the Christian convert, catechist and eventual deacon Mpengula Mbande, arguably should be regarded as the primary author of *The Religious System of the Amazulu*. Although Callaway transcribed and edited the volume, providing footnotes and occasional commentary, most of the text appeared in the words of Mbande, reflecting, at many points, Mbande's own ambiguous position on the colonial frontier as both a Zulu and a recent convert to Christianity. Mediating between the colonial mission and traditional African society, Mbande's ambivalent personal position defined the dominant perspective on Zulu beliefs and practices that emerged in Callaway's *The Religious System of the Amazulu*. As a Christian, however, Mbande mediated intercultural relations in that colonial situation by advancing his own scathing Christian critique of indigenous Zulu religion, insisting, at one point, that whatever African traditionalists said about religion "has no point; it is altogether blunt" (Callaway [1868–70] 1970: 22). Nevertheless, Mbande's account became the standard version of an indigenous Zulu religious system.

In one of his most important contributions to *The Religious System of the Amazulu*, Mbande related the "account which black men give white men of their origin". According to this creation myth, black men emerged first from the *uhlanga*, the place of the origin of all nations, coming out, however, with only a few things. They emerged with some cattle, corn, spears and picks for digging the earth. Arrogantly, with their few possessions, the black men thought that they possessed all things. When the white men emerged, however, they came out with ox-drawn wagons bearing abundant goods and able to traverse great distances. By displaying this new, unexpected, use for cattle, the whites demonstrated a superior wisdom that had been drawn from the *uhlanga*. In relation to the power and possessions of white men, black men recognized that they were defenceless. As Mbande explained:

We saw that, in fact, we black men came out without a single thing; we came out naked; we left everything behind, because we came out first. But as for the white men, we saw that they scraped out the last bit of wisdom; for there is every thing, which is too much for us, they know; they know all things which we do not know; we saw that we came out in a hurry; but they waited for all things, that they might not leave any behind. So in truth they came out with them. Therefore, we honour them, saying, "It is they who came out possessed of all things from the great Spirit; it is they who came out possessed of all goodness; we came out possessed with the folly of utter ignorance." Now it is as if they were becoming our fathers, for they come to us possessed of all things. Now they tell us all things, which we too might have known had we waited; it is because we did not wait that we are now children in comparison with them.                                                                                                                    (*Ibid.*: 79)

Therefore, Mbande concluded, Europeans had not achieved victory over Africans by their superior force of arms. Rather, their wisdom had conquered. According to Mbande, European colonizers had been "victorious by sitting still". They had not required military force. The wisdom, wealth, and virtue that whites had drawn from the *uhlanga* were sufficient to overpower the black people, who reflected among themselves, as Mbande reported, that "these men who can do such things, it is not proper that we should think of contending with them, as, if because their works conquer us, they would conquer us also by weapons" (*ibid.*: 80). In this formulation, knowledge and power, myth and military force, merged in Mbande's justification for submission to colonial rule.

In colonial situations of intercultural contact, interchange and exchange, any distinction that might be made between the religious and the secular blurred in the mediations between Africans and Europeans. In nineteenth-century missions, Christianity, as a religion, was consistently identified with European clothing, square houses and the technology of the plough, wagon and firearm. Often, it is difficult, if not impossible, to separate the political character of these engagements from the intellectual, ideological or religious dimensions. Some African questions seem obviously to be of a political nature. For example, in 1855 when the missionary bishop John William Colenso and the colonial administrator Theophilus Shepstone finished explaining the nature of God to Zulu Chief Pakade, they asked if the chief had any questions. In response, the chief asked, "How do you make gunpowder?" (Colenso 1855: 116–17). Presumably, this was a scientific, technological or military question. However, the possibility that firearms might have signified a kind of superhuman power, and were clearly identified with the religious advance of the Christian mission in southern Africa, could easily have invested this question with a "religious" content. Certainly, Chief Pakade assumed that it was a relevant question to raise in the context of a discussion about God. Accordingly, the question "How do you make gunpowder?" might very well be regarded as a nineteenth-century African religious question.

In the emergence of a secular, scientific study of religion in Europe, metropolitan theorists relied on such evidence from the colonized peripheries of empire. The manufacture of theory, the process of turning data mined from the frontiers of empire into intellectual manufactured goods at the metropolitan centre, involved a complex process of intercultural mediation. In his inaugural lectures on the science of religion in 1870, Müller demonstrated that the culture of British colonialism and imperialism permeated his understanding of the academic study of religion. "Let us take the old saying, *Divide et impera*", Max Müller proposed, "and translate it somewhat freely by 'Classify and conquer'" (1873: 122–3). More than merely a rhetorical flourish, this "old saying" provided legitimization for an imperial comparative religion that aspired to global knowledge over the empire of religion. Classification according to language gave Müller a measure of conceptual control over the library of the sacred texts of the world. But imperial conquest enabled him to develop theories of religion that were anchored in British India and British South Africa. In his last work to be published before his death, a pamphlet, *The Question of Right between England and the Transvaal*, which was printed and widely distributed by the Imperial South African Association, Max Müller asserted that the British Empire "can retire from South Africa as little as from India" (1900: 11). These two imperial possessions, he suggested, were essential for maintaining the global power and authority of the British Empire. But they were also essential for Müller's imperial comparative religion, which mediated between 'civilized' Great Britain and the 'exotic' and 'savage' peripheries of empire.

While his edition of the *Rig Veda* and his expertise in the language, mythology and religion of India were made possible by the financial support of the East India Company, Müller's imperial comparative religion rested on comparative observations that depended heavily on the British possession of South Africa. Although he observed that in the empire of religion there was "no lack of materials for the student of the Science of Religion" (1873: 101), Müller knew that those raw materials had to be extracted from the colonies, transported to the metropolitan centres of theory production, and transformed into the manufactured goods of theory that could be used by an imperial comparative religion.

In his relations with South Africa, Müller was engaged in a complex process of intercultural mediation in order to transform raw data into a theory of religion. First, Africans on the colonized periphery were drawn into this process as informants – often as collaborators, sometimes as authors – as they reported on religious innovations, arguments and contradictions in colonial contexts. As noted, the Zulu convert Mbande was drawn into this mediation, reporting local African arguments about the term *uNkulunkulu*, for example, in which Africans disagreed over whether it referred to the first ancestor of a particular political grouping, the first ancestor of all people or the supreme god who created all human beings.

Secondly, local European 'experts' on the colonized periphery synthesized these conflicts and contradictions into a 'religious system'. Relying heavily on Mbande's local fieldwork, the Anglican missionary Callaway became the leading authority in the world on Zulu religion and, by extension, on 'savage' religion in general, by publishing *The Religious System of the Amazulu*. Like other 'men on the spot' in colonized peripheries, Callaway corresponded with the metropolitan theorists in London (Benham 1896: 215, 239, 341).[2]

However, Callaway's exposition of the Zulu 'religious system' was dissected by those metropolitan theorists in the service of a third mediation, the mediation between the 'primitive' ancestors of humanity, who could supposedly be viewed in the mirror of the

Zulu and other 'savages', and the 'civilized' European. In the case of the Zulu 'religious system', for example, Müller dissected the system to find evidence for the primordial "disease of language" that had supposedly generated religious myth by mistaking metaphors for reality, *nomina* for *numina*, in ways that provided evidence for the origin of 'primitive' religious myth (Chidester 2004). What was construed as a religious system in the colony, therefore, was taken apart and reassembled in London as religious data that could be correlated and synthesized with religious data gathered from other colonized peripheries of empire and used in support of an evolutionary progression from the primitive to the civilized.

Like Müller, other nineteenth-century metropolitan theorists, such as John Lubbock, Herbert Spencer, Andrew Lang, W. Robertson Smith and James Frazer, deployed a comparative method that inferred characteristics of the 'primitive' ancestors of humanity from reports about contemporary 'savages' living on the colonized peripheries of empire. For all of their differences, they relied on the reports from local colonial experts such as Callaway, who relied on Mbande, who was struggling to work out the meaning of his own situation under colonial conditions. While paying attention to this triple mediation that linked metropolitan, settler and indigenous thinking about religion, I want to consider the roles of secular science and secular literature in this production of knowledge about African religion.

## COLONIAL DREAMS

In his popular survey of human evolution, *The Origin of Civilization and the Primitive Condition of Man*, John Lubbock explained that religion originated as the result of the primitive tendency to attribute animation to inanimate objects. To illustrate this primitive "frame of mind" and "tendency to deification", Lubbock cited evidence from southern Africa, relying on the early-nineteenth-century report from the traveller Henry Lichtenstein that the Xhosa in the eastern Cape assumed that an anchor cast ashore from a shipwreck was actually alive. In a footnote Lubbock observed, "Dogs appear to do the same" ([1870] 1889: 287). This analytical link between the behaviour of dogs and the primitive origin of religion was not uncommon in imperial comparative religion. In *The Descent of Man* (1952), Lubbock's friend and mentor Charles Darwin made this link explicit. Religion could be explained in terms of two features of dog behaviour. First, like Lubbock, Darwin observed that dogs characteristically attributed life to inanimate objects. A dog's attention to a parasol blowing in the wind, for example, suggested to Darwin that the animal assumed that objects were alive. Secondly, Darwin argued that religious devotion, the sense of submission or fear before a higher power, was analogous to a dog's devotion to its master (1952: 302–3).[3] In both these senses, therefore, by attributing animation to inanimate objects and by submitting to a higher power, the dog could provide the basic theoretical model for explaining the origin and evolution of religion.

Müller complained about this equation of canine and religious behaviour. He blamed it on a misreading of Hegel. Against Schleiermacher's definition of religion as absolute dependence, Hegel had argued that religion should rather be understood as perfect freedom. If the sense of dependence constituted religion, then the dog might be called the most religious animal. "What was considered a rather coarse joke of Hegel's", Müller complained, "has now become a serious doctrine" (1889: 69). Not only Darwin, but also other theorists developed this doctrine. In a discussion of "Animal Concepts of the Supernatural", for example, John H. King asserted that "the dog engages occasionally in rites similar to those of negro fetishism" (1892: vol. 1, 87). At stake in this controversy was a crisis over what it meant to be human. For Müller, the human was constituted by language, with speech standing as the Rubicon that no animal could ever cross. As an extension of language, religion also marked an impenetrable boundary between the animal and the human. Indicating the seriousness of this question, when Müller confronted him with this premise, Darwin reportedly declared, "You are a dangerous man" (Müller 1902: 468).

In blurring the boundary represented by speech and religion, Darwin, Lubbock and, as we shall see, the anthropologist Edward B. Tylor, established a developmental and evolutionary continuity between the animal and the human. However, because they really did not regard dogs as human beings, these theorists actually established a fundamental discontinuity between the civilized, cultured man of Britain and animals, children, women, rural peasants, the urban working class, criminals, the insane, the deaf and dumb and 'savages' on a colonized periphery of empire such as southern Africa, all of which, as Joan Leopold has noted, "represented a stage of civilization or shared cultural traits of remote ancestors" of humanity (1980: 66).

By using southern African evidence, Tylor built a theory of religion – animism, the belief in spiritual, supernatural, or superhuman beings – that explicitly linked the animal and the human by focusing on the cognitive constraints and capacities of human physiology. That theory was based not only on his analysis of the role of dreams, but also on reports from southern Africa about the originating religious significance inherent in a certain kind of involuntary physical activity that I shall identify shortly.

Like Müller, Tylor was impressed by the apparently unmediated access to 'savage' religion afforded by Callaway's The Religious System of the Amazulu. In September 1871, Tylor tried to raise funds, by making an appeal through the Colonial Church Chronicle, to subsidize the completion and publication of Callaway's work, declaring that "no savage race has ever had its mental, moral, and religious condition displayed to the scientific student with anything approaching to the minute accuracy which characterizes" The Religious System (Benham 1896: 247). In his major work, Primitive Culture, Tylor observed that Callaway's account represented "the best knowledge of the lower phases of religious belief" (1871: vol. 1, 380). Unlike Müller, however, who used Callaway's book as a resource for studying language, analysing the play of metaphors in Zulu religion, Tylor harvested evidence of the embodied origin of religion.

In standard accounts of Tylor's theory of religion, animism is thought to be derived from the 'primitive' inability to distinguish between dreams and waking consciousness.

When the 'primitive' ancestors of humanity dreamed about deceased friends or relatives, they assumed that the dead were still alive in some spiritual form. Out of dreams, therefore, evolved "the doctrine of souls and other spiritual beings in general", a doctrine that was "rational", even if it was enveloped in "intense and inveterate ignorance" (*ibid.*: vol. 1, 22–3). Certainly, Tylor found evidence of an active dream life among Callaway's Zulus. As many European reporters had observed, Zulus often saw the shade or shadow of deceased ancestors in dreams (*ibid.*: vol. 1, 430).[4] However, Callaway's volume included a detailed account about one Zulu man, an apprenticed diviner, who had become so overwhelmed with visions of spirits that he had described his own body as "a house of dreams" ([1868–70] 1970: 228, 260, 316). According to Tylor, all Zulus, as 'savage' survivals of the 'primitive', were subject to dream visions, but "as for the man who is passing into the morbid condition of the professional seer, phantoms are continually coming to talk to him in his sleep, till he becomes as the expressive native phrase is, 'a house of dreams'" (Tylor 1871: vol. 1, 443).

Although Tylor appropriated him as an archetype of the 'primitive', this particular Zulu man, who served Tylor as a 'savage' survival of the original "house of dreams" from which religion originated, can be identified as James, a convert who lived for a time at Callaway's Springvale mission station. Like so many converts, James was torn between the Christian mission and indigenous tradition. While Mbande went one way, becoming a catechist for the mission, James struggled in the other direction, striving to keep an ancestral dream alive under increasingly difficult colonial conditions. Under these conditions, the "house of dreams" was not a 'primitive' but a colonial situation, the product of contemporary conflicts in southern Africa.

In any case, the analysis of dreams did not provide the only evidence for Tylor's theory of animism. The involuntary physical phenomenon of sneezing was central to Tylor's argument. Here again Callaway's Zulu evidence was definitive. As Tylor observed, sneezing was:

> not originally an arbitrary and meaningless custom, but the working out of a principle. The plain statement by the modern Zulus fits with the hints to be gained from the superstition and folklore of other races, to connect the notions and practices as to sneezing with the ancient and savage doctrine of pervading and invading spirits, considered as good or evil, and treated accordingly.     (*Ibid.*: vol. 1, 104)

From Callaway's account, Tylor derived the ethnographic facts that Zulus thought their deceased ancestors caused sneezing; that sneezing reminded Zulus to name and praise their ancestors; that the ancestors entered the bodies of their descendants when they sneezed; and that ritual specialists, such as Zulu diviners, regularly sneezed as a ritual technique for invoking the spiritual power of the ancestors (*ibid.*: vol. 1, 98; vol. 2, 367).[5] These Zulu concepts and practices, Tylor concluded, were remnants of a prehistoric era in which sneezing was not merely a 'physiological' phenomenon, "but was still in the 'theological stage'" (*ibid.*: vol. 1, 104).

Much has been made of Tylor's 'intellectualist' theory of religion. Although primitives suffered from primordial stupidity, Tylor argued that they nevertheless exercised their limited intellectual powers to develop explanations of the world in which they lived. Unfortunately, Tylor cited a Zulu source in support of this proposition, Callaway's catechist, Mbande, who observed that "we are told all things, and assent without seeing clearly whether they are true or not" (*ibid.*: vol. 2, 387). However, Mbande's point in this statement was that most Zulus had not been exposed to Callaway's new Christian gospel. Rather than offering evidence of primordial stupidity, therefore, Mbande was announcing his recently acquired Christian commitment. In any event, Tylor's theoretical work, and his use of Zulu evidence, demonstrated that his theory of the origin of religion was based on an analysis of the body rather than the mind. More animal than human, in this respect, 'primitive' religion, as revealed according to Tylor by its survival among contemporary Zulu 'savages', had evolved out of a bodily process that was as simple, basic and involuntary as sneezing. However much it might have been theologized, sneezing marked the physiological origin of religion.

## COLONIAL ADVENTURES

Andrew Lang is included in standard histories of comparative religion for his expansive anthropological approach to myth and folklore, for his commitment to the premise that high gods stood at the origin of religion and for his vigorous polemics against Herbert Spencer's theory of ancestor worship, Müller's philological analysis of Aryan myth, and James Frazer's scheme of religious evolution (Sharpe 1986: 58–65).[6] He described himself, however, as a "hodman of letters", indicating, with characteristic humour, the humble building trade of popular literature in which he worked.

Although he engaged in often heated intellectual controversy with other imperial theorists of comparative religion, Lang seemed to hold greater affinity with popular novelists such as H. Rider Haggard and John Buchan who were linked with South Africa. Certainly, the novelists acknowledged Lang as a model and mentor. Meeting Lang in 1885, Haggard praised him as "*par excellence a litterateur* of the highest sort, perhaps the most literary man in England or America", Rising to hyperbole, Haggard identified Lang as "the tenderest, the purest and the highest-minded of human creatures, one from whom true goodness and nobility of soul radiate in every common word or act, though often half-hidden in jest, the most perfect of gentlemen" (Haggard 1926: vol. 1, 229–31). Where Haggard found human perfection, Buchan discovered a high god in Lang, noting that after reading his work in 1892, a decade before embarking on his own career in southern Africa, Lang became "the chief deity of my pantheon" (Buchan 1933: 1).

What did these adventure novelists find in Lang's comparative religion? First, Lang insisted on a global unity, a vast narrative uniformity, in the entire history of religions. Whether in southern Africa or Britain, "All peoples notoriously tell the same myths, fairy

tales, fables and improper stories, repeat the same proverbs, are amused by the same rid-
dles or devinettes, and practise the same, or closely analogous, religious rites and mysteries" (Lang 1896: 632). What provided evidence for this global uniformity of religious
narratives and practices? Like other imperial theorists, Lang relied on reports from local
experts on the colonized peripheries of empire. "Our best evidence", he held, "is from
linguists who have been initiated into the secret Mysteries. Still more will missionaries
and scholars like Bleek, Hahn, Codrington, Castren, Gill, Callaway, Theal, and the rest, sift
and compare the evidence of the most trustworthy native informants" (Lang 1906: vol. 2,
358). Of these seven scholars cited by Lang, four worked in southern Africa, suggesting,
once again, the importance of evidence from that region for theory-building in imperial
comparative religion. According to Lang, however, the narrative unity of religion was
only revealed when such evidence was tested by cross-checking accounts from other
regions of the world. Lang asked, "Does Bleek's report from the Bushmen and Hottentots
confirm Castren's from the Finns? Does Codrington in Melanesia tell the same tale as
Gill in Mangia or Theal among the [South Africans?]" (ibid.: 359). In Lang's comparative
method, evidence was validated if it was confirmed, not by additional reports from the
same region, but by reports from widely divergent areas of the globe. If local scholars in
different regions told the same stories, Lang concluded, "then we may presume that the
inquirers have managed to extract true accounts from some of their native informants"
(ibid.). In adopting Lang's notion of the global uniformity of all religious narratives, the
adventure novelists could also relate the same stories. As Haggard's hero put it in the novel
She, "All great Faiths are the same, changed a little to suit the needs of passing times and
people" (Haggard 1887a: 125).

Secondly, given this global unity of religion, myth and ritual, Lang argued that it
resulted not from intercultural borrowings or historical diffusion, but from the creative
power of the human imagination. In his 1873 essay "Mythology and Fairy Tales", Lang
argued, against Müller's philological exegesis of Aryan myth, that "there are necessary
forms of the imagination, which in widely separated peoples must produce identical
results". Similar mental and social conditions, he proposed, generated forms of imagination that produced the same narratives and practices. Clearly, Lang drew on a long history
of nineteenth-century Romantic theorizing about the creative power of imagination and
fancy to conclude that "the Aryan and the lower races have had to pass through similar
conditions of imagination and of society, and therefore of religion" (1873: 622).[7] However,
his model for the creative imagination drew extensively on reports about the myths and
rituals of the Zulus of southern Africa. The Zulus demonstrated the "necessary forms of
imagination" that had originally produced myth and ritual. Furthermore, according to
Lang, Callaway's Zulus had successfully refuted the alternative hypotheses advanced by
Müller and Spencer. With respect to Vedic myth, Müller's special province, Lang concluded that it was "plain that these tales go back to the time when our Aryan forefathers
were in the mental condition of Dr. Callaway's [African] instructor in the Zulu language"
(1873: 625; Dorson 1968: vol. 1, 200). As for Spencer's theory of ancestor worship, Lang
found that "that inquiring race, the Zulus, are as subversive of the fancy of Mr. Spencer as

of the early orthodoxy of Bishop Colenso" (1873: 630; Dorson 1968: vol. 1, 206). By exemplifying the "necessary forms of imagination", therefore, the Zulus stood as the foundation of Lang's imperial comparative religion. In writing extensively about the Zulus, with special attention to their "forms of imagination", adventure novelists such as Haggard and Buchan extended the scope of Lang's imperial comparative religion.

Thirdly, since Lang was concerned with not only the mental, but also the social conditions of myth and ritual, he developed an analysis of primitive politics in which he found that religion was politicized and politics was inevitably enveloped in a religious aura. Here again, reports about the Zulu religious polity served as Lang's model. "Among the Zulus", he noted, "we have seen that sorcery gives the sanction to the power of the chief" (1906: vol. 1, 111). In this respect, the religious resources of ritual specialists, of priests, diviners or sorcerers, supported political authority. At the same time, however, political power carried a sacred aura. As Lang recounted, "when the chief, as among the Zulus, absorbs supernatural power, then the same man becomes diviner and chief, and is a person of great and sacred influence" (*ibid.*: vol. 1, 113). In the African novels of Haggard and Buchan, this intersection between 'savage' religion and politics was arguably their central narrative theme; it definitely set a recurring and pervasive framework for dramatic action and interaction between Europeans and Africans in their adventure novels. For example, in *Allan Quatermain*, Haggard invented a Zu-Vendi society in southern Africa in which priests held such political power that "it is scarcely too much to say that they really rule the land" (Haggard 1887b: 154). Buchan's *Prester John* (1910) centred on a Christian religious movement that was also an uprising against colonial domination. Although more explicit in adventure novels, this implicit link between religion and politics formed a subtext in imperial comparative religion.

Finally, Lang's academic researches and southern African adventure novels merged in the common project of juxtaposing, often through ironic inversions, the fundamental binary opposition between savagery and civility on which imperial comparative religion was based. In his collection of satirical stories, *In the Wrong Paradise*, Lang's dedication to Haggard read: "We are all savages under our white skins; but you alone recall to us the delights and terrors of the world's nonage" (1886: frontispiece). As Haggard had his hero declare in *Allan Quatermain*, "Civilization is only savagery silver-gilt" (1887b: 13). These rhetorical turns – stating, undermining but also reinscribing the opposition between savagery and civility – were crucial to Lang's comparative religion. The truth of religion, according to Lang, was its global uniformity, imaginative origin, political character and, playing on the thematic inversion of savagery and civility, the haunting irony revealed by the history of religions that "as man advanced in social progress, he became more deeply stained with religious cruelty" (1901: 239–40). In similar terms, and engaging similar tensions in comparative religion, Lang's colleagues, the adventure novelists of southern Africa, were already imagining new myths and fictions, new folklore and history, for the global British imperial project.

## REAL AND IMAGINED

Talal Asad has proposed, provocatively, but without elaboration, that the secular 'disenchantment' of the modern West was at least in part produced through efforts directed toward the 'enchantment' of the pre-modern. Arguably, as Asad suggests, the secular "disenchantment of the world" was "a product of nineteenth-century romanticism, partly linked to the growing habit of reading imaginative literature – being enclosed within and by it – so that images of a 'pre-modern' past acquire in retrospect a quality of enchantment" (2003: 14–15).[8] Romantic adventure novels, such as the works of Haggard, were certainly engaged in such a project. But the dividing line between the real and the imagined did not correspond to any simple dichotomy between a secular reality and an imaginary religion.

According to Müller, myth might be a "disease of language", a transposition of real *nomina* into imaginary *numina*. Yet, British imperial myth and ritual were real. Present at the opening by Queen Victoria of the Colonial and Indian Exhibition in 1886, Müller reflected on the vast global power represented by that imperial ceremony:

> I feel grateful that I went and witnessed what was not a mere festivity, but an historical event. Behind the gorgeous throne and the simple dignified presence of the Queen, one saw a whole Empire stretching out, such as the world has never known, and an accumulation of thought, labour, power, and wealth that could be matched nowhere else. It is well that England should sometimes be reminded of her real greatness and her enormous responsibilities.                (1902: vol. 2, 191)

Müller's testimony hinted at the location of power in imperial comparative religion. Comparative religion was a science of symbols that could distinguish between mere ceremonies and real historical events. In his pamphlet on the South African War, Müller compares England's sovereignty, based on real historical events, with Boer claims, based, he alleges, on "prehistoric things which can have no legal value" (1900: 5). Imperial ritual, Müller suggested, was entirely different to such "prehistoric things". Since the empire relied heavily on new imperial symbols, myths and rituals, those "invented traditions" that signified British power at both the centre and periphery of empire, imperial comparative religion could certify their reality in and through the process of disempowering the alternative symbolic forms of the 'exotic' or 'savage' colonized. While the colonized allegedly acted out "mere festivity", the "disease of language", "primordial stupidity", "superstitious survivals" or a "magical mentality", according to various metropolitan theorists, British imperial ritual enacted a real historical event.

On the colonized peripheries of empire, as historian Terrence Ranger has observed, "the 'theology' of an omniscient, omnipotent and omnipresent monarchy [was] almost the sole ingredient of imperial ideology as it was represented to Africans" (Ranger 1983: 212). In South Africa, this imperial 'theology' was ceremonially enacted through transactions between British and African ritual. In 1873, for example, the British governor of

Natal, Theophilus Shepstone, invented an "enthronement ceremony" for the Zulu King Cetshwayo. Two years later and under Shepstone's patronage, Haggard transmitted colonial myths about Zulu-speaking Africans back to his European audiences. "The origin of the Zulus is a mystery", Haggard wrote; "nobody knows from whence they come, or who were their forefathers but it is thought they sprang from Arab stock and many of their customs and ceremonies resemble those of the Jews" (1882: 53). These aspects of a 'real' empire, with its theology of imperial presence, knowledge and power, generated 'real' political rituals and myths of origin.

For Tylor, scientific materialism was real. Animism, as the defining essence of religion, was not real, since it was derived from mistaking dreams for reality. Whether animism appeared among the Zulu *isanusi*, who became a "house of dreams", or among the spiritualists conducting their popular séances in London, it was a superstitious survival of the pre-modern that was out of place in the reality of secular modernity.

In building his theory of animism, Tylor intentionally disguised the colonial conditions that provided his evidence. Ignoring the social and political contexts in which his evidence was embedded was not an oversight. It was a method. According to Tylor, "savage religion" had to be abstracted from its living contexts in order to be used in an evolutionary history of human culture that began with primitive animism. "In defining the religious systems of the lower races, so as to place them correctly in the history of culture", Tylor observed in 1892, "careful examination is necessary to separate the genuine developments of native theology from the effects of intercourse with civilized foreigners" (1892: 283). Any trace of more advanced religious concepts, such as ideas of deity, morality or retribution in an afterlife, could only have entered 'savage' religion, Tylor argued, through such foreign intercourse with 'higher' races. Factoring out colonial contacts, relations and exchanges, he argued, "leaves untouched in the religions of the lower races the lower developments of animism" (*ibid.*: 298). According to this method, therefore, animism appeared as the original religion – the earliest, the lowest – only by erasing the actual colonial situations in which indigenous people lived. As a result, the theory of animism provided an ideological supplement to the imperial project.

Although it was posed as a scientific explanation of the origin and development of religion, the theory of animism also addressed nineteenth-century European dilemmas about the meaning of materiality. Despite the expansion of scientific materialism, with its implicit challenge to religious belief, the séances of spiritualism were gaining popularity in Europe, promising material proof of spiritual survival of death. For Tylor, however, contemporary spiritualist practices in Europe were a 'survival' of prehistoric religion because, like the religious beliefs and practices of indigenous people on the colonized periphery of empire, the spiritualist séance represented an unwarranted persistence in attributing life to dead matter. Accordingly, Tylor considered using the term 'spiritualism' for his theory of religion. As a European intellectual problem, therefore, the theory of animism can be situated in the context of nineteenth-century distress about the religious implications of scientific materialism and the scientific implications of a new religious practice such as spiritualism (Masuzawa 2000).

At the same time, this theory of the animation of 'dead' matter was developed in the midst of the consolidation of commodity capitalism in Europe and North America. The commodity, as Karl Marx provocatively proposed, was not dead matter because it was animated by a "fetishism of commodities", similar to 'primitive' religion, which attributed life to objects "abounding in metaphysical subtleties and theological niceties" (Marx [1867] 1974: vol. 1, 81). While supplementing the colonization of indigenous people, therefore, the theory of animism was entangled in European struggles to understand the animation of matter in capitalism at the same time that it was implicated in European dilemmas about the animation of dead matter in spiritualism.

In his theoretical arguments with Tylor, Lang eventually rejected animism as an explanation for the origin and persistence of religion. Yet, in an essay on the novels of Charles Dickens, Lang proposed that the power of his prose resided in "something primitive, an *animism*, the life of objects – knocker, stairs, house, wind, fog – all have impulses of their own". Lang found this primitive religious capacity in other secular authors, such as Wordsworth, Scott and George Sand, in which "the world is all animated and personal, everything in it has life and character". Found both in "early human thought" and the thought processes of childhood, this animistic "gleam", this "ancient mood", Lang argued, "with the associated difficulty of discerning between dreams and realities" stands as "the indispensable basis of poetry and mythology" (1917: 2–3).[9] According to Lang, animism was alive and well in the imaginative capacity of secular literature.

For Lang, the marketplace of secular literature was real. Although he was a theorist of religion, he was also a "hodman of letters", constructing books, essays and journalism for the market. His bestselling work, the series of Fairy Books, which packaged folktales from pre-modern European traditions as well as from contemporary accounts of stories told by indigenous people on the peripheries of empire, presented in secular form – as commodity, as literature – the basic terms of his theory of religion: the uniformity of narratives across societies; the creative power of the human imagination; the social conditions and particularity of myth and ritual; and the ironic juxtaposition of civility with savagery. In the secular market for imaginary literature, the adventure novelist Haggard produced bestsellers, becoming the best-paid author in Britain, while Callaway's books, not only *The Religious System of the Amazulu*, but also his collection of African folklore, *Zulu Nursery Tales, Traditions, and Histories of the Zulus* (1866–68), achieved almost no sales. In his theorizing about religion, Lang mediated between the commercially unviable work of someone like Callaway and the commercial power of the adventure novels of a popular, bestselling author such as Haggard.

This market in imaginative literature, we might assume, was a secular enterprise. However, as Gauri Viswanathan (1989) has argued with respect to colonial India, the British colonial administration easily transposed the religious aims and objectives of the Christian mission, which was designed for both the religious and cultural conversion of the natives, into 'secular' educational programmes based on initiation into the literary canon of British culture. In South Africa, secular literature, like the adventure novels of Haggard, was also doing religious work in transacting the meaning of relations between the centre of empire and the colonized periphery.

In *King Solomon's Mines* (1885), an indigenous African diviner, the *isanusi* Gagool, plays a central role, not as a "house of dreams", with no basis in reality, but as a substantial political force, effectively the ruler of a people and a territory, even if she is cast as the "evil genius of the land" (Haggard 1885: 183). The adventurers in this novel achieve success and acquire substantial wealth, but only after the death of the diviner Gagool. In this exchange between the centre and periphery of empire, the market for imaginary literature performed religious work in the way that it mediated an imperial theology through the defeat of the evil diviner Gagool by the agents of Queen Victoria's empire, which made their acquisition of wealth also a religious victory over African Zulu indigenous religious beliefs, practices and polity.

In *She* (1887a), which was dedicated to Andrew Lang, Haggard focused on the royal priestess Ayesha, ruling from the Caves of Kôr, asking, "What was her real religion?" This question is never answered, perhaps, but discussions about religion follow a trend, according to the hero, Holly, which was familiar to him from debates he had heard about the nature of religion in the nineteenth century in Britain. The human tendency to fear death and cling to life, we learn, "breeds religions". Holly tells Ayesha about his religion, based on the teachings of the "Hebrew Messiah". In this interchange, the colonial encounter is rendered not as an opposition between the secular and the religious, but between alternative ways of life. "Ah!, she said; I see – two new religions" (Haggard 1887a: 205). In *Allan Quatermain* (1887b), Haggard's imaginary Zu-Vendis, roughly based on the Zulu, are ruled by a high priest, Agon, who learns from his encounter with the British intruders into his domain that while his people subscribe to only one indigenous religion, the people of Britain have ninety-five different religions.

While presenting fictional accounts of African indigenous religion, these adventure novels mediated between Africa and the centre of empire, not by distinguishing between a 'religious' Africa and a 'secular' Britain but by rendering colonial relations in highly charged terms that raised problems about religion, religions and religious difference. In the process, Haggard knew he was intervening in the problematic production of knowledge about indigenous Zulu and other forms of African religion. In his preface to *Nada the Lily* (1892), which was dedicated to Shepstone, Haggard observed that the Zulu accounts of uNkulunkulu collected in Callaway's *The Religious System of the Amazulu* were ambivalent, since his "character seems to vary from the idea of an ancestral spirit, or the spirit of an ancestor, to that of a god" (1892: xii). In this recognition, Haggard, a bestselling novelist in the market for imaginary literature, was much more perceptive than the theorists Müller, Tylor or Lang about the fluid, contested negotiations over the meaning and force of this religious term, uNkulunkulu, on a violent colonial frontier in South Africa.

In *The Religious System of the Amazulu*, Callaway collected evidence primarily from informants who had sought refuge at his mission station in Springvale. Like the residents of other Christian missions, these informants were social outcasts or refugees from African communities (Etherington 1978: 68, 95, 102; 1987: 80). Furthermore, since they came from different regions that ranged from the remote northern Zulu territory to the eastern Cape, Callaway's informants had undergone different experiences of the expanding colonial frontier. As a result, instead of holding a single, coherent Zulu religious system, Callaway's informants asserted a spectrum of interpretive positions that can be correlated with varying degrees of colonial contact. At least seven different religious positions can be distilled from the oral testimony Callaway collected. Located in the colonial situation, Zulu religious statements can be correlated with the advance of the mission and administration, so that, for example, relatively intact political groupings to the north regarded uNkulunkulu as the ancestor of their particular tribes; political groupings broken or displaced by colonial warfare redefined uNkulunkulu as the original ancestor of all human beings; and Zulus in conversation with the mission had learned a new theological discourse in which uNkulunkulu could be understood as a supreme being (Chidester 1996: 160–65).

As a novelist, Haggard could take his choice among these different options. In *Nada the Lily*, he decided that his character, the Zulu Mopo, would understand uNkulunkulu as God. In this arbitrary decision, which was more transparently arbitrary than the decisions made on this particular question by the metropolitan theorists Müller, Tylor or Lang, the novelist nevertheless made a theoretical intervention in the study of religion. "In the case of an able and highly intelligent person like the Mopo of this story", he argued, "the ideal would probably not be a low one, therefore he is made to speak of Umkulunkulu [sic] as the Great Spirit, or God" (Haggard 1892: xii).

In this theoretical intervention, Haggard indicated that the real question was not framed by any dichotomy between the secular and the religious, but by the division between the high and the low. This division between the high and the low resonated with other divisions that bore the language of power (dominant and subordinate), the language of temporality (civilized and primitive), and the language of spatiality (familiar and foreign; near and distant; central and peripheral), in which both an imperial fiction and an imperial science of religion could be formulated.

For all of its secular, scientific aspirations, this imperial discourse about religion played a role in the 'enchantment' of the modern West. Although Asad is certainly right to suggest that the secular 'disenchantment' of the modern West was supplemented by Romantic efforts to envelop the pre-modern in mystery, the theorists of religion we have considered –Müller, Tylor and Lang – were committed to demystifying the primitive, the savage and the exotic. They presumed they were disenchanting their subjects. Yet, as we have seen, they were entangled in modes of intellectual production that mystified the relations of power – imperial and colonial, modern and capitalist – in which they worked out their theories of religion. As a result, they operated in two empires of religion: one an imperial geography, the other an imperial imaginary.

In the colonial dreams and colonial adventures we have considered, the theorists of imperial comparative religion deployed two strategies – erasure and elaboration – in their engagement with indigenous African beliefs, practices and forms of life. Tylor was a master of erasure. As we have seen, in order to distil a primitive religious mentality, he had to erase all of the social, political and military conditions under which his data were being collected. As a matter of method, as we have also seen, he insisted on erasing the intercultural exchanges in which his data were being produced as 'religious' data.

In his use of evidence, Tylor was capable of entirely erasing the meaning and significance of data supplied by 'experts' in colonial situations, such as Callaway, who provided him with his classic case of animism in the account of the Zulu diviner who became a "house of dreams". Relying on Callaway's *The Religious System of the Amazulu*, Tylor cited the Zulu diviner, the "professional seer" who becomes a "house of dreams", as a classic example of animism because "phantoms are continually coming to talk to him in his sleep" (Tylor 1871: vol. 1, 443).[10]

In Callaway's account, however, the phantoms were not coming merely to talk to the diviner; they were coming to kill him. "My body is muddled today", the seer says to his friends on awaking. "I dreamt many men were killing me; I escaped I know not how. And on waking one part of my body felt different from other parts; it was no longer alike all over" (Callaway [1868–70] 1970: 260).

The Zulu term for 'muddled' – *Dungaka, Ukudunga* – was a metaphor derived from stirring up mud in water. Although it could be applied to a state of mind, signifying a confusion of mind, it could also be applied to the disturbance of a household by a house-muddler (*Idungandhlu*) or the disturbance of a village by a village-muddler (*Idungamuzi*) (Doke & Vilakazi 1958: 175). All of these meanings, certainly, were at play, as Henry Callaway recognized, in the dreams of a Zulu man who experienced his body, his home and his village stirred up and under attack by men who were coming to kill him.

Lang was a master of elaboration. As we have seen, he drew on reports from all over the world to elaborate the 'primitive' capacity for imagination that he saw as the heart and soul of human culture, society and politics. Instead of reducing all this evidence to a single explanatory cause, such as Tylor's animism, he seemed happy to proliferate an endless array of illustrations of human cultural creativity. In this imaginative elaboration, he made common cause with Haggard.

In their elaborations, the Zulu diviner was not merely a "house of dreams". The Zulu diviner was the real force behind the royal house, the 'religious' underpinning of 'secular' politics in Africa. Most evident in the diviner Gagool, the "evil genius of the land" in *King Solomon's Mines*, the 'religious' was certainly not irrelevant in 'secular' politics. The diviner was central to the colonial drama of violence. Likewise, in *She*, we find Ayesha, both priestess and ruler, wielding imperial power. "What was her real religion?" Haggard asks. Ultimately, her religion appears to be the spiritual terror animating empire. "How thinkest thou that I rule these people?", Ayesha demands. "I have but a regiment of guards to do my bidding, therefore it is not by force. It is by terror. My empire is of the imagination" (1887a: 191).

The term "religion", therefore, meant different things to these imperial theorists. On the one hand, it referred to a mentality; on the other hand, it signified a politics. This ambiguity in late-nineteenth-century British imperial theorizing about religion was situated in the mediations and contradictions of operating in a real empire of the imagination.

## NOTES

1. See Mbiti (1975: 30).
2. See Callaway (1872; 1874).
3. See Hallpike (1986) and Verkamp (1991).
4. See also Callaway ([1868–70] 1970: 91, 126); Casalis (1861: 245); Arbousset and Daumas ([1842] 1846: 12).
5. See Callaway ([1868–70] 1970: 64, 222–5, 263).
6. See Green (1946).
7. See Dorson (1968: vol. 1, 197).
8. See Gedin (1982).
9. See Taine (1879: vol. 2, 430–41).
10. Citing Callaway ([1868–70] 1970: 228, 260, 316). See Callaway (1872: 170).

## BIBLIOGRAPHY

Arbousset, Thomas and Francois Daumas. [1842] 1846. *Narrative of an Exploratory Tour to the North-East of the Colony of the Cape of Good Hope*. Trans. John Croumbie Brown. Cape Town: A. S. Robertson.

Asad, Talal. 2003. *Formations of the Secular: Christianity, Islam, Modernity*. Palo Alto, CA: Stanford University Press.

Benham, Marian S. 1896. *Henry Callaway M.D., D.D., First Bishop of Kaffraria: His Life History and Work: A Memoir*. London: Macmillan.

Bleek, W. H. I. 1857. "Researches into the Relations between the Hottentots and Kafirs". *Cape Monthly Magazine* 1 (Jan–June): 199–208, 289–96.

Bleek, W. H. I. 1862. *A Comparative Grammar of South African Languages, Part One*. London: Trübner.

Buchan, John. 1910. *Prestor John*. Boston, MA: Houghton Mifflin.

Buchan, John. 1933. *Andrew Lang and the Border*. London: Oxford University Press.

Callaway, Henry. 1872. "On Divination and Analogous Phenomena among the Natives of Natal". *Proceedings of the Anthropological Institute* 1: 163–83.

Callaway, Henry. 1874. *A Fragment on Comparative Religion*. Natal: Callaway.

Callaway, Henry. [1868–70] 1970. *The Religious System of the Amazulu*. Cape Town: Struik. (Originally published Springvale: Springvale Mission.)

Casalis, Eugene. 1861. *The Basutos; or, Twenty-Three Years in South Africa*. London: James Nisbet.

Casanova, José. 1994. *Public Religion in the Modern World*. Chicago, IL: University of Chicago Press.

Chidester, David. 1996. *Savage Systems: Colonialism and Comparative Religion in Southern Africa*. Charlottesville, VA: University of Virginia Press.

Chidester, David. 2004. "'Classify and Conquer': Friedrich Max Müller, Indigenous Religious Traditions, and Imperial Comparative Religion". In *Beyond Primitivism: Indigenous Religious Traditions and Modernity*, ed. Jacob K. Olupona, 71–88. London: Routledge.

Colenso, J. W. 1855. *Ten Weeks in Natal: A Journal of a First Tour of Visitation among the Colonists and Zulu Kafirs of Natal*. London: Macmillan.

Comaroff, Jean and John L. Comaroff. 1999. "Occult Economies and the Violence of Abstraction: Notes from the South African Postcolony". *American Ethnologist* 26: 279–303.

Darwin, Charles. 1952. *The Descent of Man*. Ed. Robert M. Hutchins. Chicago, IL: Encyclopedia Britannica.

Doke, C. M. and B. W. Vilakazi. 1958. *Zulu-English Dictionary*, 2nd edn. Johannesburg: Witwatersrand University Press.

Dorson, Richard M., ed. 1968. *Peasant Customs and Savage Myths: Selections from the British Folklorists*, 2 vols. Chicago, IL: University of Chicago Press.

Douglas, Mary. 1975. *Implicit Meanings: Essays in Anthropology*. London: Routledge & Kegan Paul.

Etherington, Norman. 1978. *Preachers, Peasants, and Politics in Southeast Africa, 1835-1880: African Christian Communities in Natal, Pondoland, and Zululand*. London: Royal Historical Society.

Etherington, Norman. 1987. "Missionary Doctors and African Healers in Mid-Victorian South Africa". *South African Historical Journal* 19: 77–91.

Fabian, Johannes. 1983. *Time and the Other: How Anthropology Makes its Object*. New York: Columbia University Press.

Gedin, Per. 1982. *Literature in the Marketplace*. London: Faber.

Green, Roger Lancelyn. 1946. *Andrew Lang: A Critical Biography*. London: Edmund War.

Haggard, H. Rider. 1882. *Cetywayo and His White Neighbours*. London: Trübner.

Haggard, H. Rider. 1885. *King Solomon's Mines*. London: Cassell.

Haggard, H. Rider. 1887a. *She*. London: Longmans.

Haggard, H. Rider. 1887b. *Allan Quatermain*. London: Longmans.

Haggard, H. Rider. 1892. *Nada the Lily*. London: Longmans.

Haggard, H. Rider. 1926. *The Days of My Life*, 2 vols. London: Longmans, Green.

Hallpike, Christopher. 1986. *The Principles of Social Evolution*. Oxford: Clarendon Press.

Hamilton, Carolyn. 1998. *Terrific Majesty: The Powers of Shaka Zulu and the Limits of Historical Invention*. Cambridge, MA: Harvard University Press.

Hexham, Irving. 1996. "Henry Callaway, Religion and Rationalism in Nineteenth-Century Mission History". In *Missionsgeschichte, Kirchengeschechte, Weltgeschichte*, eds Ulrich van der Heyden and Heike Liegan, 439–49. Stuttgart: Franz Steiner.

Horton, Robin. 1997. *Patterns of Thought in Africa and the West: Essays on Magic, Science, and Religion*. Cambridge: Cambridge University Press.

King, John H. 1892. *The Supernatural: Its Origin, Nature, and Evolution*, 2 vols. London: Williams & Norgate.

Lang, Andrew. 1873. "Mythology and Fairy Tales". *Fortnightly Review* 13: 618–31.

Lang, Andrew. 1886. *In the Wrong Paradise*. London: K. Paul, Trench.

Lang, Andrew. 1896. "At the Sign of the Ship". *Longman's Magazine* 28: 632.

Lang, Andrew. 1901. "South African Religion". In *Magic and Religion*, 224–40. London: Longmans, Green.

Lang, Andrew. 1906. *Myth, Ritual, and Religion*, 2 vols. London: Longmans, Green.

Lang, Andrew. 1917. "Introduction". In *The Harvard Classic Shelf of Fiction*, vol. 7, ed. Charles W. Eliot, 1–4. New York: P. F. Collier & Son.

Leopold, Joan. 1980. *Culture in Comparative and Evolutionary Perspective: E. B. Tylor and the Making of "Primitive Culture"*. Berlin: Dietrich Reimer.

Lincoln, Bruce. 1999. *Theorizing Myth: Narrative, Ideology, and Scholarship*. Chicago, IL: University of Chicago Press.

Lubbock, John. [1870] 1889. *The Origin of Civilization and the Primitive Condition of Man*, 5th edn. London: Longmans, Green.

Marx, Karl. [1867] 1974. *Capital*, 2 vols. Trans. Samuel Moore and Edward Aveling. London: Lawrence and Wishart.

Masuzawa, Tomoko. 2000. "Troubles with Materiality: The Ghost of Fetishism in the Nineteenth Century.". *Comparative Studies in Society and History* 42: 242–67.

Mbiti, John S. 1969. *African Religions and Philosophy*. London: Heinemann.

Mbiti, John S. 1975. *Introduction to African Religion*. London: Heinemann.

Müller, F. Max. 1873. *Introduction to the Science of Religion: Four Lectures delivered at the Royal Institution with Two Essays of False Analogies, and the Philosophy of Mythology*. London: Longmans, Green.

Müller, F. Max. 1889. *Natural Religion*. London: Longmans, Green.

Müller, F. Max. 1900. *The Question of Right between England and the Transvaal: Letters by the Right Hon. F. Max Müller with rejoinders by Professor Theodore Mommsen*. London: Imperial South African Association.

Müller, F. Max. 1902. *The Life and Letters of the Right Honourable Friedrich Max Müller*, 2 vols. Ed. Georgina Grenfell Max Müller. London: Longmans, Green.

Nandy, Ashis. 1983. *The Intimate Enemy: Loss and Recovery of Self under Colonialism*. Delhi: Oxford University Press.

Ranger, Terence. 1983. "The Invention of Tradition in Colonial Africa". In *The Invention of Tradition*, eds Eric Hobsbawm and Terence Ranger, 211–62. Cambridge: Cambridge University Press.

Said, Edward. 1993. *Culture and Imperialism*. New York: Knopf.

Scharf, Robert. 1998. "Experience". In *Critical Terms for Religious Studies*, ed. Mark C. Taylor, 94–116. Chicago, IL: University of Chicago Press.

Sharpe, Eric J. 1986. *Comparative Religion*, 2nd edn. LaSalle, IL: Open Court.

Taine, H. A. 1879. *History of English Literature*, 4 vols. Trans. H. Van Laun. New York: Frederick Ungar.

Tylor, E. B. 1871. *Primitive Culture*, 2 vols. London: John Murray.

Tylor, E. B. 1892. "The Limits of Savage Religion". *Journal of the Royal Anthropological Institute* 21: 283–301.

van der Veer, Peter. 2001. *Imperial Encounters: Religion and Modernity in India and Britain*. Princeton, NJ: Princeton University Press.

Verkamp, Bernard J. 1991. "Concerning the Evolution of Religion". *Journal of Religion* 71: 538–57.

Viswanathan, Gauri. 1989. *Masks of Conquest: Literary Study and British Rule in India*. Oxford: Oxford University Press.

Warner, J. C. 1858. "Mr. Warner's Notes". In *A Compendium of Kafir Laws and Customs*, ed. John MacLean, 57–109. Mount Coke: Wesleyan Mission Press.

## 9

# Religion in modern Islamic thought and practice[1]

## *Abdulkader Ismail Tayob*

### INTRODUCTION

In 1985, Richard Martin edited a collection of essays (Martin 1985) on the study of Islam from the perspective of the history of religions. The essays invited and challenged specialists in the study of Islam to employ tools in the history of religions for the study of texts, symbols and traditions of Islam. The volume produced some excellent insights through case studies on early Islam, conversion, pilgrimage and hermeneutics. It was a clear demonstration that the categories and theoretical models in the study of religions could be applied to the study of Islam, and yield some fascinating results. The essays have been widely read and discussed, and other panels and discussions at international meetings have highlighted the need to develop critically similar tools and perspectives from religious studies for the understanding of Islam. In spite of the notable advance in some institutions, however, there is still only a hesitant acknowledgment that the categories developed in the wider discipline might be profitably employed for understanding Islam and Muslim societies. Graham's review of ritual theory for the understanding of Islam is one of few such studies, but his conclusion was that Islam was unique in its approach to ritual. According to Graham, none of the available theories threw light on the inherent revisionary nature of Islamic rites (Graham 1983: 70–71).

The hesitance has been shared by other text-based world religions such as Christianity and Judaism. The categories of myth and ritual have been regarded as less useful for understanding text-based religions. There was an unfortunate and widespread suspicion that these categories were better suited to small-scale religions and their very specific contexts. Religions such as Islam and Christianity were too complex and located in too many different cultural and historical locations, which warranted easy global comparisons and analyses. In other discussions, the uniqueness of Islam has been posited against Judaism and Christianity, particularly with regard to the question of secularization. The perception of the inherent and essential link between religion and politics in Islam has made it difficult to think about Islam as religion. The holism that was supposedly a unique feature of Islam, in contrast especially with the essentially secularizing possibilities of Christianity, has hindered critical reflection from within the study of religions (Van Nieuwenhuijze 1997: 2; Nasr 1994: 32). In my view, ritual, myth and secularization are not inherently problematic terms for the understanding of Islam. They cannot be uncritically applied to Islam, but they can enhance our understanding of texts, contexts, historical developments and societies in which Islam plays some minor or major role. While applying these terms and concepts to Islam, I also expect that these categories and concepts will be refined and challenged for their capacity to enhance aspects of human culture and societies.

One particular issue that was not raised in these essays, but which has become particularly prominent in recent years, has been a critical reflection of the employment of religion as an apparently neutral category of analysis. The essays in Martin's important volume assume that Islam was a religion, the understanding of which could be advanced by critically applying tools developed in the study of other religions. But the fact that religion was an invented term that conveniently (and perhaps inaccurately) covered all specific manifestations of the phenomena was not raised for critical self-reflection. The suitability of religion as a generic term was raised earlier by one of the leading scholars on Islam. In a seminal and highly influential book published first in 1962, and republished in 1978, Wilfred Cantwell Smith cast doubt on the viability of religion as a useful category: "Neither religion in general nor any one of the religions, I will contend, is in itself an intelligible entity, a valid object of inquiry or of concern either for the scholar or for the man of faith" (Smith 1978: 12). According to Smith, the idea of religion was an invention of scholars of the nineteenth century, who had attempted to locate definable dimensions of the complexity of human life. As they were inventing the boundaries of sociology, politics and psychology, they also set aside something unique in human life called religions. For Smith, the rubric of religion had failed to do justice to that important aspect of human life: "The phenomena that we call religious undoubtedly exist. Yet perhaps the notion that they constitute in themselves some distinctive entity [religion] is an unwarranted analysis" (ibid.: 17). Smith made a distinction between the religious as an orientation and experience that clearly existed within society, and some compartmentalized institution or unique aspect of human experience that could be called religion. He argued that the compartmentalized aspect of human life called religion failed to capture the meaning and essence of the religious phenomenon. And for this reason, Smith rejected the validity of religion as a useful category for studying Islam, Christianity, Buddhism and Hinduism.

It seems to me important to go beyond this distinction between religion and the religious, and raise critical questions about the way in which the terms have significantly shaped modern Islam, the objects of enquiry. This paper turns attention to the very concepts of religions and religious as they have been adopted and adapted in contemporary Muslim discourse. Without denying the complexity of the terms themselves, it points to their proliferation within Islamic discourse. Critical reflexive studies such as that of Talal Asad have turned attention to the discursive formation of the religious in the social sciences. Asad's Foucauldian analysis has brilliantly illustrated the power of concepts such as religion in European contexts for the formation of selves, communities and disciplines. Rather than looking for a clearly definable sense of religion, Asad has urged scholars to pay attention to how Muslims and Christians in particular "have had to devise very different strategies for developing moral subjects and regulating subject populations" (Asad 1986: 4–5). In much of his subsequent work, Asad has shown how the modern concepts and meanings such as religion and the religious were produced and articulated in the history of late-medieval Christianity. Using Geertz and Smith as seminal cases studies in the history and study of contemporary religions, Asad has also shown how the academic study of religion continues to discursively produce a particular sense of the religious (Asad 1993; 2001b). According to Asad, this exercise is useful but it fails to grasp the discursive dimension of religions. More trenchant critiques of the origins and effects of the discipline have come from within the discipline itself. Chidester (1996) has pointed to the colonialist dimension of the early application of religious studies on the frontier, while Fitzgerald's more recent study (2000) has highlighted its bondage to Christian theology and the mystification of the secular.

This chapter is a proposal to take a careful look at the debate around religion and the religious in the modern discourse of Islam. It abandons the search for religion and the religious in modern Islam as clearly identifiable aspects of human life. And for now, it also does not pay attention to the way in which contemporary studies of Islam such as that of Gibb, Smith and Rahman, have applied explicit and implicit theories of religions to Islam. It puts the spotlight on how the concepts of religion and the religious have played crucial roles in the production of modern Islam. This chapter explores the elaboration of religion and the religious in Muslim discourses and practices. It argues that the articulation of modern Islam in theory and practice depends to a large extent on this discursive formation around the notion of religion and the religious. Both religion and the religious as generic terms are used in the Muslim discourse itself.

Two examples of the discursive production of religion and the religious are illustrated. In the first case, the definition of religion (*din*) in the abstract has been identified in two seminal figures in modernist Islam. Both Sayyid Ahmad Khan and Jamal al-Din al-Afghani are shown to have played a leading role in how to reinterpret Islam for the modern world. Both relied on abstract definitions of religion to chart particular possibilities for Islam. They focused on the Qur'anic term *din* to speak about the religion (*al-din*) or religion in general (plural *adyan*). The idea of a generic term for religion in the Qur'an would appear to be unproblematic in its internal Islamic application. I shall show, however, that an important shift took place in the nineteenth-century use of the term. This shift introduced a more self-reflexive dimension of the essence and use of *din* in self and society. Khan searched and found an essence at the heart of religion, while Afghani focused on the social and political function of religion. In the second place, the identification of the religious (*dini* or *islami*) within societies is implicated in a process of demarcation and exclusion. The *religious* and *Islamic* in modern Islam become clear and articulated in changing social and political contexts. The *religious*, in this case *Islamic*, comes into its own when the political, the legal and social are specified. The example of Egypt shows how the religious sector was defined in the light of an increasingly growing 'secular' sector. The role of the *ulama* (learned scholars of Islam) became clarified and also circumscribed within an emerging 'religious' sector set off against the 'secular'. In both cases, I want to draw attention to the employment of religion and the religious in Muslim discourse. The transformation of Islam in the modern period has relied much more than we have conceded to the usefulness and the power of such concepts as religion (*din*) and the religious (*dini* or *islami*).

## KHAN AND GENERIC RELIGION

Sayyid Ahmed Khan was among the first Muslim intellectuals to articulate a comprehensive modern approach to Islam. Born into an elite family close to the Mughal court in Delhi in 1817, he witnessed the changing fortunes of Muslim political power. After the Indian Revolt of 1857, he was the most prominent of Muslim intellectuals to advocate support for British colonial rule. In the context of a Hindu majority, he was convinced that the British monarchy guaranteed the survival and modernization of Muslim communities in India. Until his death in 1898, he continued to hold on to this loyalist approach, and encouraged Muslims to take advantage of the new trends in science and education. He left a legacy in politics and education that continues in the Indian subcontinent and beyond.

Much has been written about Khan's modernism, but almost nothing about his reflections on religion in general and Islam as a particular instance thereof. Khan was one among a number of Muslim intellectuals who approached modernization through a conceptualization of religion. Khan's thoughts on a new definition of Islam only make sense in relation to his characterization of religion as essence: "The strangest of all strange things in this world is the conception to which people give the name religion. ... [And] the notion of religion arises in the heart of every man without any external causes, without experience and [critical] examination and without any rational proof" (Troll 1978: 252). Khan wrote mainly in Urdu on these issues, but he sometimes used English. I have located one English usage of 'religion', but in Urdu he used *madhhab* as a translation of *din*. In this sense, he used *madhhab* as a generic form of religion and referred to *madhhab islam* or *madhhab 'isawi* (Christian *madhhab*) (Khan 1898: 117). *Madhhab* is also derived from Arabic, where it is mainly used for schools of law. The significance of *madhhab* for *din* in South Asia should be subject to further investigation and reflection. For the present, I shall assume that it is an unproblematic equivalent of *din*. For Khan, religion was an innate disposition in human beings that defied classification. However, human beings were also driven by other dispositions, backgrounds and prejudices. As a unique quality, religion was indistinguishable from these other tendencies until the intellect located its true nature:

What is the true principle for establishing critically the true religion? What is this true religion? As far as man can know by his rational powers (*quwa-i aqli*), it is nothing but nature (*qudrat*) or the law of nature (*qanun-i qudrat*). ... And what is the nature or the law of nature? It is that on whose account there exists in all material and non-material things around us a wonderful connection and harmony.

(Troll 1978: 245)

And so, for Khan, while religion was in a sense beyond explanation and proof as an innate quality, true religion was identified by reason. True religion could be distinguished from the changing conditions that accompanied it. Just as the eternal laws of nature were often hidden by the diverse elements that were subject to change, true religion was obscured by tendencies that competed for human attention. As an important part of personal perception and belief, true religion corresponded to the principles of order and harmony in nature.

Khan then explored the permanent and the changing aspects of religion itself. Religion for Khan consisted of the essential and the non-essential. The first he called *ahkam-i man-susah* (values derived from texts), which contained the original values (*asli ahkam*), while the second were values derived through intellectual exertion (*ijtihadiyyat*). The former provided the foundations that reflected the harmony and order of true religion, while the latter consisted of the secondary details subject to variation and change. Khan transposed the permanent and changing within the human constitution to the structure of religions in history. In this analogy, then, the *ahkam-i mansusah* represented the permanent principles of order and harmony, while the *ijtihadiyyat* were historical accidents and could be dispensed with. Khan applied this model of generic religion to Islam. His own suggestion for the permanent element in Islam came from his fascination with modern science.

Khan expanded on his unique perspective in a lecture on Islam delivered to Muslims whose faith was shaken by the discoveries of science. He argued that a new theology (*ilm-i kalam*) was required for those exposed to modern sciences. Traditional explanations and defences developed by Muslims on the basis of Greek philosophy no longer made sense to those exposed to the new sciences (*ibid.*: 314). Reason could no longer prove or justify the existence of God. The discoveries of science, particularly the so-called eternal laws deduced from experimental sciences, provided the justification for Islam. Nature, and the eternal principles of natural harmony and order, constituted the true meaning of Islam. The new theology of Khan was captured in his categorical statement: "Islam is nature and nature is Islam" (*islam huwa al-fitrat wa 'l-fitrat huwa al-islam*) (*ibid.*: 317). This new doctrine was discovered in the experimental sciences of the nineteenth century. And it is this principle that was to be applied to historical religions (Islam).

## AFGHANI: ISLAM AND THE EVOLUTION OF HUMANITY

Jamal al-Din Afghani wrote a small tract condemning Khan's deliberations. In his *Kitab al-radd ala al-dahriyyin*, Afghani regarded Khan's thesis of naturalism as a deeply disturbing materialist philosophy. He made no distinction between the materialism of pre-modern philosophy and its contemporary imperialist resurrections led by Europe. For Afghani, the issue turned around colonialism. Whereas Khan was a loyal and unapologetic supporter of the British, Afghani was the supreme symbol of Muslim resistance against European colonialism. Jamal al-Din Afghani's origin is disputed between his own account in Afghanistan in 1838–9 and Shi'ite sources, which cite Asadabad in Iran. After an unsuccessful career in what is now known as Afghanistan, he extended his horizons to capital cities of Asia, Africa, the Middle East and Europe. He travelled extensively giving lectures to young students, and political advice to receptive sultans. As a teacher, he raised awareness among young intellectuals in Cairo, Istanbul and Iran, about the dynamic and progressive nature of Islam, on the one hand, and the need to be completely free from colonial powers on the other. As a political agitator, he advised the Ottoman and Persian sultans to take more independent positions against European powers, and to be more accountable to their own people. He pleaded and plotted for constitutional monarchies where the Sultans relinquished their absolute hold on government (Goldziher 2000).

Like Khan, Afghani's approach to the colonial powers also seemed to guide his general understanding of Islam. In the pamphlet written against Khan, Afghani set out his own general conception of religion. Afghani wrote in both Persian and Arabic, but many of his lectures were delivered in Arabic. And here the term was translated into *din*. Unlike Khan, who was concerned about the justification for belief, Afghani took an extremely functionalist approach to religion. He believed that religion was good for society because it enshrined two fundamental beliefs and six principles. The two beliefs were an acceptance of a Creator, and the consequences of reward and punishment for things done in this world. The first of six principles was a belief in the fact that human beings were terrestrial angels for the unique non-material quality that they possessed that separated them from other creatures. Secondly, every religion contained a belief in its own superiority and salvation to the exclusion of all others. Thirdly, life in this world was a preparation for a better world to come after death. The fourth, fifth and sixth principles were qualities that were generated from the beliefs: a sense of shame for committing wrong, truthfulness and trustworthiness. All the beliefs and qualities identified by Afghani were useful for building a good and powerful society. He was entirely consumed by the social and political demands of the day, and saw in religion/Islam a key to renewal. To that end, he suggested a highly functionalist approach to religion where beliefs in principle may not even matter: "religion, even if it be false and the basest of religions, because of those two firm pillars ... and the six principles that are enshrined in religions, is better than the way of the materialists, or *necheris* (the naturalists like Khan)" (Keddie [1968] 1983: 168). Taking a functionalist approach, Afghani was keen to emphasize the qualities of a generic religion that could serve the social and political goals of the day.

In a response to Ernest Renan, Afghani presented another more critical perspective of religion in general and Islam in particular. Renan's critical remarks towards Islam were part of his general thesis that Semites were less likely than Aryans to promote science, civilization and modernity. Afghani's response defended Arabs against Renan by claiming that Arabs had indeed displayed an ability and willingness to engage in philosophy in the early period: "science made astonishing progress among the Arabs and in all the countries under their domination" (*ibid.*: 184). He effectively challenged the racist remarks of Renan, which the author himself conceded in a subsequent response. But Afghani agreed with the more substantial argument that religion in general, and not only Islam, was a stumbling block to the continued development of science and civilization. While Renan had particularly singled out Islam and Semitic religions, Afghani felt that the criticism was valid for all religions. Religion may play an important role at a point in the history of a people, but dogma finally closed the door to free thinking: "If it is true that the Muslim religion is an obstacle to the development of sciences, can one affirm that this obstacle will not disappear someday? How does the Muslim religion differ on this point from other religions? All religions are intolerant, each one in its way" (*ibid.*: 185).

Afghani argued that religion was an obstacle to innovation, discovery and new knowledge. According to him, Islam and other religions claimed to have solutions and answers to all questions. This attitude created a stumbling block to further discovery and innovation. In this context, Afghani believed that there was nothing inherent within Muslim societies to set them apart from this assessment. It was only a matter of time before Muslim societies would be relieved from the yoke of religion as Christians had been in Europe. Religion/Islam was indispensable for social order until the development and proliferation of science and philosophy. A functionalist approach to religion displaced belief and commitment to a secondary level. In Afghani's life, the political goals of liberation and independence were hitched on to the shoulders of Islam/religion.

Both Khan and Afghani, in their distinctive ways, set the grounds for reform and social change within Islam. But their pamphlets and responses to each other, and to interlocutors in Europe, indicate that they relied heavily on an abstract definition of a religion as a generic concept applicable to all religions. They seemed to rely on the existing abstraction of the meaning of religion in the historical and scholarly legacy of Islam, and added a new dimension from their own contexts. In the 1960s, Smith and, following him, Izutsu discussed the meaning of *din* in Islam. Smith (1978: 103) focused on *din* as a Persian loanword in Arabic that exemplified the reification of Islam in a highly sectarian milieu. Izutsu (1964: 219–29), on the other hand, focused on the multiple meanings of the term in pre-Islamic literature and in the Qur'an. Here, he found a range of meanings from personal faith on the one extreme, to a community of faith with rituals on the other. But both seemed to focus their attention on the contrasting features of religion between faith and reification. There is one meaning of *din* that Izutsu discussed at length, namely, the notions of 'subjugation' and 'obedience' in *din* as they appeared in early Arabic usage, including the Qur'an. This sense of *din* is clear in its lexicographical meaning of authority, hegemony and debt (Ibn Manzur 1956/1375). These abstract nouns referred not only to personal belief and religious traditions, but also to hegemony in the battle field and perhaps the early state. *Din*, in addition to an attitude (faith) and a tradition, also denotes the hegemonic order of Islam within which some religions can function. Within this hegemony of the *din*, Christianity, Judaism and perhaps some other religions function as *adyan* (plural of din). Of course, Islam then takes on two forms, as a special authority and as a faith and tradition like others.[2] My reading of the Qur'an and later commentaries leads me to think that Smith and Izutsu focused too little on this crucial dimension. They seemed to have been too preoccupied with the contrasting pair of reified religion and faith.

With Khan and Afghani, we basically have a situation where Islam is no longer the dominant regime. And they give *din* an essentialist or social meaning respectively, and give up the previously self-evidently hegemonic role of Islam. This generic approach helps them to give a new meaning to Islam but, most importantly, in the case of Khan in particular, an entirely non-hegemonic significance. Their redefinition of Islam was inextricably linked to their understanding of a general conception of religion. Khan posited an enduring essence of religion together with changing and dispensable characteristics, while Afghani worked on the social and political use of religion. In the theories of change espoused by these leading modernist intellectuals, the idea of religion played a useful role in positing a general principle or social value against which Islam in particular could be re-articulated. Both were aware of the need for reform and the need to respond to European political powers and new intellectual challenges. Religion as abstraction provided a powerful instrument to think through change. It created an opportunity for Khan to posit a new foundation for Islam and, for Afghani, a justification for revolt and independence.

Both modernist traditions suggested particular approaches to Islam in the modern world. For Khan, Islam as religion could undergo substantial change as long as a core value or orientation was preserved. The forms and practices of Islam were open to transformation and reformation. On the other extreme, and with equal implications for the forms, Afghani was focusing attention on the ends to which religious might be employed. For neither of them was Islam in modernity located in a particular aspect of human social life, or related to a particular aspect of personal commitment or inner orientation. And yet, the meaning of religion in general was projected on an essence (nature for Khan) or towards a social goal (freedom for Afghani). The implications for such an articulation need further investigation and elaboration. It is clear, however, that the production of both these scholars has gone hand in hand with the conceptualization of a generic religion.

## THE *ULAMA* AND THE RELIGIOUS SPHERE

There is another more subtle discursive formation of Islam that cannot be dissociated from the modern articulation of the religious and the secular. Just as the definition of a generic religion was closely linked to the definition of Islam, the *islamic* dimension of modern society has been articulated in the shadow of a religion–secular division. In order to make the case for such an articulation, we need to recall Asad and Fitzgerald, who argued for the importance of looking at the religious and the secular as inseparable twins:

I would argue that 'religion' is a modern concept not because it is reified but because it has been linked to its Siamese twin 'secularism'. Religion has been part of the restructuration of practical times and spaces, a re-articulation of practical knowledges and powers, of subjective behaviors, sensibilities, needs, and expectations in modernity. But that applies equally to secularism, whose function has been to try to guide that re-articulation and to define 'religions' in the plural as a species of (non-rational) belief.                                          (Asad 2001a: 221)

What I wish to point out is that the secular is itself a sphere of transcendental values, but the invention of religion as the locus of the transcendent serves to disguise this and strengthen the illusion that the secular is simply the real world seen aright in its self-evident factuality.                                          (Fitzgerald 2000: 15)

Both have identified the secular as a counterpart and antithesis of the religious. The former has been regarded as the province of the rational, the material and time-bound, as opposed to the irrational, the metaphysical and the timeless. The religious and secular define each other by mutual exclusion.

The distinction between the secular and the religious in Europe has been endlessly debated in sociological literature. At the same time, obvious doubts have been raised about the validity of this contrasting pair in other cultural contexts, particular Islamic ones. My contention is that this particular contrasting pair has been constructed and invented in different configurations in Muslim contexts. If we suspended for a moment the particular content of the religious and non-religious in Europe, we can follow the changing meaning of the religious and non-religious in modern Muslim societies. One tangible way of understanding this transformation is by looking at the particular role of the *ulama* (learned scholars) in Muslim societies. As the carriers of a tradition going back more than a thousand years, their changing roles provide a good vantage point for assessing an emerging division between the religious and the non-religious. Until the Iranian revolution of 1979, studies of the *ulama* focused on their progressive marginalization and their grudging acceptance of change (Crecelius 1972; Keddie 1972, 1994). In the face of modernization, they were destined to be marginalized and eventually eclipsed by other elites. But more recently, and as a direct result of the prominent role of Islam in public life in many states, studies have focused on the continuing power and authority of the *ulama* in modern times (Schulze 1990; Van Bruinessen 1996; Skovgaard-Petersen 1997; Metcalf 2002; Zaman 2002). These studies have turned attention to the resilience of the *ulama* and their practices, even during the period of apparent decline and marginalization. I should like to focus attention on the discursive formation of the religious in the new states to show how and where the *ulama* have reinvented themselves. The discursive formation of the Islamic/religious has been an important dimension of their re-emergence in late modernity.

Egypt, its religious leaders and the famous religio-educational institute of Azhar present an illustrative example. Through its modern history, the reform of the Azhar has been an abiding concern of modernizers within and outside the institution. The state and diverse actors within and outside Egypt have championed its modernization by introducing modern subjects and modern forms of teaching, learning and certification. The resistance to these changes has been interpreted as the reaction of a stubborn traditional sector that refused to face the realities of a modern world. Looking particularly at the expertise of the *ulama* during the period of transformation, I should like to argue that a religious sphere has been in the making. The boundaries between the religious and non-religious have not been as clear as in Europe. The counter-discourse of the secular has not been prominent in Egypt to the same extent as in many countries in Europe. But the history of this institution suggests a demarcation between the religious sector as a moral discourse in public life and what are regarded as technocratic aspects of law, politics and education.

The so-called architect of modern Egypt, Muhammad Ali, and his successors tried to lay the foundations of a modern, industrialized state. On the one hand, they targeted the autonomy and independence of the *ulama* as an anomaly in a centralized state. On the other hand, they expected them to support and endorse the changes in the judiciary, education and the general economy of the country. While removed from a semi-autonomous part of public life, the sphere of learning, they were given more prominence in another. For example, while new codes were devised, *muftis* were given primary roles in the courts until the end of the nineteenth century. The first removed them from direct intervention in the legal organization of the state, while the second gave them an even more prominent role (Eccel 1984: 79; Skovgaard-Petersen 1997: 101). Between the brunt of criticism and the search for legitimacy, the *ulama* bore the burden sometimes with enthusiasm and sometimes with guarded reluctance.

Later, with the political and social changes at the end of nineteenth century, the British authorities created the first clear division between the indigenous and the general. The courts, the religious endowments (*awqaf*) and education would stay in the hands of the Khedive, while the rest would be controlled by the British. This division seemed to provide the basis for the new roles that the *ulama* could take in colonial society. These particular domains of political and social life were ostensibly unique to the Egyptians, and presented an opportunity for the Azhar to play a key role in the indigenous dimensions of social life. At least, the state and early Egyptian reformists expected this kind involvement from the *ulama* (Eccel 1984: 173). They should play a role in courts because of their expertise in Sharia; in schools because of their former roles as educators; and in charitable foundations because of the apparently 'religious' nature of these institutions. The correspondences between modern law, education and charity seemed obvious and perfectly suited for the *ulama*. The *ulama*, however, resisted these attempts in one way or another, and only agreed under pressure and in silent protest (Crecelius 1972; Marsot 1972). Their resistance seemed understandable, considering the fact that they had very little choice left. By this time, new codes were being written that left little room for earlier forms of the Sharia, a variety of different courts were established, and finally a law in 1897 prohibited all courts from consulting *muftis*. Competing institutions were established to supply the government with teachers and judges. The Dar al-'Ulum (1872) and Madrasat al-Qada' (1907) were founded in order to train teachers, judges and other civil servants. Later, even their teaching functions were clearly circumscribed. A 1923 law specifically defined a teaching role in *religion* (*din*) for Azhar (Eccel 1984: 163, 73, 88, 270–71). It was clear that the Azhar could not expect to play a meaningful and unique role in the modern state. Far-reaching legal and institutional changes were introduced that pushed the Azhar *ulama* in new and uncertain roles. It is clear that the legal changes substantially created religious sphere in which the Azhar was expected to play a role.

This particular differentiating process was apparently reversed after the revolution that ended Egyptian dependence on Britain. In a law passed in 1956, separate religious and national courts (*mahakim shar'iyyah* and *mahakim ahliyyah*) were abolished. And thus, Azhar trained personnel for the Sharia courts were in theory allowed to appear in national courts. It seemed that Azhar graduates would once again play an active role in the courts. Azhar graduates would be recognized for their Sharia training in all courts, if and when their expertise was required (*ibid.*: 316–17). What appeared to be a concession to Azhar graduates, and a move against differentiation, was in reality only a symbolic gesture. Azhar expertise was called in when the need arose, whilst in reality legal codes had replaced traditional forms of Shaira. More importantly, the number of cases that required Azhar expertise declined considerably. There has been a consistent decline in the number of 'religious' cases brought to the courts. By 1973, only 277,717 of 4,669,279 cases (5.9 per cent) had any connection with Islam (*ibid.*).[3]

The institutional changes from the end of the nineteenth century in general may be seen as an attempt to draw the Azhar and its graduates, the *ulama*, into the formal state sector within clearly definable categories. At the same time, it is clear that the state was prepared to bypass the Azhar and establish parallel institutions when it needed to do so. Against this broad institutional change, which attempted to draw the Azhar into the state structure, one may contrast the way in which Azhar has been approached by Egyptians. While the unification of the courts after the October revolution may have signalled a rejection of the compartmentalization of secular law from religious law, Azhar and its graduates continued to serve a differentiated society. Even though the distinction between legal trainees and Sharia trainees was eliminated after the revolution, these distinctions were already well established within society itself. Summarizing these developments, Eccel argued that Azhar lost its monopoly over the courts and primary education (*ibid.*: 320). The reverse side of this observation is that Egyptian society witnessed a growth in what may be called 'secular' sectors. The role of Egyptian *ulama* would have to be focused on the role of Islam in these sectors.

In contrast with the declining role of the Azhar in the judiciary and the general school, Azhar became a champion or defender of tradition, and of Islam. And this is the capacity that has given Azhar *ulama* their identity and distinctive role. The inordinate amount of attention that the state and reformers invested in Azhar provided it with an opportunity to increase its bureaucracy and its role as the moral watchdog of society. Eccel's institutional history may be complimented by Skovgaard-Petersen's (1997) extensive study of of *fatwas* (juridical opinions) from the state-appointed *Mufti* and the Azhar. Each in their own way, and supported by the Egyptian state, used individual and organizational *fatwas* to enter the public debate. Opinions have covered a wide range of topics from scientific calculations of moon sightings to savings certificates, and from insurance to sex-change operations (*ibid.*). A critical review of these opinions indicates to what extent the *ulama* and *muftis* have been approached to find creative solutions and responses to ever new scientific, social and economic changes. While their answers are never accepted by all Muslims, it is clear that the *ulama* are still expected to give an opinion on each and every novel issue. This expectation stands in stark contrast to their exclusion from the schools and the judiciary. The incapacity (or refusal) of Azhar to field candidates for the education of the society, or for filling the judiciary, can be contrasted with the way in which it has dominated these religio-moral debates in public life. Azhar has thrived in establishing itself as a state bureaucracy and for playing a key role in its *moral-religious* pronounce-ments. Both have ensured that Azhar provides employment to its graduates and increases its influence in 'secular' fields by reinventing the meaning and purpose of the religious in society.

My reading of the data and the disputes over the role of *ulama* is that the nature of the religious and non-religious were formulated and negotiated over the course of the twentieth century. The boundaries between the non-religious and the religious have been shifting with the growth of the 'secular' social and economic sectors. Developments in political organization, science and economics have forced a fundamental shift in the boundaries and jurisdiction of the *ulama* within Muslim societies. The *ulama* are no longer the producers of knowledge, nor do they serve the general bureaucracy of the state. The formation of the nation state, globalization and mercantile capitalism has forced them to change their roles and services in Muslim societies. Unlike the modernists discussed ear-lier, the *ulama* have not argued for a reinterpretation of Islam on the basis of an abstract meaning of religion. They have generally rejected these abstractions as an unacceptable imposition of Western ideas on Islam. However, they have been forced by political rulers to adapt and change to the formation of the modern state. And within these changes and adaptations, the emergence of a 'religious' sphere has been shaped. The Azhar reinvented itself as a moral religious body in relation to the secular sectors in which it has refused to participate or, more correctly, in which it has been unable to lead effectively. While the 'secular' domains were expanding, the religious domain was shaped as a moral watchdog over all areas, or a specialist organization teaching a body of knowledge called religion. My general argument is that the religion–non-religious division is an underlying ground for the transformation of the modern organization of the religious. Like the abstract defini-tion of religions in the hands of reformers, the religion–non-religious division provides a useful basis for reinventing Islam for modern social and political transformations.

The religious and the non-religious are not exclusive of each other in Egypt and most other Muslim contexts. To this extent, it makes less sense to speak of a religious–secular binary pair that define themselves in contrast to each other, as Asad and others have argued for in the history of European philosophy and politics. Nevertheless, it is possible to speak of an emerging religious sector that takes a position in relation to new spheres such as politics, society, art and economics. The distinction between the two, the religious and non-religious, is built into the framework of how Muslims think about the universal-izing role of Islam. This particular point can be illustrated by the oft-repeated claim by Muslims that Islam is a way of life:

> Islam is a comprehensive system which deals with all spheres of life. It is a state and a homeland (or a government and a nation). It is morality and power (or mercy and justice). It is culture and a law (or knowledge and jurisprudence). It is material and wealth (or gain and prosperity). It is an endeavour and a call (or an army and a cause). And finally, it is true belief and worship.          (al-Banna 1978: 2)

This particular statement is taken from one of the most influential leaders of contempo-rary Islam, and can be found in many contemporary descriptions of Islam. Most often, the statement is taken at face value to mean that there is no distinction between the religious and non-religious in Islam. And more often than not, this distinction is cast against the natural division that exists in Christianity or Europe. The statement, however, acknowl-edges the reality of many "spheres" of life that warrant systematic unification. Al-Banna should not be taken to task for the precise definition of these spheres, but they can more clearly be seen in the struggle of state and the intelligentsia coming out of the Azhar. Moreover, al-Banna's famous call must be seen as only a claim to find a bridge, Islam, that pushes back the differentiation that he witnessed. Similarly, numerous books on Islam and economics, ethics, politics and gender from within Muslim discourse were attempts to bind the fragmentation of modern experiences under the general rubric of Islam. This, at least, is the starting-point for thinking about the new role of Islam as a moral–religious cement or glue that would be distinct from spheres such as society, politics and economics generated or built on other qualitatively different criteria. The role of the Azhar *ulama* and *muftis* in making pronouncements on all sorts of 'non-religious' issues would have to keep in mind the unique role that Islam and its specialists would take upon themselves.

There is one further point that may be made about the distinctive nature of the reli-gious in Muslim societies. And this point becomes clear when we explore the substance of the *religious* contribution. This is a more tentative point that needs further observation and analysis, but I shall point to its general sense here. So far, I have characterized the new role of the *ulama* as a moral–religious oversight and adjudication over non-religious spheres. Theirs is not a substantive role pertaining to the details of the new scientific inventions or the social challenges in society. The moral–religious oversight may be lik-ened to an ethical intervention that many critics think is crucial for the future of modern society. Christian liberation theologians, progressive Muslims and Habermasian civil soci-ety activists considered it an urgent duty to invoke moral and ethical values in the critical issues facing modern societies (Casanova 1994; Gifford 1998; Hefner 2000; Herbert 2003; Safi 2003). Ethical voices are marshalled and invoked against market capitalism and state repression driven by profits and power. One may add to this, in the past few decades, the need for promoting human rights against authoritarian regimes of all shades. The similarity between these trends and the religious role of the Azhar is tempting, but misleading. In contrast with these imperatives and strategies, the religious sector emanating from Azhar is guided by a non-rational pre-eminence of *islamic* values. I have italicized *islamic* to emphasize its uniquely inviolable characteristic. For those who invoke it, the *islamic* has acquired a special quality of exclusiveness, unquestioned authority and general applicability. Usually, it refers to the invocation of a verse from the Qur'an, or a statement from the Prophet, or from the rich repertoire of texts and values from the distant past. Such pronouncements are made in a highly competitive environment. But the dominant discourse of the *islamic* is not guided by the essentialism of Khan or the functionalism of Afghani, but the pre-eminence of the uniquely and distinct religious. Some major challenges to personal laws and the rights of women, for example, are confronted by a dogmatic resistance to new interpretations. Banking interest is banned in a singular fashion, without any consideration of the banking system and the notion of value. Interest is avoided as a *religious* value, and not an economic one. Reformers would be prepared to accommodate change in the interests of social goals, or the priority of an essence, but protagonists of a specifically *islamic* position want to see a specifically *islamic* invocation. My contention is that that to all intents and purposes the *islamic* in modern Muslim societies such as Egypt is invoked as unique and exclusive, not amenable to deliberation of any kind. In this sense, its non-negotiable nature has benefited from the exclusive, non-rational nature of the religious in modern societies.

## CONCLUSION

The study of modern Islam from the perspective of religious studies would have to be attentive to the way in which the categories of religion and religious have been applied by Muslim reformers and specialists. In addition to the role of hermeneutics, myths, rituals and formation of communities, the study of religions must also be attentive to its key defining terms. The categories of religion and the religious are as much products of social changes as they are tools used by scholars of religions. Contemporary Islam, which I have called modern Islam with full consciousness, is steeped in modernity. Religion is at least one such abstraction that provides a window of analysis that highlights this modernity. But the term is not only a useful tool that analysts and specialists can use. These terms, generalized and abstracted, are used by protagonists to reinvent and reinterpret Islam in the modern world.

The concept of religion as a general idea imposes itself on contemporary reformulations of religions. Religion and its modern categories are an indispensable part of modern developments. They have played a direct and indirect role in the practice and elaboration of new possibilities and limitations. As shown in this chapter, they have been used by both so-called modernizers and traditionalists to reinvent Islam for the modern world.

The examples of Khan and Afghani illustrate this self-conscious reflection on generalized religion in order to reinterpret Islam. On the other hand, specialist scholars of Islam (*ulama*) are engaged in the elaboration of the 'religious' in a different way. This paper has highlighted the invocation and invention of a uniquely religious/Islamic aspect of modern society by the *ulama*. The 'religious' has emerged in the context of social and institutional changes of society. This particular Islamic invocation has been articulated in the simultaneous elaboration of secular sectors. The Islamic has been distinguished from these sectors while claming a totalizing judgement on them. This tension between being distinct and being relevant has obscured the emergence of the religious. But more careful observation and reflection would illustrate the nature of this religious dimension, and its far-reaching implications for change and reformation in such societies.

## NOTES

1. This is a thoroughly revised version of my lecture "Reading Religion and the Religious in Modern Islam", presented on 10 September 2004 at the Radboud University Nijmegen (www.ru.nl/contents/pages/11712/ruoratietayobbinnenwerk.pdf). I am indebted to the editor and Sa`diyyah Shaikh for their in valuable comments and suggestions for helping me to clarify my ideas for this new version.
2. The interplay between Islam as hegemonic *din* and Islam as faith and tradition can be seen in the Qur'an, and the later development of the religious tradition. In the light of the modern reformulation that I am arguing for, this changing dimension merits further study and reflection. At least in Rumi's *Fihi ma fihi* ([1207–73] 1961: 127) this distinction and interplay between hegemony and faith is clearly present.
3. Closely following the judicial sector, Azhar also lost its role in general education as well. Student numbers in the "religious" sciences (Qur'an, Sharia, theology) declined over the course of the twentieth century from 39 per cent of all students in secondary education in 1913/1914, to only 5 per cent of students in 1970/71 (Eccel 1984: 293).

## BIBLIOGRAPHY

al-Banna, Imam Hassan. 1978. *Message of the Teachings.* Trans. H. M. Najm. Durban: MYM Publications. (Originally published Islamic Party Publications (USA), 1977).

Asad, Talal. 1986. *The Idea of an Anthropology of Islam.* Occasional Papers Series. Washington, D.C.: Center for Contemporary Arab Studies, Georgetown University.

Asad, Talal. 1993. *Genealogies of Religion: Discipline and Reasons of Power in Christianity and Islam.* Baltimore, MD: Johns Hopkins University Press.

Asad, Talal. 2001a. "Reading a Modern Classic: W. C. Smith's *The Meaning and End of Religion*". *History of Religions* 40(3): 205–22.

Asad, Talal. 2001b. *Thinking about Secularism and Law in Egypt.* Leiden: ISIM.

Casanova, Jose. 1994. *Public Religions in the Modern World.* Chicago, IL: University of Chicago Press.

Chidester, David. 1996. *Savage Systems: Colonialism and Comparative Religion in Southern Africa.* Charlottesville, VA: University Press of Virginia.

Crecelius, Daniel. 1972. "Nonideological Responses of the Egyptian Ulama to Modernization". In *Scholars, Saints, and Sufis: Muslim Religious Institutions in the Middle East since 1500*, ed. N. R. Keddie, 167–209. Berkeley, CA: University of California Press.

Eccel, A. Chris. 1984. *Egypt, Islam and Social Change: al-Azhar in Conflict and Accommodation*. Berlin: Klaus Schwarz.

Fitzgerald, Timothy. 2000. *The Ideology of Religious Studies*. Oxford: Oxford University Press.

Gifford, Paul. 1998. *African Christianity: Its Public Role*. London: Hurst.

Goldziher, Ignace. 2000. "Djamal al-Din al-Afghani, al-Sayyid Muhammad b. Safdar". In *The Encyclopedia of Islam*, ed. H. U. Qureshi, J. van Lent and P. J. Bearman, 417–17. Leiden: E. J. Brill.

Graham, William A. 1983. "Islam in the Mirror of Ritual". In *Islam's Understanding of Itself*, ed. R. G. Hovannisian and S. Vryonis, 53–71. Malibu, CA: Undena Publications.

Hefner, Robert W. 2000. *Civil Islam: Muslims and Democratization in Indonesia, Princeton Studies in Muslim Politics*. Princeton, NJ: Princeton University Press.

Herbert, David. 2003. *Religion and Civil Society: Rethinking Public Religion in the Contemporary World*. Aldershot: Ashgate.

Ibn Manzur. 1956. "Muhammad b. Mukram. 1956/1375". *Lisan al-`Arab*. Cairo.

Izutsu, Toshihiko. 1964. *God and Man in the Koran: Semantics of the Koranic Weltanschauung*. Tokyo: The Keio Institute of Cultural and Linguistic Studies.

Keddie, Nikki R., ed. 1972. *Scholars, Saints, and Sufis: Muslim Religious Institutions in the Middle East since 1500*. Berkeley, CA: University of California Press.

Keddie, Nikki R., ed. [1968] 1983. *An Islamic Response to Imperialism: Political and Religious Writings of Sayyid Jamal ad-Din "al-Afghani" Including a Translation of the "Refutation of the Materialists" from the Original Persian by Nikki R. Keddie and Hamid Algar*. Berkeley, CA: University of California Press.

Keddie, Nikki R. 1994. "The Revolt of Islam, 1700–1993: Comparative Considerations and Relations to Imperialism". *Comparative Studies in Society and History* 36(3): 463–87.

Khan, Syed Ahmed. 1898. *Akhiri mazamin* (Final essays). Lahore: Rifa`ah `amm Press.

Marsot, Afaf Lutfi al-Sayyid. 1972. "The Ulama of Cairo in the Eighteenth and Nineteenth Centuries". In *Scholars, Saints, and Sufis: Muslim Religious Institutions in the Middle East since 1500*, ed. N. R. Keddie. Berkeley, CA: University of California Press.

Martin, Richard Carleton, ed. 1985. *Approaches to Islam in Religious Studies*. Tucson, AZ: University of Arizona Press.

Metcalf, Barbara D. 2002. *Traditionalist Islamic Activism: Deoband, Tablighis, and Talibs*. Leiden: ISIM.

Nasr, Seyyed Hossein. 1994. *Ideals and Realities of Islam*. London: HarperCollins (Aquarian).

Rumi, Jalal al-Din [1207–73] 1961. *Discourses of Rumi*. Trans. A. J. Arberry. London: John Murray.

Safi, Omid, ed. 2003. *Progressive Muslims: On Justice, Gender and Pluralism*. Oxford: Oneworld.

Schulze, R. 1990. "De Saoedi-Arabische Ulama en het Islamische internatiolisme". In *Schriftgeleerden in de Moderne Islam*, eds J. G. J. Ter Haar and P. S. van Koningsveld, 25–45. Muiderberg: Dick Coutinho.

Skovgaard-Petersen, Jakob. 1997. *Defining Islam for the Egyptian State: Muftis and Fatwas of the Dar al-ifta*. Ed. R. Schultze. Leiden: E. J. Brill.

Smith, Wilfred Cantwell. 1978. *The Meaning and End of religion*. San Francisco, CA: Harper & Row.

Troll, Christian W., ed. 1978. *Sayyid Ahmad Khan: A Reinterpretation of Muslim Theology*. New Delhi: Vikas Publishing House.

Van Bruinessen, Martin. 1996. "Traditions for the Future: The Reconstruction of Traditionalist Discourse within NU". In *Nahdlatul Ulama, traditional Islam and modernity in Indonesia*, eds G. Fealy and G. Barton, 163–89. Clayton: Monash Asia Institute, Monash University.

Van Nieuwenhuijze, C. A. O. 1997. *Paradise Lost: Reflections on the Struggle for Authenticity in the Middle East*. Ed. R. Schulze. Leiden: E. J. Brill.

Zaman, Muhammad Qasim. 2002. *The Ulama in Contemporary Islam: Custodians of Change*. Princeton, NJ: Princeton University Press.

# 10

# Rudolf Otto, cultural colonialism and the 'discovery' of the holy

## Gregory D. Alles

Speaking at Rudolf Otto's graveside service, Heinrich Frick recalled "Otto's own description of how he had once, in remarkable circumstances, encountered the power of the Holy with utter clarity":

> It was on his journey through North Africa, and he found himself in a poor Moroccan synagogue on Yom Kippur, just at the climax of the ceremony. What a contrast! Here was a pathetic, impoverished building with a tiny gathering of equally pathetic human beings (*Existenzen*) – and in this context the dazzling hymn of the *trisagion*, the seraphim's song of praise from the prophet Isaiah: "Holy, holy, holy is the Lord of hosts; the whole earth is full of his glory." By the flickering light of the candles the full majesty of the Lord of heaven and earth seemed to be present in the midst of our poverty and paltriness. Afterwards Rudolf Otto experienced the Holy in other religions, too, at more magnificent sacred places and in higher cultures. But it seemed to him that the contrast [between the setting and song in the synagogue] made that single impression the most shattering of all. Later he identified that experience as the precise moment (*Stunde*) when he discovered his understanding of the Holy, and he described it in moving words. (Frick 1937a: 5–6)

Three and a half decades later this moment had been reduced to a formula: "It is particularly noteworthy that Otto came to know the experience [of the holy] not primarily from reading sacred texts but on a journey as a spontaneous religious experience in a Jewish synagogue in Morocco, as he himself told me" (Ernst Benz 1971: 36).

Part of what makes this account of Otto's discovery of the Holy interesting to me is that it is so obviously wrong. First, despite situating Otto's discovery in space, Frick's account manages to efface the political context within which the experience allegedly took place, a context that we can only designate with the word colonialism. Secondly, in associating

193

the discovery of the Holy with events in a Moroccan synagogue, the account misplaced Otto's discovery of the Holy into a mystical North Africa of the European imagination; it used the trope of discovery to fabricate a simplistic genealogy for Otto's ideas, and one that is mostly false. Thirdly, although Frick actually says very little about Otto's discovery of the Holy, he does imply something about Otto's ideas. Since those ideas did not have the kind of origin that they ought to have, Frick – or perhaps Otto himself – invented the right kind of origin for them.

My first step in this chapter will be to undo the effacement, to resituate Otto's Moroccan experience in its colonial context. But that experience was neither the first nor the last travel experience that Otto identified as a profound encounter with what he saw as the experiential ground of religion. My second step, then, will be to examine this larger series. Although each experience took place within a significant political context, the strategic purposes for which Otto used the Holy varied with the shifting demands of German nationalism from the late 1890s to the late 1920s. My third step will be to ask what enabled Otto to use the Holy to meet such different demands. To answer that question I shall explore some affinities between deep structures of Otto's thought and those of his situation, affinities that, I suggest, facilitated Otto's strategic use of the Holy for a variety of political purposes, including colonial ones. That step will leave unresolved the Marx–Weber question of which come first, mental or social structures. But whatever the answer, the structures of Otto's thought and situation led to the effacement of the relations between the two. It required Otto's followers to disseminate a false genealogy for the Holy.

The lesson of the present examination should be clear: neither in origin nor of necessity was Otto's Holy, including its emphasis on alterity or otherness, a colonial conception. It emerged within a larger context of theological, ecclesiastical, social, economic and political interests. But that larger context did not preclude the strategic use of the Holy for colonial purposes, and in 1911–12 Otto did precisely that.

I

Frick's account takes the form of a *hadith* whose chain of transmission is relatively short: Frick heard the tale of the discovery of the Holy from Otto himself, and Otto certainly ought to have known. But despite its brevity, the chain is also weak. The problem is not just that travellers' tales are notoriously unreliable. It is also that the claim is at odds with the account of the same events that Otto published shortly after the events occurred (Otto 1911b: 709). From a distance of fifteen or twenty years, after the success of *Das Heilige* had transformed Otto into an international celebrity in the philosophy of religion – and a disreputable reprobate for cutting-edge German-speaking theologians such as Karl Barth – it may well have looked to Otto as if he had discovered the Holy at the moment when he heard the *trisagion* in North Africa. But that perception is similar to what Mircea

Eliade used to call a "revalorization". It re-presents the events in a new frame. The initial valorization, the contemporaneous frame, is, I think, at least as interesting as the later one. Let us consider it a little.

Like German colonialism, German travel writing during what David Blackbourn (1997) has called the "long nineteenth century" was rather different from its English counterpart. While English explorers such as Richard Burton wrote about exotic, faraway lands in Asia and Africa (Burton 1851, 1860, 1893), Germans tended to write about cities in Europe, such as Berlin and Paris, and travels among German emigrants, especially in North America (Brenner 1989). German writers could certainly denigrate the abilities of non-European people, as is clear enough from Georg Forster's comments ([1777] 1983: 19–21) on the childlike mentality of O-mai, a Tahitian prince. But, unlike Forster, they did not generally celebrate discoveries and present them as opportunities for conquest and enrichment, as English writers did. For one thing, a unified German state did not come into existence until 1871, and when it did it adamantly rejected the idea of overseas colonization, at least until 1884, when it suddenly reversed course. Instead, German classics such as Goethe's *Italian Journey* ([1829] 2002) presented travel as an opportunity to escape from business and political concerns and pursue personal cultivation unfettered by the demands of everyday life. Good examples are Goethe's geological observations and his attempts at painting.

By the beginning of the twentieth century, however, that attitude had changed. Germany was making great strides as an industrial power, and the German *Bürgertum*, the business and professional elites, had become enamoured of the colonial enterprise. As Bernhard von Bülow stated programmatically in 1897, Germany did not want to put any other country in the shade, but it did want its own place in the sun (Feuchtwanger 2001: 133). This was the time of such organizations as the Colonial Society, the Navy League and the Pan-German League (Eley 1978; Chickering 1984; Blackbourn 1997: 428–33). It was also briefly, from 1896 to 1903, the time of Friedrich Naumann's left-liberal Nationalsozialer Verein (National-Social Union), to which Otto belonged. The Verein sought to unite educated professionals (the *Bildungsbürgertum*) and labour against business (the *Besitzbürgertum*) by promoting a domestic policy that addressed the interests of workers – and, reluctantly, women – together with a foreign policy rooted in German strength (Düding 1972).

Otto's report of his encounter with the Holy in a Moroccan synagogue appeared in a piece of travel writing: a set of letters from North Africa that he sent to the Protestant theological magazine, *Die Christliche Welt*, in 1911 (Otto 1911a, 1911b). Travel letters had been extremely popular in Germany for decades, and this was not the first time that Otto had written them (Otto 1897). Nor was it at all uncommon for liberal Protestant theologians to do so. Otto's good friend Heinrich Hackmann had previously published travel accounts (Hackmann 1905, 1910).[1] So had Friedrich Naumann (1899) and many others. Unlike their predecessors, these later theological travellers, by occupation state officials, often used their travel writings to propagate their visions of German foreign policy. Otto did too.

Otto's letters from North Africa entwine reflections on two major themes: religious experience and colonial policy. They begin with a carefully crafted piece on his visit to Candelaria in Tenerife that pits a liberal Protestant emphasis on subjective religious experience against the inferior materiality of Catholic superstition (Otto 1911a). This piece concludes by insisting that genuine religious experience does *not* derive from an experience of the sublime in nature, but Otto teases his readers, breaking off suddenly and hinting that subsequent letters will discuss the matter further. That implicit promise is only partially fulfilled. In describing the Rock of Gibraltar, Otto again encounters a quasi-religious sublime, this time evoked by the recognition not of striking natural beauty but of immense political will. In his view, the adaptation of the Rock for British imperial purposes epitomizes the way the British have imposed their interests on the rest of the world. The experience of this accomplishment is not quite religious, Otto says, but it comes close (Otto 1911b: 779–80).

Otto's reflections on Gibraltar signal a shift of focus. As Otto travelled from the western edge of Africa to the eastern edge of Asia, he increasingly turned his attention away from religious experience and toward the colonial project. What propelled that shift was the inferiority he felt as a German encountering what appeared to him as the achievements of British, French and US imperialism. Discussing Friesian philosophy with young Hindus in Benares, he pressed upon them the need to learn German (Otto 1911c). In an address before the German consul in China he systematized his emerging colonial programme, later published under the title "Germany's Cultural Tasks Overseas" (Otto 1912a). What disturbed Otto most about British and French colonialism – aside, of course, from its success – was its material, economic and technical orientation and its disregard for the cultures and aspirations of colonized peoples. One hears in this concern the voice of a parochial German idealist, repeating the distinction inherited from the Napoleonic era between *Zivilisation*, which characterized the frivolous French and the materialistic British, and *Kultur*, the definitive characteristic of Germanness (Stern 1961).

Otto's letters from North Africa do not yet present a fully formed colonial programme. They merely contrast the ancient and the modern among colonized peoples and observe critically the materialistic direction of French colonialism. It is in this context that Otto describes his encounter with the *trisagion* in a Moroccan synagogue. Filth, darkness and narrowness locate the synagogue squarely in the realm of the ancient. In such settings Otto's readers do not normally encounter any sublime, whether natural or political. Instead, we encounter indolence, rote memorization, fixation on inconsequential details, an irrational attachment to markers of traditional identity and lower stages of religion (*Unterreligion*) that Otto's interlocutors reject as meaningless custom. Yet in this squalid, dark, narrow setting the sublime beauty of authentic religious experience mysteriously erupts:

*Qadoš qadoš qadoš 'elohim adonay ṣebaot*
*Male'u haššamayim wehaaretz kebodo!*
*[Holy, holy, holy, God Lord of hosts,*
*Heaven and earth are full of your glory!]*

I have heard the *Sanctus, sanctus, sanctus* of the cardinals in Saint Peter's, the *Swiat, swiat, swiat* in the cathedral in the Kremlin, and the *Hagios, hagios, hagios* of the patriarch in Jerusalem. In whatever language these words are spoken, the most sublime words that human lips have ever uttered, they always seize one in the deepest ground of the soul, arousing and stirring with a mighty shudder the mystery of the other-worldly that sleeps therein. That happens here more than anywhere else, here in this deserted place, where they resound in the language in which Isaiah first heard them and on the lips of the people whose heritage they initially were. At the same time the tragedy of this people is powerfully impressed upon the soul: they have discarded the highest and most genuine product of their nation and spirit and now sit lamenting by the side of the undecaying mummy of "their religion", standing guard over its casing and its trappings.          (Otto 1911b: 709)

In his report Otto uses this episode as one of a series of vignettes that depict an unenlightened adherence to tradition. But this Holy, this heart of culture that the French colonial project overlooks, provides Otto with a key to unlock the door to successful German colonial competition.

What should we make of these observations? I want to suggest that Otto's colonial programme emerges from the psychology of a third party in the 'contact zone' of colonialism. Otto is himself neither colonizer nor colonized but the colonizer's kin. Aspiring to equality with the colonizer, he enviously surveys the colonizer's accomplishments and at the same time confronts and negotiates his own sense of inadequacy. At one point he makes it clear that he takes the demands of Arab 'freedom fighters' more seriously than his French host does (Otto 1911b: 783). Nevertheless, he does not identify with those fighting against colonialism.[2] He may recognize the Holy among the Jews of Morocco, but he does not envisage autonomy and self-determination for them or for any colonized people. Rather, in the years before the Great War Otto saw himself as a potential colonizer. The recognition of the Holy among the Jews of Morocco helped him critique Germany's colonial rivals and so served as a prolegomenon to the formulation of his own colonial programme, a programme whose success would provide Germany with its own place in the sun, perhaps even overshadowing the British, French and US efforts. That programme belonged to a different style of colonialism from the militaristic imperialism promoted by organizations such as the Pan-German and Navy Leagues. It belonged to a German cultural colonialism.

At the time the leading German advocate of cultural colonialism – or, as he called it, ethical imperialism – was the liberal Protestant publicist, Paul Rohrbach (Mogk 1972). A frustrated theologian and geographer, a former administrator in German Southwest Africa and a prolific author, Rohrbach published a number of popular books and articles before the War with such titles as *Germany among Globally Significant Peoples* (*Weltvölkern*), "Germany's Cultural Tasks in China", *The German Idea in the World* and "Greater Germany" (Rohrbach 1908, 1910a, 1912a, 1912b). Precisely what Otto thought of Rohrbach in 1911–12 is unknown, but it is possible that he knew him and liked his ideas. When Otto gave an address before the German ambassador in China, he chose a title that echoes the title of one of Rohrbach's books (Rohrbach 1910b; Otto 1912a). Three years later, in 1915, when it looked as if Otto would have to relinquish his seat in the Prussian legislature in order to assume a professoriate at Breslau, he suggested that Rohrbach replace him (Otto 1915; cf. Otto n.d.). In 1914 Otto agreed to serve on the editorial board of Rohrbach's new journal, *Das Größere Deutschland* (Mogk 1972: 277 n95). In 1917 that journal, renamed *Deutsche Politik*, published Otto's calls to eliminate the unequal Prussian electoral system (Otto 1917a, 1917b, 1917c). What matters here, however, is not whether Otto knew Rohrbach in 1911. What matters is that Rohrbach's colonial project is commensurate with Otto's own.

Rohrbach started from the assumption that the globe was 'saturated' in the way that Bismarck had spoken of Europe as being saturated. At the beginning of the twentieth century there was no longer a realistic possibility that any European nation could establish a significant new colony in the political sense anywhere in the world. But, Rohrbach said, that did not really matter. Political colonies cost more than they yielded. The better course was to engage in an ethical or cultural colonialism in the interests of exercising political influence and becoming a preferred trading partner. A prime institution for promoting this sort of colonialism, Rohrbach thought, was the school, and a prime agent for administering schools was the Christian overseas mission. That was especially true of missions such as the Protestant Mission Society (*Allgemeiner Evangelisch-Protestantischer Missionsverein*, AEPMV), which saw its task not so much as the dissemination of Christianity as the cultivation of a more general *Bildung* or humanistic education. During a visit to China, Rohrbach had been impressed by the schools of the Mission Society run by the future Sinologist, Richard Wilhelm.

Otto, too, had visited Wilhelm and his schools in China (Otto 1912b). Perhaps for that reason he also promulgated a variety of cultural colonialism (*ibid.*). In Otto's view, a technical education that alienated students from their own cultures was debilitating. German schools should further a more general cultural education in addition to a technical one. The ideal foundation for that more general cultivation was, he thought, moral and religious, and the best way to get at that foundation was through the comparative study of religions. Otto did not deliberately evoke the Holy in his talk before the German ambassador, but he did not need to. From his earlier publications – not just his letters from North Africa but his earlier critique of Wilhelm Wundt (Otto 1910a) and before that, his discursus on the philosophy of Jakob Friedrich Fries (Otto 1909a) – it is clear that in Otto's eyes the entire realm of the moral and religious rested on the experience of a *mysterium* that was qualitatively distinct from the objects of theoretical, practical and aesthetic cognition (to use 'cognition' in its Friesian sense). A recognition of this Holy not only marked the Germans out as superior to the British and French but also linked them to colonized peoples, and it did so in a manner that ensured German superiority. It took what was allegedly the hallmark of German culture and identified it as the natural and universal bedrock of all culture. At the same time, it reserved for German thinkers the task of nurturing this dimension throughout the world, for other peoples were no more suited to the task than the Jews of Morocco, keeping their watch over a rotting corpse. What I find most striking about this colonial programme is its forthrightness. Rohrbach, Otto and others did not embark on colonialism surreptitiously and with embarrassment. They openly embraced it. Although they expressed a (patronizing) concern for colonized peoples, they justified their efforts above all by the need for Germany to compete with its European neighbours, particularly Britain (e.g. Rohrbach 1908).

If, in fact, Otto momentously discovered the Holy in a Moroccan synagogue in 1911, his subsequent behaviour did not show it. In the years leading up to the First World War he talked much more about his colonial programme than about the Holy. That programme did more than allow Otto to negotiate his frequently expressed feelings of shame and inferiority at Germany's poor showing on the world stage. On the level of social status and class it assigned the prime role in securing Germany's future greatness to people like Otto, the *Bildungsbürgertum* or educated elite, rather than either the military or the *Besitzbürgertum*, the business classes to which Otto's deceased father and several of his older brothers belonged.

Otto's colonial programme had other benefits as well. On the professional level, it served to stimulate demand for his writings. Otto had set off on his "journey around the world" to prepare a general introduction to the history of religions (Otto 1909b, 1910b; Siebeck 1909). That book was to have served as a basic textbook for a subject that, perhaps not without self-interest, Otto claimed should occupy a central position in the curriculum of every colonial school. Otto never did write that introduction, but other publications did plough colonial fields. Perhaps most notably, Otto spearheaded the publication of a series known as *Quellen der Religionsgeschichte* (Sources in the history of religions), conceived explicitly as a German counterpart to the *Sacred Books of the East* for the purposes of colonial competition (Otto 1912b; 1913b, 1913c, 1913e, 1913f).

Finally, on a more personal level, Otto acquired access to a new set of government officials, officials who were much more sympathetic to his ideas than the conservative church leaders were. In spring 1913 those officials asked Otto to lobby various groups on behalf of his colonial programme (Otto 1913a). Later in 1913 he was elected to the Prussian state legislature, where the following year he secured funding for *Quellen* (Otto 1913d, 1914). Finally, in 1915 he received the greatest prize of all, his long-sought professoriate.

II

As long ago as 1940 Wilhelm Haubold (1940: 19–21) noted that during the course of his life Otto described several memorable encounters with what he eventually came to call "the Holy". The earliest came not in 1911 but in the late 1890s, when Otto visited Egypt. Shortly afterwards he wrote to Anni Schultz, daughter of his teacher Hermann Schultz, about how profoundly he had experienced the eternal when he saw the Sphinx (Otto 1899a, 1899b). A decade later he used this experience in his *Philosophy of Religion* (1909a: 116 n1) as an example of the religious feeling of the depths and mystery (*Geheimnis*) of being and the world, a feeling beyond all symbolic expression.[3] Much later, Otto recorded a third experience in a set of letters published in *Die Christliche Welt* the year after he died: his experience of seeing the massive three-headed stone Siva on Elephanta Island in Bombay Harbour. He wrote: "Nowhere have I seen the mystery of the transcendent expressed with more grandeur or fullness than in these three heads. ... From the spirit of the religion that lived here one can learn more in an hour of viewing than from all the books ever written" (Otto 1938: 986).

In each of these experiences Otto was travelling through non-European lands whose inhabitants were living under European, but not German, domination. In each a single, very specific encounter served as a psychological catalyst, evoking in Otto a recognition of the religious transcendent. For two of the experiences the catalyst was visual, for one it was auditory. In the Egyptian and Jewish cases Otto encountered objects that he most probably took as precedent to German high culture; in the Indian case he encountered an object that was more foreign (cf. Alles 2002). But visual or auditory, own or alien, every object was pre-industrial and ancient.

To be sure, Otto did not experience religious transcendence only while travelling abroad. We can surmise from comments about the Gothic Cathedral at Ulm and the Cathedral Choir in Berlin that he experienced the Holy at home, too (Otto [1917] 1987: 88, 91 [Eng. trans., Otto 1950: 68, 71]). Perhaps the encounters overseas were particularly vivid because they were one-time occurrences. But the point I want to stress here is that these three incidents represent three different relations of the Holy to colonialism.

As we have seen, the encounter with the *trisagion* in the Moroccan synagogue played a pivotal role in the formulation of a cultural colonial programme. But by 1927, Otto, a German who had suffered deprivations under the Treaty of Versailles, tended to identify with the colonized, not the colonizer. Soon after the end of the First World War he had founded a *Religiöser Menschheitsbund*, a League of Religions, as a corrective to the League of Nations founded by Germany's old colonial competitors, England, France, Russia and the United States (Alles 1991; Obergethmann 1998). The RMB, as he called it, aimed to work for genuine peace by bringing together as equals those forces that, grounded in the religious transcendent, could alone provide the necessary moral foundation and impetus for nations to pursue peace: the world's religions. Otto also had a particular interest in the movement for Indian independence. Illness forced him to decline an invitation to meet with Mohandas Gandhi in Ahmedabad (Otto 1928: 4; cf. Otto 1933), but later, when Rabindranath Tagore visited Marburg, Otto acted as his interpreter. He also published an edition of Tagore's writings in German (Otto 1931a, 1931b). As a third party standing on the colonizer–colonized divide, Otto could shift his inclinations, and as a result his strategic use of the Holy, from one pole to the other: from colonization to resistance and presumably back again. The key was always what seemed to be in the best interests of the German nation.

Just as interesting as Otto's experiences in the Moroccan synagogue and the Elephanta cave temple is his encounter with the Sphinx. Its context is neither explicitly colonial nor explicitly anti-colonial, but that does not imply that it has no relationship to colonialism whatsoever. Even in the absence of an explicitly colonial programme, Otto found in the distant, exotic monuments of the colonized world schemas for the religious transcendent.

It is important to stress that Otto was not first attracted to what later became the idea of the Holy because of its colonial utility. What first attracted him to it was the way in which it allowed him to negotiate personal crises of faith that the historical and scientific critiques of traditional Christianity had provoked (Otto 1891; for analysis, Alles 2001). Beginning in his early university days his interest in the experiential side of religion became ever more pronounced, even creating some distance between himself and his relatives (Sonnemann 1941: 7). By the time Otto wrote to Anni Schultz about the Sphinx, religious experience had come to form the bedrock of what he called, at least in his representations to Anni, the "Schultz–Otto system" (Otto 1899c; the Schultz of the system was not Anni but her father).

Nevertheless, although personal, non-colonial motivations first led Otto to religious experience, his conceptions of religious experience always had broader resonances too, for even as a student Otto had viewed theology in the context of its service to the nation. During the summer of 1894 he filled a lengthy notebook with reflections on, of all people, Eugenio Bulgaris, a leader of the Greek Enlightenment who apparently exemplified for Otto the close relationship between liberal theology and national renewal (Otto 1894b). At the same time he had begun to discover how rhetorically useful the foreign could be in talking about transcendent realities. Reporting on his student teaching in the spring of 1894, he wrote that one of his more successful lessons was based on a picture of an elephant in a jungle. The exotic setting had fascinated his young pupils (Otto 1894a).

In these early years Otto may not have had much interest in the colonial project *per se*, but that does not mean that he had not assimilated elements of a colonial mentality. For example, we can see a colonial mentality in the conception, propounded by Hermann Schultz, among others, that religious history displayed a gradual evolution from primitive through national and moral religions to Christianity and the notion, taken over into *Das Heilige*, that primitive religions were rooted in fear. We can see it as well in Otto's realization of the rhetorical power of the foreign – and in the late nineteenth century that meant the colonized – in expressing transcendent reality. Later, Otto exploited that effectiveness in writing about the Sphinx, the Moroccan *trisagion* and the *trimurti* of Elephanta.

It would lead us too far afield to detail here the development of Otto's theoretical and practical concerns between the years 1894 and 1911: his engagement with the thought of Friedrich Schleiermacher and Jakob Friedrich Fries (cf. Almond 1984, Gooch 2000); his friendships with Wilhelm Bousset and Leonard Nelson; his activities aimed at a liberal renewal of the German church and nation in the Nationalsozialer Verein, the Friends of *Die Christliche Welt* and the Akademischer Freibund; his failed bid to become a National Liberal Party candidate in 1907 (Flathmann 1907); or even the deep bout of depression that began in 1904 and almost led him to abandon a career in theology (Otto 1904). Suffice it to say that throughout this period Otto's primary theological aim was to create a safe haven for religion secure from the ravaging critiques of the historical and natural sciences. He did this by emphasizing the distinctiveness of the religious *Weltanschauung* with its supposed roots in the primary, unquestionable data of conscious experience, an experience that he identified as the experience of a *mysterium* but, unless I am mistaken, did not yet name "the Holy". For him such a perspective had more than theological significance. Along with collaborators in the Akademischer Freibund such as Wilhelm Bousset and Leonard Nelson, Otto saw questions of *Weltanschauung* as constituting the most pressing political and social issue that the German nation faced (cf. Bousset 1909). Until the journey of 1911–1912, however, he and his associates had little explicit interest in colonialism. For example, the Friends of *Die Christliche Welt*, a group in which Otto exercised leadership, took little active interest in the AEPMV, despite repeated appeals for financial assistance, just as it seems to have taken little active interest in Otto's colonial politics after his return home in 1912 (Schwöbel 1993). Otto and his friends focused most of their attention on the embattled position of Christianity, the domestic effects of Germany's late entry into nation-building and the industrial revolution, and competition between nations on the continent of Europe.[4] These concerns, not colonialism, were the seedbed in which Otto's formulation of the experience of mystery and otherness as the ground of religion first germinated.

Let us look back at where we have been. Otto's encounters with the Sphinx, the *trisagion* and the *trimurti* present us with three different relationships of the Holy to the colonial project. Initially, Otto had little interest in an active colonial programme, although he did find it rhetorically useful to locate a particularly powerful encounter with transcendent reality overseas in the colonized world. Later he used his ideas about the role of transcendent experience and the religious–moral dimension of life to formulate a programme of active cultural colonialism. Later still he drew on the same ideas in attempting to further justice, right and a measure of autonomy for colonized peoples, including, or perhaps especially, the German people after their defeat in the First World War. The driving force in these transformations was not any relationship between the Holy and colonialism *per se*; it was Otto's commitment to the German nation and his changing views of where the good of the nation lay. But whether the good of the nation lay in pursuing colonialism, resisting it or somewhere else, Otto always made strategic use of the Holy to further that good.

Despite Frick's remarks at Otto's interment, then, what Otto seems to have discovered on his journey of 1911–12 was not so much the Holy as colonialism.[5] He became convinced that cultural colonialism was crucial for the well-being of the German nation, to say nothing of his prospects for a career. He also became convinced that theology, especially the history of religions, should stand at the centre of this project.[6]

But what allowed Otto to use the Holy for such divergent political purposes? That is the question to which we now turn.

III

According to a common definition, the sacred denotes something set apart (Durkheim), that which is different from the profane (Eliade). It is constituted by the dichotomy between the sacred and the secular. That is true of Otto's Holy, too.

Fundamental to Otto's analysis of the Holy is that it is *ganz anders*, wholly other, qualitatively different from all objects of normal experience. That characterization has justifiably evoked the quip that the Holy cannot really be wholly 'wholly other'; otherwise, we would not know anything about it (Smith 1990: 42 n9). It also led Otto into swamps of unintelligibility as he attempted to adapt Kant's notion of schematization to relate the 'irrational' (his term) and the rational elements that supposedly make up the complex category of the Holy (Reeder 1973). But however problematic, the 'wholly otherness' of Otto's Holy is, I think, key to both the colonial usefulness of the idea and to the historical effacement of that use.

Otherness was a constant feature of Otto's thought. His various programmes demanded it. Religion had to be other than science and history; Germany had to be other than Britain and France; *Bildung*, the preserve of the professional elite, had to be other than *Besitz*, the domain of business interests, which itself had to be other than the Prussian aristocracy. Each of these domains had to be other, because each of them was locked in a struggle for survival with a formidable and apparently superior opponent. If religion were not other, it could not withstand critique. If Germany were not other, it could not compete successfully in the arena of world-historical (that is, European) nations. If *Bildung* were not other than *Besitz*, if culture were nothing more than material accumulation and political power, the professional elites had no claim to superiority, nothing of value to offer. I want to add one last domain to the list, but I do so with some hesitation. That is the domain of sexual orientation. Rumours continue to circulate that Otto was homosexual. Although we cannot be certain, some evidence does seem to point in that direction (e.g. Otto 1892a, 1892b). If Otto were gay, the otherness that he associated with religion, the German nation and culture might have had a deep-rooted complement in his own self-image. He might have experienced himself as other in a world where heterosexuality was the norm and homosexuality so hidden or denied that his sexual orientation remains to this day only a matter of speculation.

In our post-Foucault, post-Said era it is easy to schematize colonialism in terms of a self–other binary pair. Colonizers make colonized peoples different from themselves, whether through romanticization or demonization, in order to dominate them. Defining people or actions – mental illness, sickness, desire, perhaps even religion or the sacred – as other is a technique of governance, power-knowledge in operation. I find these formulations crude and simplistic, but they are the default concepts that come to mind when I hear words such as colonialism, and, rightly or wrongly, I am quite willing to imagine British, French and US colonialists thinking in just this way.

Otto's definition of the Holy as *ganz anders* invites us, in fact, requires us to adopt the binary self–other pair, however crude it may be, but it also introduces variations on it. To invoke a metaphor that was worn out long ago, we might say that Otto takes a horizontal opposition – between oneself and the other inhabitants of one's world – and tips it ninety degrees. From Otto's neo-Kantian, neo-Friesian standpoint, there is a basic distinction between the apparent, phenomenal, material realm that most people take to be the self, and the real, noumenal, conscious realm that is truly the self. In important respects, then, the self, the true self, is other. It is fundamentally different from the scientific, materialistic, industrial, technological and economic interests that had come to dominate German society: what Hans Kippenberg (1997) and Todd Gooch (2000), along with many others, have been speaking of as modernity. Not just Otto's theology but his many positions depend on this opposition. It marks not so much an opposition between tradition and modernity as several more specific oppositions: Germany versus England and France; the *Bildungsbürgertum* versus the *Besitzbürgertum*, the military and the aristocracy; and religion versus science and history.

But Otto does not stop with the assertion that the self is other. To it he adds at least two more assertions. The first is the assertion that the self is nothing, the other everything. This is quite literally Otto's account of the human encounter with numinous majesty in *Das Heilige*. But that devaluation of the apparent self only takes to an infinite limit devaluations that Otto applies to other realms as well. In the international realm devaluation appears as in the devaluation of the great national powers, Germany's rivals. In the political realm it appears as the devaluation of the leaders of business and industry, whose influence in Germany had steadily outstripped that of professors throughout the second half of the nineteenth and on into the twentieth centuries. In the realm of the universities it appears as the devaluation of scientific, technical and applied fields in favour of theology and the humanities. And in the realm of the church it appears as the devaluation of conservative and orthodox leaders and laity in favour of a liberal theology rooted in genuine religious experience.

Otto does not stop with the assertion that the apparent self is nothing. He believes that it is possible to cognize the other that is the true self, although many people do not do so, and that leads to a conviction about power. Those who cognize the true self are connected with the source of genuine or legitimate power, even if, as is so often the case, they are prevented from exercising the power that is their due. That is certainly true of liberal theologians in the German church before the First World War, but it is true in other realms as well. One of them is the realm of politics. According to an odd conceit common in Otto's circles at the time, neither labour, business nor the aristocracy recognized the true good of the state. They acted in what they perceived to be their individual self-interest, and as a result their actions were conducive not to national welfare but to national disintegration. Only the *Bildungsbürgertum*, that is, the professional classes and above all professors of theology and the humanities, recognized that its own interests were the interests of the other, of the German nation. As a result, only the *Bildungsbürgertum* and those whom the *Bildungsbürgertum* were able to educate in its own ideals were in a position to govern Germany properly. That was the programme of the Akademischer Freibund, of which Otto was a local leader, as formulated by Martin Rade, editor of *Die Christliche Welt*, in the year that Otto reported to the readers of *Die Christliche Welt* his experience in the Moroccan synagogue (Rade 1912).

It is possible, of course, to 'think otherness' from a variety of political positions. Otto never adopted the position of a social democrat, communist or anarchist. He always thought otherness from the position of an out-group of the privileged, of supervisors or managers, struggling to become the in-group. That social location characterizes not only Otto's position within the church, the university and German society as a whole but also his cultural colonialism. As the example of the Sphinx shows, Otto found the otherness encountered during travel useful in illustrating the encounter with the other that is true reality. But after his journey in 1911–12 he also wanted to do more than use this otherness as a metaphor or example. He wanted very actively to manage or direct it, among other ways through the study of religions. Both in the colonized territories of Africa and Asia and at home he encountered administrators and officials who neglected the true self and its centre, the *mysterium* at the heart of all religions, and concentrated on technical development for economic benefit.[7] Their materialistic orientation presented an opportunity to a nation such as Germany, which had joined the great colonial game late. Germany could not reasonably expect to exercise political authority, but it did not need to. It could manage the cultural and moral–religious domains rooted in knowledge of the other, true reality. Otto himself contributed to this effort by addressing the innermost core. He wrote the history of religions and analysed the Holy itself.

The recognition of the true self in colonized others opens up, however, another possibility besides cultural colonialism. It also opens up the possibility of identifying with colonized peoples. Despite the suspicions of some more conservative Christian professors and students about the "temple of idols", the Religionskundliche Sammlung, that Otto founded (Benz 1971: 32–3), Otto never exactly 'went native'. He always remained a Christian theologian. But he did view the situation of Germany after the First World War as similar to that of colonized people elsewhere. He joined with them, without ever relinquishing control. Such a move is hardly unprecedented. An out-group of supervisors or managers can always ally with workers, when they see it in their best interests. That was in fact the position of the first political association that Otto joined. The Nationalsozialer Verein sought to create an alliance between an out-group of managers, the *Bildungsbürgertum*, and labour. Otto's activities after the First World War replicate something of that strategy on an international level.

Despite all these possibilities, the interweaving of self and other that is so important to Otto's programme is not without its contradictions. Indeed, the very notion of the Holy as *ganz anders* is unstable. On the one hand, consistency forces Otto to postulate that the Holy, as *ganz anders*, is different from objects of ordinary experience qualitatively, not quantitatively: in kind, not in degree. On the other hand, embedded in the very term *ganz anders* is a difference in degree, not in kind.

Here, however, I am more interested in another contradiction. At the risk of devolving into silly word-play, I might say that whoever knows the self as other denies the self as self and therefore must refuse to know it. Less abstractly, although Otto's Holy was implicated in Germany's colonial project and in much more beside, and although it had a genealogy fundamentally rooted in the structures of Protestant theology (Alles 2001), one cannot really make these observations and at the same time postulate the Holy as the Holy. To do so would be to abandon the character of the Holy as *ganz anders*. The Holy must be a *mysterium*. It must be a datum of raw experience, a primary encounter with the numinous wholly other. It must not be learned from books; it cannot be taught. It must be evoked, discovered, and where better to locate that discovery than where Europeans have so often discovered their others, the location that Otto himself found so rhetorically effective as the site of the religious transcendent: the jungle, the exotic East, or in this case a Moroccan synagogue?

A little more than three months after Otto's burial, Heinrich Frick gave the address at a memorial service for Otto held in the Aula of the University of Marburg. In it, he described Otto as an explorer, a pioneer, a discoverer of new territory (Frick 1937b: 54–5). The mythical event of the encounter with the Holy transforms Otto's journey around the world into a journey of discovery, similar to the great voyages of British seafarers such as James Cook and British explorers such as Richard Burton. Indeed, one could argue that it makes Otto's journey even greater than theirs, for Otto discovered something that must count as more significant than mere human or physical geography. He discovered the Holy.

Even without the hyperbole, such an account is deceptive in at least two ways. It imagines a discovery that did not happen, and it denies the cultural–colonial context in which the events that did happen actually occurred.

## NOTES

1. Hackmann's travel letters from Asia, begun in 1910 and published in book form in 1912, actually ran contemporaneously with Otto's.
2. The broader context is probably worth noting. Otto was in Morocco during the build-up to the second Moroccan crisis, which came to a head a month later when the German gunboat 'Panther' sailed into the harbour at Agadir. During the crisis Germany had presented itself as being on the side of Morocco against the French 'liberators'. The third of Otto's travel reports, "Vom Wege", is devoted entirely to this issue (Otto 1911b: 759–61). More broadly, his cultural-colonial attitudes parallel the stance of the German government in the Moroccan crisis.
3. In *Das Heilige* Otto is less wordy: the Sphinx evokes, almost as a mechanical reflex, the feeling of the sublime and with it that of the numinous (Otto [1917] 1987: 85 [Eng. trans. Otto 1950: 66]).
4. This orientation was typical of Germany more generally; see Blackbourn (1997: 436).
5. The traditional account may not be entirely wrong. While it is clear that Otto did not suddenly recognize the importance of the experience of transcendent reality one day in a Moroccan synagogue, it is possible that he did recognize something about that experience as a result of events in Morocco. It is possible that he realized the utility of the word *heilig*, holy or sacred, the name under which he was able successfully to present his views to the world.
6. I am using the terms 'theology' and 'history of religions' in Otto's sense rather than a contemporary one. As Otto makes clear in his *Philosophy of Religion* (Otto 1909a: v–x, 192–9), he conceived of modern theology as a *Religionswissenschaft*, whose constituents were the philosophy, psychology and history of religions.
7. In this context one might note Otto's rejection of the precursors of modern-style management, Taylorism and Fordism (e.g. Otto 1933: §5).

# BIBLIOGRAPHY

## Abbreviations

ASD      Archiv der sozialen Demokratie, Freidrich Ebert Stiftung, Bonn
GstA PL    Geheimes Staatsarchiv Preußischer Kulturbesitz, Berlin
OA       Otto Archiv, religionskundliche Sammlung, University of Marburg
UB Mbg    Universitäts-Bibliothek, University of Marburg, Manuscript Section

Alles, Gregory D. 1991. "Rudolf Otto and the Politics of Utopia". *Religion* 21: 235–56.

Alles, Gregory D. 2001. "Towards a Genealogy of the Holy: Rudolf Otto and the Apologetics of Religion". *Journal of the American Academy of Religion* 69(2) (June): 323–41.

Alles, Gregory D. 2002. "The Science of Religions in a Fascist State: Rudolf Otto and Jakob Wilhelm Hauer During the Third Reich". *Religion* 32(2) (July): 177–204.

Almond, Philip C. 1984. *Rudolf Otto, an Introduction to His Philosophical Theology.* Chapel Hill, NC: University of North Carolina Press, 1984.

Benz, Ernst. 1971. "Rudolf Otto als Theologe und Persönlichkeit". In *Rudolf Otto's Bedeutung für die Religionswissenschaft und die Theologie Heute*, ed. Ernst Benz, 30–48. Leiden: E. J. Brill.

Blackbourn, David. 1997. *The Long Nineteenth Century: A History of Germany, 1789–1918.* Oxford: Oxford University Press.

Bousset, Wilhelm. 1909. Letter to Paul Wernle. Göttingen, 6 June. Archiv RGS 798.

Brenner, Peter J., ed. 1989. *Der Reisebericht: Die Entwicklung einer Gattung in der deutschen Literatur.* Frankfurt: Suhrkamp.

Burton, Richard Francis. 1851. *Sindh and the Races that Inhabit the Valley of the Indus.* London: W. H. Allen.

Burton, Richard Francis. 1860. *The Lake Regions of Central Africa.* London: Longman, Green, Longman and Roberts.

Burton, Richard Francis. 1893, *Personal Narrative of a Pilgrimage to Al-Madinah & Meccah*, 2 vols. Ed. Isabel Burton. London: Tylston and Edwards.

Chickering, Roger. 1984. *We Men Who Feel Most German: A Cultural Study of the Pan-German League, 1886–1914.* Boston: Allen & Unwin.

Düding, Dieter. 1972. *Der Nationalsoziale Verein. Die gescheiterte Versuch einer parteipolitischen Synthese von Nationalismus, Sozialismus und Liberalismus.* Munich: R. Oldenbourg.

Eley, Geoff. 1978. "Reshaping the German Right: Radical Nationalism and the German Navy League, 1898–1908". *The Historical Journal* 21: 327–54.

Feuchtwanger, Edgar J. 2001. *Imperial Germany 1850–1918.* London: Routledge.

Flathmann, Johannes. 1907. Letter to Rudolf Otto. Hannover, 3 December. OA 952.

Forster, Georg. [1777] 1983. *Reise um die Welt.* Ed. Gerhard Steiner. Frankfurt: Insel.

Frick, Heinrich. 1937a. *Rudolf Otto zum Gedächtnis: Trauerfeier für den am 6. März 1937 heimgegangenen Professor D. Rudolf Otto und Gedächtnisrede an seinem Sarg gehalten von Professor Heinrich Frick am 10. März 1937.* Leipzig: Leopold Klotz.

Frick, Heinrich. 1937b. "Gedächtnisrede auf Rudolf Otto gehalten am 20. Juni 1937 in der Aula der Philipps-Universität". *Mitteilungen, Universitätsbund Marburg* 3: 54–63.

Goethe, Johann Wolfgang von. [1829] 2002. *Italienische Reise*, 7th edn, commentary by Herbert von Einem. Munich: C. H. Beck.

Gooch, Todd A. 2000. *The Numinous and Modernity: An Interpretation of Rudolf Otto's Philosophy of Religion.* Berlin: Walter de Gruyter.

Hackmann, Heinrich. 1905. *Vom Omi bis Bhamo: Wanderungen an den Grenzen von China, Tibet und Burma.* Halle: Gebauer-Schwetschke.

Hackmann, Heinrich. 1910. "Asiatische Reisebriefe". *Die Christliche Welt* 24: cols. 1130–36, 1180–86.

Hackmann, Heinrich. 1912. *Welt des Ostens.* Berlin: K. Curtius.

Haubold, Wilhelm. 1940. *Die Bedeutung der Religionsgeschichte für die Theologie Rudolf Ottos.* Leipzig: L. Klotz.

Kippenberg, Hans G. 1997. *Die Entdeckung der Religionsgeschichte: Religionswissenschaft und Moderne*. Munich: C. H. Beck.

Mogk, Walter. 1972. *Paul Rohrbach und das „Größere Deutschland": Ethischer Imperialismus im Wilhelminischen Zeitalter: Ein Beitrag zur Geschichte des Kulturprotestantismus*. Munich: Wilhelm Goldmann.

Naumann, Friedrich. 1899. *"Asia": Athen, Konstantinopel, Baalbek, Damaskus, Nazaret, Jerusalem, Kairo, Neapel*. Berlin-Schöneberg: Hilfe.

Obergethmann, Frank. 1998. "Rudolf Ottos 'Religiöser Menschheitsbund': Ein Kapitel interreligiöser Begegnung zwischen den Weltkriegen". *Zeitschrift für Religionswissenschaft* 6: 79–106.

Otto, Rudolf. n.d. Undated letter to Hermann Mulert. UB Mbg Hs. 797:775.

Otto, Rudolf. 1891. "Vita zum ersten Examen". Hildesheim, 29 December. UB Mbg Hs. 797:582.

Otto, Rudolf. 1892a. Letter to Albert [Brandes?]. Brockenhaus, 21 June. UB Mbg Hs. 826:23.

Otto, Rudolf. 1982b. Letter to [?] Hotzen. Munich, 18 October. UB Mbg Hs. 826:26.

Otto, Rudolf. 1894a. "Bericht über den vom 8ten Januar bis 17ten März 1894 an der Volksschule zu Erichsburg erledigten praktischen Kursus". Erichsburg, winter semester 1893–94.

Otto, Rudolf. 1894b. "Einfluß der Aufklärung auf die griechische Kirche dargestellt an dem Lebensbilde des Eugenio Bulgaris". Erichsburg, summer semester 1894.

Otto, Rudolf. 1897. "Briefe von einer Reise nach Ägypten, Jerusalem und dem Berge Athos um Ostern 1895". *Der Hannoversche Sonntagsbote. Evangelisch-lutherisches Volksblatt für Stadt und Land* 1(5): 2–3; 1(6): 2–3; 1(8): 3–4; 1(9): 3–4; 1(10): 2–4; 1(11): 3–5; 1(14): 3–4; 1(15): 3–4; 1(16): 2–4; 1(22): 4–5; 1(23): 4–5; 1(29): 3–4; 1(31): 4–6; 1(32): 4–6; 1(35): 3–6; 1(36): 3–4.

Otto, Rudolf. 1899a. Undated [but before 19 May] letter to Anni Schultz. UB Mbg Hs. 797:314.

Otto, Rudolf. 1899b. Letter to Anni Schultz. 19 May. UB Mbg Hs. 797:315.

Otto, Rudolf. 1899c. Letter to Anni Schultz. Stg. [*sic*], 30 May. UB Mbg Hs. 797:316.

Otto, Rudolf. 1904. Diary page [?] 10 October. UB Mbg Hs. 826:24.

Otto, Rudolf. 1909a. *Kantisch-Fries'sche Religionsphilosophie und ihre Anwendung auf die Theologie*. Tübingen: J. C. B. Mohr.

Otto, Rudolf. 1909b. Proposal to Paul Siebeck for *Einleitung in die Religionsgeschichte*. Göttingen, 30 June. Archiv J. C. B. Mohr, Tübingen.

Otto, Rudolf. 1910a. "Mythus und Religion in Wundts Völkerpsychologie". *Theologische Rundschau* 13: 251–75, 293–305.

Otto, Rudolf. 1910b. Letter to Martin Rade. [Toward the end of the year.] UB Mbg, Hs. 839 [#3].

Otto, Rudolf. 1911a. "Bei unserer Frau von der Kerze". *Die Christliche Welt* 25(26) (29 June): cols. 602–7.

Otto, Rudolf. 1911b. "Vom Wege". *Die Christliche Welt* 25: cols. 705–10, 724–9, 759–61, 779–83.

Otto, Rudolf. 1911c. Letter to Leonard Nelson. Benares, 1 December. Leonard Nelson Nachlaß 31, ASD.

Otto, Rudolf. 1912a. "Deutsche Kulturaufgabe im Ausland". *Der Ostasiatische Lloyd* 26(23) (7 June): 483–5.

Otto, Rudolf. 1912b. "Bericht über die Reise des Professors der Theologie D. Dr. Rudolf Otto als Stipendiaten der Kahnschen 'Stiftung für Auslandsreisen deutscher Gelehrten'". Göttingen, 29 December. GStA PK I. HA Rep. 76Vc, Sekt. 1, Tit. 8, Nr. 9, Beiheft 2.

Otto, Rudolf. 1913a. Letter to Richard Wilhelm. February. UB Mbg Hs. 797:462.

Otto, Rudolf. 1913b. "Quellen der Religionsgeschichte". Mitteilung 10. *Theologische Literaturzeitung* 38(6) (15 March): col. 190.

Otto, Rudolf. 1913c. "Quellen der Religionsgeschichte". Mitteilung 13. *Theologische Literaturzeitung* 38(9) (26 April): col. 285.

Otto, Rudolf. 1913d. Campaign speech. Stadtpark Göttingen, 8 May. *Göttinger Zeitung* 51(16369) (10 May).

Otto, Rudolf. 1913e. "Quellen der Religionsgeschichte". Mitteilung 17. *Theologische Literaturzeitung* 38(12) (7 June): cols 381–2.

Otto, Rudolf. 1913f. "Quellen der Religionsgeschichte". Mitteilung 23. *Theologische Literaturzeitung* 38(15) (19 July): col. 476.

Otto, Rudolf. 1914. Speech before the Prussian Legislature, 70th Meeting of the 22nd Legislative Period, Session 2 (2 May). *Stenographische Berichte über die Verhandlungen des Preußischen Abgeordnetenhauses* 5: cols. 5956–60 [Berlin: Preußische Verlagsanstalt].

Otto, Rudolf. 1915. Letter to Hermann Mulert. Göttingen, 22 March. UB Mbg Hs. 797:761.

Otto, Rudolf. 1917a. "Reform des Wahlrechts jetzt!". *Deutsche Politik* 2(21) (25 May): 669–72.

Otto, Rudolf. 1917b. "Jedenfalls so frühzeitig". *Deutsche Politik* 2(30) (27 July): 955–8.

Otto, Rudolf. 1917c. "Warum hat England noch keine Brotkarte?" *Deutsche Politik* 2(40) (5 Oct.ober): 1288–90.

Otto, Rudolf. 1924. "Professor Rudolf Otto on Zen Buddhism". Ed. Prajña. *The Eastern Buddhist* 3(2) (July–September): 117–25.

Otto, Rudolf. 1928. Bericht über eine Studienreise zu religionskundlichen Zwecken vom 18. Oktober bis 14. Mai 1927/28 nach Indian, Ägypten, Palästina, Kleinasien und Konstantinopel. An die Notgemeinschaft der deutschen Wissenschaft. Marburg, 6 November.

Otto, Rudolf. 1931a. "'Meine Religion' von Rabindranath Tagore". *Westermanns Monatshefte* 75: 345–50.

Otto, Rudolf, ed. 1931b. *Rabindranath Tagore's Bekenntnis*. Tübingen: J. C. B. Mohr (Paul Siebeck).

Otto, Rudolf. 1933. "Geleitwort". In *Gandhi: Der Heilige und der Staatsmann in eigenen Aussprüchen*, eds B. P. L. Bedi and F. M. Houlston, 7–16. Munich: Ernst Reinhardt.

Otto, Rudolf. 1938. "Briefe Rudolf Ottos von seiner Fahrt nach Indien und Ägypten". *Die Christliche Welt* 52(24): 985–90.

Otto, Rudolf. 1950. *The Idea of the Holy: An Inquiry into the Non-Rational Factor in the Idea of the Divine and Its Relation to the Rational*, 2nd edn. Trans. John Harvey. Oxford: Oxford University Press.

Otto, Rudolf. [1917] 1987. *Das Heilige: Über das Irrationale in der Idee des Göttlichen und sein Verhältnis zum Rationalen*. Munich: C. H. Beck.

Rade, Martin. 1912. *Der Deutsche Akademische Freibund. Oeffentlicher Vortrag nach der Konstituierung einer Ortsgruppe des Akademischen Freibundes in Heidelberg gehalten am 15. November 1911*. Munich: Buchhandlung Nationalverein.

Reeder, John. 1973. "The Relation of the Moral and the Numinous in Otto's Notion of the Holy". In *Religion and Morality*, ed. G. Outka, 255–92. Garden City, NY: Doubleday.

Rohrbach, Paul. 1908. *Deutschland unter den Weltvölkern: Materiellen zur auswärtigen Politik*, 2nd edn. Berlin-Schöneberg: Hilfe.

Rohrbach, Paul. 1910a. "Was steht für Deutschland in China auf dem Spiel". In *Deutsche Kulturaufgaben in China: Beiträge zur Erkenntnis nationaler Verantwortlichkeit*, ed. Paul Rohrbach, 32–66. Berlin-Schöneberg: Hilfe.

Rohrbach, Paul, ed. 1910b. *Deutsche Kulturaufgaben in China: Beiträge zur Erkenntnis nationaler Verantwortlichkeit*. Berlin-Schöneberg: Hilfe.

Rohrbach, Paul. 1912a. *Der deutsche Gedanke in der Welt*. Düsseldorf: Karl Robert Langewiesche.

Rohrbach, Paul. 1912b. "Das 'Größere' Deutschland". In *Der Deutsche Staatsbürger*, 2nd exp. edn, ed. Arthur Schröter, 418–61. Leipzig: Carl Ernst Poeschel.

Schwöbel, Christoph, ed. 1993. *An die Freunde: Vertrauliche d.i. nicht für die Öffentlichkeit bestimmte Mitteilungen (1903-1934)*. Intro. by Christoph Schwöbel. Berlin: Walter de Gruyter.

Siebeck, Paul. 1909. Letter to Rudolf Otto. Tübingen, 1 July. Archiv J. C. B. Mohr, Tübingen.

Smith, Jonathan Z. 1990. *Drudgery Divine: On the Comparison of Early Christianities and the Religions of Late Antiquity*. Chicago, IL: University of Chicago Press.

Sonnemann, Emil. 1941. "Meine Erinnerungen an Rudolf Otto". Bez. Bremen, 16 April. UB Mbg Hs. 797:579.

Stern, Fritz. 1961. *The Politics of Cultural Despair: A Study in the Rise of the Germanic Ideology*. Berkeley, CA: University of California Press.

# 11

# Encompassing Religion, privatized religions and the invention of modern politics[1]

## *Timothy Fitzgerald*

No tribe has a word for 'religion' as a separate sphere of existence. Religion permeates the whole of life, including economic activities, arts, crafts and ways of living. This is particularly true of nature, with which native Americans have traditionally a close and sacred relationship. Animals, birds, natural phenomena, even the land itself, have religious significance to native Americans: all are involved in a web of reciprocal relationships, which are sustained through behaviour and ritual in a state of harmony. Distinctions between natural and supernatural are often difficult to make when assessing native American concepts.      (Cooper 1988: 873–4)

... Religion and Policy, or Christianity and Magistracy, are two distinct things, have two different ends, and may be fully prosecuted without respect one to the other; the one is for purifying, and cleaning the soul, and fitting it for a future state; the other is for Maintenance and Preserving of Civil Society, in order to the outward conveniency and accommodation of men in this World. A Magistrate is a true and real Magistrate, though not a Christian; as well as a man is a true and real Christian, without being a Magistrate.      (Penn 1680: 4)

The two quotations above give us the outlines of two profoundly different meanings given to 'religion'. The first talks about religion as permeating the whole of life, and it bears comparison with religion in early modern England. I will call this holistic concept 'encompassing religion', since all practices and institutions are, in the final analysis legitimized in terms of it.[2] As such it is virtually impossible to distinguish religion from culture in the use of many anthropologists. The second quotation conveys a concept of religion as privatized and essentially distinguished from an area of life defined in non-religious terms. It is this kind of religion that is protected in modern constitutions as a human right; however, such constitutions also protect politics and the state *from* religion. It was encompassing religion against which William Penn and others such as John Locke objected, and their claims abut the essential differences between religion and politics were prescriptive, a rhetorical demand for change, rather than a description of reality. This concept of religion can be seen as the product of 'secular' thinking and also as a condition for the realization of secularity in the first place. A non-religious domain of politics, for instance, could not have been thought of unless 'religion' had been siphoned out of the totality and placed in a special essentialized category. I shall refer to this as 'privatized' or 'essentialized' religion and religions. These can be treated as two ideal ends of a spectrum, with various empirically confused examples sitting at different positions along it. However, this is not only an abstract model, but a claim about historical change.

This chapter is the small beginning of a larger enquiry into the changing meanings since the sixteenth century of categories such as 'religion', 'superstition', 'politics', 'civil society', 'secular', 'sacred', 'profane'[3] and 'economics'. One aspect of this enquiry is the influence of the colonial context on ideas. Given that these historically constituted categories do change in meaning and context, it would be methodologically inconsistent to organize the historical argument presented here *in terms of* these categories. It would be unhelpful if I was to claim, for instance, that religion impacted on politics differently in the fifteenth century as compared with the nineteenth, because this very form of words, "religion impacted on politics", smuggles in a tacit assumption that in the fifteenth century 'religion' and 'politics' were conceived as essentially separate entities or domains capable of having an impact on each other.

For example, in his interesting book on the radical Reformation, Baylor states that "Politics for the radical reformers was inseparable from religion, as it was for the vast majority of 16th century Europeans" (1991: vii). He continues:

> it would be false to stress the religious characteristic of their thinking in opposition to the political. The Christian faith and church were so integral to social life that thinking about religion was also inherently political thinking. Religious discourse in the sixteenth century had an unavoidable dimension of political reference, just as ideas about political authority and the polity were articulated in religious lan-
> guage. (*Ibid.*: xvii)

Here Baylor is (correctly) denying the separation of religion and politics in the thinking of the reformers; but he is doing it by employing those very same categories.[4] To organize the argument about the categories 'religion' and 'politics' *in terms of* those very same categories would inevitably be circular. The words 'politics' and 'politicians' hardly existed in anything like the modern sense until the late seventeenth century;[5] and 'religion' had a less generic, more specific indigenous meaning of Christian Truth. To analyse historical change as though these terms have an intuitively apprehensible constancy of meanings tends to build into the argument the tacit assumptions of our contemporary language. The most important example of this tacit modern assumption is that 'religion' is a private non-political assent to a belief in God and a future state that is essentially separated from a public non-religious domain of 'politics'. This assumption is not always merely tacit; it is made explicit in constitutions, in the laws on freedom of religion as a right, and also in academic subjects such as philosophy, sociology and political theory.

This assumption about religion has packed into it an essentialization of both domains, each having different defining characteristics that demarcate them from each other: for example, that religion is essentially non-political, spiritual rather than materialistic, other-worldly rather than this-worldly, and concerned with private faith and the salvation of the individual soul rather than the organization of the state; and that politics and the power of the state are essentially non-religious, based on legitimized violence, this-worldly rather than other-worldly, and concerned with the public organization of civil authority and the protection of private property and bodies. One result of this separation has been the interminable debate, arguably going on since the seventeenth-century deists, about the correct definition of religion, because this has implications for where the boundary between religion and non-religion is to be drawn. Frequently these debates and definitions rely on further dichotomies with slippery boundaries, such as that between nature and supernature, matter and spirit, body and soul, or scientific knowledge and pious faith. Since all of these terms are unstable in usage, they provide the possibility of an endless deferral of meaning, one set of dichotomies being implicitly or explicitly defined by another set, which in turn is defined by another set, and so on indefinitely.

This reified separation between religion and politics also allows for some kind of problematic *relationship between* them, as when we talk about the politicization of religion or the impact of religion on politics. The idea that religion can under specific circumstances become political; or that religion can have an impact on politics, only makes sense under the prior assumption that they are essentially separate and different. In modern thinking the relationship is construed in various ways, but the construals usually assume that there are two essentially distinct things that can be related in some way. It is therefore assumed to be the task of theorists and researchers to show us how in fact the relation works out in any specific cultural context. And without this assumption, it would be difficult to see how 'the secularization thesis', discussed at great length by sociologists, could be expressed (see Introduction, references to Berger 1999).

The essentialization of religion and politics as two distinct domains has been clearly imagined in some of the eighteenth-century North American state constitutions. These constitutions make religion a private and personal right, but by doing so they also establish the centrality and rationality of the non-religious state and politics. By turning religion into an object, or several objects, of constitutional legislation, the high ground of 'secular'[6] rationality is set out and enacted, and this in turn is strongly linked with the production of secular discourse in various forms, such as history (see Chapter 2). But what was it that produced secular discourse? In Chapter 2, Trevor Stack argues that it may have developed within the church in the fifteenth and sixteenth centuries and in the attempts of the Spanish to look in on the practices and institutions of American Indian culture from a higher ground, whereby to subordinate the 'data' to dominant Christian categories. Such 'looking in' on the Indians and many other colonized peoples from the 'higher ground' of European classification is consistent with the idea that the ideology of the secular as natural reason has been made possible in the first place by the construction of an essentialized idea of religions as a key aspect of colonial classification. Rather than standing on firm ground and looking out at problematic objects called religions, we are in an Alice-in-Wonderland circularity where our own secular positionality has been made possible by those religious objects themselves. We could not imagine ourselves to be occupying an essentially non-religious space unless we had been able to siphon out of that space whatever we deem to be 'religious'.

Another point to note is that, across the humanities, 'religions' are assumed to be universal both in time and place. For modern discourses on the religions of the world are ubiquitous, and there is, of course, a large publishing industry, produced by academics and others in departments of religious studies, social and cultural anthropology, sociology, philosophy and history. These discourses claim to provide knowledge of these entities. Even some historians seem comfortable with the idea that religion somehow can always be identified in ancient, medieval or modern history, in any society speaking any language (although see Bossy 1982, 1985).[7] But this sits awkwardly with the observation that, for much of the period leading up to the eighteenth-century Enlightenment, and arguably for long after, the English term 'religion' stood for Christian Truth, usually Protestant Truth,[8] as revealed in the Bible. And during much of the same period, 'politics' was not conceived as an independent domain separated from religion, and therefore in that modern sense was not articulated. How, then, did we arrive at the modern generic usage?

## THE ORIGINS OF THE MODERN RELIGION–SECULAR DICHOTOMY:
## THE CASE OF JOHN LOCKE

Probably the most famous theorist of the essential difference between religion and politics was the philosopher John Locke (1689). He was by no means the first writer to articulate a distinction,[9] and he was adding his voice to a long-running, complex argument among the European elite concerning the nature of the state and civil society. But his formulation of the problem has had the greatest impact, not least in the North American colonies.[10] Similar to the quote from Penn with which this article started, Locke defines the two domains: "The care of Souls cannot belong to the Civil Magistrate because his power consists only in outward force: But true and saving Religion consists in the inward persuasion of the Mind, without which nothing can be acceptable to God" (ibid.: 10). People make an "inward judgement" about truth and salvation, and on such matters one cannot be compelled to believe by outward force. There is this assumption of the inner mind as distinct from the outer body, religion being aligned with the inner working of the mind, and civil society with the outer, with the body. The magistrate has nothing to do with religion in this sense, because it is harmless to the state: "the Magistrate's power extends not to the establishing of any Articles of Faith, or Forms of Worship, by the force of his Laws" (ibid.: 11).

By privatizing religion as the individual's relationship with a transcendent God it became possible to think of it as a distinct domain separate from the public arena. In his *Letter on Toleration* Locke insists: "the Church is a thing absolutely separate and distinct from the Commonwealth" (*ibid.*: 25). Churches are "religious societies" and are (or ought to be) entirely private and voluntary. Locke distinguishes clearly throughout between "a Religious" matter and "a Political" one (*ibid.*: 46). The private, individualistic nature of religion is expressed in the often repeated argument that "the care of each Mans [*sic*] Salvation belongs only to himself" (*ibid.*: 58).

For Locke, as for Penn (1680), religion has nothing to do with violence, but is a peaceful, private matter. Only the state is concerned with violence. The general assumption in Locke's writing is that "religions" are Christian, voluntary churches, or private "religious societies",[11] and the only power they hold is to eject someone from membership of the society according to the rules that its membership voluntarily agreed to. But a religious society cannot use force, "For all Force belongs only to the Magistrate" (Locke 1689: 20).

Locke seeks to legitimize his argument about the meaning of religion and its essential difference from the civil government in terms of Biblical evidence, and largely on the assumption that 'religions' refer to Christian confessions. Yet at the same time he is using religion in a more generic sense. He is aware of the possibility that some will not be Christian: "No violence of Injury is to be offered to him, whether he be Christian or Pagan" (*ibid.*: 20). Pagans are described as 'superstitious' in most of the writing of the time, but, in contrast to the privacy and freedom of religion, which is concerned with the salvation of souls – "the care of each Mans Salvation belongs only to himself" (*ibid.*: 58) – the civil authority has an entirely different nature and function. For "the Political Society is instituted for no other end but only to secure every mans [*sic*] Possession of the things of this life" (*ibid.*). The expression "the Political Society" is here being newly forged. I do not mean that this is necessarily the first time the expression has ever been used, but that it is a relatively new coinage of late-seventeenth-century rhetoric. It is also here being used to refer to a non-traditional and profoundly revised idea of the Commonwealth: "*The Commonwealth* seems to me to be a Society of Men constituted only for the procuring, preserving, and advancing of their own *Civil Interests. Civil Interests* I call Life, Liberty, Health, and Indolency of Body; and the possession of outward things, such as Money, Lands, Houses, Furniture, and the like" (*ibid.*: 58).

The possession of "*outward* things" (my emphasis) implies the distinction from the *inward* things of the soul and its salvation. The duty of the civil magistrate is to defend through the fear of punishment and the possession of force, the civil interests of his subjects "by the impartial Execution of equal Laws". It seems clear to Locke that: "the whole Jurisdiction of the Magistrate reaches only to these civil Concernments ... and that it neither can nor ought in any manner to be extended to the Salvation of Souls" (*ibid.*: 9).

Political society is based on a contract between the rulers and the people, who are the supreme power in the final analysis. Again, the idea of a contract between the people and the civil magistrate is itself not new in theories of the polity, but Locke places it in a clearly separated political domain. In practice the people establish a legislative power, which "is not only the supreme power of the Commonwealth but *sacred* and unalterable in the hands where the community have once placed it" (quoted in Browning 1953: 169; emphasis added). The sacred is here extended to the central institution of the non-religious, political domain, the legislature, which in England would be the king in parliament, but which in the future American states would be the constitutionally defined arena of politics.[12]

This idea of religion as a private, non-political assent to a belief in God and a promise of a future life has become a dominating trope in contemporary discourses on religion. Its opposite, which Locke refers to as civil government or the civil governor, as the commonwealth, and as political society, does not on its own give us full access to a modern idea of the non-religious, *the secular*, for the latter needs to be combined with a number of other factors. These would include the scientific revolution of the seventeenth century, with new ideas about objectivity, time, space and matter; the importance of mathematics and measurement in the transformation of a basically Aristotelian view of the world; a new kind of distinction between the natural and the supernatural as different ontological domains; and the development in the second half of the eighteenth century of an idea of political economy as a secular domain. The separation of fact from value within this transformation has been a necessary aspect of the formulation of an idea of secular objectivity. But all of these aspects of modern ideology were in the process of being formulated in the seventeenth century and throughout the eighteenth on the basis of a number of oppositions, such as that between scientific rationality and religious faith, and Locke was one of the most important English contributors to their formulation, along with his contemporary Isaac Newton and the other members of the newly founded Royal Society.

It is not difficult to realize that Locke, among many others, was engaged in rhetorical argument to try to persuade powerful contemporaries to use terms in a certain way and to demand that these terms become transformed into legal and constitutional enforcements. There are a number of reasons why Locke should have a deep interest in this issue. One pressing issue of the day was toleration; toleration was the way that late-seventeenth- and early-eighteenth-century writers were beginning to talk about the right to practise one's 'religion' without interference from the state.[13] It is obvious that Locke was driven by this issue. But he was also a high-ranking member of a nation that was becoming a centre of colonial trade. Locke himself was appointed a member of the Board of Trade and therefore had a role in appointing governors and members of the Governor's Council of the American colonies (Clarke 1955: 335).

I am not directly concerned here with the interesting and important historiographical argument concerning the degree to which Locke did or did not directly influence the American colonial elite in their writing of state constitutions or the American Constitution itself (see Hartz 1955; Macpherson 1962; Bailyn 1965; Pocock 1975, Dworetz 1990). I want instead to clarify why the essentialization of religion and politics as separate domains was historically significant, what it was intended to achieve, what unintended ideological consequences it had, and the route by which this essentialized and reified dichotomy has passed into current uncritical ideology. Penn had very similar ideas about the need for the separation of church and state in order to relieve his Quakers from persecution, and that led him to reconceive the meanings of 'religion' and 'politics' in ways that were similar to Locke's. It also led him to found the modern state of Pennsylvania, which of course has its own constitutional history.[14] Like Locke,[15] Penn built the religion–politics dichotomy around ideas of inner and outer, soul and body, spirit and matter. In his *A Brief Account of the Rise and Progress of the People called Quakers* (1694), the series of inward–outward oppositions is expressed like this:

| | |
|---|---|
| INNER Conversion, Regeneration and Holiness | OUTWARD Schemes of doctrines, verbal creeds, new forms of Worship (p. 61) |
| The Substantial, the Necessary, the profitable part of the Soul | Religion the Superfluous, Ceremonialls, Formal Part (p. 61) |
| The Will of God's Spirit | studied Matter (p. 60) |
| Inward and experimental knowledge of God | lifeless possessions (p. 61) |
| Experiment | theory and speculation (p. 63) |
| Knowledge of the heart/the inward state | Own imaginings, glosses and commentaries on scripture (p. 63) |
| Extraordinary understanding in divine things/the Light of Christ within | Vanity of this World (pp. 63, 65) |

In *The Great Question to be Considered by the King ...* (1680), one can derive the following oppositions, which match those above:

| | |
|---|---|
| Religion | Civil society |
| Inwardness | Outwardness |
| Other-worldly salvation | This worldly governance |
| The private, individual soul, conscience | The public realm of law and magistrates |

These rhetorical oppositions are prescriptive rather than descriptive; they seek to persuade; they are forging the ideas, constructing them, inaugurating a discourse on the inner and the outer that still captivates us today. In short, the invention of religions and politics is part of the same ideological transformation that invented the private inner self of modernity. The "outwardness" of the world, however, seems to have three different meanings. First, it refers to outward actions as against inner intentions, the performance of ritual practices, the reciting of creeds, the formality of etiquette and attachment to things that are mere objects and have no inner life. The clear implication is that the inner things of the soul are closer to God and therefore more real and more authentic. This is a moral as well as an ontological distinction, in that it implies that the outer actions and possessions are relatively valueless. It is derived from the Protestant theological critique of Catholic and other forms of superstition, and a relative sundering of God and the world.

Secondly, there is the objectification of the world of solid matter, which he refers to here as "studied matter", which may reflect an awareness of the development of science and the scientific conception of the empirical observation of the material universe being developed by Galileo, Bacon, Descartes, Newton, Locke and many others. The world has been turned into an object, or a system of material processes, laid out in container time and space (see Al Azm 1972; Burtt 1932; Fitzgerald 1983: 121–42).Thirdly there is the outer world in the sense of the public realm of civil government as opposed to the privacy of inner knowledge of spirit. To what extent Penn was aware of these distinctions as he was writing is debatable.

One might say that these ideas were circulating and various individuals gave them various formulations.[16] What they all involved in one way or another was a profound reconfiguration of the dominant worldview of what I call *encompassing religion*. The idea of privatized religion(s) could be seen as implicated in the origins of the modern metaphysical mind–body duality. It gradually took the place of the Aristotelian metaphysics lying behind the view of religion as an all-encompassing truth, in which each created kind or species participates by degree in the totality. We can see the radical nature of this change clearly in the way American state constitutions were formulated in the later eighteenth century. In eighteenth-century American constitutions, religion, as I show later, appears as one contentious item within a complex constitutional statement of the values, principles and procedures of the non-religious political process that they represent and specify. Written constitutions of this kind fundamentally define modern politics as the public world of natural rationality, and religion appears as a problematic item that has been quarantined from the state through various measures, in particular tolerance, freedom of conscience or opinions, freedom of worship and freedom of religion. Arguably American constitutionalism in the eighteenth century was the arena in which the modern domain of politics as public shared reality was most powerfully defined and institutionalized.[17]

That Locke had a vast indirect influence few would deny, although Penn was influential too, and anyway there were several generations responsible for embedding these ideas in wide public discourses, especially in the American colonies and their debates about the meaning of liberty and the definition of political authority. However, one can at least say that, given that a whole system of new ideas about space, time and causality were forming, partly in the colonial context of maps, compasses, exploration, the rationalization and globalization of trade and the development of nationalistic consciousness, Locke's articulation of those ideas was especially clear and representative. Given those reasons, he needed to discredit and destroy an entirely different discourse on religion, one that had been dominant in one form or another for centuries, and that for many of *his* contemporaries would have been as self-evidently true as the discourse on the separation of religion and politics seems to *our* contemporaries.

## ENCOMPASSING RELIGION

The more general *encompassing* discourse against which individuals such as Locke and Penn were arguing was that religion means Christian Truth, that Christian Truth is all-encompassing and universal, and that nothing exists or could exist (in the proper sense of the word 'exists') outside religion. Religion was not an object covered by a clause in a constitution but encompassing Truth, and what we today have separated out as 'religion', 'politics' and 'economics' were embedded in different configurations within the totality.

Locke set out to destroy the validity of this. In one place Locke exemplified this totalizing ideological perspective with the Biblical description of ancient Israel:

> the Commonwealth of the *Jews* ... was an absolute Theocracy; nor was there, or could there be, any difference between that Commonwealth and the Church. The Laws established there concerning the Worship of One Invisible Deity, were the Civil Laws of that People, and a part of their Political Government; in which God himself was the Legislator. (1689: 52)

But Locke denied that this view of the matter is Christian, since the gospels brought in a new dispensation: "But there is absolutely no such thing, under the Gospel, as a Christian Commonwealth. He prescribed unto his Followers no new and peculiar form of Government; nor put he the sword into any Magistrate's Hand, with the Commission to make use of it in forcing men to forsake their former Religion, and receive his" (*ibid.*: 52). It is clear that Locke is attacking the dominant ethos of the hierarchical commonwealth encompassed by religion. More specifically, Locke's *First Treatise on Government* targeted Sir Robert Filmer's *Patriarcha*, probably published in 1680, whose principles denied the possibility of the separation of religion and politics that Locke wished to achieve. Filmer, who supported the divine right of kings, argued that civil power is from God, "by the divine law" (1991: 5–6). For Filmer, God, the Father of all, ordained a patriarchy in the family, and this is essentially the same as patriarchy in the state. "It follows that civil power not only in general is by divine institution, but even the assignment of it to the eldest parent" (*ibid.*: 7) and, he continues, "To confirm this natural right of regal power, we find it in the Decalogue that the law which enjoins obedience to kings is delivered in the terms 'honour thy father' [Exodus, xx, 12] as if all power were originally in the father" (*ibid.*: 11). Filmer holds that the natural duties of a father over one family are identical in kind to those of a king over the whole commonwealth (*ibid.*: 12).

God, the Father of Humankind, gave Adam lordship not only over Eve but over the whole world. Adam's family was the first commonwealth, and he had absolute power and authority over his family. This patriarchal power was divided by Noah after the Flood between his three sons. After the "confusion of Babel" the regal power descending from Adam was further dispersed throughout the world. All true Kingship is legitimized by this descent (*ibid.*: 10). Even after the true natural father or his line disappear, the right of the father descends to the title of prince or king.

In Filmer's theory, the idea deriving from theorists such as Bellarmine and Suarez of civil authority being based in the free consent of an original contract was denied by reference to Biblical authority. The Bible was generally the final authority for people who we today might call political theorists, even though Aristotle was also an important source. Filmer's arguments arose in the specific context of Charles I's claim to a divine right of kings. However, in order to appreciate the revolutionary nature of the challenge from writers such as Locke and Penn, we need to be able to see Filmer as one specific representative of a general view of the whole social order as rooted in, and encompassed by, the scheme of Christian revelation, and a divinely instituted patriarchy.

## 'THE RELIGIOUS' AND 'THE SECULAR'

During the sixteenth and seventeenth centuries, and right up into modernity, the most common use of the term 'the religious' has been to refer to a special class of virtuosi within the Catholic Church – the monks, friars and nuns – as distinct from the *secular clergy*; it referred to a specialized branch of Christendom, *a status* (Cross 1958: 1364–5; Bossy 1985: 170). One also finds references to the religious houses, meaning abbeys, monasteries and convents: the houses of 'the religious'. The bishops, in their obsequious letter to Henry VIII as part of their Preface to *The Institution of a Christian Man*, make reference to "the clergy of this your most noble realm, as well religious as other" (Lloyd 1825: 26). Here 'religious' refers to the monks, friars and nuns, the religious clergy, also called the Regulars. The "other" here refers in contrast to the *secular* priests. To be a secular in medieval England was not equivalent to the modern idea of the secular as non-religious. To be a devoted Christian, to be baptised and confirmed, to practice self-mortification and to serve the church would in today's language be called religious, but in the late sixteenth century these characteristics were in principle and by definition shared equally by all Christians, regardless of whether or not they were of a religious or secular status.

It could be argued that the religious were so-called because in principle their full-time withdrawal from the world exemplified service to God, and in that sense offered the most radical vision of the sacredness of service to God available. These renouncers most effectively symbolized the reality of the redemptive soteriology of the cross. The orders of Benedictines, Dominicans, Franciscans and others were, in a sense, 'other worldly' in distinction from 'this world'. Yet they were also an integral part of the universal church, and the church bridged the other-worldly–this-worldly distinction. It was, after all, the duty of all Christians to symbolically carry their cross, so in one sense the religious were not doing something qualitatively different from those 'seculars' such as Thomas More who wore a hair shirt and whipped himself in his study. A better way of expressing this might be to say that the whole doctrine of the church was based ultimately on a redemptive other-worldly soteriology, while simultaneously ordaining a ritual order in this world, along with the sacralization of power hierarchies. Within this overall world order 'the religious' had a specific status and function.

The older sense of the religious and the secular as two branches of the clergy is still current usage in referring to the Catholic orders, and perhaps within some sections of the Anglican Church too.

## CANON LAW AND SECULAR LAW

For many centuries in English, and deriving from Latin, there was a distinction between canon or church law and secular or common law. Again, this is not the same as the modern distinction between religion and the secular. The modern distinction is based on an *opposition* between the religious and the non-religious. As I argued earlier, politics in the modern state is supposed to be non-religious, and religion is supposed to be non-political. Whatever positive definitional attributes some people might wish to give to 'religion' or 'politics' in their generic modern forms, at base they define each other by what the other is not. In contrast, the medieval ecclesiastical and secular authorities were both *encompassed* by Christendom and Mother Church. It would have been meaningless to medieval and early modern Christian subjects to have been told that the secular is non-religious. After all, in general in modern usage one could not say that the secular priesthood were not 'religious', although one could have said that they were not 'the religious'. If the pope was a prince, was he religious or secular? If the king was addressed as 'sacred monarch' and as God's vicar on earth, as he or she regularly was in England, did this make the king a religious or secular figure? (One might ask the same question about property, the legislative assembly, and rights as they are represented in modern constitutions.)

The medieval encompassment of all institutions under the wing of the Holy Church, or at the cosmological level under the all-encompassing glory of God, can be understood when we turn to Cross's entry on "Toleration" in the *Dictionary of the Christian Church*:

> Christianity, which claims to be the only true religion, has always been dogmatically intolerant. Dissent ('heresy') within its own ranks, has been anathematized time and again in the history of the Church. St. Augustine went so far as to demand corporal punishment for heretics and schismatics; and this became the normal procedure in the Middle Ages when, owing to the intimate connection between Church and state, Catholic and citizen were virtually synonymous terms, and the heretic was thus considered a revolutionary endangering the foundations of society. The regular penalty in the Middle Ages was death. (Cross 1958: 1364–5)

The historian R. W. Southern, like many others, has made the same point (Southern 1970: 16–17). The medieval distinction between church and state can be usefully approached from the angle of the exercise of authority. In particular, Logan (1968) strengthens the view that I am arguing for here that the distinction is only intelligible as a division of functions within an ideological totality. He shows that the degree of cooperation between the two authorities reveals how they both shared the same ends:

> The exclusion of a person from normal society constituted in medieval Europe a penalty inflicted by both secular and ecclesiastical authorities ... ex-communication severed a person from the Christian community; it removed him from the communion of the faithful. In a unitary Christian society this amounted, at least in theory, to nearly complete ostracism ... Amidst the dashing of candles and the tolling of bells he was cursed and cut off from the church's body ... henceforth to be treated as a pagan.
> (Logan 1968: 13)

While we can accept that ecclesiastical and civil courts were clearly distinguished as organizations, it also seems clear that they acted in concert towards a transcendental goal of unity, and that the unity was both spiritual and temporal, for the conservation of the temporal order was a sacred duty (*ibid.*: 15).

Logan's study goes up to the 1530s, yet this procedure "continued in use in to the next century and forms part of the ecclesiastical and legal history of those years. The reforming legislation forbade appeals to Rome, it is true, but the legislation had little effect on the internal machinery of the ecclesiastical courts. They continued to function by pre-Reformation procedure" (*ibid.*: 17).[18] We can see then that the secular was either a status of churchmen (the secular priests) or a power invested in institutions and officeholders that was subordinated to, and encompassed by, religion. The secular was not non-religious in the modern sense at all. It was all about religion, because religion meant Christian Truth. Tawney, among others, noted that, at the beginning of the seventeenth century, this medieval synthesis was still dominant (1926: 19–22 and *passim*). O'Gorman (1997: 163ff.) has weighed up the extent to which what he calls the confessional state continued to dominate England in the eighteenth century (see below). When we use the term 'secular' today, as in 'secularism' and 'secularization', we are talking about an entirely different cosmology, ideology and set of dominant values.

## RELIGION: THE COMMONWEAL

The idea of the commonweal as the "politic body" was also not equivalent to 'the secular' in today's usage and meaning. The commonweal or commonwealth is perhaps best understood as religion seen under the view of the organization of society and human relations in this world. The commonweal was God's hierarchy on earth, and ordered relations between rulers and subjects, seniors and juniors, men and women, adults and children, and all others. As already pointed out, the English word 'religion' in the sixteenth century and for long afterwards had a meaning virtually identical with Christian Truth revealed in the Bible. In their address to the King in the publication of *The Institution of a Christian Man*, the bishops refer to "the right institution and education of your people in the knowledge of Christ's true religion" (Lloyd 1825: 23).

Religion was not in *opposition* to the secular, and it would be equally wrong to think of the idea of the commonweal in the sixteenth and much of the seventeenth centuries in England as 'the secular' in today's meaning of 'non-religious'. The commonweal was conceived as based on a hierarchy of sacred duties determined by degree and rank. Sir Walter Raleigh had put it in this way:

> that infinite wisdom of God, which hath distinguished his angels by degrees, which hath given greater and less light and beauty to heavenly bodies, which hath made differences between beasts and birds, created the eagle and the fly, the cedar and the shrub, and among stones given the fairest tincture to the ruby and the quickest light to the diamond, hath also ordained kings, dukes or leaders of the people, magistrates, judges, and other degrees of men.　　　　　　(Quoted in Tillyard [1943] 1998: 19)

The idea that the commonweal was the equivalent of modern secular politics, standing in opposition to and separate from religion, would be entirely misleading. The commonweal and all 'politic' order and governance, were encompassed by religion. The *commonweal* was the form in human relations that religion (Christian Truth) took. It was based on a detailed analogy with the human body, with individual rank being represented by parts of the body, identified by their nature, qualities and functions (see e.g. Williams 1967: pt II).

That there was no separation between 'religion' and 'society' can be seen immediately in the first sentence from Tyndale's treatise on vocation: "As pertaining to good works, understand that all works are good which are done within the law of God, in faith and with thanksgiving to God" (Williams 1967: 292). Tyndale's understanding of good works in effect conserves the status quo, "degree high or low". He goes on to say that the apostle, the shoemaker and the kitchen page all submit themselves to Christ when they submit to their master (*ibid.*: 292–3).

Tyndale, like many other of his contemporaries, used the analogy of the body to talk about the order of the commonweal or 'politic body', where sin and the breaking of laws are hardly distinguishable (*ibid.*: 293). As one would expect of hierarchy, based on deference and senior–junior relations rather than 'social stratification' or 'class' in the nineteenth-century sense,[19] masters have duties to their servants too (*ibid.*: 294). The same analogy of fathers to sons is advocated for landlords and tenants. And this analogy also relates us all to Christ as sons to father. By the use of such analogical relationships the commonweal and all its degrees is bound up with God, who is the highest degree, the father of all. It indicates where Filmer's *Patriarcha* derived from.

One of the ways the distinction between the spiritual and the temporal was conceived in the sixteenth and seventeenth centuries was in the distinction within parliament, and therefore government, between Lords Spiritual (bishops) and Lords Temporal. However, in the understanding of the time both the spiritual and the temporal as categories of people were subsumed in the higher unity of God and his redemptive purposes, and in the higher unity of the commonweal. Thus they were all members of parliament, they were all members of the church, bishops helped formulate state policy, church ministers read state edicts in the form of sermons in their churches, and the king was God's anointed ruler on earth.

'Religion' and the 'Commonweal' are two different ways of talking about the same thing, which is the divine order of the world. Some readers will think this naive, and will assume that hegemonic ideas held by an elite are not descriptions of the way people generally did think, but rhetorical attempts to persuade the lower classes to accept and internalize their submission. And it is true that the dominance of a discourse does not mean that there were no alternative ways of thinking available. Yet I quoted Baylor (1991) earlier as evidence that even the radicals of the German Reformation did not separate religion from politics. It seems that this top-down concept of obedience to one's station is at least recognized if not loved as rhetorical necessity by the lower orders, and seems to have been internalized by those poor petitioners who submitted "A Supplication of the Poore Commons" (1546) to their "most dear lord" King Henry: "they say your highness's laws are God's laws, and that we are as much bound to observe them as the Law of God given by Moses. Truth it is, most dear lord, that we are bound by the commandment of God to obey your highness and all your laws set forth by your High Court of Parliament" (Williams 1967: 287).

The nature of church, kingship and the state render the modern English-language discourse of 'religion and politics' uncharacteristic until the eighteenth century, although the distinction itself was broached by the English sectarian radicals, clearly articulated by the late seventeenth century, and from an early date written into some American state charters and constitutions. For the king, referred to by such epithets as "our most dread sovereign Lord", "the king's royal majesty", and in other places quite frequently "our most sacred king" was in 1534 both the head of state and also the head of the Church of England.[20] We can arrive at a sense of awe at the exercise of this divinely blessed kingly power when we consider the statement put out by the cowed Abbot and monks of Peterborough Monastery soon before the dissolution in 1534, which legitimized the king as God's representative on earth (*ibid.*: 777–8).[21]

The relation between the authority of the Catholic Church and the subordinate authority of the state (the church-state) was reformulated by Henry VIII into an identification of "the Christian religion and duty" with the power of the national state embodied in the king (the state-church). It was to the King's "laws and decrees" that the subjects made absolute submission, not to the Bishop of Rome. Kinney comments that "obedience is always a holy act" (Kinney 1975: 47). Obedience of a servant to a master, of a wife to a husband, of a pupil to a teacher, of a subject to a prince, of lower degree to higher degree, was analogous to the obedience of a Christian to God. The whole deferential social order was wrapped in divinity and teleologically determined by God's scheme of redemption.

Kinney writes that in such different kinds of writing as Spenser's *The Faerie Queene*, or "a sermon transforming Essex's uprising into a morality play of good and evil", or *A*

*Philosophical Discourse Entitled the Anatomie of Mind* by Thomas Rogers (1576), there are common themes that envisage creation as "a single fabric, woven with purpose and beauty by a single artist", in which order on earth is analogous with order in heaven, in a world in which everything and every person has its rightful place. "For Elizabethans, man's security and contentment rested in his wholehearted acceptance of due order and degree" (Kinney 1975: 46). Obedience, as the willing submission of the individual to the order of the whole, is fundamental. The homilies preach against the individual prioritization of self-interest, and insist on the acceptance of God's order. The subordination of the interests of the individual to those of the state-church had to be turned upside down by Locke and other powerful rhetoricians in order to arrive at the modern liberal dominance of rational self-interest and the rights of individuals. Rebellion had cosmic significance (*ibid.*: 44).

## POLITIC NOT POLITICS

The commonweal was frequently referred to as 'the politic body' and, like other uses of 'politic' as an adjective this implies fitting, well-ordered and God given, although it can also have more negative connotations, in the sense of crafty or cunning.[22] Divine purpose was realized through submission to one's status and duties in the creation of a harmonious whole. This was a politic state of affairs. Worship could be politic too. King Henry's Preface to *The Articles about Religion* (1536) and *The Institution of a Christian Man* (1537) (both republished in Lloyd 1825: xv–xxxii) concerns salvation and the order of the polity. Henry mentions several times the question of salvation and also "the honest ceremonies and good and politic orders" and the need for "unity and concord" (*ibid.*: xvi.) Henry says that he and his bishops have divided the Articles into two; those that are directly necessary to our salvation, and those less important practices "as have been of a long continuance for a decent order and honest policy, prudently instituted" (*ibid.*: xvi).

The words 'politic' and 'policy' here are a long way from contemporary usages such as 'politics' and indicate not a domain but an attribute. For 'politics' as a contemporary noun implies a secular, in the sense of non-religious, domain separated off from another domain named 'religion'. The prolonged attempts by various intellectuals to imagine religion and politics as separate required that both politics and religion should have different natures or essences, made highly explicit as I showed not only by Penn (1680) and Locke (1689) but also by the Anglican Divine William Warburton ([1748] 1766). By being essentially separated, they can then be thought of as having problematic interrelations. But this modern usage cannot make much sense when referring to an idea of a totality of human relations made by and for God, in which the king is head of the church, and the bishops (Lords Spiritual) are in the parliament with the rest of the nobility (Lords Temporal), and play a leading role in government; and the ministers read state-authorized homilies in the form of sermons on civil obedience.

A *politic* action is one that is suitable and appropriate to the circumstances, and thus as relevant to those actions that we might today judge to be 'religious' as to those we might judge to be 'political'. This does not mean that the word 'politician' and the expression 'political power' were not occasionally evident. For example, Filmer himself uses these terms in his discussion of, and disagreement with, the Jesuit Suarez's claim that "Adam had only economical power, but not political" ([1680] 1991: 16). This "economical power" is used by Suarez in the standard way of the time to refer to the domestic situation, the power of a father over his household, and distinguished from "political power", which Suarez defines as power over a community of families. These early examples of the political and economical are different from modern usage because for both of these theorists politics and economics are not separated out as distinct and autonomous non-religious domains, but as gradations of power within the encompassing legitimization of God and the Bible. Filmer also refers to "the politicians and civil lawyers", and despite Filmer's holistic intentions it is tempting to see these as early modern beginnings of significantly shifting usage. This would mean a shift in the direction that Locke and others were trying to make explicit.

One difference with later theorists is that the sixteenth- and seventeenth-century writers were talking from the inside out, that is to say, they were talking from within a worldview that they took to be the way things are, the order of things, the Truth. They had not yet turned it into a *comparative sociological theory*. However, in *The Dialogue between Pole and Lupsett* (1539?) attributed to Thomas Starkey (Williams 1967: 295–302; Mayer 1989), there patently is a theory of the commonweal. Starkey is certainly advocating a conservative vision of the commonweal, but he has a more abstract theoretical style. Starkey was an Anglican priest who advised Henry VIII and his Chancellor Thomas Cromwell (Mayer 1989: viii; Zeeveld 1948: 111–27).

Pole, one of the conversants who speaks most in defence of the commonweal, develops the body analogy very explicitly; he refers to "the true commonweal" as "the politic body", as civil order, as politic law, the politic state, commonalty (Williams 1967: 296–302). The analogy with the body anchors the "politic state" in the "order of nature" (*ibid.*: 297).

As the head of state is the "heart", so the head and the eyes and ears are "the under officers by princes appointed" whose responsibility is to the "weal" or well-being of the body. Craftsmen and warriors are the hands, ploughmen and tillers the feet (*ibid.*: 297). Like Tyndale, Pole draws an analogy with disease "when the parts of the body agree not together: the head agreeth not to the feet, nor feet to the hands: no one part agreeth to the other: the temporalty grudgeth against the spiritualty, the commons against the nobles, and subjects against their rulers" (*ibid.*: 299).

## RELIGION AND POLITICS IN EIGHTEENTH-CENTURY NORTH AMERICA

Penn went to America to found Pennsylvania with a King's Charter in 1682. He promised the subjects their full civil and religious liberties. Nearly a hundred years later, in 1774–75, after considerable parliamentary interference in the government of the colony, deputies appointed by the General Assembly took their grievances against the king-in-parliament to the Continental Congress. There followed various stages of constitutional development, and in September 1776 a specially convened convention adopted a state constitution (Hough 1872: 217). This was criticized by some republicans within the Pennsylvania opposition for lacking "the legitimate checks and balances necessary for a stable equilibrium of political power" (*ibid.*: 218). Eventually, a new constitution was agreed in 1790. The Bill of Rights section:

> re-enacted the old colonial provision copied into the first Constitution, respecting freedom of worship, rights of conscience, and exemptions from compulsory contributions for the support of any ministry. The recognition of a God and of a future state of rewards and punishments were still demanded of all holding office, but a belief in the divine inspiration of the Old and New Testaments was not included.
>
> (*Ibid.*: 220)

A desire for this degree of toleration was not unanimous in the late-eighteenth-century colonies. There were those like John Swanwick, himself a Philadelphia man, who in his open letter *An Act for the Establishment of Religious Freedom* (Swanwick 1786) politely expressed alarm at the degree of toleration being granted in Virginia. Swanwick did not deny some degree of separation of church and state, but his objections to it are fundamentally that it is too extreme in its liberality, one might say too loose in its definition of 'religion', and that it ought to make more provision for protecting and promoting the Christian faith:

> By this act ... a door is opened wide for the introduction of any tenets in religion, however degrading to Christianity, or how tending to its destruction; that all countenance or support of government to it is withdrawn, and ... the legislature of Virginia may be held and administered by men professedly atheists, Mahometans, or of any other creed, however unfriendly to liberty or the morals of a free society.     (*Ibid.*: iii)

Swanwick seems like an Enlightenment man, and his view of Christianity is of a gentle rational kind that guarantees civil liberties. There is a degree of ambiguity in his argument, for he also seems to be arguing for the establishment of a state religion on the grounds that without it the civil society can have no principles of cohesion and will fall into anarchy. His language throughout implies the separation of religion from politics, and yet at the same time the Christian (Protestant) religion is essential for holding political society together.

Swanwick reprints the Virginia Act in his open letter. The Act begins with an appeal to freedom of thought as a natural right, and insists that nobody can be forced to pay taxes to subsidize a particular form of religion, since everyone should be free to give "his contributions to the particular pastor whose morals he would make his pattern". Both civil and ecclesiastical rulers have tyrannically imposed and set up "their own opinions and modes of thinking" on people (*ibid.*: v). This state of affairs is unacceptable; our civil rights have no dependence on our religious opinions, and to stop someone holding office on that basis is an infringement of his "natural right". The civil magistrate should not be obliged "to intrude his powers into the field of opinion" since this "destroys all religious liberty" and would tend to result in the imposition on others of the civil magistrate's private opinions. The civil governor has no authority in the matter of religious opinions, a domain where his opinion is his own private one. This constitutional argument concerning the lack of qualifications of the civil magistrate to legislate on religious matters was made by Locke and Penn in the late seventeenth century.

Swanwick does not wish to return to the pre-enlightened times and he seems to accept the conceptual distinction between civil government and religion. He refers instead to "the mild spirit of an enlightened Christianity becoming more and more diffused" (*ibid.*: 7) and to the Christian revelation as "the purest and most luminous of all that have been given to men", a form of words that again suggests the possibility of other, non-Christian claims to revelation. He contrasts "true religion" to enthusiasm (*ibid.*: 8), to the "debasing system of materialism" (*ibid.*), and also to the "despotic rage" typical of "Mahometan princes" (*ibid.*: 14), to "the continual massacres of Greek and Roman kings and chiefs" and infidels such as Genghis Khan, and to Catholic superstition (*ibid.*: 17). In contrast, Christianity, by which he means mild rational Christianity, that is to say, liberal Protestant Christianity, has given us "certain civil or political rights" (*ibid.*: 14). In countries where the Christian revelation is unknown, "there are no comparable civil blessings": "Despotic governments have generally taken the firmest root among nations that were blinded by mahometan or pagan darkness, where the throne of violence has been supported by ignorance and false religion" (*ibid.*: 18).[23]

The habit of interchanging 'religions' with 'superstitions' is evident here in Swanwick's writing at the high point of the American Enlightenment. A good example of this can be found in the fascinating writings of Samuel Purchas about a century and a half earlier ([1613] 1626). One point of transition from religion as Christian Truth to generic religions came from the multiplication of 'religions' reported and described by travellers and voyagers in their letters and journals. Purchas, who had admired the collections of travel writings collected and translated by Richard Hakluyt ([1599] 1809), retold many of these stories in his own words plus others that he himself collected and translated in *Purchas his Pilgrim Or Relations of the World and the Religions Observed in all Ages and places Discovered, from the Creation unto this Present. Contayning a Theologicall and Geographicall Historie of Asia, Africa, and America, with the Ilands adjacent. Declaring the ancient Religions before the Flood, the Heathenish, Jewish, and Saracenicall in all Ages Since, in those parts professed, with their severall opinions, Idols, Oracles, Temples, Priests, Fasts, Feasts, Sacrifices, and Rites Religious: Their beginnings, Proceedings, Alterations, Sects, Orders and Successions. With brief Descriptions of the Countries, Nations, States, Discoueries; Private and Publicke Customes, and the most remarkable Rarities of Nature, or Humane industrie, in the same.* The title is a good summary of the contents and notable for its reference to the religions of the world "observed in all Ages and places". That Purchas can suggest that there is more than one religion suggests a stage in the process of the transformation towards a modern usage. The fourth edition of 1626 has a dedicatory epistle to Charles I, in which Purchas points out that the first edition of 1613 had been dedicated to Charles's father James I. Purchas recounts that King James had told him (Purchas) that he had read his book seven times and kept a copy on his bedside table. If this was true, then it brings home vividly the importance to the English and their rulers of the growth of foreign trade and commerce generally, and knowledge of other peoples in the world.[24]

The contents of the book indicate a well developed vocabulary of religion and religions, for example: "Asia: The First Booke. Of the first beginnings of the World and Religion: and of the Regions and Religions of Babylonia, Assyria, Syria, Phoenicia, and Palestina". Chapter IIII (Purchas [1613] 1626: 17) is explicitly a "History of Religions".

We seem to have here a modern discourse on world religions as early as 1613. However, it is clear that the idea of religion is thoroughly Christian and monotheistic, and only applied to the superstitions of the pagans by analogy, rather in the modern style of 'pseudo-religions' or 'quasi-religions' (see Smith 1994 and the discussion in Fitzgerald 2000: 98ff.). False religions, or superstitions, are those barbaric or pagan practices, and accounts of the meaning of life and death and right and wrong, that are *fallen* versions of true religion. The whole structure of the book is based on the Christian Bible, and the assumption of an overriding and encompassing Fall and Redemption narrative. The whole of history is encompassed by this divine narrative. The first five or six chapters might be called the theory and method section, and they make it clear that Biblical Christianity frames the whole collection of narratives. The point is that the 'religions' in the plural are 'superstitions', and the two words oscillate throughout the text as alternatives. There is only one true religion, and this religion can explain, on the basis of the Bible, how these fallen versions of religion can be found in so many different forms all over the world. The religions of the world are represented as mistakes, misunderstandings and superstitions, resulting from lack of contact and a falling away from the true sources of revelation. The existence of these religion-like superstitions must be explained according to the revelation of true religion. This is a pilgrimage, and Purchas refers to himself as a pilgrim, reading thousands of journals and travel narratives, travelling around the world in his imagination, collecting and translating and reproducing a vast range of data about the cultures, customs and beliefs of the different regions of the world. It is virtually an attempt to theorize a history of the world on the basis of ethnography interpreted through deduction from Biblical narrative.[25] It provides us with a prime and early example of the combination of confessional and secular writing. The confessional aspects still largely encompass the secular, but point towards modern travel writing and anthropology.[26]

Returning to the late eighteenth century, Swanwick therefore represents a position between, on the one hand, the pre-Enlightenment commonweal in which the civil society is encompassed by, and embedded in, religion; and the full constitutional construction of secular political civil society in which 'religion' is one item of natural rights, alongside all the others.[27] It is a matter of degree. For Swanwick a minimal reference to Christian themes such as Christ, salvation and a future life of rewards and punishments should be required for officeholders for the cohesiveness of the civil society. Yet four years later in his own Pennsylvania, much of the Christian nuance was undermined by excluding from that 1790 Constitution the necessity of belief in the divine inspiration of the Bible, which further severed the increasingly abstract concept of religion and religions from its semantic moorings in encompassing Christian Truth, and gave it a universal, ahistorical appearance useful for colonial classification purposes.

The 1838 Pennsylvania Constitution was a ratification of the 1790 Constitution with amendments. When one looks at the index and summary of the Articles, bearing in mind the structural similarity of one Constitution with another, one can see clearly how much the modern domain of politics has been constructed through constitutionalism. American constitutionalism should perhaps be considered the arena where the modern conception of the political, non-religious state, the secular location of rational humanity, was formed in its earliest and most explicit manifestations. The Constitution itself is a sacred document. 'Religion' is put in a special place as though to quarantine it. It is reduced to Sections 3 and 4 of Article IX in the Declaration of Rights:

> 3. That all men have a natural and indefeasible right to worship Almighty God according to the dictates of their own consciences; that no man can of right be compelled to attend, erect, or support any place of worship, or to maintain any ministry against his consent; that no human authority can, in any case whatever, control or interfere with the rights of conscience; and that no preference shall ever be given, by law, to any religious establishments or modes of worship.
> 4. That no person, who acknowledges the being of God and a future state of rewards and punishments shall, on account of his religious sentiments, be disqualified to hold any office or place of trust or profit under this Commonwealth.
> (Hough 1972: II, 236–7)

"The commonwealth" has been turned upside down, and it is now the equivalent of the 'civil governor' or the political society, as Locke and Penn had both argued it should be. Religion does not encompass the order of hierarchy, but has become a privatized essence freely available to any individual (even though all language is about men [and savages] and not about women). Toleration means separation of church and state, the privatization of religion, and the investment of sacrality in rights. Religion is not the sacred; *the right to practice a religion freely* is sacred. The Constitution lays out the basis of the political society and its sacred principles and its "inherent and indefeasible rights": "all men are born equally free and independent"; "all power is inherent in the people"; "inviolate rights" such as life, liberty, property, reputation, free and equal elections, trial by jury, freedom of the press, of thought, of expression, due course of law, freedom from unreasonable interference by the state, the right to sue the commonwealth (unthinkable under the older meaning), and others. This is the construction, the articulation, of the modern world; but its contrived and invented aspects are disguised by the concept of natural reason.

In his *Notes on the State of Virginia*, published in London in 1787, Thomas Jefferson, who referred to "the sacred fire of freedom and self-government" (Bailyn 2002: 25) gives a history of the colony since the first attempt of Sir Walter Raleigh to found a colony in Virginia under Queen Elizabeth (*ibid.*: 180ff.). The first settlers were "of the English church". They possessed the powers of making, administering and executing the laws. They were intolerant of all other sects and churches, and Quakers were banned outright. Baptism according to Anglican rites was compulsory. The Anglicans were in complete control for about a century. However, "Other opinions began then to creep in, and the great care of the government to support their own church, having begotten an equal degree of indolency in its clergy, two thirds of the people had become dissenters at the commencement of the present revolution" (*ibid.*: 262). Jefferson defends the present constitution, based on enlightened principles of natural reason and rights. He refers to the previous Anglican "religious slavery" (*ibid.*: 264) and compares it to the present establishment of civil freedom. Many of the arguments he makes are strikingly similar to those of Locke and Penn a hundred years earlier. The "rights of conscience" are not answerable to the civil authorities, but only to God: "The legitimate powers of government extend to such acts only as are injurious to others. But it does me no injury for my neighbour to say there are twenty gods or no god. It neither picks my pocket nor breaks my leg" (*ibid.*: 265).

Elsewhere his language sounds Lockean too (*ibid.*: 141). This fundamental distinction between civil government and religion, which Locke, Penn and others had argued, are clearly established in the thinking of Jefferson. Simultaneously, he imagines many religions in the world; there are "probably a thousand different systems of religion" of which "ours is but one of that thousand" (*ibid.*: 267). The only way that anyone can decide which is the true religion is through reason and free enquiry (*ibid.*). Only one of these can be right, but deciding which one is not in the competence of the civil administrator, but must be left to the free rational intelligence of the individual to decide through open and free debate. Choosing one's religion can only be a matter of personal choice, and cannot be forced.

Jefferson, like Locke and Penn one hundred years earlier, is attacking the idea that any one form of Christianity or any religion at all can determine the nature of the civil government. We can see a clearly privatized concept of religion, its truth assessed according to rational principles, separated from the civil government whose job is to maintain social order. It has nothing to do with religion. Jefferson also has a concept of religions that are multiple, an idea that derives from the multiplicity of different Christian churches and sects, but extending the association of 'religion' to belief in gods and the superstitions of Catholics and other peoples.

On the other hand, the indigenous Americans, Jefferson's own colonial others, who are referred to as "Indians", "Aborigines" and "Savages", do not have either civil government or religion (*ibid.*: 150). They have "never submitted themselves to any laws, any coercive power, any shadow of government". Yet they avoid anarchy because "Their only controls are their manners" (*ibid.*), and also that innate sense of right and wrong that "in every man makes a part of his nature" (*ibid.*: 151).

## THE ESSENTIALIZATION OF 'RELIGION' AND 'POLITICS'
## AS A COLONIAL PIZZA EFFECT?

The concept of private religion as essentially distinct from public politics may have originated in seventeenth-century England, at least in so far as it is represented in the English language,[28] but, given that dissent from the dominance of the established church was one of the prime motives for the establishment of colonies, then such a separation was simultaneously in the minds of many settlers. In England, the increasing demand for the separation of church and state was not the ideology of a new class in the Marxist sense, since 'the middling orders' who supported many of the non-conformist churches were not themselves conscious of being a class and, as O'Gorman points out, English society was still dominated by the idea of degree and the value of deference, represented by "minor variations of speech, dress, and manners which are often too subtle and too varied to be conveyed in documentary evidence" (1997: 115). Nevertheless, dissenters such as the Quakers were explicitly in favour of egalitarianism in dress and manners, objected to hat etiquette and honorific language, and seem typical of the relationship between the religion of the heart, severe criticism of ritualism and hierarchy, trade, a more democratic concept of private property and an emerging colonial world order.

However, the development of this kind of thinking in England could be exaggerated, and there is good reason to believe that it was the American dissenters who first most effectively institutionalized this idea of modern politics as non-religious, by making it central to their constitutions. For England during the century of Enlightenment was still to a large extent a "confessional state", and the extent to which it had become a political state in the modern sense of 'non-religious' or separated from religion is arguable. O'Gorman weighs up both sides of the equation. On the one hand it could be said that "England in the early eighteenth century was a confessional state, a state in which one official confession of faith, Anglicanism, was established by statute and enforced through the law – a faith, moreover, in theory accepted and practiced by the vast majority of the population" (1997: 163).

The Test and Corporation Acts and the Licensing Act had maintained the church's dominance and established status. O'Gorman says that, for J. C. D. Clark, who takes a strongly revisionist stand, "the structural foundations of eighteenth century society were the monarchy and the aristocracy as well as the Church". The period was one of hierarchy, patriarchalism and faith, rather than liberalism, individualism and secularism. It should be thought of more as an age of monarchy and aristocracy, rather than of reform, protest and modernization (*ibid.*: 171). This "revisionist" picture of eighteenth-century England suggests that "the church was the dominant social force in the eighteenth century ... Anglicanism was much more than a 'political theology'; it was a pervasive social cement binding all orders of society" (*ibid.*: 165). O'Gorman, quoting J. C. D. Clark with reservations, writes: "The ideology of the confessional state thus legitimised social hierarchy, underpinned social relationships and inculcated humility, submission and obedience" (*ibid.*).

On the other hand, however, the church may have appeared stronger than it really was. Various bits of legislation such as the Toleration Act, and the repeal by the Whigs of the Occasional Conformity Act of and the Schism Act had undermined the church's all-embracing position and introduced an element of voluntarism, religious pluralism, and apathy (*ibid.*: 169). Commercial values had widely penetrated British society by the middle of the eighteenth century, intersecting with values from other sources, such as law and politics. A corporate theology of a graded hierarchy in which duties are assigned by birth gave way for many people to individual conscience and personal responsibility. (*ibid.*: 170). And though parliament was still dominated by the figure of the king, the two-party system of Whigs and Tories, combined with state finance and the increase in trade and commerce, would surely have corresponded better to the separation and privatization of religion than to the continued dominance of the state-church (*ibid.*: 172–3).

This ambiguous picture points to a slower rate of transition compared with the American states. It suggests that the encompassing religion was still a kind of reality, but that the separation of religion and politics was an idea that had not achieved hegemony but was common currency. The position of William Warburton, an Anglican bishop who was in favour of the monopoly of the church, gives us some insight into this halfway house. In his work *The Alliance between Church and State* ([1748] 1766), we find the idea of their separation but interdependence implied by the title. It is interesting to find the expression "modern Politics" on the first page. The expression "their politic alliance", the older adjectival usage, can be found in the preface dedicated to Warburton's patron, the Earl of Chesterfield. But here "modern politics" sounds like the reified domain of contemporary rhetoric. Furthermore, Warburton distinguishes between the essence of church and state in modified Lockean terms. "The only subjects worth a wise Man's serious notice, are RELIGION and GOVERNMENT" (*ibid.*: iii), he tells Chesterfield, and goes on to distinguish them: "the object of Religion being Truth ... requires Liberty; and the object of Government, Peace ... demands submission ...".

However, Warburton argues that this separation requires an alliance between the two spheres such that the Church of England and the nation state are essentially distinct yet complementary, and provide a combination necessary for stability: "they seem naturally formed to counteract one another's operations" (*ibid.*: iv). Their "Natures" (*ibid.*: iv) and their "Agency" are different, but "there seems to be no more reason against their POLITIC ALLIANCE than we see there was against the *physical union* of the Soul and the Body" (*ibid.*: iv).

Here Warburton makes two pieces of metaphysical speculation mutually supportive by drawing an analogy between them, as has been noted in the cases of both Locke and Penn. He not only convinces us that religion and government (or church and state) are things that have essentially different yet complementary natures, but he also virtually takes for granted the by now well-established discourse on the existence of two other essentially different but complementary things, the soul and the body. Church and state are distinct but complementary in a way analogous to soul and body. There is a whole library of rhetorical contestation here, for how can a non-material entity such as the soul have a physical relationship? This was a great problem for Locke, Descartes, Spinoza and Kant, and also to the Scottish common sense philosophers such as Thomas Reid, who were concerned about philosophical issues such as theory of perception and theory of knowledge. One only has to think of the different ways these supposed entities – a soulless body and a bodiless soul, brought into mutual relations in order to provide the other with what it lacks – have already been debated by Warburton's time by philosophers and theologians, and this library of contestation has been compressed into an assumption and slipped neatly into his own text as an encapsulated strategy to support another essentialization of imaginary entities: religion and government or politics. He is therefore embedding his argument about church and state within a further dualism that could not have existed in the same senses in the late medieval period, except in the minds of some very rare individuals, but not at the 'official' level of a bishop of a national religion.

The idea of secular (in the sense of non-religious) scientific knowledge of a material world that is objective and external to the observer presupposes some idea of the observing subject who can stand back from the world and make factually true propositions about it. This idea of the possibility of objectivity has been fundamental for Enlightenment concepts of the natural and social sciences. Not only does it turn the world into an object, or a system of objects, and us into master observers, it turns all other peoples and their visions of reality into objects subordinated to our master gaze and method.

Arguably as already suggested it was the North American colonies that brought these ideas about the essential difference between religion and politics into realization first and most emphatically, and that they were re-exported from North America not only to other colonial societies but also back to England. And we have the evidence of the chapters in this book that the separation of religion and politics has been exported from Western colonial powers such as Britain and America to different parts of the world as part of the logic of colonial control and global capitalism, as well as Enlightenment mastery.

## CONCLUSION

In this chapter I have argued that in contemporary rhetoric on religion there are two general conceptions of religion that are in conflict. They both derive from Christianity, and project an internal ideological hostility between a holistic concept of Christendom, which I have called encompassing religion, and a privatized Protestant inward piety or faith that makes possible the idea of a secular (in the sense of non-religious) world. These opposed ideologies still oscillate in contemporary discourses.

One is of encompassing religion, where nothing properly exists outside religion since it represents Truth, which is all-embracing. In this model, 'politics' and 'economics' are embedded, and all 'facts' are subordinated to Christian redemptive values that give them meaning. This model of religion is hierarchical, and all things that exist have their proper place and function within the teleological whole. Individual persons exist in so far as they find their proper subordinate place in this context of hierarchical relationships. That which opposes it is pagan superstition and belongs in Hell.

This idea of religion became, in colonial-era travel writing of the early kind represented by Samuel Purchas (that is to say, early seventeenth century), multiple (religions) and interchangeable with superstitions (superstitions are fallen religions). Other peoples or 'nations' came to be identified as having 'religions' rather by analogy to the way that the English nation had Christian Truth, a Protestant yet still hierarchical conception articulated by the idea of the commonweal. This idea of national religions is reflected in the way that twentieth-century structural–functional anthropologists have claimed that small-scale societies in Asia and Africa have holistic cultures. In Purchas, nations and religions are also close to what today we might call ethnic identities. I suggest, although cannot substantiate this here, that these ideas developed powerfully in the era of European empires, notably the British and French, with their contradictory ideologies of imperial hierarchy, cultural essentialism and commercial and religious individualism. This latter aspect of individualism feeds into the second main idea of religion, which emerges out of the former. Although still clearly operational, these discourses are under dissolution in a world increasingly dominated by American neo-colonialism and consumer capitalism.

The second concept of religion, which I would argue is hegemonic today, cuts across the first, or stands it on its head. The idea of religion as a private soteriological belief essentially separated from politics, or the idea of religious societies having essentially different purposes and characteristics from political societies, has become institutionalized in Western liberal democracies and exported through the processes of colonization to many societies where no such distinction was conceivable in the local language. This idea of religion was powerfully articulated, (in the English language at least) in the seventeenth century, and was developed and transformed into a conception of secular, rational, political 'man', especially through the American constitutional process, which produced the most powerful charter for representing this political essence. At the same time, and as an integral part of this discourse, a notion of the secular as the non-religious, the natural, the rational, was generated as the superior ground from which to observe and order the world. This idea of religions as privatized personal choices first made the idea of markets as aspects of nature possible, and then the religions became commodities themselves.

Through the processes of colonialism and world domination these parochial European representations have assumed the appearance of universals, different representations dominant at different periods of the imperial and colonial eras. Yet they are contradictory and can generate a whole range of ideological representations in different contexts, depending on the needs of the moment and who is deploying them. Today these English language discourses on religion are present, usually unanalysed, in the media and in public debates about nationalism, ethnic identity, minority culture and the relation between democracy and non-Western forms of world construction. My hypothesis is that the term 'religion' is sliding constantly between these different and even contradictory notions in the contemporary rhetoric of academics, politicians, community leaders, corporate bosses and the media. To the extent that the English-language discourses have been appropriated into the rhetorics of other non-European languages, any number of further variations may have been generated. This instability explains why discourses that represent 'religion' and 'politics' as natural aspects of all human societies, are not only analytically dubious, but ideologically volatile.

## NOTES

1. This chapter is based on English-language texts, mainly English and North American. The story needs to be told from the point of view of other languages and cultures. I believe that the importance of Scotland in this story about the separation of religion and politics and of church and state may be great, as indicated for example by the story of Jenny Geddes (Lothian 1995; thanks also to information received from sculptor Professor Merilyn Smith), but I have not had the space required to follow this up. I am grateful to colleagues for reading and commenting on earlier drafts of this chapter: John Drakakis, Steven Ingle, Neil Keeble, Jairo Lugo, Brian Murdoch and Colin Nicolson. It has been impossible for me to acknowledge all the invaluable comments I have received, but to the extent that I have been able to incorporate them into an already long chapter it has been improved considerably. I have also benefited from comments from participants in various seminar and lecture forums that are too numerous to list.

2. It seems significant that William Purchas ([1613] 1626) in his retelling of the proto-ethnography on indigenous Americans deriving from travel journals and other sources, could find their practices worthy of being called 'religion', although with the nuance of fallen religion or superstition, whereas one hundred and fifty years later Thomas Jefferson (1787) could find no sign of either religion or civil society among them.

3. See Fitzgerald (2007) for a discussion of the ubiquitous confusion between the religion–secular and sacred–profane dichotomies, and the need for their analytical separation.

4. Another example of this problem can be found in R. W. Swanson's *Church and Society in Medieval England* (1989). In the preface Swanson makes a point of apologizing for what he calls the anachronism of his title, pointing out that "the church was society" (*ibid.*: ix). Yet he has a whole chapter on "The Church and the Political Order" that subverts this point and creates methodological confusion (*ibid.*: ch. 3).

5. Both John Drakakis and Neil Keeble have pointed out (pers. comm.) that in Italian in the writing of Machievelli a distinction is already mooted, and this is reflected in late-sixteenth-century English drama, for example Marlowe's *The Jew of Malta*, where the challenge of 'politics' and 'politicians' to 'religion' is represented.

6. As I go on to explain, the term 'secular' to indicate a materialist, atheistic, non-religious rationality was not generally used in this way until after 1850; in the late-seventeenth-century writings of Locke the non-religious magistracy conforms to natural reason, as does the non-political religion. This Enlightenment rendering of natural reason is only dependent on God, if at all, in the remotest deistic sense, and for many eighteenth-century thinkers is simply 'in the nature of things'. Religion has become imagined as 'belief' understood as propositional, but the belief is about the supernatural as distinct from the natural, which is the domain of scientific knowledge.

7. I have been greatly helped in my understanding, as far as it goes, of late medieval and early modern Europe by John Bossy (1982, 1985) and his critical approach to language and its historiographical context. However, Bossy does not in these works show much interest in the colonial context.

8. Although Chillingworth (1638) reveals how English Catholics saw it. For them, Christian Truth was mediated by the Catholic Church, and Protestants are heretics.

9. I have already mentioned the influence of Machiavelli and early signs of a distinction in late-sixteenth-century English drama with the characterization of the scheming 'politician' who uses

'religion' cynically for 'political' ends. The Protestant trend towards intense inwardness, combined with the execution of Charles I (Charles VI of Scotland), the era of republicanism, and the failure of godly rule all contributed to its articulation. Neil Keeble points out (pers. comm.) that Milton's *Paradise Lost* contributed to this trend to separate the inner kingdom from the outer fallen world.

10. I am aware that the claim by a historian such as Louis Hartz (1955) that Locke provided the basis of American revolutionary thought has been challenged by such writers as Bernard Bailyn (1967), John Dunn (1969) and J. G. A. Pocock (1975), all of whom argue for a greater influence from the Machiavelli–Harringtonian tradition of republicanism. Also, Garry Wills (1979) has argued for the importance of the Scottish Enlightenment thinkers. On the other hand, Dworetz (1990) has argued strongly for Locke's primary influence. My focus must be limited to the separation of religion and politics and the corresponding construction of an essentially non-religious domain of politics as central to the definition of human rationality; and an essentialized and privatized domain of 'religion' licensed by the state.

11. It is true that one can find various references to "becoming religious", to "religious fraternity" and to "religious duties" in John Bunyan's *The Pilgrim's Progress* ([1678, 1684] 1984: 60; 84/5), usages that are not referring to monastic orders, suggesting that the modern usage was earlier and more prolific among radical Protestant Christians than among the members of the elite Anglican hierarchy. This was in the context of a world represented as a pilgrimage, in which a major trope is the distinction between true inner religion as personal faith and outer show of apparent religion, the following of mere "ordinances". However, while the world is represented in Bunyan as profane in the sense of fallen there is little sense of the modern idea of a neutral system of matter with no moral implications. And there is no usage in *The Pilgrim's Progress* of such words as 'civil' or 'political', the kinds of words that Locke was using at around the same time or soon after to refer to a non-religious state or politics. See Fitzgerald (2007) on the confusion between the 'secular' and the 'profane', and the 'sacred' and the 'religious'.

12. It seems important to note that 'religion' and 'the sacred' are not coterminous in this discourse.

13. Neil Keeble has pointed out to me (pers. comm.) that the idea of toleration first appears in early-seventeenth-century radicals and sectaries such as Barrowists, Brownists and Baptists.

14. "One of the leading ideas of William Penn in his colonizing work was toleration, and the record of Pennsylvania in this was better than that of any other American colony" (Clarke 1955: 344).

15. And later Warburton; see the discussion below. The modern dichotomy between the self and the external world, between observer and observed, is surely in the process of emergence.

16. Burtt (1932) directly connects Newton and his concept of an external, material world made of indivisible particles contained in infinite time and space with Cartesian dualism. Al Azm (1972) argues that the theses in Kant's antinomies in the *Critique of Pure Reason* substantively represent the Newtonian view of a material reality 'external' to a knowing subject, particularly as expounded by the Newtonian Clarke in his correspondence with Leibniz. The antitheses significantly correspond with Leibniz's critique of the Newtonian view. I have argued that the Cartesian dualism inherited by Newton and embedded in much modern thought (despite the implications of quantum mechanics and relativity theory) became internalized in the seventeenth- and eighteenth-century Enlightenment as natural rationality and common sense (see Fitzgerald 1983: 121–42).

17. In his important book *Imagined Communities*, Benedict Anderson has argued that the origins of nationalism was in the New World (1991: xiii). There seem to be many significant parallels between the invention of 'nations' and the invention of 'religions', including the colonial context, but I do not have the space to pursue this here.

18. See Penn (1680: 4) and Cross (1958: 1365).

19. O'Gorman emphatically (and I would think rightly) denies the existence of modern class consciousness in eighteenth-century England, and instead asserts an "integrated set of hierarchies, ascending and descending in minute gradations" (1997: 115). This is one of the reasons why in my view we have to look to the dissenting, more egalitarian American colonies for the earliest and most unambiguous institutionalization and constitutionalization of the separation of religion and politics.

20. This language was used to address the Stuarts, William and Mary, and the Hanovers through the eighteenth century. The contemporary monarch Queen Elizabeth II is still head of state and head of the church.

21. See also, for example, Thomas Cromwell's *First Injunctions* of 1536 (Williams 1967: 805–8) and McCoy (2002).
22. The *Oxford English Dictionary* gives prudent, judicious, expedient, shrewd, skilfully contrived, cunning and scheming.
23. One can perhaps see here the transition from the older opposition between religion (Christian Truth) and superstition (the fallen religion of 'the other') to the more modern dichotomy between European/Western rationality and the irrational native of the colonies. The irony is that it is a colonial native (although a white one) who is thinking in this way. It exemplifies the obvious point that white Americans were not colonized at all in the same sense in which indigenous Americans were colonized.
24. Purchas's book is very much about maps, compasses, designs of ships, speeds and lengths of voyages and geography, as well as what we now tend to call 'cultures'. The transition in concepts of space and time is shown in his placing of the Garden of Eden within a Mercator Map of the region we call the Middle East. Benedict Anderson's discussion of 'The Map' (1991: 170ff.) is germane, as is much of his argument, for example "Apprehensions of Time" (*ibid.*: 22ff.). The imagining of 'religions' and 'nation states' overlaps.
25. Stack has indicated a source of secular writing within the church's need to take a superior stance in the objectifying need to describe and classify indigenous American practices. It may be also that travel writing in the colonial context had a similar effect, producing a descriptive prose style that offered a higher place from which to describe and classify the customs of the natives. There is not enough space to do justice to Purchas's interesting book, which is a rich source of early ethnography.
26. The reports in Purchas of the indigenous people of America are to be found in *The Eighth Booke: Of New France, Virginia, Florida, New Spaine, with other Regions of America Mexicana; and of their Religions*. He records that there is one Virginian called "Tomocomo" who is now in London (Purchas [1613] 1626: 843). Purchas claims that "no people have there been found so savage which have not their Priests, Gods and Religion" (*ibid.*: 840). In contrast, in his *Notes on the State of Virginia* (1787: 150), Thomas Jefferson seems not to be able to find either religion or politics among the indigenous people
27. The centrality of politics as the explicit arena of action and reality, in contrast to the quarantining of religion, is indicated by George Washington's words when he was submitting the draft Constitution: "the Constitution...is the result of a spirit of amity, and of that mutual deference and concession which the peculiarity of our political situation rendered indispensable" (Hough 1872: 22). The Constitution only mentions 'religion' in Article I of the Amendments, where it merely says that "Congress shall make no law respecting an establishment of religion, or prohibiting the free exercise thereof; or abridging the freedom of speech, or the press; or the right of the people to peaceably to assemble, and to petition the government for a redress of grievances" (*ibid.*: 38). The historian Bailyn gives an idea of the way that 'politics' has been essentialized and prioritized when he says that, for John Adams, the "defence of bicameralism" was the central issue, and "involved nothing less than the nature of political man" (2002: 13).
28. The importance of Scotland in this process deserves more knowledge and attention than I have been able to give it here. The role of the Stuart kings, as kings both of Scotland and England, and the attempts of James VI in the early seventeenth century to impose on the Scottish Presbyterian church the episcopacy of England, may have raised the issue of church and state relations in a different but significant context that I cannot explore here.

## BIBLIOGRAPHY

Al Azm, S. J. 1972. *The Origins of Kant's Arguments in the Antimonies*. Oxford: Clarendon Press.
Anderson, Benedict. 1991. *Imagined Communities: Reflections on the Origin and Spread of Nationalism*. New York: Verso.
Bailyn, Bernard. 1965. *Pamphlets of the American Revolution*. Cambridge, MA: Harvard University Press.

Bailyn, Bernard. 1967. *The Ideological Origins of the American Revolution*. Cambridge, MA: Harvard University Press.

Barlow, Frank. 1963. *The English Church, 1000-1066: A Constitutional History*. London: Longman.

Baylor, Michael G., ed. 1991. *The Radical Reformation*. Cambridge: Cambridge University Press.

Berger, Peter, ed. 1999. *The Desecularization of the World: Resurgent Religion and World Politics*. Washington DC: Ethics and Public Policy Center & Wm. B. Eerdmans Publishing Company.

Bossy, John. 1982. "Some Elementary Forms of Durkheim". *Past and Present* 95: 3–18.

Bossy, John. 1985. *Christianity in the West, 1400-1700*. Oxford: Oxford University Press.

Browning, Andrew, ed. 1953. *English Historical Documents Vol. VIII, 1660-1714*. London: Routledge.

Bunyan, John. [1678, 1684] 1984. *The Pilgrim's Progress*. Ed. with an introduction and notes by N. H. Keeble. Oxford: Oxford University Press.

Burtt, E. A. 1932. *The Metaphysical Foundations of Modern Science*, 2nd edn. London: Routledge.

Chillingworth, William. 1638. *The Religion of Protestants A Safe Way to Salvation, Or, An Answer to a Book entitled Mercy and Truth, Or, Charity Maintain'd by Catholiques, which pretends to prove the Contrary*. Oxford: Printed by Leonard Lichfield.

Clarke, Sir George. 1955. *The Later Stuarts 1660-1714*, 2nd edn. Oxford: Clarendon Press.

Cooper, G. 1988. "North American Traditional Religion". In *The World's Religions*, ed. Stewart Sutherland, 873–82. London: Routledge.

Cross, F. L. 1958. *Dictionary of the Christian Church*. Oxford: Oxford University Press.

Dunn, John. 1969. "The Politics of Locke in England and America in the 18th Century". In *John Locke: Problems and Perspectives*, ed. John Yolton. Cambridge: Cambridge University Press.

Dworetz, Steven M. 1990. *The Unvarnished Doctrine: Locke, Liberalism, and the American Revolution*. Durham, NC: Duke University Press.

Filmer, Sir Robert. [1680] 1991. *Patriarcha and Other Writings*. Ed. Johann P. Sommerville. Cambridge: Cambridge University Press.

Fitzgerald, T. 1983. *Philosophical Issues in Agnosticism since Hume and Kant*. PhD thesis. University of London.

Fitzgerald, T. 2000. *The Ideology of Religious Studies*. Oxford: Oxford University Press.

Fitzgerald, T. 2007. *Discourse on Civility and Barbarity: A Critical History of Religion and Related Categories*. New York: Oxford University Press.

Gwatkin, H. M. 1908. "Religious Toleration in England". In *Cambridge Modern History V: The Age of Louis XIV*, ed. Adolphus W. Ward, 324–37. Cambridge: Cambridge University Press.

Gwatkin, H. M. 1917. *Church and State to the Death of Queen Anne*. London: Longmans, Green.

Hakluyt, Richard. 1809. *Hakluyt's Collection of Early Voyages, Traffiques, and Discoveries of the English Nation, A New Edition, with Additions*, 5 vols. London. [This is a republication of Hakluyt's *The principal navigations, voyages, traffiques and discoveries of the English nation, made by Sea or Overland to the Remote and Farthest Distant Quarters of the Earth, at any time within the Compasse of These 1600 yeres: divided into Three Severall Volumes, according to the Positions of the Regions, Whereunto they were Directed*, 3 vols (London, 1599).]

Hartz, Louis. 1955. *The Liberal Tradition in America*. New York: Harcourt, Brace and World.

Hill, Christopher. 1972. *The World Turned Upside Down: Radical Ideas during the English Revolution*. Harmondsworth: Penguin.

Hough, Franklin B., ed. 1872. *American Constitutions: Comprising the Constitution of Each State in the Union, and the United States, with the Declaration of Independence and Articles of Confederation*, 2 vols. Albany, NY: Weed, Parsons.

Jefferson, Thomas. 1787. *Notes on the State of Virginia*. London (microfilm).

Jensen, Merrill, ed. 1955. *American Colonial Documents to 1776, English Historical Documents Vol. IX*. London: Eyre and Spottiswoode.

Katz, Stanley. 1969. "The Origins of American Constitutional Thought". *Perspectives in American History* 3: 474–90.

Kinney, A. F., ed. 1975. "Homily on Obedience (1559)". In *Elizabethan Backgrounds: Historical Documents of the Age of Elizabeth I*, ed. Arthur F. Kinney, 44–70. Hamden, CT: Archon Press.

Kirby, Ethlyn Williams. 1935. "The Quakers' Efforts to Secure Civil and Religious Liberty, 1660-1696". *Journal of Modern History* 7: 401–21.

Lloyd, C., ed. 1825. *The King's Book: A Necessary Doctrine and Erudition for any Christian Man: set forth by the King's Majesty of England*. London.

Locke, John. 1689. *A Letter Concerning Toleration*, 2nd edn. London.

Logan, F. D. 1968. *Excommunication and the Secular Arm in Medieval England: A Study in Legal Procedure from the 13th to the 16th Century*. Toronto: Pontifical Institute of Medieval Studies.

Lothian, Murdoch. 1995. *The Cutty Stool*. Glasgow: Hughson Gallery.

McCoy, Richard C. 2002. *Alterations of State: Sacred Kingship in the English Reformation*. New York: Columbia University Press.

Macpherson, C. B. 1962. *The Political Theory of Possessive Individualism*. Oxford: Oxford University Press.

Mayer, T. F., ed. 1989. *Thomas Starkey: A Dialogue between Pole and Lupset*. London: Offices of the Royal Historical Society, University College, London.

O'Gorman, Frank. 1997. *The Long Eighteenth Century: British Political and Social History 1688-1832*. London: Arnold.

Pangle, Thomas L. 1988. *The Spirit of Modern Republicanism: The Moral Vision of the American Founders and the Philosophy of Locke*. Chicago, IL: University of Chicago Press.

Penn, William. 1680. *The Great Question to be Considered by the King, and this approaching Parliament, briefly proposed, and modestly discussed: (to wit) How far Religion is concerned in Policy or Civil Government, and Policy in Religion? With an Essay rightly to distinguish these great interests, upon the Disquisition of which a sufficient Basis is proposed for the firm Settlement of these Nations, to the Most probable satisfaction of the Several Interests and Parties therein. [By one who desires to give unto Caesar the things that are Caesar's, and to God the things that are God's.]* (microfiche). Edinburgh: National Library of Scotland.

Penn, William. 1694. *A Brief Account of the Rise and Progress of the People called Quakers in which their fundamental Principles, Doctrines, Worship, Ministry and Discipline are Plainly Declared to Prevent the Mistakes and Perversions that Ignorance and Prejudice may make to abuse the Credulous ... etc.* London.

Pocock, J. G. A. 1972. "Virtue and Commerce in the 18th Century". *Journal of Interdisciplinary History* 3 (Summer): 119-34.

Pocock, J. G. A. 1975. *The Machiavellian Moment*. Princeton, NJ: Princeton University Press.

Purchas, Samuel. [1613] 1626. *Purchas, his Pilgrimage; or, Relations of the World and the Religions observed in all Ages*. London.

Purchas, Samuel. 1625. *Hakluytus Posthumus or Purchas his Pilgrimes, contayning a History of the World in Sea Voyages and Lande Travells, by Englishmen and others*, 4 vols. London.

Smith, J. E. 1994. *Quasi-religions: Humanism, Marxism and Nationalism*. Basingstoke: Macmillan.

Smith, W. C. 1962. *The Meaning and End of Religion*. New York: Macmillan.

Southern, R. W. 1970. *Western Society and the Church in the Middle Ages*. Harmondsworth: Penguin.

Starkey, Thomas. [1539?] 1989. *A Dialogue between Pole and Lupset*. London: Offices of the Royal Historical Society, University College, London.

Swanick, John. 1786. *Considerations of an Act of the Legislature of Virginia, Entitled, An Act for the Establishment of Religious Freedom. By a Citizen of Philadelphia*. Microfilm. Philadelphia, PA.

Swanson, R. W. 1989. *Church and Society in Late Medieval England*. Oxford: Blackwell.

Tawney, R. H. 1926. *Religion and the Rise of Capitalism*. London: John Murray.

Tillyard, E. M. W. [1943] 1998. *The Elizabethan World Picture*. London: Pimlico.

Tyndale, William. 1848. *The Parable of the Wicked Mammon*. Ed. H. Walter. London: Parker Society. Reprinted in *English Historical Documents: 1485-1558. Vol. 5*, ed. C. H. Williams, 292 (London: Routledge, 1995).

Warburton, William [1748] 1766. *The Alliance between Church and State: Or, the Necessity and Equity of an Established Religion and a Test Law Demonstrated in Three Books*, 4th edn. London.

Williams, C. H., ed. 1967. *English Historical Documents: 1485-1558. Vol. 5*. London: Eyre and Spottiswoode.

Wills, Garry. 1979. *Inventing America: Jefferson's Declaration of Independence*. New York: Vintage Books.

Zeeveld, W. G. 1948. *Foundations of Tudor Policy*. Cambridge, MA: Harvard University Press.

# 12
# Colonialism and the myth of religious violence

## William T. Cavanaugh

The idea that religion has a peculiar tendency toward violence has inspired a host of scholarly books exploring this thesis. At the same time, a significant group of scholars has been questioning whether 'religion' even exists, except as an intellectual construct of highly dubious value. The first group of scholars carries on as if the second group did not exist. In this chapter I shall bring the two together.

This may sound as though I am setting up a tedious border skirmish among academics who thrive on haggling over definitions, but I am convinced that there are important implications for the study of colonialism. Once we begin to ask what the 'religion and violence' arguments mean by 'religion', we find that their explanatory power is hobbled by a number of indefensible assumptions about what does and does not count as 'religion'. Certain types of practices and institutions are condemned, while others are arbitrarily ignored. Why? My hypothesis is that 'religion and violence' arguments serve a particular need for their consumers in the West. These arguments are part of a broader Enlightenment narrative that invents a dichotomy between the religious and the secular and constructs the former as an irrational and dangerous impulse that must give way in public to rational, secular forms of power. The argument that religion causes violence sanctions a dichotomy between non-Western, especially Muslim, forms of culture on the one hand, which – having not yet learned to privatize matters of faith – are absolutist, divisive and irrational, and Western culture on the other, which is modest in its claims to truth, unitive and rational. This dichotomy, this 'clash of civilizations' worldview, in turn can be used to legitimize the use of violence against those with whom it is impossible to reason. In short, their violence is fanatical and uncontrolled; our violence is controlled, reasonable and often regrettably necessary to contain their violence.

I shall begin by examining two prominent academic arguments that religion is inherently prone to violence, and show how the arguments fail. I shall then place these arguments in the context of Western colonialism. I do not suggest that arguments that religion causes violence are deliberately constructed with imperialistic purposes in mind. I suggest instead that just as Timothy Fitzgerald, Richard King, Russell McCutcheon and others have shown that the development of the concept 'religion' was linked with European colonialism, so the argument that religion causes violence continues to lend itself to the promotion of ideologies that favour Western culture over that of our supposedly less rational, non-Western others.

## I. RELIGION AND VIOLENCE

### Mark Juergensmeyer, *Terror in the Mind of God*

The work of sociologist Mark Juergensmeyer is perhaps the most prominent contemporary scholarship on the question of religion and violence. His most thorough work on the subject, the book *Terror in the Mind of God: The Global Rise of Religious Violence* has been issued in an updated edition with a new preface after the attacks of 11 September 2001. Juergensmeyer contends that "Religion seems to be connected with violence virtually everywhere" (Juergensmeyer 2000: xi). This, he claims, is true across all religious traditions, and it has always been so (*ibid.*: xii). He does not think this is an aberration. "Rather, I look for explanations in the current forces of geopolitics and in a strain of violence that may be found at the deepest levels of the religious imagination" (*ibid.*: 6). The argument, then, is built on a combination of empirical observations about some violent behaviours in the face of globalization on the one hand, and contentions about the transhistorical essence of religion on the other. For the latter, Juergensmeyer concentrates on the propensity of religion to divide people into friends and enemies, good and evil, us and them. More specifically, religious images of struggle and transformation – or 'cosmic war' – have a tendency to foster violence when transferred to 'real-world' conflicts by 'satanizing' the other and ruling out compromise or peaceful coexistence.

The first part of Juergensmeyer's book consists of case studies of what he takes to be religious violence. Abortion clinic bombers, Timothy McVeigh, Protestants and Catholics in Belfast, Zionists, Muslim fundamentalists, Sikh militants and the Japanese Aum Shinrikyo all come under scrutiny. This section is full of interesting interviews and empirical observations. Juergensmeyer does a good job being as fair to his subjects as possible and lets them present their own views. In the second part of the book, Juergensmeyer attempts to explain the underlying logic of religious violence. He begins by describing the acts of these groups as "performance violence". Their acts are "deliberately intense and vivid", "savage", "meant purposely to elicit anger" and "deliberately exaggerated" (*ibid.*: 119–20). Juergensmeyer wants to distinguish between acts of violence done for utilitarian purposes and those whose main purpose is symbolic. "I can imagine a line with 'strategic' on the one side and 'symbolic' on the other, with various acts of terrorism located in between." The takeover of the Japanese embassy in Peru in 1997 would be closer to the "strategic,

242

political side" and the Aum Shinrikyo gas attack in 1995 would be closer to the "symbolic, religious side" (*ibid*.: 123). One thing that distinguishes religious violence from secular violence is the former's tendency to pursue symbolic targets – defined as those "intended to illustrate or refer to something beyond their immediate target" – rather than those with long-term strategic value. As such, acts of religious violence can be "analyzed as one would any other symbol, ritual, or sacred drama" (*ibid*.).

This attempt to distinguish religious from secular political violence according to the symbolic–strategic axis begins to break down in the course of Juergensmeyer's own analysis, for he must admit the symbolic nature of politics. For example, Juergensmeyer states that symbolic acts can actually weaken a secular government's power. "Because power is largely a matter of perception, symbolic statements can lead to real results" (*ibid*.: 132–3). Here Juergensmeyer wants to maintain his distinction between the symbolic–religious and the real–political, but he gives the game away by admitting that "real" power largely rests on "mere" perception. Likewise, he refers with approval to Pierre Bourdieu's work on power and symbol, from which he gleans that "our public life is shaped as much by symbols as by institutions. For this reason, symbolic acts – the 'rites of institution' – help to demarcate public space and indicate what is meaningful in the social world" (*ibid*.: 144). Rather than conclude, as Bourdieu does, that the political can be just as symbolic as the religious, however, Juergensmeyer concludes that "Public ritual has traditionally been the province of religion, and this is one of the reasons that performance violence comes so naturally to activists from a religious background" (*ibid*.: 125). In the face of evidence that not just religion but politics is symbolic, Juergensmeyer seems to claim that whatever is symbolic about politics must be the purview of religion. The argument oscillates between saying explicitly "religion employs symbolism" and saying implicitly "if it's symbolic, it must be religious". Much clarity could be won for this chapter of Juergensmeyer's argument if he simply dropped the term 'religion' and set out to analyse the symbolic power of violence. Doing so would, among other gains, render explicable the appearance of the Unabomber in this chapter. The Unabomber is used to illustrate the way that symbolic violence today requires media exposure, despite the fact that the Unabomber would appear to have had no affiliation with any group or ideas that Juergensmeyer would consider religious.

Once Juergensmeyer has made the symbolic–strategic distinction, he moves on to analyse the heart of the religious warrior's symbolic universe: the notion of 'cosmic war'. "What makes religious violence particularly savage and relentless" is that it puts worldly conflicts in a "larger than life" context of "great battles of the legendary past" and struggles between good and evil (*ibid*.: 146). Essential to religion is a larger drama of the establishment of order over chaos and evil. Worldly political conflicts – that is, "more rational" conflicts such as those over land (*ibid*.: 153) – are of a fundamentally different character than those in which the stakes have been raised to cosmic proportions. If the stakes are thus set high, the "absolutism of cosmic war makes compromise unlikely", thus increasing the intensity of the violence (*ibid*.: 154). According to Juergensmeyer, conflicts are likely to be characterized as cosmic war under any of the following conditions: (i) "the struggle is perceived as a defense of basic identity and dignity"; (ii) "losing the struggle would be unthinkable"; and (iii) "the struggle is blocked and cannot be won in real time or in real terms". As an example of worldly political conflict turning into cosmic war, Juergensmeyer offers the Arab–Israeli conflict, which "was not widely regarded as a sacred battle from the perspective of either side until the late 1980s" (*ibid.*: 161–3).

Once again, however, keeping the notion of cosmic war separate from ordinary worldly political war is difficult or impossible on Juergensmeyer's own terms. What he says about cosmic war is virtually indistinguishable from what he says about war in general:

> Looking closely at the notion of war, one is confronted with the idea of dichotomous opposition on an absolute scale… War suggests an all-or-nothing struggle against an enemy whom one assumes to be determined to destroy. No compromise is deemed possible. The very existence of the opponent is a threat, and until the enemy is either crushed or contained, one's own existence cannot be secure. What is striking about a martial attitude is the certainty of one's position and the willingness to defend it, or impose it on others, to the end.
>
> Such certitude on the part of one side may be regarded as noble by those whose sympathies lie with it and dangerous by those who do not. But either way it is not rational. (*Ibid.*: 148–9)

War cuts off the possibility of compromise, and in fact provides an excuse not to compromise. In other words, "War provides a reason to be violent. This is true even if the worldly issues at heart in the dispute do not seem to warrant such a ferocious position" (*ibid.*: 149). The division between mundane war and cosmic war seems to vanish as fast as it was constructed. War itself is a "worldview"; indeed, "The concept of war provides cosmology, history, and eschatology and offers the reins of political control" (ibid.: 155). "Like the rituals provided by religious traditions, warfare is a participatory drama that exemplifies – and thus explains – the most profound aspects of life" (*ibid.*). Here we have moved from religion as a contributor to war to war itself as a kind of religious practice.

At times, Juergensmeyer admits the difficulty of separating religious violence from mere political violence. "Much of what I have said about religious terrorism in this book may be applied to other forms of political violence – especially those that are ideological and ethnic in nature" (*ibid.*: 217). This is an important admission, leaving aside the question of what political violence that is *not* ideological would look like. Nevertheless, Juergensmeyer provides a summary of what distinguishes religious from secular violence. First, religious violence is "almost exclusively symbolic, performed in remarkably dramatic ways". Secondly, religious violence is "accompanied by strong claims of moral justification and enduring absolutism, characterized by the intensity of religious activists' commitment". Thirdly, cosmic war is "beyond historical control". Although some secular ideas such as class conflict seem similar; they are thought to take place only on the social plane and within history. So in Maoism, persons can be separated from their class roles and re-educated. In cosmic war, satanic enemies cannot be transformed, but only destroyed. Fourthly and finally, secular conflicts have sought conclusion within their participants' lifetimes, but religious activists can wait for hundreds of years, or even for fulfilment in some trans-temporal realm. Therefore there is no need for religious activists to compromise their goals, nor to "contend with society's laws and limitations" when they are "obeying a higher authority" (ibid.).[1]

One could almost refute these four attempts to separate religious from secular violence using only Juergensmeyer's own words. First, Juergensmeyer himself states that all terrorism, even that of leftists and separatists motivated solely by political gain, exemplifies "performance violence" (ibid.: 216–17). There is no reason to suppose that Basque separatists killing policemen or the United States dropping nuclear weapons on civilian targets in Japan are any less symbolic or dramatic than Muslim Palestinians bombing Israeli buses, or Israeli punitive raids on Palestinian neighbourhoods. Secondly, as we have seen above, Juergensmeyer himself writes of the absolutism of all war. Certainly the wars fought by nation states for supposedly mundane ends are couched in the strongest rhetoric of moral justification and historical duty: witness "Operation Infinite Justice", the US military's first name for the war on Afghanistan. Nor is there any warrant for supposing that the commitment of a US Marine – semper fidelis – is any less 'intense' than that of a Hamas militant, as if such a thing could be measured at any rate. Thirdly, Juergensmeyer's own words quoted above indicate that war produces an all-or-nothing struggle against an enemy one is determined to destroy. In the clash of civilizations we are currently witnessing, the Pentagon does not seem any more interested in re-educating al-Qaida than the latter is in re-educating the Great Satan. Fourthly and finally, again in Juergensmeyer's own words, "The concept of war provides cosmology, history, eschatology, and offers the reins of political control". US leaders have given every indication that the 'war against terror' will stretch indefinitely into the future. As Juergensmeyer also points out, war shuts down the possibility of compromise. He offers no empirical evidence that the presence or absence of belief in a trans-temporal realm has any effect on one's willingness to flout human conventions regarding the conduct of war. Nor, by Juergensmeyer's own standards, does belief in a trans-temporal realm distinguish religion from non-religion; some of what counts as 'religion' for Juergensmeyer – Theravada Buddhism, for example – does not appear to have any such belief.

In a chapter on martyrdom, Juergensmeyer appeals to the work of René Girard to explain the connection between religion and violence. Juergensmeyer has many interesting suggestions about violence, symbolism and social order, but his analysis is hobbled by the term 'religion'. According to Juergensmeyer, martyrdom is a form of self-sacrifice, and is therefore linked with sacrifice, which is the "most fundamental form of religiosity". In Girard's famous work on sacrifice, intragroup rivalries are kept from threatening the coherence of the group by focusing the group's aggression on a sacrificial victim. Juergensmeyer accepts this analysis, but claims, pace Girard, that war is the context for sacrifice rather than the other way around. War is the basic dynamic that preserves group identity by erecting antinomies of we versus they, order versus chaos, good versus evil, truth versus falsehood. Furthermore, "Warfare ... organizes social history into a storyline of persecution, conflict, and the hope of redemption, liberation, and conquest".

In the next sentence, however, the subject changes from 'warfare' in general to 'cosmic war': "The enduring and seemingly ubiquitous image of cosmic war from ancient times to the present continues to give the rites of sacrifice their meaning" (*ibid*.: 169–70). Juergensmeyer seems to acknowledge that Girard's theory – and Juergensmeyer's own emendation of it – applies to societies in general, even supposedly secular ones.[2] Talk of sacrifice in war is endemic to modern nation states; *dulce et decorum est pro patria mori*. Nevertheless, Juergensmeyer wants to identify the social role of war in asserting order over chaos with 'religion'.[3] Again, the argument oscillates between "religion contributes to violence understood in terms of symbolism" and "if it's violence understood in terms of symbolism, it must be religious".

Juergensmeyer could stop this oscillation by providing a definition of religion that would help distinguish it from symbolism in general or public ritual in general, but he offers none. When he reports that Gerry Adams and the IRA leadership emphatically consider their struggle against the British to be anti-colonial, and not religious (*ibid*.: 37), it is unclear by Juergensmeyer's standards how one would begin to decide this question. Juergensmeyer contends that those Catholics in Ireland who identified religion with the church would not think of the struggle as religious, "But those who thought of religion in the broadest sense, as part of a society's culture, saw the Republican position as a religious crusade" (*ibid*.: 41). If the conflict in Northern Ireland only becomes a religious conflict when religion is construed as some unspecified dimension of culture in general, then it seems we are left with two choices: either reconfigure the book as an exposition of the cultural or symbolic dimensions of violence, or, if something more specific is meant by 'religion', define 'religion' and drop all the examples, such as that of Northern Ireland, that do not fit the more specific paradigm. Unfortunately, Juergensmeyer takes neither of these two roads to clarity.

If one takes the title of the book – *Terror in the Mind of God* – one might expect that 'religion' might specifically denote belief in a God. However, of the three figures pictured beneath the title on the front cover – Aum Shinrikyo leader Shoko Asahara, Oklahoma City bomber Timothy McVeigh, and terror mastermind Osama bin Laden – only the last one professes belief in a God. Aum Shinrikyo is a non-theistic melange of Buddhist, yogic, Taoist and other practices, and McVeigh was a self-described agnostic. Juergensmeyer nevertheless identifies McVeigh as a "quasi-Christian" because he had some contacts with the anti-government militia group Christian Identity (*ibid*.: xii, 30–36). Although he was an agnostic, Juergensmeyer writes that McVeigh's action was "quasi-religious" because it involved a symbolic target and was set in the context of a larger historical drama of government versus the people, slavery versus liberty (*ibid*.: 127, 164–5). Similarly, the two high school students who gunned down their classmates in Littleton, Colorado in 1999 were involved in the "quasi-religious 'trenchcoat' culture of gothic symbolism" (*ibid*.: 11). By what standard this tragedy could be associated with religion is anybody's guess. Without some independent idea of what distinguishes religion from symbolism in general, the argument is always in danger of being thrown into reverse. Instead of showing how religion contributes to violence, whatever is violent and kooky gets identified as religious.

In Juergensmeyer's earlier book *The New Cold War?: Religious Nationalism Confronts the Secular State*, he writes "Secular nationalism, like religion, embraces what one scholar calls 'a doctrine of destiny.' One can take this way of looking at secular nationalism a step further and state flatly, as did one author writing in 1960, that secular nationalism *is* 'a religion'" (1993: 15). Juergensmeyer cites Ninian Smart's contention that secular nationalism is a "tribal religion", and goes on to suggest that religion and secular nationalism be seen as two species of the genus "ideologies of order" (*ibid.*: 30–31). Unfortunately, Juergensmeyer does not take his own suggestion seriously. He sees the difficulty of separating 'religious' violence out from other ideologically motivated but 'secular' types of violence, but he nevertheless proceeds to build his book around a dichotomy between "reason and religion", secular nationalism and religious nationalism (*ibid.*: 201).

Juergensmeyer's work is full of interesting empirical studies of the ideologies of violent groups and individuals. The attempt to build a general theory about religious – as opposed to non-religious or secular – violence, however, is confused, and arbitrarily serves to focus our attention on certain kinds of violence and away from others. Juergensmeyer's treatment of McVeigh is a good example of how this dynamic works. McVeigh spent three and a half years in the US Army. After participating in the slaughter of a trapped group of Iraqi soldiers in the 1991 Gulf War, McVeigh is reported to have walked around taking snapshots of Iraqi corpses for his personal photo collection. When searching for the source of McVeigh's violence, however, Juergensmeyer does not mention his army training, but hones in instead on the fact that, although McVeigh was not affiliated with Christian Identity, he read their newsletter and made several phone calls to their compound on the Oklahoma/Arkansas border. He also once got a speeding ticket on the access road to the compound (2000: 30–36). On this, and the fact that McVeigh read William Pierce's novel *The Turner Diaries*,[4] Juergensmeyer builds the case for the agnostic McVeigh as a religious warrior.

One can imagine the reaction of a typical Middle Eastern Muslim, who might well wonder why we need to track down small bands of Christian survivalists for evidence of divisive ideologies of total struggle against evil, when the Pentagon – with its annual budget approaching half a trillion dollars – is rife with such thinking. Indeed, as Juergensmeyer himself indicates, war and preparations for war require such a 'worldview' and raise the stakes to an all-or-nothing battle of us versus them. This is not, of course, to say that there is no value in studying fringe groups that do violence in the name of their beliefs, including Christian beliefs. It is rather to indicate that the theoretical divide between 'religious' and 'secular' violence is incoherent and distracts attention from the violence of, for example, the putatively secular nation state.

## Charles Kimball, *When Religion Becomes Evil*

Charles Kimball's *When Religion Becomes Evil* was chosen as the Top Religion Book of 2002 by *Publishers Weekly*, and it has reached an audience beyond the academy. It is a generous, well-intentioned and balanced book, full of evidence of violence done in the name of faith, but also of more hopeful signs that the 'major religions' have resources within them to prevent evil being done in their name. Nevertheless, the book is marred by the principal problem from which the 'religion and violence' genre suffers: its inability to provide any convincing way to distinguish the religious from the secular. As a result, certain kinds of violence may be, willy-nilly, tacitly condoned.

The force of Kimball's argument rests on the following claim, which appears in the first paragraph: "It is somewhat trite, but nevertheless sadly true, to say that more wars have been waged, more people killed, and these days more evil perpetrated in the name of religion than by any other institutional force in human history" (2002: 1). One would think that the rest of the book would be devoted to proving such a claim, but Kimball apparently considers it too trite and obvious to need proving. The rest of the book is devoted to finding the root cause of the violence of religion and is organized around five 'warning signs' to alert us to when religion is about to unleash its capacity for evil.

What would be necessary to prove the claim that religion has caused more violence than any other institutional force over the course of human history? One would first need a concept of religion that would be at least theoretically separable from other institutional forces over the course of history. Kimball does not identify those rival institutional forces, but an obvious contender might be political institutions: tribes, empires, kingdoms, fiefs, states and so on. The problem is that religion was not considered something separable from such political institutions until the modern era, and then primarily in the West. What meaning could we give to either the claim that Roman religion is to blame for the imperialist violence of ancient Rome, or the claim that it is the Roman 'state' and not Roman religion that is to blame? Either claim would be nonsensical, because there was no neat division between religion and politics; Roman religion was largely a matter of duty to the emperor and to the gods of Roman civic life. Similar comments apply to ancient Israel, Confucian China, Charlemagne's empire, Aztec civilization and any other pre-modern culture. Is Aztec religion or Aztec politics to blame for their bloody human sacrifices? Any attempt to prove Kimball's 'trite' claim about the destructive influence of religion in history would get bogged down in hopeless anachronism.

It is not simply that religion and politics were jumbled up together until the modern West got them properly sorted out. As Wilfred Cantwell Smith (to whom, with two others, Kimball's book is dedicated) showed long ago in his landmark 1962 book *The Meaning and End of Religion* (1962), 'religion' as a discrete category of human activity separable from 'culture', 'politics' and other areas of life is an invention of the modern West. In the course of a detailed historical study of the concept 'religion', Smith was compelled to conclude that in pre-modern Europe there was no significant concept equivalent to what we think of as 'religion', and furthermore there is no "closely equivalent concept in any culture that has not been influenced by the modern West" (*ibid.*: 19). Smith still contends that it is possible to be 'religious' without the concept, but other scholars have taken the anti-essentialist implications of his historical study to their logical conclusion. Richard King (1999), Russell McCutcheon (1997) and many others have focused on the way that the concept of religion was invented by modern Western scholars and bureaucrats, often in the interests of colonialist pursuits.[5] Jonathan Z. Smith argues "Religion is solely the creation of the scholar's study .... Religion has no independent existence apart from the academy" (1982: xi). Timothy Fitzgerald (2000) argues that there is no coherent concept of religion, and the term should be scrapped as itself a form of mystification.

Fitzgerald's conclusion is controversial, but it represents one increasingly significant solution to the problem of the definition of religion, a problem almost universally recognized by those who study religion. After two hundred years of *Religionswissenschaft*, the 'scientific' study of religion, there is nothing close to agreement on what religion is. Yet very few of those who argue that religion has a tendency towards violence even pause to consider the problem.

At the beginning of his first chapter, Kimball describes how flustered his students become when he asks them to write a definition of religion. Kimball acknowledges the problem, but treats it as a merely semantic difficulty: "Clearly these bright students know what religion is"; they just have trouble defining it. After all, Kimball assures us, "Religion is a central feature of human life. We all see many indications of it every day, and we all know it when we see it" (2002: 15). Well, no we do not. A survey of religious studies literature finds totems, witchcraft, the rights of man, Marxism, liberalism, Japanese tea ceremonies, nationalism, sports, free market ideology and a host of other institutions and practices treated under the rubric 'religion' (see Fitzgerald 2000: 17). Kimball, on the other hand, recognizes none of these practices as religious. He deals with the problem of the definition of religion by recommending a comparative empirical analysis that begins by "[g]athering data and organizing the facts about a particular religion" (2002: 18). After doing so, we may make some conclusions about what all religions have in common (*ibid.*: 22–3). The problem with this approach is that it begs the question about what qualifies as a religion to begin with. How do we know which phenomena qualify as religions so that we may begin our comparative analysis of them? Kimball mentions Hinduism, Buddhism, Judaism, Christianity, Islam, Shinto, Zoroastrianism, Manichaeism, Native American religions and "indigenous tribal religions" (*ibid.*: 21–3). How did he arrive at this list? Why Shinto, when there is widespread scholarly doubt about its status as a religion, even among those who accept the usefulness of the category 'religion' (Mullins *et al.* 1993: 4)? Why Native American 'religion', when scholars acknowledge that Native American tribes do not traditionally distinguish between religion and the rest of life?[6]

Some might wish to excuse Kimball and others on the grounds that virtually every scholarly concept has some fuzzy edges. We might not be able to nail down, once and for all and in all cases, what a 'culture' is, or what qualifies as 'politics', for example, but nevertheless the concepts remain useful. All may not agree on the periphery of these concepts, but enough agreement on the centre of such concepts makes them practical and functional. Most people know that 'religion' includes Christianity, Islam, Judaism and the major 'world religions'. Whether or not Confucianism or Shinto fits is a boundary dispute best left up to scholars who make their living splitting hairs.

This appears to be a common-sense answer, but it misses the point rather completely. In the first place, when some scholars question whether the category of religion is useful at all, it is more than a boundary dispute. There are some who do not believe there is a centre. In the second place, and much more significantly, the problem with the 'religion and violence' arguments is not that their working definitions of religion are too fuzzy. The problem is precisely the opposite. Their implicit definitions of religion are *unjustifiably clear* about what does and does not qualify as a religion. Kimball, for example, subjects the violence of Hinduism to close scrutiny, but passes over the violence of other kinds of nationalism in silence, despite a telling acknowledgement that "blind religious zealotry is similar to unfettered nationalism" (2002: 38). How are they different? Forms of 'secular' nationalism do not appeal to God or gods, but neither do some of the institutions Kimball includes in his list of religions, such as Theravada Buddhism.

Kimball is typical of those who make the argument that religion is prone to violence in that he assumes a sharp distinction between the religious and the secular, without explicitly analysing or defending such a distinction. This is not a peripheral issue; the entire force of the argument rests on this distinction. In making this assumption, however, Kimball and others ignore the growing body of scholarly work that calls the distinction into question. The case for nationalism as a religion, for example, has been made repeatedly from Carlton Hayes's 1960 classic *Nationalism: A Religion* to more recent works by Peter van der Veer (1999), Talal Asad (1999), Carolyn Marvin (Marvin & Ingle 1999) and others. Kimball and others who make the 'religion and violence' argument might wish to defend the religion–secular distinction against these other lines of argument, but in fact they do not. The argument that religion is prone to violence goes on as if "we all know religion when we see it", while arbitrary and undefended decisions are made as to what constitutes a religion and what does not.

We need not accept the judgements of the authors I have cited to see the problem. We need only to look at Kimball's own "warning signs" for when a religion is apt to turn evil. The middle five chapters of Kimball's book are each devoted to one of these warning signs, with an introductory chapter and a concluding chapter added at each end. According to Kimball, religion is likely to turn violent when it displays any of these features: absolute truth claims, blind obedience, the establishment of the 'ideal' time, the belief that the end justifies any means and a declaration of holy war. Religion does not necessarily exhibit these features, but "[t]he inclination toward these corruptions is strong in the major religions" (Kimball 2002: 6). At the same time, Kimball holds out hope that correctives from within the religions will be marshalled to prevent violence.

What happens if we take seriously Kimball's own passing reference to the similarity between religious zealotry and nationalism, and search nationalism for the five warning signs? The first, absolute truth claims, is a regular feature of the discourse of nation states at war. As Kimball himself states, George W. Bush, while "determined to keep the 'war on terrorism' from descending into a conflict between Christianity and Islam", invoked a "cosmic dualism" between good nations, led by the United States, and the forces of evil: "You had to align with the forces of good and help root out the forces of evil or be counted as adversaries in the 'war on terrorism'" (*ibid.*: 36). Are not claims to the universal goodness of liberal democracy absolute truth claims? If not, what distinguishes them from being 'absolute'?

The second warning sign, blind obedience, depends on the rather subjective adjective 'blind'. Obedience is rigidly institutionalized for those whose job is to do violence on behalf of the nation-state. In the armed forces there is, for example, no allowance for selective conscientious objection, that is, the individual soldier deciding on the basis of conscience that any particular war is unjust. Once inducted, the soldier must fight in any war his or her superiors deem necessary, and the soldier must fight as he or she is ordered. Is this 'blind' obedience in the service of violence?

The remaining three warning signs also seem to apply to nationalism. The third warning sign, the establishment of the 'ideal' time, is so broadly defined that "making the world safe for democracy" or Francis Fukuyama's "end of history"[7] would seem to qualify. The history of modern warfare between nation states is full of evidence of the fourth warning sign – the belief that the end justifies any means – from the vaporization of innocent civilians in Hiroshima to the practice of torture by over a third of the world's nation states, including many democracies.[8] As for the fifth sign, the declaration of holy war, what counts as 'holy' is unclear, but arguably the battle of good versus evil that President Bush believes his nation is leading would fit. 'Secular' nationalism, then, would appear to exhibit – at times – all five of the warning signs.

## II. TESTING THE DISTINCTION

There is plenty of important empirical and theoretical work to be done on the violence of certain groups of self-identified Christians, Hindus, Muslims and so on, and there are no grounds for exempting their beliefs and practices from the causal factors that produce violence. For example, it is certainly the case that, under certain circumstances, particular construals of Muslim or Christian beliefs contribute to violence. Juergensmeyer's and Kimball's books contain a wealth of empirical data on various ideologies and the production of violence. Where their arguments – and others like them – fail is in trying to separate a category called 'religion' with a peculiar tendency toward violence from a putatively 'secular' reality.

Although I have focused on two prominent books for brevity's sake, I could easily multiply examples of this conceptual confusion. Religious studies scholar Richard Wentz's book *Why People Do Bad Things in the Name of Religion* identifies 'religion' not only with Christianity and Islam, but also with faith in technology, secular humanism, consumerism and devotion to Monday-night football (1993: 13–21). Wentz defines 'religion' so broadly that he concludes: "Perhaps all of us do bad things in the name of (or as a representative of) religion" (*ibid.*: 37). If this is the case, then 'religion' picks out nothing more distinctive than "whatever people deem really important". In a book on public religion, historian Martin Marty argues that religion has a particular tendency to be divisive and therefore violent (2000: 25–6). When it comes to defining what 'religion' means, however, Marty begs off giving a definition, since "[s]cholars will never agree on the definition of religion" (*ibid.*: 10), and instead gives a list of five 'features' that mark a religion. He then proceeds to show how 'politics' displays all five of the same features. Religion focuses our ultimate concern, and so does politics. Religion builds community, and so does politics. Religion appeals to myth and symbol, and politics 'mimics' this appeal in devotion to the flag, war memorials and so on. And so on down the list (*ibid.*: 10–14). Marty offers five defining features of 'religion', shows how 'politics' fits all five, and yet continues to act as if the five features help us distinguish what is religion from what is not.

What these studies make clear is that the attempt to separate out a 'secular' sphere from a 'religious' sphere with a peculiar tendency towards violence is incoherent. There is no reason to suppose that so-called secular ideologies such as nationalism, patriotism, capitalism, Marxism and liberalism are any less prone to be absolutist, divisive and irrational than belief in, for example, the biblical God. As Marty himself implies, belief in the righteousness of the United States and its solemn duty to impose liberal democracy on the rest of the world has all the ultimate concern, community, myth, ritual and required behaviour of any so-called religion.[9] Recently revived debate over a ban on flag burning is replete with references to the 'desecration' of the flag, as if it were a sacred object (Stolberg 2003). Carolyn Marvin and David Ingle's book *Blood Sacrifice and the Nation* (1999) is a detailed analysis of American patriotism as a civil religion – focused on the flag totem – whose regeneration depends on periodic blood sacrifice in war. 'Secular' nationalism of the kind we are currently witnessing can be just as absolutist, divisive and irrationally fanatical as certain types of Jewish, Christian, Muslim or Hindu militancy.

An objection can be raised that goes something like this: certainly secular ideologies can get out of hand and produce fanaticism and violence, but religious ideologies have a much greater tendency to do so precisely because the object of their beliefs is claimed to be absolute. The capitalist knows that money is just a human creation, the liberal is avowedly modest about what can be known beyond human reason, the nationalist knows that her country is made up of land and mortal people, but the religious believer claims divine sanction from a god or gods who are, in some sense, *absolute*, far surpassing mere human creation. Indeed, nationalism only becomes fanatical when divine sanction is claimed, when it is believed that we live in God's country. Using this criterion of absoluteness (or sometimes 'ultimacy') we can distinguish between religious and secular ideologies and their respective proclivities toward violence.

The problem here is that what counts as 'absolute' is decided *a priori* and appears immune to any empirical testing. How people actually behave is ignored in favour of theological descriptions of their beliefs. Of course Christian orthodoxy would make the theological claim that God is absolute in a way that nothing else is. The problem, as the first table of the Ten Commandments makes plain, is that human beings are constantly tempted to idolatry: to putting what is merely relative in the place of God. It is not enough, therefore, to claim that worship of God is absolutist. The real question is, what god is actually being worshipped?

But surely, the objection might go, nobody really thinks the flag or the nation or money or sports idols are their 'gods'; that is just a metaphor. However, the question is not simply one of belief, but of behaviour. If a person claims to believe in the Christian God but never gets off the couch on Sunday morning and spends the rest of the week in obsessive pursuit of profit in the bond market, then what is 'absolute' in that person's life in a functional sense is probably not the Christian God. Matthew 6:24 personifies mammon as a rival god, not in the conviction that such a divine being really exists, but from the empirical observation that people have a tendency to treat all sorts of things as absolutes.

Suppose we apply an empirical test to the question of absolutism. 'Absolute' is itself a vague term, but in the 'religion and violence' arguments it appears to indicate the tendency to take something so seriously that violence results. An empirically testable definition of 'absolute', then, might be "that for which one is willing to kill". This test has the advantage of covering behaviour, and not simply what one claims to believe. Now let us ask the following two questions: what percentage of Americans who identify themselves as Christians would be willing to kill for their Christian faith? What percentage would be willing to kill for their country? Whether we attempt to answer these questions by survey or by observing American Christians' behaviour in wartime, it seems clear that, at least among American Christians, the nation state – Hobbes's "mortal god" – is subject to far more absolutist fervour than 'religion'. For most American Christians, even public evangelization is considered to be in poor taste, and yet most endorse organized slaughter on behalf of the nation as sometimes necessary and often laudable. In other countries or other traditions the results of this test might be very different. The point is that such empirical testing is of far more usefulness than general theories about the violence of 'religion'.

We must conclude that there is no coherent way to isolate 'religious' ideologies with a peculiar tendency towards violence from their tamer 'secular' counterparts. People kill for all sorts of things. An adequate approach to the problem would be resolutely empirical: under what conditions do certain beliefs and practices – *jihad*, the "invisible hand" of the market, the sacrificial atonement of Christ, the role of the United States as worldwide liberator – turn violent? The point is not simply that "secular" violence should be given equal attention to 'religious' violence. The point is that the distinction between 'secular' and 'religious' violence is unhelpful, misleading and mystifying, and should be avoided altogether. Self-identified Christians, Muslims, Hindus and others would still be subject to scrutiny, but a fuller and more adequate picture of violence would emerge. The beliefs of the Jim Joneses and Osama bin Ladens of the world are a significant part of the problem of violence in the twenty-first century. At least equally significant is the evangelical zeal with which 'free trade', liberal democracy, and American hegemony are offered to – or forced on – a hungry world.

## III. NEO-COLONIALISM AND THE MYTH OF RELIGIOUS VIOLENCE

The myth of religious violence has long had an important role in the foundational story of the modern state. When Europe was wracked by irrational fanaticism and violence, the story goes, the European state was the first political system to recognize that religion must be privatized, so that a public sphere of universal reason could be opened to everyone. When Catholics and Protestants in the sixteenth and seventeenth centuries began killing each other over beliefs that are beyond rational adjudication, the state stepped in as peacemaker. The lesson learned by liberalism – a lesson to be exported militarily, if necessary, to other more primitive lands – is that there is something essentially irrational and therefore prone to violence in religion. A secular public order is to be preferred as a step towards peace. It follows from this story that those political orders that have not learned to separate out religion from an undue influence in the public sphere are therefore less rational than their Western counterparts.

This story is false in that it treats 'religion' as an isolatable cause to which the state was a response. In fact, however, the wars of the sixteenth and seventeenth centuries were about the triumph of the modern sovereign state over against a medieval ecclesiastical order that was as 'political' as it was 'religious'.[10] As Wilfred Cantwell Smith and his successors have shown, religion was not simply separated out from politics but was *invented* in the sixteenth and seventeenth centuries. The religion–secular dichotomy was a creation of the modern state, which secured its unrivalled sovereignty by domesticating the church. It is crucial to note that the origins of the sovereign state *predate* the Reformation and the rise of Christian division. It is also crucial to note that the state did not arise as peacemaker. On the contrary, as Michael Howard sums up the evidence, "the entire apparatus of the state primarily came into being to enable princes to wage war" (2000: 15).[11]

Nevertheless, the myth of religious wars and the liberal state as peacemaker continues to mark the 'clash of civilizations' worldview that attributes Muslims' animosity toward the West to their inability to learn the lessons of history and remove the baneful influence of religion from politics. Juergensmeyer, for example, sets up a "new Cold War", pitting the "resurgence of parochial identities" against "the secular West" (1993: 1–2): "Like the old Cold War, the confrontation between these new forms of culture-based politics and the secular state is global in its scope, binary in its opposition, occasionally violent, and essentially a difference of ideologies" (*ibid.*: 2). Although he tries to avoid demonizing "religious nationalists", Juergensmeyer sees them as essentially "anti-modern" (*ibid.*: 5). The particular ferocity of religious nationalism comes from the "special relationship between religion and violence". The question then becomes "whether religious nationalism can be made compatible with secular nationalism's great virtues: tolerance, respect for human rights, and freedom of expression" (*ibid.*: 8). Given the war between "reason and religion", however, Juergensmeyer is not optimistic; "there is ultimately no satisfactory compromise on an ideological level between religious and secular nationalism" (*ibid.*: 201).

Despite its incoherence, the idea that religion is prone to violence thus enforces a binary opposition between "the secular West" and a religious Other that is essentially irrational and violent. The conflict becomes explicable in terms of the essential qualities of the two opponents, not in terms of actual historical encounters. So, for example, Juergensmeyer attempts to explain the animosity of the religious Other toward America.

> Why is America the enemy? This question is hard for observers of international politics to answer, and harder still for ordinary Americans to fathom. Many have watched with horror as their compatriots and symbols of their country have been destroyed by people whom they do not know, from cultures they can scarcely identify on a global atlas, and for reasons that do not seem readily apparent.　　　　　(2000: 179)

Nevertheless, Juergensmeyer is able to come up with four reasons "from the frames of reference" of America's enemies. First, America often finds itself cast as a "secondary enemy": "In its role as trading partner and political ally, America has a vested interest in shoring up the stability of regimes around the world. This has often put the United States in the unhappy position of being a defender and promoter of secular governments regarded by their religious opponents as primary foes" (*ibid.*: 180). Juergensmeyer cites as an example the case of Iran, where "America was tarred by its association with the shah" (*ibid.*). The second reason often given is that America is the main source of "modern culture", which includes cultural products that others regard as immoral. Thirdly, corporations that trade internationally tend to be based in the United States. Fourthly and finally, the fear of globalization has led to a "paranoid vision of American leaders' global designs" (*ibid.*: 181).

Juergensmeyer acknowledges that "Like all stereotypes, each of these characterizations holds a certain amount of truth" (*ibid.*). The fall of the Soviet Union has left the United States as the only military superpower, and therefore "an easy target for blame when people have felt that their lives were going askew or were being controlled by forces they could not readily see. Yet to dislike America is one thing; to regard it as a cosmic enemy is quite another" (*ibid.*: 182). The main problem, according to Juergensmeyer, is "satanization", that is, taking a simple opponent and casting it as a superhuman enemy in a cosmic war. Osama bin Laden, for example, had inflated America into a "mythic monster" (*ibid.*).

The problem with Juergensmeyer's analysis is not just its sanitized account of colonial history, where America just happens to find itself associated with bad people. The problem is that history is subordinated to an essentialist account of 'religion' in which the religious Others cannot seem to deal rationally with world events. They employ guilt by association. They have paranoid visions of globalization. They stereotype, and blame easy targets when their lives are disrupted by forces they do not understand. They blow simple oppositions up into cosmic proportions. Understanding Muslim hostility toward America therefore does not require careful scrutiny of America's historical dealings with the Muslim world. Rather, Juergensmeyer turns our attention to the tendency of such 'religious' actors to misunderstand such historical events, or blow them out of proportion. Understanding Iranian Shiite militancy does not seem to require careful examination of US support for overthrowing

Mohammed Mossadegh in 1953 and for the Shah's twenty-six-year reign of terror that was to follow. Instead, Juergensmeyer puzzles over why 'religious' actors project such mundane things as torture and coups and oil trading into factors in a cosmic war.

The danger of Juergensmeyer's analysis is that it calls attention to anti-colonial violence, labelled 'religious', and away from colonial or neo-colonial violence, labelled 'secular'. Kimball's analysis suffers from the same bias. Kimball's indictments only apply to certain kinds of violence, and I fear that the argument as a whole can be used actually to legitimize other kinds of violence. In his chapter on holy war, for example, Kimball tells the story of the development of Christian thinking and practice on war as a fall from an original commitment to non-violence to a compromised stance of justifying bloodshed. According to Kimball, the "overwhelming evidence suggests that the followers of Jesus were pacifists for the first three centuries" (2002: 158). The ensuing story of Christian attitudes toward war is one of "how the religious ideal is easily compromised and antithetical behavior justified" (*ibid.*: 157). As the Just War doctrine developed, it served to support those in power and, furthermore, says Kimball, it "also had no obvious connection with the Christian faith" (*ibid.*: 161).

Given his narrative of the Just War tradition as a falling away from the original pacifism of Jesus and the early Christians, one might expect that Kimball – a self-identified Christian – would count himself a pacifist. He says otherwise in the same chapter:

> Perilous situations, at times, may indeed warrant the decisive use of force or focused military action. But such action must not be cloaked in religious language or justified by religion. There is no doubt, in my view, that the attacks of September 11 and the prospect of additional mass murder through terrorism required swift and decisive action. The immediate potential for catastrophe – from the loss of life to widespread suffering resulting from economic and political instability – was, and remains, a real and present danger. While there are legitimate bases for collective military action in the community of nations, an appeal to religion is not one of them.
>
> (*Ibid.*: 156)

Although Kimball is not a pacifist, he is clearly trying to limit violence, not justify it. The problem is that there remain, in Kimball's view, perfectly legitimate non-religious, or 'secular', ways of justifying violence. Far from a condemnation of violence, Kimball's analysis results in a selective condemnation of *certain kinds* of violence, labelled 'religious'. The problem is not violence as such; there are still, occasionally, good reasons for bombing and shooting people. To qualify as good, these reasons must be 'secular'. 'Secular' violence, however regrettable, is sometimes necessary. 'Religious' violence, on the other hand, is always reprehensible.

There is a pro-Western bias built into the analysis. Those who have not yet learned to disassociate religion from the use of force are threats to the peace of the world and must be dealt with as such. *Their* violence – being tainted by religion – is uncontrolled, absolutist, fanatical, irrational, divisive. *Our* violence – being secular – is controlled, modest, rational, beneficial, peacemaking and sometimes regrettably necessary to contain *their* violence. It is no secret who the primary 'they' are today. In this worldview, we in the West are threatened by a Muslim culture whose primary point of difference with ours is its stubborn refusal to tame religious passions in the public sphere. We in the West have long ago learned the sobering lessons of religious warfare and have moved toward the secularization of the use of force. Now we only seek to share our peaceful solution with the Muslim world. Regrettably, it is sometimes necessary to bomb them into democracy.

Kimball would certainly reject this crude programme. He is a scholar of Islam who has spent many years among Muslims and others in the Middle East trying to foster mutual understanding. Despite his sympathy for Muslim ways, however, he is clear that the Muslim world must change, and it must look more like our world:

> While many Muslims call for some type of Islamic state, others work toward other goals. Given our pluralist, interdependent world, some Muslims argue for secular democratic states as the best model for the future .... Muslims living in Western democratic countries have an especially important role to play in openly discussing and debating viable, alternative social and political structures for the future. All of the above begs the question: Is it really possible to fashion an Islamic state in the twenty-first century? We will likely find out in the coming decade. Having spent a great deal of my professional life at the intersection of religion and politics in the Middle East, I have grave doubts. At some level, any state in which rights and status are tied to a particular religious tradition will relegate some of its citizens to second- and third-class status. *(Ibid.: 111)*

The problem is not that Kimball has certain views about what is best for the Muslim world. The problem is that those views help frame the argument about 'religion and violence' that masquerades as an objective, descriptive analysis of certain kinds of violent behaviour. The framing of the argument is determined by a built-in bias toward condemning only certain kinds of violence. The choice of which kinds of violence are condemnable is arbitrary and based on a deep bias toward the Western Enlightenment way of narrating the world. Violence on behalf of the Muslim *umma* is always reprehensible. Violence on behalf of the Western nation state is sometimes necessary and often praiseworthy.

The argument that religion is prone to violence is a significant component in the construction of an opposition between "the West and the rest", as Samuel Huntington puts it (1993: 192). Huntington's famous thesis about the "clash of civilizations" was first put forward by Bernard Lewis in an article entitled "The Roots of Muslim Rage":

> It should by now be clear that we are facing a mood and a movement far transcending the level of issues and policies and the governments that pursue them. This is no less than a clash of civilizations – the perhaps irrational but surely historic reactions of an ancient rival against our Judeo-Christian heritage, our secular present, and the worldwide expansion of both. *(Lewis 1990: 60)*

As in Juergensmeyer, actual historical issues and policies and events are transcended by a consideration of the irrationality of the Muslim response to the West. The West is a monolithic reality representing modernity, which necessarily includes secularity and rationality, while the Muslim world is an equally monolithic reality that is ancient, that is, lagging behind modernity, because of its essentially religious and irrational character. This opposition of rational and irrational, secular and religious, Western and Muslim is not simply descriptive, but helps to create the opposition that it purports to describe. As Roxanne Euben writes in her study of Islamic fundamentalism, this opposition is part of a larger Enlightenment narrative in which defining reason requires its irrational other:

> [E]mbedded in the Enlightenment's (re-)definition and elevation of reason is the creation and subjection of an irrational counterpart: along with the emergence of reason as both the instrument and essence of human achievement, the irrational came to be defined primarily in opposition to what such thinkers saw as the truths of their own distinctive historical epoch. If they were the voices of modernity, freedom, liberation, happiness, reason, nobility, and even natural passion, the irrational was all that came before: tyranny, servility to dogma, self-abnegation, superstition, and false religion. Thus the irrational came to mean the domination of religion in the historical period that preceded it. (Euben 1999: 34)

The problem with grafting Islamic fundamentalism into this narrative, according to Euben, is that it is incapable of understanding the appeal of fundamentalism on its own terms. It dismisses rather than explains (*ibid.*: 14–15). It also exacerbates the enmity that it purports to describe. As Emran Qureshi and Michael Sells put it:

> Those who proclaim such a clash of civilizations, speaking for the West or for Islam, exhibit the characteristics of fundamentalism: the assumption of a static essence, knowable immediately, of each civilization, the ability to ignore history and tradition, and the desire to lead the ideological battle on behalf of one of the clashing civilizations. (Qureshi & Sells 2003: 28–9)

In other words, the opposition of 'religious' violence to 'secular' peaceableness can itself be a tool of neo-colonial violence. In his book *Terror and Liberalism*, contributing editor to *The New Republic* Paul Berman's call for a "liberal war of liberation" to be "fought around the world" (2003: 191) is based on the contrast between liberalism and the "mad" ideology of Islamism (*ibid.*: 182).[12] Similarly, Andrew Sullivan, in a *New York Times Magazine* article entitled "This *Is* a Religious War", justifies war against radical Islam on epistemological grounds. He labels it a "religious war", but not in the sense of Islam versus Christianity and Judaism. It is rather radical Islam versus Western-style "individual faith and pluralism" (2001: 44). The problem with the Islamic world seems to be too much public faith, a loyalty to an absolute that excludes accommodation to other realities. "If faith is that strong, and it dictates a choice between action or eternal damnation, then violence can easily be justified" (*ibid.*: 47).

At root, the problem is epistemological. According to Sullivan, it took Western Christians centuries of bloody "religious wars" to realize "the futility of fighting to the death over something beyond human understanding and so immune to any definitive resolution" (*ibid.*: 46–7). The problem with religion is that authoritative truth is simply not available to us mortals in any form that will produce consensus rather than division. Locke, therefore, emerges as Sullivan's hero, for it was Locke who recognized the limits of human understanding of revelation and enshrined those limits in a political theory. Locke and the founding fathers saved us from the curse of killing in the name of religion. "What the founders and Locke were saying was that the ultimate claims of religion should simply not be allowed to interfere with political and religious freedom" (*ibid.*: 53). In theory, we have the opposition of a cruel fanaticism with a modest and peace-loving tolerance. However, Sullivan's epistemological modesty applies only to the command of God and not to the absolute superiority of our political and cultural system over theirs. According to Sullivan, "We are fighting for the universal principles of our Constitution". *Universal* knowledge is available to us after all, and it underwrites the "epic battle" we are currently waging against fundamentalisms of all kinds. Sullivan is willing to gird himself with the language of a warrior and underwrite US military adventures in the Middle East in the name of his secular faith. Sullivan entitles his piece "This *Is* a Religious War", although the irony seems to elude him entirely. On the surface, the myth of religious violence establishes a dichotomy between our peace-loving secular reasonableness and their irrational religious fanaticism. Under the surface lies an absolute 'religious' devotion to the American vision of a hegemonic liberalism that underwrites the necessity of using violence to impose this vision on the Muslim other.

Sam Harris's book about the violence of religion dramatically illustrates this double standard. Harris condemns the irrational religious torture of witches (2004: 87–92), but provides his own argument for torturing terrorists (*ibid.*: 192–9). Harris's book is charged with the conviction that the secular West cannot reason with Muslims, but must deal with them by force. In a chapter entitled "The Problem with Islam", Harris writes: "In our dialogue with the Muslim world, we are confronted by people who hold beliefs for which there is no rational justification and which therefore cannot even be discussed, and yet these are the very beliefs that underlie many of the demands they are likely to make upon us" (*ibid.*: 128). This is especially a problem if such people gain access to nuclear weapons:

There is little possibility of our having a *cold* war with an Islamist regime armed with long-range nuclear weapons ... In such a situation, the only thing likely to ensure our survival may be a nuclear first strike of our own. Needless to say, this would be an unthinkable crime – as it would kill tens of millions of innocent civilians in a single day – but it may be the only course of action available to us, given what Islamists believe.                                                                                   (*Ibid.*: 128–9)

Muslims then might interpret this act of 'self-defense' as a genocidal crusade, thus plunging the world into nuclear holocaust. "All of this is perfectly insane, of course: I have just described a plausible scenario in which much of the world's population could be annihilated on account of religious ideas that belong on the same shelf with Batman, the philosopher's stone, and unicorns" (*ibid.*: 129). In other words, if we have to slaughter millions through a nuclear first strike, it will be the fault of the Muslims and their crazy religious beliefs. Before we get to that point, Harris continues, we must encourage civil society in Islamic countries, but we cannot trust them to vote it in:

> It seems all but certain that some form of benign dictatorship will generally be necessary to bridge the gap. But benignity is the key – and if it cannot emerge from within a state, it must be imposed from without. The means of such imposition are necessarily crude: they amount to economic isolation, military intervention (whether open or covert), or some combination of both. While this may seem an exceedingly arrogant doctrine to espouse, it appears we have no alternatives.
>
> (*Ibid.*: 151)

Harris's book is a particularly blunt version of this type of justification for neo-colonial intervention, but he is by no means isolated. His book is enthusiastically endorsed by such academic stars as Alan Dershowitz, Richard Dawkins and Peter Singer. Indeed, Harris's logic is little different in practice from the Bush doctrine that America has access to liberal values that are "right and true for every person, in every society", that it must use its power to promote such values "on every continent", and that America will take pre-emptive military action if necessary to defend such values.[13] Today the US military is attempting, through the massive use of violence, to liberate Afghanistan and Iraq from religious violence. It is an inherently contradictory effort, and its every failure will be attributed in part to the pernicious influence of religion and its tendency towards violence. If we really wish to understand its failure, however, we will need to question the very myth of religious violence on which such military adventures depend for legitimization.

## NOTES

1. Although Juergensmeyer does not divide this summary into four separate points, I have done so to clarify my response to each point.
2. According to Girard "There is no society without religion because without religion society cannot exist". Even 'secular' societies are religious (Girard 1977: 221).
3. Juergensmeyer tries to tighten the link between war and religion by saying that "the task of creating a vicarious experience of warfare – albeit one usually imagined as residing on a spiritual plane – is one of the main businesses of religion". In the next sentence, however, he acknowledges that "Virtually all cultural traditions have contained martial metaphors" (2000: 156). How then are we supposed to distinguish religion from other cultural traditions?
4. Pierce's novel describes a battle between patriotic freedom fighters and the US government. Although

Pierce scorned Christian Identity, he founded another group called the Cosmotheist Community (Juergensmeyer 2000: 30–33).

5. See, for example, McCutcheon (1997), King (1999) and Peterson & Walhof (2003).

6. For example, G. Cooper writes, "No tribe has a word for 'religion' as a separate sphere of existence. Religion permeates the whole of life, including economic activities, arts, crafts and ways of living" (1988, quoted in Fitzgerald 2000: 81).

7. US State Department official Francis Fukuyama (1992) argues that with the fall of communism history has now ended, in the sense that there are no viable alternatives remaining to the dominance of liberalism.

8. In May 2004, photographic evidence of the abuse of Iraqi prisoners by American soldiers touched off an international furore, and brought to light the US Army's own findings of the beating and torture of Iraqi prisoners (Jehl & Schmitt 2004).

9. And yet for Marty (2000: 26), Ronald Reagan's designation of the Soviet Union as the "Evil Empire" is evidence of the divisive tendencies of 'religion', as opposed to the more obvious candidates of nationalism or patriotism.

10. I make this argument in more detail in my book *Theopolitical Imagination* (2002: ch. 1).

11. Charles Tilly writes: "War made the state, and the state made war" (1975: 42).

12. Berman takes issue with Huntington's "clash" thesis, saying that only Islamists see the conflict in such epic terms. "They also looked upon every new event around the world as a stage in Judaism's cosmic struggle against Islam. Their ideology was mad. In wars between liberalism and totalitarianism, the totalitarian picture of the war is always mad" (Berman 2003: 182).

13. *The National Security Strategy of the United States of America*, September 2002, prologue and p. 15.

# BIBLIOGRAPHY

Asad, Talal. 1999. "Religion, Nation-state, Secularism". In *Nation and Religion: Perspectives on Europe and Asia*, eds Peter van der Veer and Hartmut Lehmann, 178–91. Princeton, NJ: Princeton University Press.

Berman, Paul. 2003. *Terror and Liberalism*. New York: W. W. Norton.

Cavanaugh, William T. 2002. *Theopolitical Imagination*. Edinburgh: T. & T. Clark.

Cooper, G. 1988. "North American Traditional Religion". In *The World's Religions*, ed. Stewart Sutherland, 873–82. London: Routledge.

Euben, Roxanne L. 1999. *Enemy in the Mirror: Islamic Fundamentalism and the Limits of Modern Rationalism*. Princeton, NJ: Princeton University Press.

Fitzgerald, Timothy. 2000. *The Ideology of Religious Studies*. Oxford: Oxford University Press.

Fukuyama, Francis. 1992. *The End of History and the Last Man*. New York: Free Press.

Girard, René. 1977. *Violence and the Sacred*. Trans. Patrick Gregory. Baltimore, MD: Johns Hopkins University Press.

Harris, Sam. 2004. *The End of Faith: Religion, Terror, and the Future of Reason*. New York: W. W. Norton.

Hayes, Carlton. 1960. *Nationalism: A Religion*. New York: Macmillan.

Howard, Michael. 2000. *The Invention of Peace: Reflections on War and International Order*. New Haven, CT: Yale University Press.

Huntington, Samuel. 1993. "If Not Civilizations, What?". *Foreign Affairs* 72 (November/December): 191–4.

Jehl, Douglas and Eric Schmitt. 2004. "Army Reveals Other Abuses". *New York Times* (5 May): A1

Juergensmeyer, Mark. 1993. *The New Cold War?: Religious Nationalism Confronts the Secular State*. Berkeley, CA: University of California Press.

Juergensmeyer, Mark. 2000. *Terror in the Mind of God: The Global Rise of Religious Violence*. Berkeley, CA: University of California Press.

Kimball, Charles. 2002. *When Religion Becomes Evil*. San Francisco, CA: HarperSanFrancisco.

King, Richard. 1999. *Orientalism and Religion: Postcolonial Theory, India, and "The Mystic East"*. London: Routledge.

Lewis, Bernard. 1990. "The Roots of Muslim Rage". *Atlantic Monthly* 266 (September): 47–60.

Marty, Martin. 2000. *Politics, Religion, and the Common Good*. San Francisco, CA: Jossey Bass.

Marvin, Carolyn and David W. Ingle. 1999. *Blood Sacrifice and the Nation: Totem Rituals and the American Flag*. Cambridge: Cambridge University Press.

McCutcheon, Russell. 1997. *Manufacturing Religion: The Discourse on Sui Generis Religion and the Politics of Nostalgia*. Oxford: Oxford University Press.

Mullins, M. R., Shimazono Susumu and Paul L. Swanson, eds. 1993. *Religion and Society in Modern Japan*. Berkeley, CA: Asian Humanities Press.

Paterson, Derek and Darren Walhof, eds. 2003. *The Invention of Religion: Rethinking Belief in Politics and History*. Piscataway, NJ: Rutgers University Press.

Qureshi, Emran and Michael A. Sells. 2003. "Introduction: Constructing the Muslim Enemy". In *The New Crusades: Constructing the Muslim Enemy*, eds Emran Qureshi and Michael A. Sells, 1–50. New York: Columbia University Press.

Smith, Jonathan Z. 1982. *Imagining Religion: From Babylon to Jonestown*. Chicago, IL: The University of Chicago Press.

Smith, Wilfred Cantwell. 1962. *The Meaning and End of Religion*. New York: Macmillan.

Stolberg, Sheryl Gay. 2003. "Given New Legs, Old Proposal is Back". *New York Times* (4 June): A28.

Sullivan, Andrew. 2001. "This *is* a Religious War". *New York Times Magazine* (7 October): 44–7, 52–3.

Tilly, Charles. 1975. "Reflections on the History of European State-Making". In *The Formation of National States in Western Europe*, ed. Charles Tilly, 3–83. Princeton, NJ: Princeton University Press.

van der Veer, Peter. 1999. "The Moral State: Religion, Nation, and Empire in Victorian Britain and British India". In *Nation and Religion: Perspectives on Europe and Asia*, eds Peter van der Veer and Hartmut Lehmann, 3–9. Princeton, NJ: Princeton University Press.

Wentz, Richard E. 1993. *Why People Do Bad Things in the Name of Religion*. Atlanta, GA: Mercer University Press.

# Index

Printed in the United States
96305LV00001B/89-134/A

9 781845 532673